insider picks

manila by day

- shops & services
- lunch-outs & light bites
- recreation & activities

Encyclea
Publications

Insider Picks: Manila By Day

First Edition

Published by Encyclea Publications, an imprint of Asiatype Inc.
Unit 114, 11th Floor, Columbia Tower, Ortigas Avenue,
Greenhills, Mandaluyong City, Metro Manila, Philippines 1550
Tel/Fax (+632) 744-6262

ISBN: 978-971-0321-32-2

Distributed by Asiatype Distribution Inc.
Ground Floor, Columbia tower, Ortigas Avenue, Greenhills
Mandaluyong City, Metro Manila, Philippines 1550
Tel (+632) 744-5677, 744-0077
Fax (+632) 721-0383
Email: contact@asiatype-distribution.com
www.asiatype-distribution.com

For updates, inquiries, and feedback: www.insiderpicks.ph

WRITERS: **Cecile Jusi-Baltasar** (Different Bookstore, A, JT's Manukan, Likha Diwa Sa Gulod, New Hatchin Japanese Grocery, Salcedo Weekend Market, Silahis Arts and Artifacts); **Lori Baltazar** courtesy of dessertcomesfirst.com (Astralis, BBQ, DST, Kanin Club, Peanut Butter Company, Purple Feet, Tsumura); **Cherie Altea-Bitanga** (Choto Stop, Haiku, Hana, Inagiku, Kukifuji, Malcolm's, Nanbentei, Nanohana, Sango, Seryna, Shinjuku, Shokuji, Tsukiji, Yamazaki); **Carla Casanova** (Aussie Café & Resto, Café Juanita, Caruz); **Clarissa Concio-Tiglao** (Bulan, Messy Bessy, Skate of the Nation, Venus & Mars, Village Pantry, The); **Stephanie Dychiu** (ATHAG, Be Beautiful For Him Salon, Belliya's Candles, Club Intramuros Golf Course, Cockfighting, Danilyn's, Figlia, Geo Shop, Good Qi Circle, Grand Thrift Shop, Ikea, Institute of Inner Studies, Jay Cee Kay Stationers and Engravers, MSM US Surplus, Mabini Street Antique Shops, Makati Golf Club, Manila Yacht Club, Michi Calica Fresh Flowers, Navales Dental, Oasis Acupuncture, Pateros Day Trip, Popular Bookstore, Solidaridad Bookshop, Tiong Hwa Food Products, Twinkle Ferraren Swimwear, Video 48, Yash Antique Shop and Kulintangan Antiques, Yin & Yang Shop of Harmony); **Kage Gozun** (Aloha Boardsports, Beadazzled Jewelry, Bohemia Cakes, Borders, Cartimar, Fresh Manila, I Love You Store, Iiideas, J&S Surf Shop, Lung Center Weekend Market, Manila Seedling Bank, Mosayko Pilipino, Reading Room, The, Salcedo Weekend Market, Stoked, Inc., Tiendesitas' Pet Village;); **Cynthia Hauck** (Lopez Museum); **Carren Jao** (ACTS, Aqualogic, Finale, Jackfruit, King Louis, Lay Bare, Manila Contemporary, Pablo Gallery, SLab, Human Heart Nature, Azta, Filipinas Heritage Library, Galleria Duemila); **Candice Lopez** (Carla & Elaine's, Dezato, Indie Shoppe, Indigo Baby, Machiavelli Chocolatier, Next9, Ninyo Fusion Cuisine, Pedala, Punch Drunk Panda); **Adrian Sun** (Van Gogh is Bipolar); **Anna Villar** (Avilon Zoo, Bahay Tsinoy, Fun Ranch, La Mesa Eco Park, Malabon Zoo, Manila Ocean Park, Museo Pambata, Philippine Air Force Museum, Philippine Science Centrum); **Ceia Ylagan** (Buffet Bags); and **Asiatype editorial.**

EDITOR: Jenina F. Alli
COVER DESIGN: Japhet Sanota
TEMPLATE DESIGN: Manny Quilop
PAGE LAYOUT: Mhanny Sula

In A Nutshell...

A daytime city guide bred by word of mouth, *Insider Picks: Manila By Day* isn't an attempt to cover all that the metro has to offer (especially since today's café is tomorrow's barber shop in these fickle parts). It is, rather, an inspired pursuit of premium alternatives: places and things well beyond the "same old, same old" whether they're quirky holes-in-the-wall or old-timers with perks and goodies many don't know about.

Insider Picks: Manila By Day—chockfull of secrets too delicious not to share!

CONTENTS

SHOPS & SERVICES

Apparel, Accessories

Moms, Kids

Personal Care

Home, Garden

Lifestyle, Specialty Shops

Collectibles, Gift Ideas

Books, School/Office Supplies

Tech, Electronics, Automotive

F&B, Food Prep, Ingredients

LUNCH-OUTS & LIGHT BITES

East

West

Shops & Services

Whether they're out-of-the-way stores or part of Manila's homogenous map of malls, these shops embody, in their own respective ways, the art of the truly worthwhile find.

LEGEND U B V

U - UNIQUE isn't limited to kitsch quaint stores but can also refer to mainstream shops with a product or service not found among its peers.
B - BARGAIN isn't just about cheap prices but great value for money.
V - VARIETY refers not only to the astounding range and diversity of products but also to the value added by that range and diversity.

Aling Mila's

U B V

SPECIALTY: Affordable and unique Halloween costumes and accessories.

This *sari-sari* store is a godsend for eleventh-hour Halloween needs. It closes later than malls do and boasts Halloween décor and costumes that can rival a department store's. Full costumes range from ghouls to corpse brides. The only thing missing? Adult sizes.

PRICES: Tombstones, P90; fiberglass jack-o'-lantern with light, P450; a set of hanging haunted-house accessories, P600; children's costumes, P750.

PAYMENT: Cash. ADDRESS: Aguirre Ave. cor. N. Jacinto, Parañaque
OPEN: Daily, 5 a.m. – 9:30 p.m.

Ang Pambansang Tshirt

U B V

SPECIALTY: Graphic shirts advocating local tourism and patriotic love.

Pambansang Tshirt promotes tourist hot spots like Cebu and Boracay as well as less-traveled provinces like Batanes and Donsol using modern imagery. Roosters appear as black silhouettes against geometric patterns in bold citrus colors; Bohol's Chocolate Hills get posterized to look like a watercolor painting; and coconut-tree silhouettes in white, yellow, or hot pink are set against a backdrop of fire-engine red.

PRICES: Men's shirts and women's baby tees start at P350.

PAYMENT: Cash, credit card. WEBSITE: angpambansa.com
ADDRESS: Team Manila Studio, 146-B Jupiter Ave., Makati
T: 899-1570 OPEN: Daily, 10 a.m. – 7 p.m. See directory for resellers.

Anicete's

U B V

SPECIALTY: Made-to-measure suits for men. Anicete's offers affordable, quality work and does subcontracted work for some well-known, pricier tailor shops. You get your suit after about two weeks.

PRICES: Labor is P2,000 and up for a suit if you source your own fabric.

PAYMENT: Cash. ADDRESS: Sampaguita St., Mapayapa Village, Commonwealth, Quezon City OPEN: Mon – Sat, 10 a.m. – 5 p.m.

Aum Jewels

U B V

SPECIALTY: Bespoke designer concept jewelry.

Though Aum Jewels carries RTW pieces, it primarily offers commission services for handcrafted jewelry by store owner and chief jewelry designer Paul Syjuco. Aum's collection is a younger, more hip, and more character-driven take on fine jewelry. You can bring your own stones or jewelry for redesigning, though Aum keeps a variety of gems at hand. If they don't have what you want, they will source it out for you. You can get your order approximately four to six weeks from confirmation of design and downpayment, but allowances can be made to meet tight deadlines.

PRICES: There are no additional design charges, so customized orders aren't more expensive than those on display at the store. An initial 50% non-refundable deposit is requested to begin an order. Rings, P5,000 and up; earrings, P18,000 and up. For bespoke pieces, clients can set the working figure.

PAYMENT: Cash, credit card. ADDRESS: Lobby, TriNoma Mall, EDSA cor. North Ave., Quezon City T: 943-1524 OPEN: Daily, 11 a.m. – 8 p.m.

Baubles, Bangles, N' Beads (online)

U B V

SPECIALTY: Limited-edition handpainted bangles, shoes, and bags.

The wooden handpainted bangle, their flagship product, started out with abstract tropical-themed designs and colors like drawings of *gumamela* flowers or dotted patterns reminiscent of tribal tattoos. Now they feature commemorative designs inspired by historical figures (the bangles had an

I Love Cory line) and pop culture (painted faces of Hollywood icons like Marilyn Monroe). Just recently, the bangles have been joined by moon-cut, round-toe flats from the brand Ichigo, with each pair also intricately handpainted with a bevy of patterns, from peacock feathers to tropical sceneries. Accepts orders for customized designs.

PRICES: P350–500 a bangle.

PAYMENT: Cash, bank deposit, G-Cash. WEBSITE: baublesbanglesnbeads.multiply.com EMAIL: handpaintedbangles@yahoo.com M: 0923-531-9662, 0929-626-3120 OPEN: By appointment.

Beadazzled Jewelry

U B V

SPECIALTY: Handmade accessories made with semiprecious stones and healing crystals.

Beadazzled Jewelry is run by husband-and-wife team Raffy and Zu, the former a goldsmith and the latter a certified gemologist. Together they design accessories out of crystals and semiprecious stones, sourcing the materials and creating each piece by hand. Smaller items are phone charms and rings; necklaces can be ordered as sets as well as individual pieces. The couple are well-versed in the healing properties of crystals and can tell you which stones are best for focus, relaxation, weight loss, etc. They can also work within your design preferences or budget. Stone appraisal and identification also on offer.

PRICES: P150 and up for small pieces; custom jewelry can go up to 6 figures.

PAYMENT: Cash, credit card. EMAIL: beadazzled.jewelry2003@gmail.com ADDRESS: 2/L Pergola Mall, Aguirre Ave. cor. Elsie Gaches St., Phase 1, BF Homes, Parañaque T: 659-2896 M: 0915-783-2243 OPEN: Tue–Sun, 11 a.m.–7 p.m.

Beadlady Craft Café

U B V

SPECIALTY: One-of-a-kind handcrafted polymer clay bead accessories.

Big hits include beads that look like dainty cupcakes and chocolate truffles with bite marks, Moroccan-inspired clay medallions set in brass filigree, and French-inspired pieces with photo-transfer designs on polymer clay tiles wrapped with filigree. Decorated like a quaint French patisserie, the store has an eye-catching cherry red door against a talcum white façade and a bay window. Delicious pastel colors bathe the naturally lit interiors, flanked on one side by a wall display of handcrafted fashion and home accessories and on the other by paintings and prints by local artists. There's a nook serving native brewed coffee and desserts where customers can plunk down with their purchases to start working on their DIY bead kits.

The shop also caters to bead artisans looking for special materials and supplies; it has a mini library dedicated to bead work and a workshop studio on the second floor where bead artists are given access to tools, work space, and workshops on clay art, print making, wire working, and resin bead making.

PRICES: Necklace with pendant charms, P350 and up; big bead accents for charm bracelets or cocktail rings, P250 and up. Workshops, typically P1,600 per head for one half-day session, inclusive of tools and materials.

PAYMENT: Cash. WEBSITE: beadlady.multiply.com ADDRESS: Shop 54, Cubao Expo, Gen. Romulo Ave., Araneta Center, Cubao, Quezon City OPEN: Tue – Thu, 12 nn – 8 p.m.; Fri, 12 nn – 9 p.m.; Sat/Sun, 10 a.m. – 9 p.m.

Binky's Beads

U B V

SPECIALTY: Personalized semiprecious stone bracelets.

Binky's Beads designer Binky Illusorio makes one-of-a-kind bracelets and necklaces with beads that are handcarved from semiprecious stone (turquoise, agate, jade, malachite, sodalite, topaz, and cloisonné). Only sterling silver is used for the clasps and closures, so that even if the pieces aren't strictly "fine" jewelry, they won't tarnish and can last long enough for your kids to inherit them. Illusorio has a personal approach with clients, finding out more about their personalities and determining what materials and design suit them before starting on a piece—though she also accepts design requests. Illusorio occasionally participates in bazaars and trade shows, keeping her bead business small so that she can have the time and creativity to keep producing unique and inspired pieces.

PRICES: Bracelets start at P1,900; necklaces at P2,500.

PAYMENT: Cash. EMAIL: bbi1970@yahoo.com T: 724-2222 OPEN: By appointment.

Boo Boo Shop, The

U B V

SPECIALTY: On-hand and made-to-order anime, manga, and J.Pop themed clothes, accessories, costumes, plushies, and props like armors and weapons. Perfect for cosplay and other costume needs.

The Boo Boo Shop started out as an online store, with custom orders and measurements being consolidated online. Items they have on-hand can be shipped within a week of payment, made-to-order costumes are typically completed after about three weeks. You can have items shipped or pick them up at designated meet-up points.

PRICES: Highly variable depending on your specs, but a regular anime outfit averages at P1,200. Plus shipping.

PAYMENT: Bank deposit, G-Cash, PayPal, Western Union. WEBSITE: thebooboshop.multiply.com EMAIL: the_booboo_shop@yahoo.com ADDRESS: Bldg. 04, Unit 13, BLPC, Pag-asa, Quezon City M: 0905-263-2497 OPEN: By appointment.

Buffet Bags (online)

U B V

SPECIALTY: Custom-made women's leather bags.

Buffet Bags offers custom-made bags made of durable leatherette with classic crocodile, iguana, and *banig* designs. The bags are designed for everyday use and flexible enough in style for the evening. Bags are lined with expertly tailored fabric that matches the bag's leatherette make. Most designs have clasp closures, but you can request for zippers. New moms can choose from a wide line of corporate baby bags equipped with bottle holders and compartments for diapers and baby wipes. Other products include checkbook holders, wallets, and pouches that come in various colors, from pastels to metallic. Orders are confirmed upon 50% downpayment.

PRICES: Wallets, pencil cases, pouches, and checkbook holders, P150 and up; shoulder bags, totes, clutches, corporate baby bags, P300–1,200.

PAYMENT: Cash, bank deposit. WEBSITE: buffetbags.multiply.com EMAIL: ninabcruz@yahoo.com M: 0918-944-1307

Chikarahats (online)

U B V

SPECIALTY: Anime, manga, and J.Pop fun animal character head gear, fleece aviator hats, furry ski caps, etc. Perfect for cosplay, costume needs, or simply adding campy funk to an outfit. Accepts custom orders.

PRICES: P120 and up.

PAYMENT: Bank deposit, PayPal, Western Union. WEBSITE: chikarahats.webs.com EMAIL: chikarahats@yahoo.com

Clear Shoe Box Project (online)

U B V

SPECIALTY: Clear but thick plastic shoe boxes for standard-sized men's and women's shoes.

PRICES: P75 a box.

PAYMENT: Cash, bank deposit. WEBSITE: clearshoeboxproject .multiply.com M: 0917-881-1610

Crate

U B V

SPECIALTY: Limited-edition and retro-designed sneakers.

Considered the first "by sneakerheads, for sneakerheads" retailer in the country, Crate carries brands like Nike, Nike SB (Skate Board), Adidas, Puma, and New Balance. Major sneaker stores have the same brands but carry the athletic line, while Crate homes in on limited-edition items with distinct retro design cues found in Western skateboarding subcultures. Whereas most sneakers have the hard court in mind, Crate's pieces were built for the pavement. Here you won't find the usual line of aerodynamic footwear that features innovative shocks and "breathable" material. Instead, you'll see hi-tops with flat-bottom rubber platform soles in whimsical color ways like tangerine-brown-neon-green, using materials like suede, canvas, and nylon. Special shoe orders are accepted on one condition: the type of shoe must not be available in major sports apparel retailers and sporting goods stores.

PRICES: Prices average between P5,200 and P6,500 a pair, with the occasional collector's item at P8,000 and up.

PAYMENT: Cash. WEBSITE: cratemakati.multiply.com ADDRESS: 132 LRI Design Plaza, Nicanor Garcia St. (Reposo), Bel Air, Makati M: 0917-891-7683 OPEN: Tue–Sat, 1 p.m.–7 p.m.

D'Franz

U B V

SPECIALTY: Goth, rock, and thrasher wear and accessories.

D'Franz is home to almost everything rocker rebel. Shirts hang from racks and walls featuring hardcore, grind core, heavy metal, grunge, pop rock, and yes, even emo bands. Available here are tokens from all streams of alternative—from grunge, skater, and goth to Rastafari. Goth bags and bracelets sit alongside '80s Vans sneakers, boarding footwear, heavy-duty guitar straps, fan knives, brass knuckles, beanies, military caps, biking gloves, and skateboard accessories. D'Franz doesn't have a signage or even a makeshift door sign, just a glass-walled store front. But as a shop that looks like the walk-in closet of a mosh-pit body slammer, it's an oddity that's hard to miss along Alabang-Zapote Road's rather uneventful stretch of concrete.

PRICES: Shirts start at P150, genuine Vans sneakers go for P1,400 (about P500 cheaper than mall prices).

PAYMENT: Cash. ADDRESS: Along Alabang-Zapote Rd., Las Piñas (towards Las Piñas, away from SLEX). From SM South Mall, it's about two buildings before Mini Stop, on your right. M: 0928-431-7152 OPEN: Daily, 10 a.m. – 10 p.m.

Defacto Industry

U B V

SPECIALTY: Custom-made locally designed jeans (where made-for-model skinny jeans can look good on less-than-perfect bodies).

Here you'll be asked to decide what fit you prefer—skinny, boot, straight, baggy, or even a hybrid of different cuts (e.g., "pelvis-clinging low-risers, skinny from hip to knees, then wide elephant leg onward"). If you're not sure what looks good on you, the people at Defacto will recommend a cut that flatters your height and body type.

Next is choosing fabric. The shop has so much more fabric swatches than even most jean retailers in malls. Take your pick from raw, stretch, and textured in varying levels of thickness like "thick and stiff" for a dressier tailored look or "soft and relaxed" for a casual look. After that is color—monotone dark navy, stone-washed or sand-blasted indigo, shiny, muted, etc. Last is the color of thread you'd like for the seams; you might also want some thread or patch work as design accents (an embroidered dragon, perhaps, or multicolored swirls). Defacto has pocket designs like padded pouch pockets tailor-fit to your MP3 player or cellphone. Finally, get yourself measured. You'll get your jeans in about a week. The shop accepts back jobs until your new pair of Defactos fits perfectly.

PRICES: Typically P1,800–4,000 a pair; north of P4,000 for orders with highly specialized embellishment.

PAYMENT: Cash. WEBSITE: defactory.multiply.com EMAIL: defacto.industry@gmail.com ADDRESS: V8 Indie Boutique, Unit 112, Mile Long Bldg., Amorsolo cor. Herrera Sts., Legaspi Village, Makati M: 0917-812-2529, 0920-429-1393 OPEN: Daily, 10:30 a.m.–8 p.m.

Designer Soirée

U B V

SPECIALTY: By-invitation sales for significantly marked-down designer togs and accessories.

Designer Soirée doesn't run a store but holds variably located, intimate sales similar to exclusive trunk shows. Items are new and of current stock, but the bargain prices owe largely to Designer Soirée's connections with and access to international showroom factories. Brands brought in include Miu Miu, Tory Burch, Braziliano Praia, Karrots Cases, and Phillip Lim—many of which aren't in Manila. Text or email to get on their mailing list.

PRICES: 50%–70% lower than boutique SRP.

PAYMENT: Cash. EMAIL: designerssoiree@gmail.com M: 0915-901-2543

Dumask (online)

U B V

SPECIALTY: Vintage-style statement accessories whose designs revolve around found objects and chunky accents from a bygone romantic era.

Miniature sunglasses are made into pendants, coats of arms into rings, lockets into charms. There are accessories that also make use of "conventional" materials like Swarovski crystals, beads, and semiprecious stones, but the resulting product is still one that's kitsch and time-worn. Each piece is one-of-a-kind and there are no remakes.

PRICES: Large puppy locket charm necklace with purple glass beads, P280.

PAYMENT: Cash. WEBSITE: dumask.multiply.com

Figlia

U B V

SPECIALTY: Custom-made ladies' shoes.

The cobblers of local shoe retail brands Celine and Figlia can hew any shoe you want, whether it's a design you saw on a celebrity, a favorite style you can't find anymore, or your own inspired creation. Just bring a photo of the shoe in mind and go to their office to have your feet measured. Costs vary depending on materials. There will be a number of fittings to ensure comfort is not sacrificed for style. Production takes about three weeks.

PRICES: Minimum of P5,500 a pair.

PAYMENT: Cash. ADDRESS: Suite 1801 Centerpoint Bldg., Julia Vargas Ave., Ortigas Center, Pasig T: 633-7691 OPEN: Mon–Fri, 9 a.m.–6 p.m. by appointment.

Figura

U B V

SPECIALTY: Bespoke designer men's shoes in innovative materials.

Figura is the local distributor and proprietor of Tenorio Manila, the only custom-made designer label for men's shoes. You can have your feet measured at home and have your pairs flown to you; returning customers can have their old Tenorio Manila pairs cleaned and refinished free of charge. The shoes are made with a technique that maximizes leather by assembling small leather cut-outs with fine expert stitching. As a result, each pair fits like second skin. Exotic materials like fish scales, patent cow hide, ostrich leather, sheepskin, metallic leather, lizard belly skin, kidskin, and juvenile calf leather are married with design-savvy embellishment such as gold foil detailing or perforated dragons to create truly unique foot pieces for men.

PRICES: P7,000 and up for men's leather shoes.

PAYMENT: Cash, credit card. WEBSITE: philippineshoes.com
EMAIL: figurashoes@gmail.com, jehanmachacon@philippineshoes.com
ADDRESS: Figura Showroom, Apartment 904 Prince Plaza 1, Legaspi St., Legaspi Village, Makati M: 0917-541-5401, 0918-836-6746, 0919-396-8656 OPEN: By appointment.

Graphic Designed Lifestyle

U B V

SPECIALTY: Limited-edition men's and women's tops, accessories, and lifestyle items with graphic prints and designs of Filipino urban subculture.

A brand under local design consortium Team Manila, Graphic Designed Lifestyle (GDL) produces apparel, accessories, and lifestyle items inspired by everything Manila—from patriotic themes to everyday urban scenes. A shirt gives the mug of national hero Jose Rizal post-modern rendition with bold Warhol-esque colors; wallet prints are Photoshopped to look like sticky rice wrapper; and there are stickers of local urban terms and slang ("Pssst!", "Askals," and the word "Chismis" on the famed Rolling Stones tongue logo).

PRICES: Graphic shirts and baby tees start at P350. Printed tote bags, P200 and up. Small accessories like lanyards, wristlets, P100; wallets P150 and up.

PAYMENT: Cash, credit card. WEBSITE: teammanilalifestyle.com
ADDRESS: Team Manila Studio, 146-B Jupiter Ave., Makati T: 899-1570 OPEN: Daily, 10 a.m.–7 p.m.

Hatah Hatah (online)

U B V

SPECIALTY: Anime, manga, and J.Pop fun animal character head gear, fleece aviator hats, furry ski caps, etc. Perfect for cosplay, costume needs, or simply adding campy funk to an outfit. Accepts custom orders. You can have items shipped or pick them up at designated meet-up points.

PRICES: P150 and up, plus shipping.

PAYMENT: Bank deposit, G-Cash, PayPal. WEBSITE: hatahhatah .multiply.com M: 0927-794-3254, 0923-559-8669

Hoseki

U B V

SPECIALTY: High-end concept jewelry.

Hoseki has three distinct signature collections. The Filipiniana collection executes traditionally Filipino themes in a modern way, like sculpted gold ylang-ylang set against geometric tribal tattoos. This collection shows masterful and creative use of corals and pearls. The Oriental collection depicts themes like Japanese blooms and Chinese dragons, and prominently uses Burmese jade and exotic wood. The Avant Garde collection reinterprets works of prestigious Filipino post-modern visual artists.

PRICES: Dangling mother-of-pearl earrings with exotic pearls and gems, P35,000 and up; necklaces with pearls and gems, P40,000 and up.

PAYMENT: Cash, credit card. WEBSITE: hosekijewelryart.com
ADDRESS: LG/L Podium, 18 ADB Ave., Ortigas Center, Mandaluyong
T: 634-1736 OPEN: Daily, 10 a.m. – 8 p.m.

I Love You Store

U B V

SPECIALTY: Vintage clothing and accessories, and limited-edition retro items from local prestige designers.

Sitting above a restaurant-cum-bar, this quirky treasure trove revels in the art of eclectic and rare finds. Everything from one-off dresses to kitschy knickknack is displayed in a seemingly haphazard manner.

PRICES: Statement name tags P150; pins and trinkets, P200 and up; clothing, P850–3,000.

PAYMENT: Cash. ADDRESS: Cubao Expo, Gen. Romulo Ave., Araneta Center, Cubao, Quezon City M: 0917-499-5223 OPEN: Tue –Sat, 3 p.m. onward; Sun, by appointment.

Indie Shoppe (online)

U B V

SPECIALTY: Kitsch and cult-cool women's apparel and accessories.

Indie Shoppe carries mostly women's clothing, accessories, and collectibles that evoke urban whimsy reminiscent of the '80s. Among their bestsellers are sling purses fashioned from the colorful cartridges of old cassette tapes, jelly toy cameras that look like little Lomos (though they do take pictures), vintage-style tees bearing old-school logos of popular consumer brands like Coca-Cola, Apple, or Dunkin Donuts, and "stress buns" (stress balls that convincingly resemble either a savory dinner bun or a donut). Orders are confirmed upon 50% downpayment. Get your orders via shipment or via meet-up point in Robinsons Place Ermita.

PRICES: Cassette purse, P350; vintage shirt, P150–200. Plus shipping.

PAYMENT: Cash, bank deposit, G-Cash. WEBSITE: indieshoppe.multiply.com EMAIL: indieshoppe@yahoo.com M: 0927-904-8214

J2 Jeans

U B V

SPECIALTY: Custom-made jeans.

They give you a choice of denim variants, thread colors, and pocket designs. They can even make maternity jeans with wide elastic waistbands that grow with the belly. J2 Jeans is well stocked with the wash or cut of the moment and can easily understand trendy embellishment you want done. They can also advise you on what cut works best with your body type. You can either go to their shop or have them come to you (at minimal extra charge, depending on how far you live). Your jeans are done after three to five days.

PRICES: A pair starts at P1,500.

PAYMENT: Cash. WEBSITE: j2engineeredjeans.multiply.com EMAIL: totallychicclothing@yahoo.com ADDRESS: 1204 Asturias cor. Dapitan Sts., Sampaloc, Manila (behind U.S.T.) M: 0918-949-6907 OPEN: By appointment.

Jewel Thief (online)

U B V

SPECIALTY: Handcrafted concept accessories and jewelry inspired by antiquated Tuscan art. Cocktail rings, cuff bracelets, and neck pieces are handmade from handcut gemstones and Baroque pearls set in silver or silver-gilt (i.e., silver gilded with gold).

PRICES: From P6,500 for a cocktail ring to P34,000 for a silver cuff.

PAYMENT: Cash, credit card. WEBSITE: jewelthief.com.ph EMAIL: marly@jewelthief.com.ph M: 0917-526-5692

Jewelmer

U B V

SPECIALTY: South Sea fine pearl jewelry from a major South Sea pearl distributor to prestige jewelry boutiques all over the world.

Since its inception in 1979, Jewelmer, a company founded by a French perliculture specialist and a Filipino entrepreneur, has been engaged in South Sea pearl farming with the vision of creating the most lustrous pearls in the world. The company currently has its own South Sea pearl farms in preserved areas of Palawan.

South Sea pearls are the biggest and most sought after in the world with sizes ranging from 8 mm to 18 mm; all too rarely, a Baroque South Sea pearl can reach as much as 26 mm. The surface of a Palawan South Sea pearl sometimes has irregularities that are natural to pearls and used as one of many measures of authentication.

Each Jewelmer piece uses high-quality gemstones to adorn a pearl, and each pearl is hand-selected and handcrafted in 18K gold. A certificate of authenticity comes with each piece to guarantee the origin and unaltered state of the pearls—here you will find round pearls as well as oval, button, Baroque, semi-Baroque, semi-round, drop, circled, and semi-circled.

Apart from visiting Jewelmer stores, you can also order online through their website; orders are confirmed upon 50% downpayment.

PRICES: Several factors determine the pricing of a Jewelmer piece, chief among which are the kind of pearl used and its size, any accompanying gems, and the design and designer behind the piece. Each piece is a unique combination of these factors, and so prices are remarkably variable. We saw a 50-bead choker of silver-talcum 11 mm South Sea pearls retailing at about P100,000. South Sea pearls are highly prized fine jewelry abroad, and getting them at Jewelmer assures international-grade quality along with value for money.

PAYMENT: Cash, credit card. WEBSITE: jewelmer.com EMAIL: retail@jewelmer.com ADDRESS: 2/L Filipino Zone of Greenbelt 5, Ayala Center, Makati T: 757-6641 OPEN: Daily, 11 a.m. – 8 p.m. See directory for other branches.

Kangol Hats

U B V

SPECIALTY: High-fashion men's headwear like fedoras, messenger caps, berets, and pull-ons made of luxe material like wool, angora, and tweed. This British headwear brand has adorned many a celebrity head—from the Beatles' to Brad Pitt's.

PRICES: Hats start at P1,800.

PAYMENT: Cash, credit card. ADDRESS: Bratpacks, Greenbelt 5, Ayala Center, Makati ADDRESS 2: 2/L Archaeology Wing, Power Plant Mall, Rockwell, Makati OPEN: Daily, 11 a.m. – 9 p.m.

Love Me Vintage (online)

U B V

SPECIALTY: Quirky, one-off, pre-loved but well-maintained vintage duds for style mavens who know how to play around with fashion.

PRICES: Tops, P250 – 500; bottoms, P350 – 550; bags, P500 – 700.

PAYMENT: Cash WEBSITE: lovemevintage.multiply.com EMAIL: lovemevintage@yahoo.com M: 0915-846-3586

Lucky Doll (online)

U B V

SPECIALTY: Remarkable range of vintage-inspired lingerie, hosiery, corsets, sexy costumes, and intimate wear calling to mind the burlesque queens and pin-up girls of '40s and '50s Americana.

Seasonal items arrive on schedule. By October, for example, the Sexy Santa collection was already online. Mainstays are the Bondage and Exotic Dancer lines. The Bondage Line is a leather and chain collection spanning all kinds of S&M items: from dominatrix corsets to fur-trimmed cuffs. Exotic Dancer Wear offers metallic, body-cling "hooker" dresses and jumper G-strings. Costumes beyond typical Japanese school girl include Sexy Genie, Trampy Gypsy, Gothic Nurse, and Flirty French Maid. The rest of the collection are teddies, corsets, chemises, and all manner of intimate wear.

The store's extensive size chart shows you the proper way to measure yourself. You can have ill-fitting products changed. The one and only item for men is a skin-tight bondage coverall with a strategically located cut-out. You get your orders two days after confirmation of payment.

PRICES: Lingerie sets, teddies, and exotic dance wear, P480–650; costumes, P1,200 and up; Bondage "starter" kit of leather cuffs, soft leather whip, leather mask, ball gag, and leather thong, P1,600 (items also sold individually). Plus shipping.

PAYMENT: PayPal, G-Cash, bank deposit. WEBSITE: luckydollstore.multiply.com

---

Mush Pomato (online)

U B V

SPECIALTY: Polymer clay dessert-themed accessories. Accepts custom orders. You can have items shipped to you or you can pick them up at designated meet-up points. Orders are typically ready after a week.

PRICES: Earrings and rings start at P150; pendants, P250. Plus shipping.

PAYMENT: Bank deposit, G-Cash. WEBSITE: mushpomato.multiply.com EMAIL: jaynwayn@yahoo.com, mushpomato@gmail.com
M: 0927-794-3254, 0923-559-8669

Naluzzi's

U B V

SPECIALTY: Made-to-measure men's suits and formal wear. Chief tailor Renato "Mang Boy" Naluz is a top pick among prominent male newscasters for their suits. He also does specialty dress shirts, like the Mexican guyabera.

PRICES: Suits, P7,000 and up; specialty dress shirts, P3,000. Prices are for labor and materials.

PAYMENT: Cash. ADDRESS: 2/L Atrium Bldg., Makati Ave., Makati
T: 811-4352, 811-4292 OPEN: Mon–Sat, 10 a.m.–5 p.m.

Panopio

U B V

SPECIALTY: Fashion-forward fine jewelry locally handcrafted from fine metals, natural stones, and exotic materials like coral and shell.

PRICES: Gemstone drop earrings with coral, P35,000 and up; engagement rings, P12,000 and up; GIA (Gemological Institute Of America) certified diamond rings, P200,000 and up.

PAYMENT: Cash, credit card, lay-away plans.
WEBSITE: panopiojewellery.multiply.com ADDRESS: G/L Manila Peninsula, Ayala cor. Makati Aves., Makati T: 812-3456 M: 0917-813-0598 OPEN: Daily, 10 a.m. – 8 p.m.

Paul Smith & Dot Dot Dot Warehouse

U B V

SPECIALTY: Discounted designer wear from previous seasons (Paul Smith, Dot Dot Dot, Eley Kishimoto, Chloé, and McQueen).

PRICES: As much as 50% off SRP.

PAYMENT: Cash. ADDRESS: 41 Sta. Maria St., Barangay Kapitolyo, Pasig T: 631-9631 OPEN: By appointment.

Playculture Tees (online)

U B V

SPECIALTY: Men's and women's tees with geek humor and references to '80s sci-fi pop culture, video games, comic books, and anime.

Geeks, leets (gaming elite), sci-fi junkies, and those who grew up in the '80s will get a kick out of Playculture Tees' shirt collection. Basic round-neck shirts and baby tees get geek-pimped with graphic logos of famous old-school cartoons, video games, and sci-fi shows—like a lone silhouette of a Star Wars X-wing fighter craft. A typical "Beware of Dog" sign gets a twist: this time the sign reads "Beware of Pet Cat" with a red Thundercats beacon. Some plain shirts feature humorous concept text like "Time Space

Warp *Ngayon Din*!" and "All My Base Are Belong To You" (a play on the poorly translated English phrase "All your base are belong to us" that first appeared in a 1991 Sega game and mutated into an iconic blunder). Yet other shirts put a grown-up spin on a childhood favorite, like the famous Sesame Street biped typewriter with "WTF" on its paper feed instead of the alphabet of the day.

PRICES: Men's shirts start at P350, women's at P250.

PAYMENT: Cash. WEBSITE: playculture.multiply.com EMAIL: info .playculture@gmail.com

Sarto Manila

U B V

SPECIALTY: Reasonably priced European-cut bespoke suits.

Apart from being able to boast a high batting average when it comes to perfect-at-first-fitting, Sarto Manila has a sartorial knowledge of fit, fabric, and design and a personalized and collaborative approach with each client. Just like the tailors of London's Savile Row, birthplace of the bespoke suit, Sarto doesn't rely on ready-made patterns and creates each suit from scratch. You can bring a magazine page of a suit you want copied or discuss with them what you want and don't want. They also carry luxe fabrics like cashmere—truly a one-stop shop for those who want to suit up.

PRICES: Gun metal gray suit with colored pin stripes (long-sleeved dress shirt, pants, and suit jacket), P9,000 for labor and materials. Prices can go lower or higher depending on fabric and cut.

PAYMENT: Cash. EMAIL: sartomanila@gmail.com ADDRESS: E. Rodriguez cor. Doña Juana Aves., New Manila, Quezon City M: 0917-535-0814, 0917-521-2295 OPEN: By appointment.

Schu Factory Outlet

U B V

SPECIALTY: Discounted brand new women's shoes from previous seasons.

PRICES: 50%–70% off SRP. Heels can go for under P500.

PAYMENT: Cash. ADDRESS: G/L Security Land Bldg., 6797 Ayala Ave. cor. V.A. Rufino St., Salcedo Village, Makati T: 840-4924 OPEN: Daily, 10 a.m.–7 p.m.

Simple Shoes (online)

U B V

SPECIALTY: Eco-friendly casual-chic footwear for men and women.

These planet-friendly shoes are made from recycled tires, organic cotton, and recycled water bottles. The designs are anything but hippie tree-hugging yokel, however, and are actually very chic, with adorable maryjanes for women and sneakers for men. The natural silk sneakers keep feet cool when the weather is warm and warm when it's cold. The 100% vegan collection uses no animal byproduct and is made with pesticide-free hemp. Even the shoe boxes are eco, made of recycled paper and starch glue.

PRICES: P2,500–3,500 a pair.

PAYMENT: Credit card, bank deposit. WEBSITE: simpleshoes.multiply.com See directory for resellers.

Sports Warehouse

U B V

SPECIALTY: Year-round sale on brand new designer athletic brands (Adidas, Puma, Converse, Fila, New Balance, Sisley, Gas, Vans).

PRICES: 40%–70% off SRP.

PAYMENT: Cash, credit card. ADDRESS: G/L Club Six Fifty, E. Rodriguez Jr. Ave., Libis, Quezon City T: 638-2671 OPEN: Daily, 11 a.m.–8 p.m.

Stoic Clothing

U B V

SPECIALTY: Kitsch and retro/vintage-inspired women's apparel and accessories (think Marcia Brady dresses and high-waist bodycon skirts). Whether you're a flower child trapped in the body of a Gen X-er, or one of the gifted few who can pull off '80s-style polka dots, Stoic is your haunt.

Kindred-spirit fashion brands consigned at Stoic include Föfa (funky faux leather bags), Methilation (of-the-moment boots, sandals, and shoes), Verve Sense Soothers (anti-stress personal care products), and locally designed accessories that range from artfully gaudy to "goth in technicolor."

PRICES: Vintage-style dresses, P600 and up.

PAYMENT: Cash. WEBSITE: stoicclothing.multiply.com, methilation.multiply.com, fofashion.net, verve-lifestyle.com EMAIL: stoicclothing@gmail.com ADDRESS: Shop 23 Cubao Expo, Gen. Romulo Ave., Araneta Center, Cubao, Quezon City M: 0908-863-1231, 0917-994-7866, 0906-299-8013 OPEN: Tue–Thu, 1 p.m.–8:30 p.m.; Fri/Sat, 1 p.m.–9:30 p.m.; Sun, 1 p.m.–8 p.m.

Switchrings (online)

U B V

SPECIALTY: Funky rings with interchangeable designs.

Canadian-born Switchrings are made of two colored outer hoops joined at the base and a detachable inner C-shaped wedge bearing the design or pattern of your choice. You can mix and match wedges and hoops to create several color and design combinations from just a few rings. Switchrings are also available at Chocolate Clothing stores.

PRICES: Switchrings, P195 each.

PAYMENT: Cash. WEBSITE: switchring.multiply.com See directory for Chocolate Clothing Co. store branches.

Trilogy Boutique

U B V

SPECIALTY: Concept and high-street urban and casual wear and accessories from indie labels (e.g., Junk Food, Christy's Crown Series Hats, Obey, Incase Bags, Gourmet Footwear, Alternative Apparel, Lego Watches, Andy Warhol Watches, Wize & Ope, Anthology).

Trilogy throws in some dining with your shopping through in-store café Canteen (see Lunch-Outs & Light Bites), and also holds events like video launches and art exhibits. Check their website or twitter page for updates.

PRICES: Andy Warhol watches, P5,000 and up; Christy's Crown suede fedoras and caps, P1,800 and up; one-off graphic tees, P700 and up.

PAYMENT: Cash, credit card. WEBSITE: thetrilogyboutique.com, twitter.com/trilogyboutique; they also have a Facebook page. EMAIL: trilogyboutique@gmail.com ADDRESS: 110 Alvion Center, Rada St., Legaspi Village, Makati T: 328-1071 OPEN: Mon–Fri, 11 a.m.–8 p.m.; Sat/Sun, 10 a.m.–5 p.m.

Twinkle Ferraren

U B V

SPECIALTY: Custom-made women's swimwear. Twinkle Ferraren has been designing swimsuits since 2005 and can customize exactly to your size. Go to her website to choose your design, then email your requirements. After checking availability of fabric and embellishments, she'll give you a price quotation. She also makes cover-ups and resort wear.

PRICES: P1,500–5,000 for a bikini or a maillot.

PAYMENT: Cash. WEBSITE: t-w-i-n-k-l-e.com EMAIL: twinkle.ferraren@gmail.com ADDRESS: Cloud Lounge, Feron Bldg., 9590 Kamagong cor. Bagtikan Sts., Makati T: 899-6278, 899-6281 OPEN: By appointment.

Über Finds

U B V

SPECIALTY: Bargain designer vintage pieces from Europe, Singapore, and Hong Kong.

The pre-loved items are from stylists, private shoppers, celebrities, and fashionistas. A friend of the store owners who has vintage stores in Europe also supplies Über Finds with obscure high-street brands, mostly in smaller Asian sizes that are hard to move in Europe. New pieces are thrown in for a collection that is both retro and updated.

THAT VINTAGE LV, REAL OR BOOTLEG?

The Louis Vuitton monogram is intact all throughout a bag. If part of the L or V is eaten by a seam, then that, dear shopper, is no LV.

PRICES: 20%–50% off SRP for pre-loved designer items, 10% off for new designer items. Non-branded vintage items, P200–550 (tops, skirts), P500–1,000 (dresses, jeans). There's also a P99 rack.

PAYMENT: Cash, credit card, and lay-away plans for designer items in the five-digit (or more) price bracket. WEBSITE: uberfinds.multiply.com ADDRESS: 42 Esguerra St. cor. Eugenio Lopez Ave., South Triangle, Quezon City T: 799-2434 OPEN: Mon–Sat, 1 p.m.–11 p.m.; Sun, by appointment.

Vintage Restore

U B V

SPECIALTY: Custom-made retro-design bags and professional restoration/repair of vintage designer bags.

PRICES: Vintage-inspired handcrafted bags, P6,000–9,000; vintage bag restoration and repair, P2,500 and up.

PAYMENT: Cash. WEBSITE: vintagerestore.multiply.com ADDRESS: 2/F, 122 Doña Consolacion Bldg., Jupiter St., Bel Air, Makati T: 890-4326 OPEN: By appointment.

Anthem

U B V

SPECIALTY: Dressy and casual shoes that are locally made using imported and very soft Italian leather. Ideal for tweens and teens, with a line from cult pop brands like Paul Frank (of Julius the Monkey fame), Tokidoki (anime and J-Pop), and Harajuku Lovers (by pop star Gwen Stefani).

PRICES: Casual open-toed footwear like flip-flops and sandals, P580–1,300; casual urban, rubber soled shoes, P1,700 and up; dress shoes, P2,200 and up.

PAYMENT: Cash, credit card. ADDRESS: 3/L Greenbelt 5, Ayala Center, Makati OPEN: Daily, 10 a.m. – 8 p.m.

Boon, Inc.

U B V

SPECIALTY: Innovative bathing, feeding, storage, and child-mobility product lines for babies and kids from a U.S. design studio committed to making parenting easier.

Boon products look like toys but have serious ergonomics and multifunctionality. Potties come with storage compartments, bath toys double as scrubs, and kiddie bean bags can store clothes. Above all, products adhere to high safety standards: items are free of toxins and made with blunt edges and rounded corners, while bath products are non-water-absorbent to prevent the growth of mildew, mold, and bacteria. Boon is available at all Rustan's Department Store branches and Babyland branches. Pre-orders are accepted for locally unavailable items.

PRICES: Interlocking plates and bowl set (for babies 9 mos and up), P799; rounded toddler utensils, P299 a pair; toilet-training potty with side storage compartments, P2,899; bath toys and scrubbies, P699 for a set; kiddie bean bag with storage, P3,000–5,000.

PAYMENT: Cash, credit card. WEBSITE: booninc.com EMAIL: melissa.j.so@gmail.com ADDRESS: G/L Midland Manor II, 31 Ortigas Ave., Greenhills, San Juan T: 724-9316 M: 0920-951-8009

Legend: U=Unique, B=Bargain, V=Variety

Club Princess

U B V

SPECIALTY: Royal makeovers, miniature beauty products, and accessories for tweens and teens.

Glittery, whimsical, and done in delicious candy pastels, Club Princess is a little girl's haven of accessories, miniature beauty products, nail care, glitter tattoos, and royal makeovers. Such is the level of "royal treatment" here that if they run out of the product you want to buy, they will usually offer you or your little girl a makeover or some other treatment on the house for your trouble. The shop also throws private princess parties for a maximum of 20 people, where you can have the place to yourself and your little girl's guests for the day with a set party package of treatments and goodies.

PRICES: Royal makeover, P395; glitter tattoo, P95; Buy the Bucket, P50 (set of fancy accessories, clips, Band-aid strips with colorful cute prints). Private party packages, P9,800 and up for 10 people (includes use of shop, royal makeovers, treatments, and giveaways.)

PAYMENT: Cash, credit card. ADDRESS: G/L B1-08 Bonifacio High St., Bonifacio Global City, Taguig T: 856-2821, 900-2739 M: 0917-839-8858, 0917-846-2193 OPEN: Mon–Thu, 12 nn–9 p.m.; Fri/Sat, 12 nn–12 mn; Sun, 12 nn–11 p.m.

Kiddie Salons

They come with kiddie distractions like race-car seats, cartoon DVDs, toys, and a staff trained in cheering up squirming tots while carefully snipping their hair off.

CUTS 4 TOTS
Glorietta T: 817-0108
V-Mall Greenhills T: 727-6087
The Block SM North EDSA
T: 442-0021
TriNoma T: 916-6114

KIDS HAIR SALON
Robinsons Galleria T: 634-3266
Rustan's Makati T: 817-6682
SM Southmall T: 805-1292
Podium T: 637-5462
Market! Market! T: 843-7821
SM City Manila T: 522-4047

Coco and Jam (online)

U B V

SPECIALTY: Educational freeplay toys (kids age 2 and up) and anti-slip baby and toddler sock shoes.

Partnering with leading toy companies in the U.S. and Europe, the shop specializes in non-mechanical freeplay toys that stimulate children's creativity and imagination. Bilibo, a bestseller, is a sturdy plastic toy formed by two detachable half-shell pieces. Tots can rock in it, clamber over it, or use it as any prop of their choice in make-believe games. Even the battery-run toys are educational. The Teach-a-Tot dolls narrate step by step how they brush their teeth, dress up, etc.

The latest hot item, Bical Baby Grippers for babies and toddlers, is a line of washable, non-toxic, and anti-microbial shoes that fit and breathe like a sock but have flexible non-slip rubber soles. They're especially for toddlers who've just learned to walk and who'll eventually discover running. Parents don't have to worry as much about their little ones slipping and falling. Coco and Jam is consigned at several branches of Hobbes & Landes. You can also order online, where shipping is free for purchases upward of P3,500.

PRICES: Bilibo, P1,800; Bical Baby Grippers, P1,450 a pair.

PAYMENT: Cash, credit card. WEBSITE: cocoandjam.com EMAIL: cocoandjam@gmail.com, info@cocoandjam.com T: 634-2556

Dash

U B V

SPECIALTY: Kids wear with attitude (the anti-Disney apparel).

PRICES: Jeans, P1,200 and up; playsuits, P900 and up; Busquets backpacks, P1,200 and up.

PAYMENT: Cash, credit card. ADDRESS: 3/L Greenbelt 5, Ayala Center, Makati OPEN: Daily, 10 a.m. – 8 p.m.

Florsheim Kids

U B V

SPECIALTY: Top-quality dress shoes for kids to tweens.

A top American shoe brand, Florsheim has always been known for durability and comfort, the latter of which is elusive among mid-range and department-store-bought dress shoes. Florsheim Kids features a good collection of school shoes, loafers, and leather dress shoes for both boys and girls in classic designs and sizes that even young adults can fit into. Made of genuine napa leather with thermo plastic rubber insoles, the shoes are durable but pliant enough to conform to your foot's natural curvature. They're perfect for kids who are past drastic growth spurts and need a a pair that will last—all with the comfort of second skin.

PRICES: P2,500 per pair.

PAYMENT: Cash, credit card. ADDRESS: 3/L Greenbelt 5, Ayala Center, Makati OPEN: Daily, 10 a.m. – 8 p.m.

Hoodieholic (online)

U B V

SPECIALTY: Authentic branded American West Coast style funky hoodies, with a limited-edition, handpainted line featuring psychedelic, gothic, and Kawaii pop designs. Brands include Billabong, O'Neill, Vurt, Etnies, Forever 21, Wet Seal, Kirra, Roxy, Ripcurl and Delias. All products are U.S.-imported and brand new with tags still intact.

PRICES: 30%–50% lower than commercial retailers.

PAYMENT: G-Cash, bank deposit. WEBSITE: hoodieholic.multiply.com M: 0917-479-6478, 0920-222-2277

Indigo Baby (online)

U B V

SPECIALTY: All-natural, organic, aromatherapy line of baby bath and body products, DEET-free insect repellent, breastfeeding ponchos.

Indigo Baby's bath and body line uses organic and all-natural ingredients ensured to be safe for newborns, free from Parabens, artificial perfumes, petrochemicals, Lanolin, and other unnecessary synthetic ingredients. Most of the products contain lavender and blue chamomile, known to calm the fussiest of babies. One of its carrier products, the Jar of Hope First Aid Gel, is used to relieve diaper rash, cuts, bruises, insect bites, even baby's colicky, irritable moments. Another effective and popular product is the Shoo Fly Insect Don't Bother Me Repellant, a light, non-greasy milk lotion using a cocktail of lavender, geranium, eucalyptus, and citronella essential oils.

Indigo Baby also carries other parenting accessories such as the Boncho or breastfeeding ponchos, and Nappy Clutch, a stylish take on changing pads that fits any handbag or can be worn fashionably around one's wrist. Other items to check out: reusable Milk Trays made for storing breastmilk, made of flexible BPA-free plastic, durable enough for the freezer, and with 16 1-ounce cavities that fit any bottle opening; and the Fridge-to-Go, a collapsible carrier that keeps breastmilk, juice, and food chilled with built-in surround cooling for six to nine hours. Order online or visit the showroom.

PRICES: Jar of Hope First Aid Gel, P325; Shoo Fly Insect Don't Bother Me Repellant, P575 (250 ml); Boncho, P565; Nappy Clutch, P750; Milk Trays, P1,165 (set of 2); Fridge-to-Go, P1,800.

PAYMENT: COD, bank deposit, G-Cash, Smart Money, or PayPal. WEBSITE: indigomanila.multiply.com EMAIL: indigo.manila@gmail.com ADDRESS: 120 Capt. Manzano St. by N. Domingo on Pinaglabanan, Brgy. Pedro Cruz, San Juan T: 725-9285 M: 0922-849-9892 OPEN: Showroom, Mon – Fri, 9 a.m. – 5 p.m.

Jump

U B V

SPECIALTY: Hip, design-savvy urban footwear for kids and teens.

An offshoot of established hip and edgy footwear store Shoe Salon, Jump has the same level of style savvy, only in much smaller sizes. Well-heeled kids, tweens, and young teens can now sport Ipanema and Grendha sandals and slippers, Nike Air Force One rehashes, and Papillon sandals at their next playdate or high school soirée.

PRICES: P2,500 and up for a pair.

ADDRESS: 3/L Greenbelt 5, Ayala Center, Makati OPEN: Daily, 10 a.m. – 8 p.m.

Levels of Discovery

U B V

SPECIALTY: Furniture and home accessories especially designed for children from birth to age 12.

Levels of Discovery, a U.S.-based children's furniture design and manufacturing company and retailer, caters to parents looking to stamp their homes with their child's personality. Available through local distributor Mavinix Inc., Levels of Discovery carries designs that go well beyond typical blue and pink pieces. Probably only here can you find a leopard-print chaise longue miniaturized to fit your little preschooler, or an heirloom kiddie rocking chair with built-in paint palette, supplies storage, and photo slot.

Multifunctionality is another key product feature. A toilet trainer potty can transform into a chair once your tot has been trained, and most benches and big furniture also act as storage bins. When it comes to child safety, Levels of Discovery claims that its products are tested by an independent, internationally recognized testing laboratory based on safety standards issued by U.S. child safety boards and quality-control agencies. Paint used on the furniture is continually re-certified to ensure compliance with all standards for lead or heavy metal content.

PRICES: Rocking chairs, P5,000–7,000; toy box bench with storage, P7,000; kiddie chaise longue with storage compartment, P8,000 and up.

PAYMENT: Cash, credit card. WEBSITE: levelsofdiscovery.com
ADDRESS: Unit 303 Cityland III, VA Rufino cor. Esteban Sts., Legaspi Village, Makati T: 494-1949, 216-1229 M: 0917-790-7377 OPEN: By appointment.

Loot Fairy (online)

SPECIALTY: Customizable loot bags, loot-bag toys, and Ecobloks (environment-friendly wooden toys for kids ages 3 and up).

Loot Fairy specializes in loot-bag creations and eco-savvy "open-ended" toys handcrafted from wood that are said to promote a child's creativity and imagination. Loot-bag designs are fully customized. A typical bag can contain a set of wooden "transformers," colorful maracas, handmade bookmarks, fun-shaped wooden magnets, a miniature coffee-table set, a miniature handyman tool set, and a small board game. (Loot-bag toys can be bought individually.) There are also more "grown-up" toys such as kiddie zips (fabric strips for twirling and spinning much like those in ribbon gymnastics). Another eco-savvy product line is Ecobloks, wooden building blocks in multiple shapes and sizes made from scrap mahogany (i.e., no new trees are cut in manufacturing). Ecobloks are machine-cut but hand-finished to ensure that each piece is free of splinters and sharp edges.

PRICES: Custom drawstring canvas loot bag with individually printed guest names, P125. Loot-bag toys like wooden transformers, P60 a piece; handpainted maracas, P130 a pair; small board game, P15. Multicolored kiddie zips (with 50" to 57" tails, for ages 10 and below), P475 a pair; Ecobloks, P350 (set of 19), P850 (set of 52).

PAYMENT: Cash, bank deposit. WEBSITE: lootfairy.multiply.com
EMAIL: lootfairy@gmail.com M: 0918-944-8332

Nanay Manila (online)

SPECIALTY: Pentatonic handmade wooden lyre.

Nanay Manila, an advocate of the Waldorf non-traditional method of child education, offers handmade wooden lyres—maybe not the most popular of instrument choices, but touted as one that is easy for both parents and young kids to learn and bond over before bedtime.

PRICES: Pentatonic handmade wooden lyre with hard-back leather case, tuning key, and songbook, P8,000.

PAYMENT: Cash, credit card. WEBSITE: nanaymanila.com EMAIL: myquaintlife@yahoo.com T: 716-6007 M: 0917-540-4455

Next9 (online)

U B V

SPECIALTY: Baby slings and leak-proof cloth diapers.

Locally made ring slings (fabric baby slings fastened by two rings), light and durable for "baby-wearing," are put through a 250 lb pull test to ensure that they can handle a baby's weight. Innovative all-in-one diaper line Tushy Wushy combines the absorption rate of cloth diapers with the function of a waterproof diaper cover. Next9 also sells nursing covers and maternity wear.

PRICES: Ring slings, P1,000–1,500; washable and reusable diapers, P1,000 (pack of 3 in different colors).

PAYMENT: Cash, bank deposit, G-Cash. WEBSITE: next9.org EMAIL: info@next9.org T: 331-8590, 722-5436 M: 0917-532-5643

Pick A Diaper (online)

U B V

SPECIALTY: Generic, affordable diapers for delivery. Also does meet-ups where you can pick up your order at the following spots: (Makati) Ineng's Link between Landmark and Shangri-La (weekdays, 12:30 p.m.), Citibank Valero entrance (weekdays, 9 a.m.–3 p.m. except lunch), (Taguig) Market Market (Fridays, 5:30 p.m.), (Parañaque) UCPB Sucat, SM Bicutan, McDo BF, and Evangelista.

PRICES: P100 and up for a pack of 30 pcs.

PAYMENT: Cash. WEBSITE: pickadiaper.multiply.com ADDRESS: 2 San Dionisio Ave., San Dionisio Village, Sucat, Parañaque T: 825-4519 (look for Lei Sta. Ana) M: 0917-957-0002

PinoyBaby (online)

U B V

SPECIALTY: Eco-friendly baby and parenting products.

Carrier product is the Thirsties Diaper Cover, a breathable, reusable leak-proof cover for cloth diapers imported from the U.S. Also available is the Thirsties Fab Fitted Diaper, a modern take on cloth diapers which fits like a disposable. Since PinoyBaby Store promotes natural parenting, it also distributes organic bath and body products for baby and mommy, baby pouches, and natural (wooden) toys. Get your orders via delivery or arranged pick-up.

PRICES: Thirsties Diaper Cover, P799 (pack of 4); Thirsties Fab Fitted Diaper, P940 (pack of 4); Starter Set (with assorted diapers and covers), P2,650. Plus shipping.

PAYMENT: Cash, bank deposit, G-Cash. WEBSITE: store.pinoybaby.com EMAIL: info@pinoybaby.com

Proud Mama (online)

U B V

SPECIALTY: Extensive line of baby, kiddie, and mommy implements that are both pretty and practical.

A recent topseller, Funky Feet line is a collection of baby socks with fashionable prints like maryjanes, flats, sneakers, and loafers. Another unique item is the car seat slip covers, made of machine-washable fabric and waterproof lining. They preserve your car seat for subsequent kids, come in prints that camouflage small milk stains, and are easy to remove and put back on. Other items for modern parents: bug-repelling non-toxic Citronella wrist bands; bra extenders that accommodate cupsize upgrades during nursing months; mobile coolers for breast milk; and fashionable nursing dresses. Get your orders via delivery or arranged pick-up.

PRICES: Funky Feet, P500 (5 pairs), P320 (3 pairs); nursing dresses, P1,500 (plus P500 for custom designs); nursing cover-ups, P650; repellant wrist bands, P200 (good for 120 hours).

PAYMENT: Cash, bank deposit, G-Cash. WEBSITE: proudmamastore .multiply.com EMAIL: proudmamastore@gmail.com M: 0929-419-6387, 0922-830-0407 See directory for resellers.

Roots and Wings (online)

U B V

SPECIALTY: Modern parenting gear like dual sling baby carriers, nursing corsets, fashionable nursing bras, and belly bands.

The Saya Baby Carrier has a dual-sling design that takes the form of a pouch sling with the comfort and security of a baby wrap and has five basic carrying positions. The Corsierre is a three-in-one bra-cami-corset top that works as a feeding bra while offering tummy support and the sexy look of a corset. The shop also distributes La Leche League nursing bras, Babylegs (stylish baby leg/arm covers), and other mommy items like the Transition Tubes (belly bands for the expanding pregnant belly).

PRICES: Saya Baby Carrier, P950 and up; La Leche League nursing bras, P950 and up; Babylegs, P600 a pair; Transition Tubes, P250.

PAYMENT: Cash, bank deposit, PayPal. WEBSITE: rootswingsinc.com EMAIL: info@rootswingsinc.com ADDRESS: Unit 23 GVT Kaimito St., Valle Verde I, Pasig T: 671-5826 M: 0917-892-0195 OPEN: Mon–Fri, 10 a.m.–5 p.m. by appointment.

Shop Familia

U B V

SPECIALTY: Imported high-end gear and wear for babies to tweens.

Shop Familia's clothing collection reads like a "who wore what" of Hollywood kiddie couture, with brands like Zutano, Kaiya Eve, and Umi worn by celebrity tots like Heidi Klum's daughter and David Letterman's son. Shop Familia also carries Weil Baby feeding gear, a U.S.-based pediatrician-developed line of BPA-free nursing bottles clinically proven to reduce colic. Training spouts and cups that help your child transition from bottle feeding and orthodontic pacifiers are also available.

PRICES: Formal dresses, P3,000 and up; printed onesies and rompers, P900 and up; hand stitched suede baby shoes, P1,400 and up. Weil Baby feeding set, P3,000 (4 bottles, extra nipples, cleaning kit).

PAYMENT: Cash, credit card, bank deposit, G-Cash. WEBSITE: shopfamilia.com.ph ADDRESS: G/L La'O Centre Bldg., 1000 Arnaiz cor. Makati Aves., Makati T: 836-2021 M: 0915-893-9752. OPEN: Daily, 10 a.m. – 7 p.m.

Smile Shoppe (online)

U B V

SPECIALTY: School humor baby tees and T-shirts with cartoon character depictions of "Mr. Blue Eagle" or "Little Miss Cheerleader." Themes are also taken from the movie of the moment, like "Little Miss Gryffindor" (of Harry Potter fame) and "Little Miss Cullen" (of Twilight fame).

PRICES: Shirts, P250 and up.

PAYMENT: Bank deposit, G-Cash. WEBSITE: smileshoppe.multiply.com

Sugarfree and Blue

U B V

SPECIALTY: Anime cosplay outfits and accessories for tweens and up.

PRICES: Anime cosplay hoodies, tops, and head gear, P600 and up.

PAYMENT: Cash, bank deposit, G-Cash. WEBSITE: sugarfreeandblue.multiply.com ADDRESS: 2/L Festival Supermall, Filinvest, Alabang, Muntinlupa T: 659-2513, 727-0160 OPEN: Daily, 10 a.m.–8 p.m. See directory for other branches.

Tarte Tatin

U B V

SPECIALTY: "Little Parisian" apparel for little girls and tweens.

Local brand Tarte Tatin is all about chic and whimsical, devoid of shmaltzy ruffles. Signature items include opaque stockings and leggings in several colors, sailor tops, riding pants, tunics, kaftans, sleek cropped jackets, and ballerina skirts made diaphanous with layers of tulle and a petticoat.

PRICES: Tops, P800 and up; diaphanous petticoat skirts, P1,500 and up.

PAYMENT: Cash, credit card. ADDRESS: 3/L Greenbelt 5, Ayala Center, Makati OPEN: Daily, 10 a.m.–8 p.m.

Tot Couture (online)

U B V

SPECIALTY: Chic felt baby shoes and bibs in a wide range of prints (zebra stripes, ladybug spots, comic crossbones, and dainty designs like paisley and Pucci-esque patterns) for ages 1 to 12 months. Some of the shoes and bibs come in matching prints.

PRICES: Baby shoes, P300–350 a pair; bibs, P150. Plus shipping.

PAYMENT: Bank deposit, G-Cash. WEBSITE: totcouture.multiply.com EMAIL: totcouture@gmail.com

Toy Kingdom and Toys R Us

U B V

SPECIALTY: Top two retailers of the newest toy releases for kids of all ages. These two stores are always the first to bring in the biggest toy hits in the U.S. They were the only ones who were fully stocked with those metal toy scooters and waveboards that were all the rage with kids.

PRICES: Standard manufacturer's SRP. But range is astoundingly wide—there are small toys no more than P100, as there are techy collectibles like 4D space shuttle models priced at P8,500.

TOY KINGDOM WEBSITE: toykingdom.ph ADDRESS: UG/L Bldg. A, SM Megamall, EDSA cor. Julia Vargas Ave, Ortigas Center, Mandaluyong T: 636-1822 OPEN: Daily, 10 a.m. – 9 p.m.
TOYS R US WEBSITE: toysrus.com.ph ADDRESS: 4/L Robinsons Galleria, EDSA cor. Ortigas Ave., Quezon City T: 395-2110 OPEN: Daily, 10 a.m. – 9 p.m.

Youji & Me

U B V

SPECIALTY: Imported baby gear and eco-friendly "analog" baby toys.

Youji & Me retails "progressive parenting" brands like Boikido and Wee Gallery. France-based Boikido is a line of handmade wooden toys designed for children to actively use their imagination. Wee Gallery, on the other hand, is all about fun visual stimulation. They have flash cards with eye-catching black and white animal sketches on laminated boards sturdy enough to endure a baby's handling and biting. This retail store is also one of the few that carry the Easy Expression-hands-free pumping bra for busy nursing moms.

PRICES: Boikido toys, P1,500 and up; Wee Gallery wall graphics and canvases, P2,000 – 3,050; hands-free pumping bra, P2,000.

PAYMENT: Cash, credit card. WEBSITE: youjiandme.com ADDRESS: 3/L Greenbelt 5, Ayala Center, Makati T: 756-3838, 756-0767 M: 0917-539-6854 OPEN: Daily, 10 a.m. – 8 p.m.

Amistad Spa

U B V

SPECIALTY: Boutique-style spa with luxe Persian-inspired interiors, separate facilities for men and women, and a music lounge with floor where guests can relax on plush floor cushions and enjoy some savory deli sandwiches, various teas, and fruit platters after or in between treatments. The massages on offer are your standard shiatsu, Swedish, stone, etc. but the therapists are well-trained in all of them.

PRICES: Massage, P700 and up (1 hr, 20 mins); dry body oil and essential oil, P400 and up (100 ml).

WEBSITE: amistad-spa.com EMAIL: info@amistad-spa.com
ADDRESS: 1091 Quezon Ave., Sta. Cruz, Quezon City T: 794-5943
OPEN: Mon–Fri, 3 p.m.–3 a.m.; Sat/Sun, 1 p.m.–3 a.m.

Amuin Wellness

U B V

SPECIALTY: Spa and aromatherapy products using homegrown natural ingredients like lemongrass, mango, and lemon. Formulated by the Tagaytay's bed-and-breakfast spa Nurture Spa, products come in dark brown canvas totes, gift packs, or customized spa-on-the-go travel kits.

PRICES: Fruit-based scrubs and moisturizers, P350 and up (250 ml); dry body oil and essential oil, P400 and up (100 ml).

WEBSITE: amuinwellness.com ADDRESS: 2/L Air-Rich Bldg., Km. 19.5 East Service Rd., Sucat, Parañaque T: 838-0073 M: 0918-888-8772, 0920-9505724

ATHAG

U B V

SPECIALTY: *Hilot* therapy.

The *manghihilot* has been the village doctor of small communities in the Philippines earlier than the 16th century, before the Spaniards arrived.

Now, people in remote barrios that have no hospitals or doctors still rely on the *manghihilot* to diagnose and relieve maladies. Today's *manghihilot* commonly treats sprains, muscle pains, migraines, asthma, and arthritis. Frequently, people with no ailments still go for a round of *hilot* to improve blood circulation and remove toxins from the body. ATHAG—Association of Traditional Health Aid Givers—is dedicated to the practice of this Philippine "ancient healing art." At the clinic, a diagnosis is first done before treatment is applied. To avoid waiting, set an appointment before you go.

PRICES An hour of *hilot* therapy, P550.

PAYMENT: Cash. EMAIL: athag*hilot*@yahoo.com ADDRESS: 2/L Jacinta Bldg., EDSA Guadalupe, Makati T: 381-5456, 381-5466 OPEN: Daily, 9 a.m. – 8 p.m.

AZTA

U B V

SPECIALTY: Edgy, urban Asian pop hair styles on the cheap.

Inspiration from the F4 rage in 2004 gave birth to this chain of hip barbershops that could give spiky anime haircuts similar to those seen on the famed Taiwanese boyband stars of hit TV soap Meteor Garden. Named after the Filipino word "asta," meaning "the way one carries oneself," Azta gives its customers a salon atmosphere worlds away from the old ladies gossiping endlessly in cramped spaces reeking of perming solution. Instead, it provides an urban space and a friendly staff well aware of current hair trends. Azta consistently keeps its quality through feedback from customers and instituting its own Research, Training, and Quality Assurance (RTQ) Group. In partnership with international hair care brands Davines and Tigi Bed Head, Azta launches bi–annual seminars that update the staff with trends in the beauty industry. If you find yourself dissatisfied with the service, head on back within three days for a free back job.

PRICES: Basic haircuts start at P200 for women and P150 for men. Other specialty services: dreadlocks (P3,500 for shoulder-length hair, P800 for monthly maintenance thereafter), cornrows (starting at P1,500), and hair extensions (at P300/lock).

PAYMENT: Cash, credit card. WEBSITE: aztaurbansalon.multiply.com EMAIL: azta_urban_salon@yahoo.com OPEN: Daily, 10 a.m. – 9 p.m. ADDRESS: 2/L SMRC Bldg., Katipunan Ave. cor. B. Gonzales St., Loyola Heights (in front of Miriam College), Quezon City T: 434-6733 OPEN: Mon – Fri, 12 nn – 9 p.m.; Sat – Sun, 10 a.m. – 9 p.m. See directory for other branches.

Be Beautiful For Him

U B V

SPECIALTY: Waxing services, and purportedly the most thorough and painless Brazilian wax in town.

Be Beautiful For Him opened its doors in 1965 before bra-burning and the feminist movement became trendy. But longevity is always a good sign. For 44 years, this little salon has shampooed, manicured, and massaged an impressive clientele of politicians, politicians' wives, newscasters, fashion models, megastars, tycoons, their children, and their children's children. It's a power list tonier salons would kill to have. No wonder the owners don't see the need to update furniture or do PR. They don't have to. Be Beautiful For Him does business the old-fashioned way—personalized service at an affordable price. Prices of manicures, pedicures, waxing, facials, and haircuts are fantastic value given the skill and tenured experience of the staff. Call to make an appointment—the place fills up fast.

PAYMENT: Cash. ADDRESS: 8485 Kalayaan Ave., Makati T: 895-7305, 890-0772 OPEN: Mon – Sat, 9 a.m. – 6 p.m. Home service by appointment.

Bright Smile

U B V

SPECIALTY: Professional teeth whitening/lightening at lower prices.

PRICES: P2,000 for 1 session, P3,000 for 2 sessions (a session takes about 30 minutes).

PAYMENT: Cash. ADDRESS: 5/L Casman Bldg., 1198 Quezon Ave., Quezon City T: 387-0000, 415-1809 M: 0927-341-9220, 0939-247-6985, 0922-793-5564 OPEN: By appointment.

Brow Haus

U B V

SPECIALTY: Eyebrow construction—i.e., grid-technology-aided brow trimming and shaping (or re-shaping) according to face shape, eye shape, nose, chin, skin and age group. Therapists are trained in Singapore, where the establishment is based.

Here, threading and tweezing done for brow construction is less painful due to specialty tools and therapist training. Other services include Add A Color, where brows are either lightened or darkened with natural vegetable dye, and a host of lash enhancements (color, curl, extensions).

PRICES: Brow construction, P580; Add A Color, P900; lash enhancements, P1,800 and up; Brow Reconstruction (for damaged brows from shaving or over-plucking).

PAYMENT: Cash, credit card. WEBSITE: browhausmanila.multiply.com, twitter.com/BrowhausManila Also on Facebook. ADDRESS: 2/L Serendra, High Street, Bonifacio Global City, Taguig T: 90 1-0597, 501-3998 M: 0917-577-1352, 0917-847-2112 OPEN: Daily, 10 a.m. – 10 p.m.

Dental Spa Manila

U B V

SPECIALTY: Standard as well as cosmetic dental services (veneers, whitening) in a spa environment. You're given a robe, comfy bedroom slippers, and a welcome drink before you hop on the dentist's chair. A masseuse kneads away the tension on your shoulders and back before your dental procedure, then proceeds to give you a leg and foot massage while your dentist works on you. Truly a unique way to get your teeth done.

PRICES: Basic dental services with integrated massage, P2,500 and up.

PAYMENT: Cash, credit card. WEBSITE: dentalspamanila.com EMAIL: dentalspamanila@yahoo.com ADDRESS: Suite 1503 Medical Plaza Bldg., Amorsolo cor. de la Rosa Sts., Legaspi Village, Makati T: 893-6769 M: 0918-459-2683, 0917-533-9097 OPEN: Mon–Fri, 9 a.m. – 5 p.m.

Human Heart Nature (online)

U B V

SPECIALTY: 100% organic, Philippine-grown beauty products.

Human Heart Nature is priced competitively with mainstream, mass-marketed beauty products. Coming from their work in the nation-building movement, Gawad Kalinga, the owners made the conscious decision to have smaller profit margins so they could pass on more affordable prices to consumers. With its products, Human Heart Nature pushes the green agenda in the Philippines by providing a viable means of livelihood for Philippine organic farmers and quality products for their distributors. Bestsellers include the Honey Facial Cleanser and Make-up Remover (with antioxidants and Vitamin C), Citronella Bug Spray (safe enough for kids), and the Aloe Vera Kid's Shampoo in Banana scent. Products are sold online and through distributors.

PRICES: Honey Facial Cleanser and Make-up Remover, P90 (100 ml); Citronella Bug Spray, P100 (100 ml); Aloe Vera Kid's Shampoo, P33 (50 ml). Delivery within Metro Manila is free for orders above P750.

PAYMENT: Cash, credit card, G-cash. WEBSITE: humanheartnature.com EMAIL: customer.service@humanheartnature.com ADDRESS: Units A–B, 2 Feria Rd., Commonwealth Ave., Quezon City T: 494-3580, 408-5608 OPEN: Daily, 10 a.m. – 8 p.m.

I-Lash Extensions

U B V

SPECIALTY: Eyelash extensions in varying length and thickness, good for three months. Colored lashes (brown, blue, violet) also available.

Choose among short, medium, and long, as well as from natural to the more dramatic "mascara" for your lash extensions' length and thickness. Each extension is a pair of lash strands aligned with, then glued carefully to, your natural lashes. The procedure takes an hour and half your first session, so make sure you settle into a comfy position because you can't open your eyes once it has started. Check out website for promos and updates.

PRICES: Extensions are priced by thickness, not length. Fine extensions, P550; mascara extensions, P1,000–1,250. Half off for retouching (ideally done within 3 weeks of first application).

PAYMENT: Cash. WEBSITE: ilashsalon.multiply.com
EMAIL: ilashsalon@gmail.com ADDRESS: Unit GB-02, 2/L Greenlanes Arcade, Greenhills Shopping Center, Greenhills, San Juan (Entrance is beside Japan Home Center, right across Globe Hub, Connecticut Carpark.) T: 710-4626 OPEN: Daily, 10 a.m.–8 p.m.

Ilog Maria (online)

U B V

SPECIALTY: Fresh honey; organic skin care, bath and body, spa, and wellness products from honeybee-based ingredients like honey, beeswax, pollen, propolis, royal jelly, and bee venom.

Ilog Maria's commitment to quality is extraordinary. At the wake of the debilitating typhoon that was Ondoy, the family-run, Cavite-based business devoted its energy to rehabilitating its bee farms. A lot of the damage has been resolved, but the farm is not yet in fighting form. As a result, Ilog Maria has regulated its honey to one pot per customer so they can still meet much of the demand without compromising the purity of the honey, and they choose to remain outlet-free to keep prices low.

Legend: U=Unique, B=Bargain, V=Variety

Many swear by the efficacy of their products. The Propolis Throat Spray freshens breath, prevents colds, coughs, fever, and flu; and soothes sore throat, smoker's cough, and canker sores (singaw). Propolis Ointment is effective against bacterial and fungal skin infections, rashes, itching, mild to moderate psoriasis, wounds, burns, and bug bites. Fresh Frozen Royal Jelly induces relaxation and anxiety relief, helps hormonal balance, and can take the place of HRT. Half a teaspoon of their Fresh Bee Pollen every day ups your metabolism and energy and can even help burn fat.

The website has extensive literature on each product, and your orders arrive with flyers about each item's use and ingredients. Orders arrive after a day or two upon confirmation of payment.

PRICES: Propolis Throat Spray, P82.50 (30 ml); Propolis Ointment, P110 (25 g); Fresh Bee Pollen, P110 (50 g).

PAYMENT: Cash, bank deposit, G-Cash. WEBSITE: ilogmaria.com
EMAIL: info@ilogmaria.com

Institute of Inner Studies

U B V

SPECIALTY: Pranic healing.

As a generalization, what Indians call prana is the energy that animates the earth and the human body. It can be absorbed from the sun, the air, the ground, and other people. When a person is experiencing illness or disharmony, toxic energy and blockages can be drained from him and more prana can be directed at him by a pranic healer to renew vigor. People who undergo treatment sometimes find themselves feeling emotional and mildly disoriented, because their chakras (areas of the body that absorb energy) were opened up. The feeling passes naturally and ideally leads to a better sense of well-being. The Thursday pranic healing sessions at the Institute of Inner Studies are free of charge, but donations are appreciated.

PRICES: Treatment sessions on days and times outside of the regular Thursday session cost P500.

PAYMENT: Cash. ADDRESS: Room 206, Evekal Bldg., 855 Arnaiz Ave. (Pasay Rd.), Makati T: 819-1874, 812-2326 OPEN: Regular session OPEN: to all, Thu, 3:30 p.m. – 7 p.m.; other days and times by appointment.

Lay Bare Waxing

U B V

SPECIALTY: Affordable cold sugar wax hair removal system, said to be quicker and less painful than hot wax systems.

Lay Bare's cold waxing system uses a mixture of sugar, *calamansi*, and honey. The two most popular procedures in the salon are the underarm wax and the Brazilian wax. Aside from competitive pricing, Lay Bare also has a number of discount programs. Check out website for promos. Appointments can be made via phone or online.

PRICES: Underarm wax, P150; Brazilian wax, P450. As much as 50% less than prices at upscale salons and most waxing establishments.

PAYMENT: Cash, credit card. WEBSITE: lay-bare.com EMAIL: info@lay-bare.com OPEN: Daily, 10 a.m. – 9 p.m. ADDRESS: G/L Loyola Heights Condominium, Esteban Abada cor. Fabian St., Quezon City T: 473-6864, 434-0774 See directory for other branches.

Leyende (online)

U B V

SPECIALTY: Organic bath and body products.

Products are handmade, natural, and organic—no harsh chemicals, no residue from pesticides, herbicides, and chemical fertilizers. This means less chances of allergies and skin problems. Hardly any animal by-products are used and most of the ingredients are plant-based, tried and tested by both scientific and alternative medicine communities. Leyende's raw ingredients come from organically accredited farms and companies such as Plamil UK,

Legend: U=Unique, B=Bargain, V=Variety

Rain Forest Remedies, Honeybiz Australia Ltd., and Agbang Karite Africa, among others. Even the packaging uses reusable and recycled materials.

Leyende offers a comprehensive product line that includes Clear and Present Shampoo (made of pure aloe vera gel, organic egg whites, tea tree extract, and castor oil), Face Canvas Moisture Glider (with organic mango butter from India), Kiss Kiss Balm Balm (made of pure grade-A beeswax with organic calendula extract), Clouds in my Coffee soap (with *barako* granules), and Once Bitten Chocolate soap (with raw Brazilian chocolate). Order online or through its online list of resellers and distributors.

PRICES: Clear and Present Shampoo, P450 (280 ml); Face Canvas Moisture Glider, P450 (60 g); Kiss Kiss Balm Balm, P200 (15 g); Clouds in my Coffee soap, P130 (100 g); Once Bitten Chocolate soap, P150 (100 g).

PAYMENT: Cash, bank deposit, G-Cash. WEBSITE: leyende.com, leyende.multiply.com EMAIL: info@leyende.com ADDRESS: 27/L Burgundy Corporate Tower, 252 Sen. Gil Puyat Ave., Makati M: 0915–671-3154

Navales Dental

U B V

SPECIALTY: Cosmetic dentistry.

During a Navales Smile Makeover, Doctor Mitsy Navales studies your face—bridge of the nose, jawline, skin tone, laugh, how you talk, etc.—before she designs the smile that brings out your best, be it through porcelain crowns, realignment, or veneers. She spot-treats according to the needs of individual teeth. And because she's also a pediatric dentist, you don't need to worry as much about pain.

PRICES: P5,000 and up, depending on the extent of work to be done.

PAYMENT: Cash, credit card. WEBSITE: navalesdental.com EMAIL: info@navalesdental.com ADDRESS: 1710 Medical Plaza Bldg., Amorsolo cor. De La Rosa Sts., Legaspi Village, Makati T: 751-8101, 817-4824 OPEN: Mon/Wed – Sat, 9 a.m. – 5 p.m.

Neo Day Spa

SPECIALTY: Extensive line of specialty spa treatments such as Pre- and Post-Natal Massage, Lactation Massage (ease new moms into lactation), Yogassage (massage incorporating yoga positions), Caviar Facial (using premium black caviar from Biodroga, an upscale German skin care line), Ingham Reflexology, and Pearl Body Scrub. The pre-natal, post-natal, and lactation massages are done by certified pre-natal masseuses.

PRICES: Yogassage, P1,750 (90 mins); Pre-natal Massage, P1,150 (60 mins); Caviar Facial, P2,000 (90 mins).

PAYMENT: Cash, credit card. WEBSITE: neo.ph ADDRESS: G/L Net One Center, 26th St. cor. 3rd Ave., Bonifacio Global City, Taguig T: 815-8233, 815-6948 OPEN: Daily, 11 a.m. – 11 p.m. ADDRESS 2: Ki by Neo Day Spa, 35 Wilson cor. Washington Sts., Greenhills West, San Juan T: 584-6789, 584-6066 OPEN: Daily, 1 p.m. – 11 p.m.

Oasis Acupuncture

U B V

SPECIALTY: Acupuncture.

The World Health Organization has affirmed acupuncture's effectiveness in treating hypertension, pain, depression, and reproductive, respiratory, and digestive disorders. Dr. Ed Concepcion, owner of Oasis, is one of the most sought-after acupuncturists in the country. After training in Western medicine, he studied acupuncture in China and has specialized in it for almost 20 years. An appointment with him has to be made about three to four months in advance, there is a full staff of other acupuncture doctors.

PRICES: First session, P700; plus P10 per needle used. Number of needles depends on diagnosis before treatment. An average of 20 needles is used per session. Succeeding sessions, P650, plus cost of needles.

PAYMENT: Cash. WEBSITE: oasisacupuncture.org ADDRESS: Centro Maginhawa, 97 Maginhawa St., Teacher's Village, Quezon City T: 921-7649, 434-8490 OPEN: Mon – Sat, 9 a.m. – 11 a.m., 2 p.m. – 4 p.m.

Legend: U = Unique, B = Bargain, V = Variety

Sanctuario Spa

U B V

SPECIALTY: Indigenous Filipino and Oriental massage therapy and spa treatments using herbal concoctions and herbal baths. House special is the traditional *hilot* with virgin coconut oil

Located in Malate, Sanctuario Spa's main branch is a tranquil 1940s colonial-style house adorned with local antiques, art work, and ethnic linens. The lush grounds boast two whirlpools, a sauna, a steam room, a salon, a café, a Turkish Hammam scrub room, an Indian massage room, and outdoor massage villas. Sanctuario also offers novelty treatments like the Sacred Tantric Massage, Vishnu 4-Hand Massage, and Lava Stone Massage, and alternative healing like Acupuncture and Reiki, Xiamen Foot Reflexology, Bentosa Cupping, regional *hilot* specialties, exotic pampering treatments, and a full range of salon services. They also sell the organic oils, creams, and scrubs that they use, and have a unique line of occult items like amulets, charms, tumble stones, crystals, Mala beads, and Wiccan spells.

PRICES: Massage, P845–1,500; traditional Filipino healing therapies, P855–1,900; acupuncture, P4,555 (3 sessions); Reiki, P955 (1 hr).

PAYMENT: Cash, credit card. WEBSITE: sanctuariospa.com
ADDRESS: 1826 Jorge Bacobo St., Malate, Manila T: 450-1127 OPEN: Sun–Thu, 3 p.m.–12 mn; Fri/Sat, 3 p.m.–3 a.m. ADDRESS 2: 30 Sgt. Esguerra Ave., South Triangle, Quezon City T: 920-9963, 920-9970 OPEN: Sun–Thu, 3 p.m.–12 mn; Fri/Sat, 3 p.m.–3 a.m.

Strip

U B V

SPECIALTY: Bikini waxing, Brazilian waxing, and Boyzilian waxing (yes, Brazilian for boys!)

Strip, a Singapore-based franchise of waxing salons, has especially trained therapists who can work fast to minimize pain while giving you smooth and hair-free legs, arm pits, and nether regions. You get your own stripping kit (wax, spatulas, and wet wipes), which has 16 spatulas, so the therapist never has to double dip. Once a spatula is dipped in wax then touches your skin, it is discarded. Each treatment also comes with one cream to soothe post-waxing itch and irritation, and another to treat ingrown hairs and let hair grow out finer. For men, the Boyzilian comes with a squeeze toy and pain-relieving ointments. Check out their Twitter page for promos and updates.

PRICES: Brazilian, P1,200 (less 25% on Mondays); Boyzilian, P1,900.

PAYMENT: Cash, credit card. WEBSITE: twitter.com/stripmanila, stripmanila.multiply.com ADDRESS: 2/L Serendra, Bonifacio High St., Bonifacio Global City, Taguig T: 856-9145 M: 0917-847-2112 OPEN: Daily, 10 a.m. – 10 p.m. ADDRESS 2: 4/L Greenbelt 5, Legaspi St., Ayala Center, Makati T: 501-3997 OPEN: Sun – Thu, 11 a.m. – 9 p.m.; Fri/Sat, 11 a.m. – 10 p.m.

Venus & Mars (online)

U B V

SPECIALTY: Natural emu oil and emu oil-based products.

Historically used by Australian aborigines to treat burns, wounds, bruises and muscle and joint pains, emu oil is a rich source of antioxidants, Linoleic Acid (helps ease muscle pain), Oleic Acid (anti-wrinkle), and Terpinces (skin softeners), making it an all-around skin tonic. Venus & Mars mixes refined emu oil with high-grade all-natural ingredients to create a hypoallergenic skin care line. For purists, 100% premium Emu Oil is available in 30 ml and 50 ml bottles, and can be used as a moisturizer, makeup base, insect bite ointment, and relief for diaper rash, eczema, and psoriasis. Bestsellers include the emu soaps (with goat's milk, olive oil, and beeswax), the Happy Pores Toner (infused with the healing properties of cucumber), and the Emu Radiance Face Cream (can be used as a light foundation).

PRICES: V&M special soaps, P100 (60 g); glycerin soaps, P135 (100 g); creams and lotions, P225–390 (15–50 ml).

PAYMENT: Cash, bank deposit, G-Cash. WEBSITE: venusandmars08.multiply.com EMAIL: vandm08@yahoo.com M: 0927-924-0961

Legend: U=Unique, B=Bargain, V=Variety

105 Rada

U B V

SPECIALTY: Upscale furniture and homeware from high-street shops Scandinavia Trends, Curate, and Kitchen Studio.

105 Rada is home to Scandinavia Trends and Curate (both furniture and home accessory shops) and Kitchen Studio (specializes in customized kitchen assembly, design, and modular sets). Scandinavia Trends carries strong Danish brands known for their originality and timelessness, while Curate carries offbeat luxe pieces from Italian design houses. Both Scandinavia Trends and Curate carry the aesthetic sensibilities of their birth countries: subdued yet rich colors and clean lines for the Dane, artfully loud for the Italian. Common in both, though, is a strong commitment to ergonomics and aesthetics. Kitchen Studio, on the other hand, has been creating bespoke kitchens, cabinets, and shelves in a diversity of materials and themes. The showroom is but a sample of how they can mix and match designs and parts to come up with a kitchen that is truly one-of-a-kind.

PRICES: European designer homeware begets European prices, so expect to spend about P2,000 for a simple implement like a tea infuser (though so sleek it looks like a space-age art object).

PAYMENT: Cash, credit card. ADDRESS: 105 Rada, G/L RCI Bldg., 105 Rada St., Legaspi Village, Makati SCANDINAVIA TRENDS T: 813-3446 WEBSITE: scandinavia-trend.com EMAIL: info@scandinavia-trend.com OPEN: Mon–Sat, 10 a.m.–6:30 p.m. CURATE T: 473-3303 WEBSITE: curateworld.com EMAIL: info@curateworld.com OPEN: By appointment. KITCHEN STUDIO T: 894-0848 WEBSITE: kitchenstudioinc.net OPEN: Mon–Sat, 10 a.m.–6:30 p.m.

A-11

U B V

SPECIALTY: Limited-edition furniture and home accents from prominent Filipino designers, some from salvaged ancestral house parts and furniture.

A-11 was originally a 1940s split-level wooden house in a genteel tree-lined neighborhood. Now, it is a lifestyle boutique with items arranged and stacked to look like personal belongings rather than merchandise at a store. A-11 has no signage, so call for landmarks.

PRICES: Small home accents like vases and water jugs, P300 and up; desk lamps with unique European country fabric shades, P2,000 and up.

PAYMENT: Cash, check for big purchases (dining sets, furniture)
ADDRESS: 2680 F.B. Harrison St., Pasay T: 833-8357 OPEN: By appointment.

Angelino's Antiques

U B V

SPECIALTY: Second-hand vintage and salvaged heavy wooden furniture.

Without a store sign, this bodega gets lost amidst the steel and glass establishments dotting Libis. Inside, however, are nice finds for vintage buyers on a budget. The items are made from local hardwood and carry designs that would be at home in old Spanish houses. If you're prepared to sift through dust and cramped aisles, you can get to a well-preserved traditional narra birthing chair, a garden bench fashioned from a real kalesa, or a table hewn from the trunk of an acacia tree—all in need of just a little sanding and buffing.

PRICES: Vintage birthing chairs, garden kalesa benches, and Chinese wardrobe cabinets, P5,000 and up.

PAYMENT: Cash only. ADDRESS: 183 E. Rodriguez Jr. Ave., Bagumbayan, Quezon City T: 912-4410

Artemis

U B V

SPECIALTY: Contemporary furniture and statement home pieces made of woven seaweed and seagrass. Also features furniture imports from the following upscale brands: Donghia (contemporary furnishings from New

York, Hollywood clientele), Schumacher (American brand of modern ottomans and armoires), Jim Thompson (prestigious Thai silk company), Pierre Frey (traditional French fabric and wallpaper designer and manufacturer), and Gaston y Daniela (prestigious furnishing fabric brand in Spain).

PRICES: Seagrass accent lounge seat, P14,000; seagrass living room set, P85,000 and up.

PAYMENT: Cash, credit card. EMAIL: artemis1995@pldtdsl.net ADDRESS: 2245 Don Chino Roces Ave. (Pasong Tamo) cor. Sabio St., Makati T: 867-2381, 843-1142 OPEN: Daily, 10 a.m.–7 p.m.

Azcor

U B V

SPECIALTY: Architectural and decorative light fixtures that use local materials to accent sleek and contemporary designs. The resulting pieces are modern continental yet distinctly Asian.

PRICES: Table lamps start at P7,000, stand lamps at P8,500. A typical chandelier with 6 arms, P23,000–30,000.

PAYMENT: Cash, credit card. WEBSITE: azcor.com.ph ADDRESS: 1014-C Almeda Arcade, Arnaiz Ave. (Pasay Rd.), Makati T: 843-1963 to 64, 844-4490 or 96 OPEN: Daily, 10 a.m.–7 p.m. ADDRESS 2: 4/L Bldg. B, SM Megamall, Mandaluyong T: 633-1656, 633-4944 OPEN: Daily, 10 a.m.–8 p.m.

Bangkal Thrift Shops

U B V

SPECIALTY: Easy-to-refurbish second-hand furniture and home accessories of retro-inspired design.

In the area you will find Bangkal Bodega, a warehouse of second-hand PX goods and "Stateside" items and considered the mother lode of Bangkal's *segunda mano* industry. Around it, dotting the arterial network formed by Evangelista, Apolinario, and Hizon Streets, are several small, home-based shops that sell from their garages or sala turned showrooms precious thrift finds like art deco home accents, salvaged furniture made of hardwood like narra and mahogany, used European designer furniture, chinaware from England, vintage chandeliers from Prague, a few local antiques, and undervalued art works of prominent artists (like a P5,000 Malang print).

Pickings may not be as great as they were in the '90s, but Bangkal is still worth a gander. After all, going home with a ratty but authentic Mies van der Rohe chair makes an entire day of sifting through someone else's refuse well worth it. You can get a free map featuring Bangkal's flea market route from Fat Michael's, a kitsch restaurant within the area serving homespun Continental dishes.

PRICES: Art deco couches, P3,000 and up; period pieces like traditional Filipino daybeds and writing tables, P3,000 and up; designer chairs and home accessories, P800–3,000; vintage publications and art books, P200 and up.

PAYMENT: Cash. ADDRESS: Gen. Del Pilar cor. Gen. P. Santos Sts. (Bangkal Bodega); Apolinario, Hizon, and Evangelista Sts. for home-based Bangkal thrift shops; Barangay Bangkal, Makati OPEN: Mon–Sat, 9 a.m.–6 p.m.

Belliya's Candlelight

U B V

SPECIALTY: Citronella buckets (natural insect repellant, stylish and fragrant alternative to the unglamorous katol); votive candles that have been used as stress relievers, sleep inducers, aphrodisiacs, and party giveaways; scented candles with themed designs; eco-friendly candle stands and holders made from recycled wax.

For bulk orders, Belliya's can create customized packaging and append little messages and quotes on each candle. They deliver within Alabang (Tue–Thu) and Makati (Mon–Sat) given a minimum purchase of P500. Though they don't have a store, they join bazaars almost every month. Call, email, or check their website for bazaar schedules, orders, and delivery or pick-up details.

PRICES: Citronella pails, P380 each; refills, P280.

PAYMENT: Cash. WEBSITE: belliyas.com EMAIL: info@belliyas.com ADDRESS: 88 Roxas-Chua Circle, Pacific Village, Alabang, Muntinlupa T: 805-1163, 887-1281 M: 0918-942-2305, 0920-922-2696

Berde Tile and Foundry

U B V

SPECIALTY: Cold forged metals, art tiles, and slate plating.

There are three unique branded product lines and services under Berde's roof. First is Orum Cold Forged Metals, a cost-effective alternative to achieving the look of authentic metal finishes without the design limitations of real metal. This service uses aluminum, bronze, brass, copper, and iron sheets on plywood, PVC, concrete, even cardboard.

Second is Mimo Custom Art Tiles, which boasts the technology to put any image onto ceramic tiles, limestone tiles, and carpet tiles in high resolution and size—from floor tile to mural. All tile designs and sizes are customizable.

Last but not least is SlateLite, which infuses slate into fiberglass panels. The result is a product that has the same veneer as slate but is more lightweight, more flexible, easier to cut and reshape, and easier to install using commercial adhesives. Commonly used for wall panels, SlateLite is water-resistant and can be used for areas like fountains and hot tubs.

PRICES: Forged Metal starts at P500 per wall panel; art tile, P6,000 each; SlateLite starts at P2,290 per wall panel.

PAYMENT: Cash, credit card. WEBSITE: berde.com.ph EMAIL: info@tileandfoundry.com ADDRESS: Berde Showroom, G/L, LRI Business Plaza, 210 N. Garcia St., Bel Air, Makati T: 776-2281 to 85 OPEN: Daily, 10 a.m.–7 p.m.

Borders

U B V

SPECIALTY: Furniture and accents by Cebu-based international designers. Borders enjoys rapid turnover of its showroom pieces, mostly furniture made of wrought iron, sculpted rattan, and leather. Beyond that are home accents such as decorative wall panels, lacquer trays, Celadon bowls, etc.

PRICES: Home accents, P500 and up; big furniture like beds and modular L-sofas, P40,000 and up.

PAYMENT: Cash, credit card. WEBSITE: borders.com.ph EMAIL: sales@borders.com.ph ADDRESS: G/L, La Fuerza Bldg., Don Chino Roces Ave. (Pasong Tamo), Makati T: 893-2905, 893-2908 OPEN: Daily, 10 a.m. – 7 p.m. ADDRESS 2: 3/L Filipino Home Zone, Greenbelt 5, Ayala Center, Makati T: 729 7762 OPEN: Daily, 10 a.m. – 8 p.m.

Cardinal Ceramics

U B V

SPECIALTY: Ceramic and porcelain tableware at outlet prices.

Cardinal Ceramics has done commissioned pieces for five-star restaurants and hotels in Manila and for distinguished international ceramic retailers like Villeroy & Boch. Though offering deeply discounted prices here, Cardinal Ceramics has a long-standing reputation for high-quality tableware that even the so-called "rejects" offered at this factory outlet would be welcome pieces in any respectable hostess' home. The brand specializes in dainty blue and white tableware (reminiscent of Netherlands' famous Delftware) as well as elegant all-white pieces. Products run the gamut from tea sets, carafes, demitasses, coffee cups, mugs, serving dishes, flatware for full-course meals, ramekins, and even non-dining ware like scent diffusers, center piece containers, votives, and vases. Recent additions to the store's product line is a selection of imported Indian clothes, textiles, bags, and accessories.

Legend: U=Unique, B=Bargain, V=Variety

PRICES: As much as 85% lower than lifestyle and home accessory shops. A mug originally retailing at P200 can sell for as low as P60. Mid-sized flatware go for P300 and up for a set of 6; tea sets go for P700 and up for a tea pot and 6 cup-saucer pairs; small pieces like ramekins start at P50.

PAYMENT: Cash. WEBSITE: cardinalceramics.com ADDRESS: 121 Sacred Heart St., San Antonio Village, Makati T: 899-3730, 899-6394, 890-4216 OPEN: Daily, 8 a.m. – 6 p.m. ADDRESS 2: PSCOR Bldg., Elizalde cor. Elsie Gaches Sts., BF Homes, Parañaque T: 842-3917 OPEN: Daily, 8 a.m. – 6 p.m.

Cirkulo Laminates

U B V

SPECIALTY: Wall panel laminates made with indigenous materials like crushed young bamboo for a modern indigenous look.

Cirkulo laminates are bamboo panels laminated with various finishes and looks (some finishes look like woven mats, others have sleek pinstripes). Panels are chemically treated against termites, fungus, and mold. These panels can be used as wall or door accents, or as full coverage for table tops, counter tops, cabinet doors, and room partitions.

PRICES: A 2'×2' panel starts at P1,200.

PAYMENT: Cash, credit card. EMAIL: hmt_mnl@pldtdsl.net, hmtrading@pacific.net.ph ADDRESS: HM Trading, 2nd Ave., Santa Maria Industrial Estate, Bagumbayan, Taguig T: 839-2251 to 54 OPEN: Daily, 9 a.m. – 5 p.m. by appointment.

Contemporaneo

U B V

SPECIALTY: Custom-made and innovatively designed wooden furniture.

Exhibiting fine workmanship in hardwood furniture, Contemporaneo accepts commissioned work yet also carries a wide range of existing designs that trade in traditional for a more modern aesthetic. An example of this would be a minimalist, modular L-shaped sofa frame in bleached and agitated wood, or a high-back Moroccan chair with wooden cut-out strips for the back rest.

PRICES: Mahogany 4-seat dining room set, P45,000; narra and kamagong queen-sized bed, P85,000.

PAYMENT: Cash, check, credit card. EMAIL: contemporaneophil@yahoo.com, muebles_de_lizamyr@yahoo.com, muebles@pldtdsl.net.ph
ADDRESS: MC Home Depot, 167 Ortigas cor. Meralco Aves., Pasig
T: 641-5203, 643-3847, 641-5203 OPEN: Daily, 10 a.m. – 8 p.m.
ADDRESS 2: 32nd St., cor. Bonifacio Drive, Bonifacio Global City, Taguig M: 0922-837-8230 OPEN: Daily, 10 a.m. – 8 p.m.

Custom-Made Handcraft Traditions

U B V

SPECIALTY: Home accessories and lifestyle items handcrafted from non-timber forest resources.

PRICES: Cube-shaped *banig* beanbag made from handwoven pandan, P1,995 (16"×16"×11"); journal jackets handwoven from indigenous textiles, P195.

PAYMENT: Cash. ADDRESS: 92 A Masikap Ext., Diliman, Quezon City T: 929-3665 M: 0927-878-7002 OPEN: Mon – Fri, 9 a.m. – 5 p.m. by appointment.

Danilyn's

U B V

SPECIALTY: Custom-made modern furniture and fine home furnishings.

Danilyn's has been known among professional designers, interior decorators, and distinguished commercial establishments as a reliable source of custom-built modern furniture and home accessories. Some of the company's clients include reputable names in the local furniture and interior design industry, such as Artemis, Budji Layug, and Kish International. Other distinguished

Legend: U = Unique, B = Bargain, V = Variety

clients include Coconut Palace, Malacañang Palace, and Shangri-La Plaza Hotel. If you have a photo of a piece you want recreated, email it to them along with measurements and other relevant info. It's best to call before emailing so you can explain your needs and budget in detail.

PRICES: Drapery, typically P7,000; big 5-seat sofas, around P20,000. Prices vary widely depending on style, size, and materials.

PAYMENT: Cash. WEBSITE: danilyns.com EMAIL: danilynsmail@yahoo.com ADDRESS: Block 7, Lot 9 Gladiola St., T.S. Cruz Subdivision, Almanza Dos, Las Piñas T: 850-4638, 850-4639, 809-2269 OPEN: By appointment.

Dapitan Arcade

U B V

SPECIALTY: "Shabby chic" export-overrun rattan and abaca handicrafts, wicker and wrought iron home accessories, and country-themed tableware.

Resembling a covered court, the roofed quadrangle houses about 76 stalls à la tiangge layout, with a few more vendors spilling out onto nearby sidewalks and streets. This poor man's Pottery Barn is jampacked with stalls and isn't air-conditioned, so be prepared to rummage in the heat and dust. Another thing, stalls aren't organized according to product category or in any kind of order. A good idea would be to comb through the entire area first and note down the stall numbers that interest you so you can go back and make your purchases after your round. If you look hard enough, you might come across unique finds and collectibles like recreations of Matryoshka dolls (those Russian nesting dolls in graduated sizes). Stocks are refilled and new items are brought in during the Christmas season, so choices are especially varied around this time. But prices also jump and vendors are less relenting as they take advantage of the holiday rush. To get the best of both inventory and price, come to Dapitan Arcade around end of September to first week of October—you'll be in time for new arrivals but ahead enough of last-minute gift buyers to haggle and get as much as 45% off.

PRICES: Flatware, P30 each; P250 and up each for big serving platters similar to lacquerware. Abaca lanterns, P65 and up; 5-pot wrought iron hanging plant holder, P250; Buddha busts, P300 and up; imitation Matryoshka dolls, P500 and up per set of 7; Kokeshi doll recreations (handcarved and handpainted traditional Japanese limb-less dolls), P150 and up for each; large leather jewelry boxes (about 8"×10"), P400–600; multi-bulb upright canvas lamps, P1,200–1,800; 5-drawer narra bureau (about 48"×60") with mother of pearl accents, P19,000.

PAYMENT: Cash. ADDRESS: Kanlaon cor. Dapitan Sts., Sta. Mesa Heights, Manila T: 411-0252 (arcade administrator) OPEN: Daily, 7 a.m.–7 p.m.

Designs Ligna

U B V

SPECIALTY: Upscale custom-made wooden furniture with innovative design; furniture embellished with local and exotic natural materials like handcut coconut shells, hand-crushed bamboo, and abaca.

The company has over 40 years' worth of experience in engineering and designing wood ("ligna" in Latin). In-house teams of designers and craftsmen (some of whom have been with the company for 30 years) are highly trained in Scandinavian designs (clean lines, sleek geometric shapes) as well as carrying out custom designs. Designs Ligna uses timber only from sustainable sources such as white ash (the same durable wood used to make American baseball bats), solid maple, teak, and Philippine mahogany. It is also one of the very few local furniture manufacturers that can veneer its own items with wood and leather. Local exotic materials such as vines, shells, bark, leaves, coconut shells, bamboo, wicker, malacca poles, abaca, and seagrass are used as furniture embellishment.

PRICES: Beds from theme collections, P100,000 and up (queen size); narra cabinet, P18,000; seagrass and abaca lounge chair, P14,000 and up.

PAYMENT: Cash, credit card. EMAIL: makatisales@designsligna.com, mari_gomez@designsligna.com ADDRESS: 2/L Almeda Arcade Bldg., Arnaiz Ave. (Pasay Rd.), Makati T: 845-3027 OPEN: Daily, 10 a.m. – 7 p.m. See directory for other branches.

Dexterton

U B V

SPECIALTY: A vastly extensive line of high-end European concept furniture and home accessories.

Dexterton houses a full line of building-, home-, and furniture-related products in an eight-story showroom in Quezon City and a new auxiliary showroom in Makati. The store carries items from both prestige lines like Philippe Starck and Ludwig Mies van der Rohe (of Barcelona chair fame) and obscure but trend-shaping studios like Kartell (famous for their acrylic chairs). Dexterton also has an extensive range of bathroom and kitchen fixtures from brands used in upscale restaurants, hotels, and resorts.

PRICES: Acrylic chairs, P6,000 to P20,000 each; animal-print lounge chair, P40,000; lamps, P7,000 and up; small-scale utilitarian items like shower heaters, P5,000 and up.

PAYMENT: Cash, credit card. WEBSITE: dexterton.com.ph ADDRESS: 157 Sgt. E. Rivera St., Quezon City T: 362-1111, 361-6006 M: 0917-858-1838, 0917-858-5838 OPEN: Daily, 10 a.m. – 8 p.m. ADDRESS 2: 3/L Greenbelt 5, Ayala Center, Makati T: 960-8999 M: 0917-505-6168 OPEN: Daily, 10 a.m. – 8 p.m.

DST

U B V

SPECIALTY: Ovenproof ceramics, dishware, restaurant ware, porcelain, and kitchen accents on the cheap.

Plates come in varied sizes, shapes, and designs (though, peculiarly, none of them is round); ramekins are in an astounding array of sizes. Most notable are their tea sets for one. Painted with idylls depicting rural Oriental life, the tea pot comes with a strainer to keep errant tea leaves from swirling in your drink. A three-piece genius of an accompanying cup is comprised of the cup itself, a (detachable) strainer of sorts built into the cup, and a cover for keeping your tea hot. As a bonus, the cover flips upside down and can be used as a "parking slot" for the strainer while you drink. All DST plates are ovenproof, so they can go straight from the oven to the table then to the refrigerator.

PRICES: Teapot and cup set, P350 and up; coffee cups with saucers, P350 (set of 6); ramekins, P300 and up (set of 4 in graduated sizes).

PAYMENT: Cash. ADDRESS: 204 Del Monte Ave., Quezon City
T: 414-0928 M: 0917-455-7292 OPEN: Daily, 10 a.m. – 8 p.m. Also available at San Lorenzo Weekend Market every Sunday, 7 a.m. – 2 p.m.

Garden Strips in the City

U B V

SPECIALTY: Long stretches of roadside vendors selling a wide variety of gardening and landscaping needs, from potted plants and path pebbles to outdoor fountains and topiaries.

This entry isn't about a store as much as it is about three streets in the city that serve as accessible one-stop hubs for gardening and landscaping needs. These streets are Katipunan (White Plains) in Quezon City, Concha Cruz Street in Parañaque, and Daang Hari in Las Piñas.

The Katipunan garden strip spans about a kilometer from the corner of Boni Serrano (Santolan) to Temple Drive. It is perhaps the most diversified of the three since, apart from potted plants and a host of gardening needs, it also has two big koi fish and pond stores, one sizeable area with nothing but several tall heaps of different types of pebbles, garden stones, and sand, and ornamental plants beyond the usual potted mums and carnations. Among the three, only here will you find those upright, reed-like pygmy bamboo plants sleek enough to look at home in a swanky bachelor's pad.

On the other hand, what Concha Cruz and Daang Hari lack in exotic choices, they make up for in convenience. Southerners don't have to go all the way to the "mainland" and subject themselves to traffic jams just to get a few pots and seedlings. Pickings here are nothing to scoff at in the first place. Concha Cruz, which stretches out well over eight blocks from the corner of Elizalde St. going towards Alabang-Zapote Road, has enough variety for all kinds of green thumbs, whether you're one who wants some flowers, a landscape hobbyist, or a chef looking to plant his or her own herb garden. There's even a smattering of small shops selling overrun outdoor furniture from Cebu. Daang Hari more or less gives you similar pickings and prices as those of Tagaytay and Cavite streetside garden vendors, and has a substantial range of fruit and vegetable seedlings.

PRICES: Prices in Katipunan and Concha Cruz are pretty standard, with potted herbs starting at P50, potted flowers at P100, and large decorative clay pots (enough for a small tree) at P300 and up. Daang Hari's prices are lower by about 10%.

PAYMENT: Cash. KATIPUNAN ADDRESS: From Katipunan cor. Boni Serrano (Santolan) to cor. Temple Drive, Quezon City CONCHA CRUZ ADDRESS: Concha Cruz cor. Elizalde Sts., Parañaque DAANG HARI ADDRESS: Daang Hari, about 3 km down towards Cavite, Las Piñas

---

Hamburg International

U B V

SPECIALTY: Modernist fixtures and fittings both sleek and flexible enough to mix and match when designing your dream bathroom.

Hamburg International carries prominent European bathroom fixture and fittings brands such as Rain Sky (shower fitting that pours out water, mist, even fragrances that you can program beforehand) and Villeroy & Boch (famous for multifunctional and sleek metal bathroom consoles that combine the functions of a beauty salon, fitness room, and dressing room).

PRICES: Tap fittings start at P2,500; bathroom sinks and ceramic fixtures start at P15,000; bigger implements like bathtub systems and modular bath consoles go north of P120,000.

PAYMENT: Cash, credit card. EMAIL: hisc@pldtdsl.net ADDRESS: G/L, BMG Centre, San Antonio St., Paseo de Magallanes Commercial Center, Makati T: 854-1442 OPEN: Daily, 10 a.m. – 7 p.m.

Heima

U B V

SPECIALTY: Contemporary trends and kitsch-cool graphic prints fused with classic furniture and home accessory designs; generally all manner of home ware with counterpoint concept themes like vintage modern, graphic minimalist, Neo-Asian, and modern glam.

There's an underlying aesthetic coherence amidst Heima's motley crew of items that evokes fantasy and whimsy. Think Tim Burton's Alice in Wonderland, or, in design parlance, Martha Stewart on psychedelic 'shrooms. A few pieces that speak to Heima's look would be the "Happy Couch," a huge two-seater upholstered in a patchwork of various imported harmoniously mismatching fabrics; or the love seat in the shape of a woman's oversized pair of fat, plump lips; or restored traditional writing tables with the classic brass handles but redone in colors that match your iPod. Heima also features Wall Arts by MDM designs and eco-friendly items from Indie Art & Brown Label and Beansprout Inc. A popular novelty item in their eco line, the Sun Jar is a solar-powered LED night light that comes in cute, jelly-colored jars. They easily sell out, so call first to check for availability.

PRICES: Happy Couch, P30,000; concept design benches and standard-sized two-seaters, P12,000 and up; Sun Jars, P900 and up.

PAYMENT: Cash. WEBSITE: heimastore.multiply.com, heimastore.com EMAIL: heimastore@yahoo.com ADDRESS: G/L Shop 33, Cubao Expo, Gen. Romulo Ave., Araneta Center, Cubao, Quezon City T: 911-3540 OPEN: Daily, 1 p.m. – 9 p.m. ADDRESS 2: Unit 229 LRI Design Plaza, 210 Nicanor Garcia St. (Reposo), Bel Air 2, Makati T: 798-0027 M: 0917-810 4346 OPEN: Daily, 1 p.m. – 9 p.m.

liideas

U B V

SPECIALTY: Choice home furnishings and accents from Indonesia, Cambodia, Singapore, and the Philippines.

In support of up-and-coming Asian artists and designers, liideas (the three I's stand for Inspired Interior Ideas) showcases Filipino- and Asian-designed wooden furniture, modern Asian pieces, along with room accents such as pillows, vases, screens and floor rugs. Pressed bamboo and woven leather are only a few of the ingenious materials used here. But there are also timeless items made with stainless steel, glass, and marble.

PRICES: Soaps in various scents (pear, coffee, rose are popular), P250 a slice; canopy bed, P54,550; Victoria Tufted armchair, P25,300.

PAYMENT: Cash, credit card. EMAIL: philippines_iiideas@yahoo.com ADDRESS: Unit 507 Parc Royale Condo., Julia Vargas Ave., Ortigas Center, Pasig M: 0917-532-7316 OPEN: Daily, 10 a.m. – 6 p.m.

Ikea Distributors

U B V

SPECIALTY: Everything IKEA—furniture, bathroom and kitchen items, office supplies, storage solutions.

Ikea gained world renown for being the pioneer of flat-pack (i.e., ready-to-assemble) lightweight yet durable furniture. Today, the Scandinavian brand's popularity continues because of one key factor: looking high-end minimalist yet retailing at affordable prices. Ikea pieces have streamlined designs that focus on function. Yet for all their pragmatism, they're also very pretty. A child's aluminum loft bed, with space underneath for a table, is a reprieve from bulky double-decks. Storage boxes in stainless steel can act as living room decoration. Even their spatulas look good! Ikea has four local distributors that can accommodate orders for items that aren't on-hand. Below are the distributors' details.

PRICES: Brushed aluminum storage boxes with lid (set of 2), P550; table, wall, and floor lamps, P450–2,000; aluminum loft bed, P11,000 and up.

PAYMENT: Cash, credit card, bank deposit (for online vendors)

5 Corners

WEBSITE: ikeaph.multiply.com EMAIL: ikeaph@gmail.com
ADDRESS: 120 Kamias Road, Quezon City M: 0920-927-6514
OPEN: Mon–Fri, 8 a.m.–5 p.m.; Sat/Sun, 10:30 a.m.–7:30 p.m.
ADDRESS 2: 129 Katipunan Ave. (near cor. Santolan), Quezon City
OPEN: Daily, 10:30 a.m.–7:30 p.m.

Pinoy Ikea (online)

WEBSITE: pinoyikea.multiply.com EMAIL: levibal@yahoo.com
ADDRESS: 36 Finance St., Diosa Village, Project 8, Quezon City
M: 0917-832-3031 OPEN: Viewing by appointment.

Mayflower 1620

EMAIL: rooms101@gmail.com ADDRESS: 23 A Cavalry Hills St., Rolling Hills, 9th St., New Manila, Quezon City T: 774-1780 M: 0917-825-2407 OPEN: Daily, 10 a.m.–7 p.m. ADDRESS 2: 4977 Enrique St., Palanan, Makati T: 833-5590 M: 0917-813-1201 OPEN: Daily, 10 a.m.–7 p.m.

Mobler

WEBSITE: newmanila23.multiply.com, mobler.com.ph EMAIL: mobler.wilson@gmail.com, newmanila23@gmail.com ADDRESS: 2/L Wilson Square Bldg., 199 Wilson St., Greenhills, San Juan OPEN: Daily, 10 a.m.–7 p.m.

Kartini Asia

U B V

SPECIALTY: Gardening and landscape design implements; Balinese, Indian, and Indonesian garden and indoor furniture and home accessories; decorative rocks and boulders; exotic flower plant seedlings and arrangements.

If you don't have anything particular in mind, it is best to call and make an appointment with store owner Nina Malvar, who handled a landscape firm for many years before putting up this shop. This garden shop also serves snacks and savory meals from a limited menu at the in-house coffee shop, and has an in-house spa with a signature massage called Pijat (a mix of Balinese long strokes, Philippine *hilot*, and Thai stretching).

PRICES: Outdoor Southeast Asian wood furniture, P20,000 and up; antique door panels with elaborate handcarving, P60,000 and up; antique landscaping wall stones, P2,000 each.

PAYMENT: Cash, credit card. WEBSITE: kartiniasia.com EMAIL: kartini_nm@yahoo.com ADDRESS: Alabang Town Center, Madrigal Ave., Alabang, Muntinlupa T: 807-4356, 807-7579 M: 0917-816-1368 OPEN: Daily, 10 a.m.–10 p.m. ADDRESS 2: 12 Palace cor. Seoul Sts., BF Homes International, Las Piñas T: 788-0242, 825-1498 OPEN: Daily, 10 a.m.–10 p.m.

Komodo Manila

U B V

SPECIALTY: Furniture, home accessories, and architectural details in teakwood and other Indonesian woods.

Teakwood is known for its durability even under extreme weather conditions, heavy humidity, and prolonged sun exposure. As such, teakwood furniture is commonly found in upscale resorts, spas, and hotel poolsides. Komodo Manila carries over 250 conventional designs on teakwood and other Indonesian exotic solid woods spread out among indoor and outdoor furniture, flooring, decking, doors, and wall panels. They also offer Indonesian natural stones as home accents and accept custom orders. They can provide you with literature and the necessary information on how to clean, maintain, and annually restore your teakwood furniture.

PRICES: Intricately carved teakwood door panel, P50,000 and up; lush cushioned seats, P8,000 each; poolside recliner, P24,000. Small home accessories like trays and plant boxes, P2,000–5,000.

PAYMENT: Cash, credit card. WEBSITE: komodo-online.com EMAIL: inquiry@komodo-online.com, luismendez@komodo-online.com ADDRESS: FMF Compound, 126 Pioneer St., Mandaluyong T: 636-3640, 631-1221 OPEN: Daily, 10 a.m.–8:30 p.m. ADDRESS 2: LRI Design Plaza, 210 N. Garcia St., Bel Air, Makati T: 403-0677 OPEN: Daily, 10 a.m.–8:30 p.m.

Living Space

SPECIALTY: Recreations of iconic designer furniture.

A lot of the pieces here might look familiar. You've either seen them in glossy design magazines or in movies. Living Space boasts a wide selection of recreated designer furniture that are nevertheless made with quality materials meant to be as durable as their muses. They are sourced from reputable manufacturers that export to Europe and North America.

PRICES: The Barcelona chair with ottoman, currently retailing at north of P100,000, can be recreated here for P45,000.

Legend: U=Unique, B=Bargain, V=Variety

PAYMENT: Cash, credit card. WEBSITE: www.livingspace.com.ph EMAIL: info@livingspace.com.ph ADDRESS: Penthouse, 201 Del Monte Ave., Masambong, Quezon City T: 566-9293, 566-6768 OPEN: By appointment. ADDRESS 2: Suite 223A, 2/L LRI Design Plaza, 210 Nicanor Garcia St., Bel Air II, Makati OPEN: Mon–Sat, 10 a.m. – 7 p.m.

Malatumbaga

U B V

SPECIALTY: Reclaimed ancestral building materials and salvaged ancestral house parts (hardwood posts, hand-hewn beams, solid wooden floor planks, clay roof and floor tiles, clay bricks, adobe, piedra china, and stone pavers). Also offers restoration, installation, refurbishing, and refitting services of ancestral materials.

PRICES: Prices are highly variable depending on the age of the house part, the rarity of the raw material, the history of the house or neighborhood it was from. A typical 12' beam could start as low as P1,500 for hand-hewn varieties from local hardwood, yet reach as high as P15,000 for centuries-old varieties from endangered wood.

PAYMENT: Cash, check. WEBSITE: malatumbaga.com, ancestralbuilding.materials.com EMAIL: info@malatumbaga.com, sales@malatumbaga.com ADDRESS: 37 Angeles St., Alabang Hills Village, Alabang, Muntinlupa T: 807-2511 OPEN: Daily, 10 a.m. – 6 p.m.

Manila Seedling Bank

U B V

SPECIALTY: Extensive line of gardening needs, from organic soil and rare herbs to accents like ponds, mini-falls, and topiaries; landscaping services.

The Manila Seedling Bank compound is a collection of stalls and shops devoted to gardening. The stalls are located behind the Manila Seedling Bank building; vehicle entrance is along Agham Road. Mega Orchids Landscaping specializes in just that—landscaping and orchids. Several garden accents of different sizes are available, from small marble fountains to near life-sized iron elephants. Bird's Nest Garden focuses on exotic flowering trees, vines, and ferns. The stall next to them is the best place to find fresh herbs of all sorts. If you ask for an herb that they might not yet have in stock, they can source it for you. Green Passion Garden is notable for their extensive collection of garden ponds, mini-falls, and topiaries.

PRICES: Garden ponds begin at P750; herb seedlings are upwards of P30; Topiary to order at P5,000.

PAYMENT: Cash, check (depending on vendor). ADDRESS: Quezon Ave. Extension Cor. EDSA, Quezon City OPEN: Daily, 9 a.m.–6 p.m. Although some stalls open and close earlier without warning.

Messy Bessy (online) U B V

SPECIALTY: Environment-friendly cleaning products for delivery.

Messy Bessy is the first line of Filipino household products that is safe, non-toxic, and bio-degradable. Its products feature all-natural ingredients that are just as effective as their commercial counterparts. Gift packs with assorted products are bundled up in cute, reusable *bayong*s. Products are priced lower and discounts are given to returned bottles to promote recycling. Messy Bessy donates a portion of sales revenues to HOuSE, a non-profit organization that helps disadvantaged adults.

PRICES: Most products come in standard sizes (P60 to P450) and refill sizes (P350 to P1,000). Bayong-bundled gift packs, P750 (Minty Orange Surface Cleaner, Eucalyptus All-Purpose Scrub, Aloe & Green Tea Hand Wash + Dishwashing Liquid).

PAYMENT: Cash. WEBSITE: messybessy.com EMAIL: buymessybessy@gmail.com T: 502-7176 M: 0917-560-7178 See directory for resellers.

Mosayko

U B V

SPECIALTY: Handcrafted mosaic lamps, candle holders, mirrors, religious icons, and table top décor.

Mosayko is a play on the Tagalog phrase "Mosaic ko" meaning "My mosaic" which is what this Filipina artist specializes in—handmade mosaics that can be purchased "off the rack" or custom-made. Artist Denise Celdran made a go of creating tiled pieces at the start of the new millennium, receiving success during various road shows and markets in Europe. In Manila, her handcrafted art covers light boxes, lamps, mirrors, and religious icons. She recently branched out to tiling mosaics on bathrooms and has even been commissioned to do an entire swimming pool.

PRICES: For prices of the items and quotations on personalized art, contact Denise Celdran.

PAYMENT: Cash, check for regulars. WEBSITE: mosayko.com EMAIL: deniseceldran@yahoo.com M: 0917-820-2081 OPEN: By appointment.

MSM U.S. Surplus

U B V

SPECIALTY: Used furniture and toys from the US.

MSM is where the forsaken trappings of American life go to die—and be rescued by Pinoy homes. Baby grand pianos, La-Z-Boys, sofas, mattresses, closets, mountain bikes, washing machines, televisions, computers, lawn mowers, lamps, rubber rafts, mag wheels, desks, coffee tables, drum sets, guitars, kitchen gadgets, strollers, stuffed animals, books—all in one big messy pile. It's like looting your neighbor's home in the aftermath of a tornado. Parents should know this is where they can get cheap top-notch toys for fickle children; and vintage collectors will salivate over the wood-paneled stereo systems, ancient video game consoles, and outdated office equipment. Restoration and re-upholstery are necessary, but that's what shabby chic is all about. MSM can deliver upon request, at extra cost.

PRICES: Pianos, P40,000–85,000; mountain bikes, P5,000–25,000; 20" TV, P2,500; plush sofas, P12,000–25,000.

PAYMENT: Cash, credit card. ADDRESS: 809 Scout Borromeo St., South Triangle, Quezon City T: 929-9221 OPEN: Mon–Sat, 9:30 a.m.–7:30 p.m.; Sun, 9:30 a.m.–6 p.m.

Noble House

U B V

SPECIALTY: Chinese antiques.

With a little over 25 years in the industry, Noble House's reputation as a trusted antiques shop of luxe Chinoiserie can largely be attributed to the taste and savvy of its owner, half-Kashmiri, half Portuguese-Chinese Ruby Nazir, who grew up right above an antique shop on Hong Kong's Hollywood Road. The furniture and home accessories in the shop run a wide gamut, from writing desks to Buddha sculptures. The items are sourced from Kuala Lumpur, Hong Kong, Macau, and China; but a majority come from old homes in Shanghai, where the pieces are especially unique owing to the presence of Dutch, French, and English expatriates from decades ago.

PRICES: Small handcarved jewelry boxes, P2,500–12,000; 19th-century Chinese antique armoires, P35,000 and up; Shanghai multi-paneled screens and dividers with preserved details or lattice work, P45,000 and up.

PAYMENT: Cash, credit card. EMAIL: noblehouse@pldtdsl.net ADDRESS: Suite 110, G/L LRI Design Plaza, 210 Nicanor Garcia St., Makati T: 812-7005 OPEN: Daily, 10 a.m.–7 p.m.

Legend: U=Unique, B=Bargain, V=Variety

Orientique

U B V

SPECIALTY: Antique pieces and teak furniture from Indonesia and India.

With a network of suppliers from all over Asia, Orientique offers antique furniture and home accessories sourced from Indonesia, India, Pakistan, and China, with a special focus on teakwood antiques. They also accept orders for reproduction pieces, and can turn cannibalized house parts into modern utilitarian pieces (e.g., doors into table tops).

PRICES: Burmese teakwood gazebo used for traditional Indian weddings, P65,000; handcarved matrimonial cabinet from India, P165,000.

PAYMENT: Cash, credit card. WEBSITE: orientique.net ADDRESS: 2 Pines cor. Sheridan Sts., Mandaluyong T: 746-6839, 746-6850 M: 0927-403-5496 OPEN: Daily, 10 a.m. – 7 p.m. See directory for other branches.

Ramon Orlina

U B V

SPECIALTY: Custom-made glass sculpture, functional sculpted furniture, and glass jewelry.

The first local artist to sculpt from huge glass blocks using the cold method (i.e., no heat application to soften the glass) with self-improvised tools, Ramon Orlina has been creating functional art glass pieces like sculpted furniture and light installations for more than 30 years. Many of his works grace prestigious commercial spaces, but it is his functional pieces and jewelry that home owners find especially unique. One such piece is a love seat infused with mild steel and a polyurethane finish. The paper-thin seat seems to float and looks too fragile to carry the weight of one person, let alone two—it's more art installation than something to sit on. But the steel infusion makes the seat durable and strong enough to bear the weight of two people, showing Orlina's expertise in design and engineering.

PRICES: Orlina can create something based on a client's working figure.

PAYMENT: Cash, check. WEBSITE: orlina.com EMAIL: orlina@pldtdsl.net, ramon.orlina@gmail.com ADDRESS: Orlina Atelier, 2170–2174 Ilaw ng Nayon cor. Blumentritt Sts., Sampaloc, Manila T: 749-6438, 781-5918, 781-9471 M: 0917-880-5108 OPEN: By appointment.

Silahis Arts and Artifacts

U B V

SPECIALTY: Handmade Philippine products made from indigenous Philippine materials (wooden salad bowls, heavy wooden furniture, and musical instruments made from bamboo; jewelry and home décor made from anahaw leaves, shells, and natural fibers).

Shelves of cultural artifacts spill over to the mezzanine level which houses jewelry (from neck pieces with simple shell pendants to chunky, glittery earrings and rings) and Filipino costumes. On the second floor are Oriental ceramics, fabric, and primitive art, including maps.

PRICES: Coconut husk bowl, P100; anahaw *bayong* (woven tote), P35; yakal wood 4-poster cabinet, P67,000; neck pieces, P170 and up.

PAYMENT: Cash, credit card. WEBSITE: silahis.com EMAIL: export@silahis.com ADDRESS: 744 Calle Real del Palacio (Gen. Luna), Intramuros, Manila T: 527-3841 to 42 OPEN: Daily, 10 a.m.–7 p.m.

Sindo

U B V

SPECIALTY: Concept furniture and home accessories that fuse contemporary Western designs with Asian influences; innovative use of wicker, rattan, abaca, leather, wrought iron, stone, coconut shells, rattan peel, and bamboo.

PRICES: Living room modular sets comprised of an L-shaped couch, two ottomans, and a coffee table, P50,000–80,000; accent pieces like Tatami floor chairs in rattan skin, P9,000 and up each; breakfast trays, vases, and small decorative items, P900 and up.

PAYMENT: Cash, credit card. WEBSITE: sindo.com.ph EMAIL: sindo.ph@gmail.com, sindo_ph@yahoo.com ADDRESS: 4/L, Bldg. A, SM Megamall, EDSA, Mandaluyong T: 634-7975 OPEN: Daily, 10 a.m.–8 p.m.

Trip Shop, The

U B V

SPECIALTY: Bargain-priced surplus and slightly used home items from Japan, Australia, and the U.S.

Find everything from old models of upscale American audio gear to slightly used hotel mattresses. A lot of the damages in the overrun items are forgivable, and the used items are clean and still have enough use in them to get your money's worth. Just thoroughly inspect items that specifically need to be in good condition (e.g., electrical appliances).

PRICES: Bulky furniture, P2,500 and up; pre-used hotel mattresses, P2,000–8,000; branded golf sets (Callaway, Mizuno, Lynx), P2,800 and up; branded home theater systems, P1,500–7,000.

PAYMENT: Cash. WEBSITE: caloycalica.tripod.com
EMAIL: caloycalica@yahoo.com ADDRESS: 14-D Liberty Ave. cor. EDSA, near Camp Crame, Quezon City T: 415-8383 M: 0922-822-4217, 0921-476-2060 OPEN: Daily, 10 a.m.–7 p.m.

Wallprints

U B V

SPECIALTY: Digitally printed visual art wallpaper panels with modern visual art and abstract graphic designs.

PRICES: P4,000 per 1×2.7 m roll.

PAYMENT: Cash. EMAIL: wprints@gmail.com ADDRESS: G/L J&L Bldg., 251 EDSA, Greenhills, Mandaluyong T: 726-8376 OPEN: Daily, 10 a.m.–8 p.m.

Weaves of Asia

U B V

SPECIALTY: Imported heritage linens and designer fabrics for upholstery and drapery; local exotic fabrics like *piña*, *jusi* blends, and local silks.

PRICES: Expect to spend no lower than P1,000 per meter on the fabrics.

PAYMENT: Cash, credit card. EMAIL: admin@weavesofasia.com, sales@weavesofasia.com ADDRESS: 32 Jupiter St., Makati T: 897-6405/06 M: 0917-835-1356 OPEN: Daily, 10 a.m. – 7 p.m.

Yin & Yang Shop of Harmony

U B V

SPECIALTY: Feng shui charms and consultation.

The Mandarin Hotel is perceived to be a vortex of good luck, hence the flood of businessmen and politicians at its Chinese New Year parties. At its lobby is the Yin & Yang Shop, the go-to destination for sensible feng shui advice and top-quality luck ornaments. Since geomancy at the shop is treated like a science, there are rational explanations underlying each item. Based on your birth chart and specific goals, the items you need can be identified. Jade Mandarin Ducks on a Plate ward off third parties in a relationship. Trend Eight Lucky Coins can be kept inside checkbooks or accounting books if you're having trouble collecting receivables. The Master Protection Pendant protects the safety of those born in the year of the Ox, Dragon, Dog, Horse, or Goat, and those whose first name or last name starts with C, K, L, M, N, P, T. Yes, that specific. Longer consultations on career, marriage, money, or the layout of your home can be arranged, as well as appointments with international geomancer Joseph Chau when he's in town.

PRICES: Mandarin Ducks on a Plate, P4,888; Trend Eight Lucky Coins, P1,288; Protection Pendant, P13,888.

PAYMENT: Cash, credit card. EMAIL: yinyangmandarin@yahoo.com ADDRESS: G/L Mandarin Oriental Hotel, Makati Ave., Makati T: 752-5882 OPEN: Mon – Sat, 11 a.m. – 8 p.m.

Legend: U=Unique, B=Bargain, V=Variety

AC+632

U B V

SPECIALTY: Collectible and limited-edition home and fashion accessories from local and international avant garde designers.

The store's name, taken from the telephone area code of Manila, is a concept store of everyday items that metamorphose after a mad dose of haute-couture treatment. Take the homely umbrella. Here, what once was a purely utilitarian apparatus can come in premium leather or lace and given an intricately sculpted handle, consequently becoming something more than protection from the rain. Not exactly a miser's haunt, AC+632 is where you go to spoil yourself with that one impractical and decadent bauble that gives your predominantly department-store-furnished room or closet an instant style upgrade. The store carries a curated line of home and fashion accessories as well as collectibles and art pieces from prestigious local designers as well as from around the globe.

PRICES: Limited-edition designer umbrellas, P9,000.

PAYMENT: Cash, credit card. ADDRESS: 2/L Greenbelt 5, Ayala Center, Makati T: 758-2564 OPEN: Daily, 11 a.m. – 8 p.m.

Adora

U B V

SPECIALTY: Euro-style upscale department-store fare with a motley crew of local and foreign designer products and equally diverse price points—in a nutshell, it's SM for millionaires.

Occupying about 2,500 sqm of opulent retail space are products and brands covering a typical department store's mix—some are sourced locally, some are from well-known design houses abroad, some are first-timers in the Philippine retail scene, some are non-branded yet choice fashion and crafted pieces from China, Turkey, Brazil, France, and Thailand at prices lower than their more designer counterparts. Adora is also the first to bring in luggage prestige brand Rimowa (purportedly the lightest luggage in the world), along with fashion heavyweights Chloe and Givenchy. Even their homeware is sheer luxury—from organic votives to 600 thread-count bed linens.

PRICES: Here you'll find accessories under P500, as well as sweaters north of P30,000. A non-branded exotic snakeskin minaudière retails at less than P4,000, while a high fashion clutch is tagged at north of P100,000.

PAYMENT: Cash, credit card. WEBSITE: adora.ph/ EMAIL: info@adora.ph ADDRESS: 2–3/L Greenbelt 5, Legaspi St., Ayala Center, Makati T: 687-4809 OPEN: Mon–Thu, 11 a.m.–8:45 p.m.; Fri–Sun, 11 a.m.–9 p.m.

All About Pets

U B **V**

SPECIALTY: Professional pet grooming that includes nail clipping, deticking spray, nail filing, oral cleaning/toothbrush, cologne spraying, hair trimming, ear cleaning, hair clipping, ear plucking, hair styling, ear cleaning with otitis, ordinary bath, deticking, medicated bath. Also has veterinary services, behavioral counseling, dietary planning, and pet supplies.

PRICES: Standard grooming (with bath, nail clipping, and ear cleaning), P450 and up.

PAYMENT: Cash. WEBSITE: allaboutpetsclinic.com EMAIL: info@allaboutpetsclinic.com ADDRESS: 9 JRM Bldg., Sct. Borromeo St., South Triangle, Quezon City T: 376-7387 OPEN: Mon–Sat, 9 a.m.–6 p.m.; home service by appointment.

Aloha Boardsports

U B V

SPECIALTY: Surfboards and Nike SB (Skateboarding).

Aloha Boardsports is the exclusive distributor of several surfboard and bodyboard brands in the Philippines, including Southpoint, Walden, Mactavish, 7S, Firewire, Morey and Victoria skimboards. To compliment the wide range of boards are apparel brands Volcom, Rip Curl, Lost as well as all around surf brand Dakine. Aloha Boardsports also began their distribution of Nike SB (Skateboarding), available only through their satellite skate shop, Five-0, which also carries skateboard brands Sector 9, Stereo, Alien Workshop and Anti-Hero. Their warehouse doubles as a retail store and often hosts major sales events with discounts of up to 50% off on selected merchandise.

PRICES: Nike SB skateboards, P2,800–4,900; surfboards, upwards of P21,000.

PAYMENT: Cash, credit card. WEBSITE: alohaboardsports.com
ADDRESS: 3/L Power Plant Mall, Rockwell Center, Makati OPEN: Daily, 10 a.m.–8 p.m. See directory for other branches.

Animal House

U B V

SPECIALTY: Professional pet grooming, extensive veterinary care using modern amenities, pet microchipping, and dog training.

Animal House, with more than 10 branches in the city, is a one-stop shop for veterinary treatments, vaccinations, grooming, boarding, and pet purchases (food, medicine, and supplies). Laboratory and diagnostic facilities include X-rays, Ultrasound, ECG's, dental scalers, and full surgical console. Their grooming is no less extensive, with nail polishing, tooth-brushing, milk baths , and anal sac draining as extras to the standard bath, trim, nail clipping, and ear cleaning. They use different shampoos and conditioners for different breeds, since some products, for instance, are best for shaggy coats while others are short and wavy hair.

Pet owners are required to present proof of anti-rabies shots before their pets can be groomed. Some animals get hostile when handled by strangers. So to side with caution, the animals are muzzled during grooming. The owners, however, are encouraged to be around to help placate their pets. With complete grooming, Animal House throws in anal sac draining as a complimentary service. This is the removal of accumulated dirt and discharge around the anus to prevent abscess.

Dog training and obedience services are also offered, as is microchipping (implant of a permanent identification and tracking number).

PRICES: Full grooming (with bath, hair trimming, ear cleaning, nail clipping, and anal sac draining), P480 and up.

PAYMENT: Cash, credit card. WEBSITE: animalhouse.com.ph EMAIL: anihouse@skyinet.net ADDRESS: 737 Aurora Blvd., New Manila, Quezon City T: 726-8112 OPEN: Mon–Sat, 9 a.m.–10 p.m.; Sun, 9 a.m.–4 p.m. See directory for other branches.

Asia Pro K9 Dog School

U B V

SPECIALTY: Home service dog training that teaches basic to advanced obedience, indoor and outdoor toilet training, behavior correction, and some tricks.

PRICES: A basic training module for standard commands and signals (heel, halt, sit, stand, come, shake hands, down, stay, foot, no, relax) starts at P6,000 for 15 sessions.

PAYMENT: Cash. M: 0915-939-0039

Aszoo Dog Training

U B V

SPECIALTY: Professional house-call dog training that teaches basic to advanced obedience, indoor and outdoor toilet training, behavioral correction, tricks, and guard work.

Den Valenzuela, owner and training director of Aszoo Dog Training Services, has been teaching and training dogs of various breeds and sizes for over 10 years. Apart from the basic obedience course, other training programs on offer are Advanced Obedience and Guard Work. Advanced Obedience teaches canine commands and signals for walk slow, walk fast, creep, head, flat right, flat left, inside, and out. Guard Work teaches technical security commands for attention, watch, search, apprehension, attack, bomb sniffing, and control poisoning prevention. All courses are offered with a guarantee that should the dog not learn within the specified training period of a course, training continues free of charge.

PRICES: Basic and Advanced training courses, P6,000 each for 15 sessions. A joint package of Basic and Advanced training, P 8,500 for 30 sessions.

PAYMENT: Cash. WEBSITE: aszook9.webs.com EMAIL: aszoo_denv@yahoo.com ADDRESS: 89 Engineering St., Rivera Court, Project 8, Quezon City T: 929-0342, 455-6212, 566-1292 M: 0928-662-7920 OPEN: By appointment.

Bohemian Nation

U B V

SPECIALTY: Wide range of handcrafted Indian and Tibetan antique furniture, home accessories, and chunky gemstone accessories.

Bohemian Nation is a high-end depot of antique Tibetan and Indian salvaged house parts and furniture, home accessories, and fashion accessories—all personally handpicked by the well-traveled couple who own the shop. People can choose among book shelves, tables, screen dividers, sofa benches, doors, and window panels, or among smaller accent pieces like tapestry, terra cotta Buddha heads, oil burners, and light fixtures.

All of the pieces bear strong design cues from their places of origin: door and window panels from India, for example, are intricately carved with figures from Hindu mythology, while Tibetan cabinets made from Himalayan soft woods like pine carry signature bamboo, dragon, and floral patterns found in Tibetan monasteries. As for the women's Indian accessories, there's a wide variety among rings, neck pieces, and earrings. Each piece reflects ornate metalwork and is accented by medium to large and richly colored semiprecious gemstones like topaz, amethysts, onyx, peridot, and lemon quartz. As with the furniture, accessory stocks are kept to a minimum so that each buyer ends up with a truly unique piece.

PRICES: Tibetan decorative door panels (with sizes starting at about 12"×24"), P2,000 and up; Indian carved door panels (with sizes starting at about 18"×30"), P8,000 and up; tapestries, P2,500–8,000; Indian rings, P1,200–4,500; Indian chokers and drop necklaces, P6,500–21,000.

PAYMENT: Cash, check, credit card. WEBSITE: bohemiannationtradingco.com EMAIL: info@bohemiannationtradingco.com ADDRESS: The Serenity Place, Westgate Center, Filinvest Corporate City, Alabang, Muntinlupa T: 771-2389 OPEN: Daily, 10 a.m.–8 p.m.

Bombproof Gear

U B V

SPECIALTY: Wide variety of locally made, designed, and sourced outdoor equipment for camping, hiking, surfing, and skateboarding.

Bombproof Gear calls itself an old-school homegrown Pinoy outdoor brand designed to equip and dress all types of outdoor adventurists: surfers, skateboarders, mountaineers, hikers, trekkers, backpackers, adventure racers, rafters, spelunkers, and rock and wall climbers. The brand prides itself in its strongly fraternal sense of customer service: not only can you buy equipment from the shop, but you can have gear designed, manufactured, or sourced for you, whether money is no object or you only have enough budget for used items. True to its patriotic battle cry, its in-mall (and one and only) shop is largely populated by local brands such as Tribu (for mountaineering sandals, waterproof and quick-dry jackets and backpacks, tents, and sleeping bags), Team Manila (for skater and surfer board shorts and T-shirts printed with Pinoy witticisms), and its own label (for board shorts, surfer rash guards, backpacks, waterproof and quick-dry jackets and cargo pants, sleeping bags, and tents). There's also a small selection of imported goods, especially among camping gear, outdoor gadgets, skateboard parts, and surfboard parts.

PRICES: Tribu waterproof and quick-dry jacket and cargo pants, P1,000 and P1,300, respectively; Bombproof Gear large hooded sleeping bag,

P1,500; solar charging panels, P2,000; Team Manila board shorts, P700 and up. Imported skateboard parts, P500 and up (for small parts like shock pads and truss heads), P2,500 and up (for a set of wheels), P3,500 and up (for decks).

PAYMENT: Cash, credit card. WEBSITE: bombproof.multiply.com ADDRESS: 3/L Robinsons Galleria, EDSA cor. Ortigas Ave., Quezon City T: 634-1760 M: 0919-319-9770, 0922-878-9049 OPEN: Daily, 10 a.m. – 8:30 p.m.

Bow and Wow

U B V

SPECIALTY: Organic pet food and all-natural pet grooming items.

The premium on organic pet food which you don't usually find in commercial pet food brands comes from high-protein content through the use of fresh meats, low carbohydrate content, absence of grains and other fillers, and the use of fruits, vegetables, and other health-promoting botanicals. The pet superstore has dietary supplements made from carrots, alfalfa, and parsley and canned food made from salmon, tuna, and trout. Even their grooming and lifestyle line—ear wipes, shampoos, hair detanglers, doggie blankets, and puppy diapers—are preservative-free.

PRICES: Organic dog food, P2,500 and up (13.5 kg); all-natural pet shampoos, P450 and up (12 oz); puppy diapers, P550 and up (12 pcs).

PAYMENT: Cash, credit card. ADDRESS: LG/L Greenbelt 5, Ayala Center, Makati OPEN: Daily, 10 a.m. – 8 p.m.

Cartimar

U B V

SPECIALTY: Pets and pet supplies; PX Goods; Korean, Japanese groceries.

Cartimar is a complex of buildings known for its PX goods sold at cheaper prices, from branded cosmetics to designer running shoes (allegedly "export overruns" but more likely great looking knock-offs). Korean and Japanese grocery stores line one section of the dry goods section. The most popular is Masan, which stocks everything from imported Potong ice cream to frozen edamame.

But what Cartimar has really become synonymous with is the wide selection of pets and pet supplies at negotiable prices. The pet section comprises two main buildings of four rows each with a small extension towards the back. Stalls are numbered by row and easy to locate. Birds, puppies, kittens, exotics and their corresponding accessories are found here at negotiable prices. Take your time and comparison-shop to make sure you make the best deal. As a general rule, the stalls in the extension fronting the back parking lot are more willing to give bigger discounts. Hans Pet Haus specializes in bird feed and is a cheap place to get parrot feed by the kilo instead of the overpriced brands found inside vet clinics. Off through a wide alley is Aqualand, with a focus on fish and waterplants. Do a little research before purchasing the more exotic marine life, just to be sure you aren't participating in some shady wildlife trade. The same rule applies for exotics sold throughout the complex. Cartimar has been subject to numerous raids in the past, which has made for stricter rules and regulations. Whenever possible, ask if the animal in question is registered.

Next to Aqualand Alley is the garden center with a limited choice of plants and pottery. While not extensive, it does have all the basics and is conveniently located next to the parking lot.

PRICES: Roasted seaweed, P59 (pack of 12); frozen edamame, P120; large collapsible dog cage, P6,500; blue macaws, P95,000; African gray parrots, P35,000; young ball python, P6,000; whippet P18,000; mini schnauzer, P25,000; fruiting *calamansi* plant, P250; lemon scented conifer, P350; potting soil P50–150.

PAYMENT: Cash. ADDRESS: Cartimar Ave., Mabolo, Pasay OPEN: Daily, 9 a.m.–7 p.m.

Collective, The

U B V

SPECIALTY: Compound of small, independent shops that advocate the eco lifestyle, individuality, and all things counter culture.

The compound hasn't met its quota of tenants yet but it already has a smattering of truly unique indie shops worth checking out and a bustling night scene. During the day, drop by Hocus, a bike-refurbishing shop that also does custom silk-screen printing on shirts, posters, and any printable surface; Wabi-Sabi, a noodle house and vegetarian grocery; Rituals, a concept "*sari-sari*" store of organic goods, eco-friendly, and vegetarian goods available in fractional portions (e.g., half a sachet, one and a half bottles, etc.); and Sundae, a women's clothing store of retro duds and old-school Nike and Vans shoes that are particularly hard to find for female feet.

PRICES: Prices are about 15% lower than at simliar shops in more commercial areas. Rituals is especially able to retail at rock-bottom prices because they don't spend much on packaging and encourage customers to bring their own containers.

PAYMENT: Cash. ADDRESS: 7274 Malugay St., Makati (from EDSA southbound, turn right at Buendia, right at Chino Roces, left at Yakal, left at Mayapis, then left at Malugay). OPEN: 11 a.m. onward.

Dart Tiglao's Dog Training

U B V

SPECIALTY: Intensive, single-session, house call dog training for specific dog issues (foundations of good dog behavior, toilet training, hyperactivity, severe aggression, and introduction to commands).

PRICES: P1,000 for one 5-hour session.

PAYMENT: Cash. EMAIL: dart@kokoro-works.com M: 0919-375-3630

Dogmaster Canine School

U B V

SPECIALTY: Home service dog training that teaches basic to advanced obedience, indoor and outdoor toilet training, behavioral correction, and tricks.

PRICES: A basic training module for standard commands and signals (heel, halt, sit, stand, come, shake hands, down, stay, foot, no, relax) starts at P6,000 for 15 sessions.

PAYMENT: Cash. T: 356-8617 M: 0916-849-5939

Echo Store

U B V

SPECIALTY: Eco–friendly lifestyle products.

ECHO Store, ECHO being an acronym for Environment & Community Hope Organization, is a business that espouses three values: health, fair trade, and care for the environment. Hence the tag as a "sustainable lifestyle" shop. As a retailer, it carries pretty much the same product categories as others—food, apparel, personal care. But it's where their products are sourced from and what they're made of that make the store unique. Organic bath and body products are made by small cottage-industry cooperatives in rural communities; apparel and accessories handcrafted by women from the urban-poor community of Payatas and the Correctional Institute for Women are recreated by-products of discarded or unused items such as tire rubber, tarp, and old newspapers; Neo-Trad (short for Neo Traditional) is a line of contemporary lifestyle items that feature the artistry of Philippine indigenous and cultural communities; and food items are from homegrown all-natural ingredients (e.g., *malunggay* pasta, brown rice). ECHO Store also carries products from local brands that share the store's advocacy, such as Ilog Maria Honeybee Farms, Z.E.N. health and beauty products, Holystic Haven skincare, and Messy Bessy cleaning solutions.

PRICES: Ilog Maria Anti-bacterial Throat Spray (a bestseller!), P150; organic and hypoallergenic feminine wash, P70; Propolis (ointment for skin irritation, safe even for young tots); Federico's Island Wine: Duhat (black plum flavor), P295; *Barako* Coffee, P175; *Tablea* Chocolate, P120; Muscovado rocks, P60. You can also opt for goody baskets comprised of an assortment of products, costing anywhere from P550 to P3,200.

PAYMENT: Cash, credit card. EMAIL: echolifestyle.store@gmail.com ADDRESS: G/L Serendra Piazza (facing Market! Market!), Taguig T: 901-3485 OPEN: Daily, 12 nn–10 p.m.

Expedition Plus

U B V

SPECIALTY: High-end branded outdoor gear: MSR, Petzl, North Face.

With the exception of North Face, top-of-the-line outdoor gear brands carried in this store like MSR, Deuter, and Petzl may be obscure for the non-trekker but are considered heavyweights by the outdoor hardcore. These brands, pegged at much higher price points than gear found in malls, are designed to endure extreme weather conditions yet are lightweight. These are the same brands used by Mount Everest hikers. Products not currently in stock can also be specially ordered for you.

PRICES: North Face lightweight Tadpole tent, P40,000; Petzl 3-piece headlamp set, P2,500; MSR all-weather stove and cook set, P7,500.

PAYMENT: Cash, credit card. EMAIL: ofortexp@info.com. ph ADDRESS: Unit 242, Mile Long Bldg., Amorsolo St., Makati T: 894-4092 OPEN: By appointment.

Firma

U B V

SPECIALTY: Luxe Asian-themed and vintage Filipino home and fashion accessories.

Oriental luxe is the running theme among Firma's collection of local designer homeware, with a special focus on lamps, throw pillows, and draperies. Though contemporary in design, each piece carries a retrospective element that would make it look at home in China's decadent opium houses or Vietnam's chic coffee boutiques. The Vintage Filipino line carries white marble coasters and hotplates, place mats, stationery, postcards, and pillows depicting graphics of Filipino cigarette labels from the 1800s to the early 1900s. Chunky costume jewelry and art pieces crafted by some of the country's most illustrious designers are also available.

PRICES: Pinoy vintage pillow, P1,480; pillows in silk with embroidery, beads, and tassels, P2,480–3,980; necklaces, 5,980.

PAYMENT: Cash, credit card. WEBSITE: firma.com.ph EMAIL: firma@eastern.com.ph ADDRESS: Unit 12, North Syquia, 1991 M.H. del Pilar St., Malate, Manila T: 524-8740 See directory for other branches.

Geo Shop

U B V

SPECIALTY: Eco-friendly grocery items like *malunggay* pasta noodles and chemical-free home cleaning solutions.

Organically grown produce, eco friendly items, and all things "sustainable" tend to come from scattered small-scale producers who are hard to pin down. Fortunately, the Geo Shop has gathered quite a lot of them in one place. The store is worth a once-a-month trip for stocking up on organic soap, shampoo, rice, snacks, sauces, juices, coffee, tea, sweets, herbal cures, and home cleansers that come from different provinces all over the Philippines. Every item you buy helps the economy of the small community that it came from. Bonus: A tarot card reader often hangs out at the store.

PRICES: Veggie noodles in squash, *malunggay*, *pechay*, spinach, or carrot, P20 a pack. Tasty spiced coconut vinegar, P40 a bottle. Powdered *barako* coffee, P70 a pack. Organic multipurpose cleaners, P135 a bottle. Organic rice, P65 a kilo. Tarot card reading, P250 per 30-minute session.

PAYMENT: Cash. ADDRESS: Stall 22 Cubao Expo, Gen. Romulo Ave., Araneta Center, Cubao, Quezon City T: 438-4243 M: 0919-222-3556 OPEN: Daily, 10 a.m.–7 p.m.

Legend: U=Unique, B=Bargain, V=Variety

Gran Trail Cycles

U B V

SPECIALTY: Full set-up bikes, bike parts, accessories, and repair for cross-country, mountain, and urban bikers.

This bicycle boutique is the exclusive distributor of Niner bikes, the serious biker's wheel of choice and a brand whose innovative suspension, chain work, and wheel sizing have produced bikes that are lightweight, durable enough for long travels and extreme terrain, pedal-efficient, and aerodynamic. The store carries other premium two-wheelers such as Cannondale, Fuji, Haro, GT, Mortop, Mavic, and Shimano, including parts and accessories. Gran Trail Cycles offers everything from all-terrain bikes (for mountains, cross-country races), commuter bikes (for inner city travel), to even hybrid bikes (takes design cues from both all-terrain and road bikes). The store also does bike repair, wash, and customization, and has a modest selection of sports apparel and gear like long boards to frisbees.

PRICES: Top-of-the line performance bikes like Niners, Fujis, and Mavics start north of P40,000. But Gran Trail holds regular sales and promos, and can slash as much as 25% off the original SRP. Those new to the sport can start with local in-house brands, which go for P10,500 and up.

PAYMENT: Cash, credit card. WEBSITE: grantrail.multiply.com; they're also on Facebook EMAIL: grantrailcycles@gmail.com ADDRESS: 4018 West Gate, Filinvest Corporate City, Alabang, Muntinlupa T: 772-1225 OPEN: Mon – Sat, 10 a.m. – 7 p.m.; Sun, 10 a.m. – 5 p.m.
ADDRESS 2: 1009 Alrose Bldg., Metropolitan Ave., Makati. OPEN: Mon – Sat, 10 a.m. – 8 p.m.

Guitar 911

U B V

SPECIALTY: Custom guitars and repair services like fretboard replacement and guitar restoration.

Besides being a guitar repair shop for both amateur and professional musicians, which harps on affordable services such as guitar action/

intonation repair and circuitry check and repair, Guitar 911 specializes in building one's dream guitar. Whether it is designing and building a guitar by parts or performing a custom paint job, one can expect a one-of-a-kind creation. Guitar 911 provides the service of one of the metro's best luthiers, Mang Doro Taneo, who was trained by industry legend Mang Rudy of RJ Music Store fame. Many of its clients are guitar players from professional bands, owing likely to the fact that Guitar 911 is partly owned and run by musicians Kelvin Yu and Jugs Jugueta of local rock band Itchyworms.

PRICES: Guitar action/intonation repair, P350; circuitry check and repair, P500; designing and building a guitar by parts, custom neck at P6,000, custom body at P5,000; custom paint job, P5,000.

PAYMENT: Cash. WEBSITE: guitar911.com.ph EMAIL: guitar911.com.ph@gmail.com ADDRESS: 35 Sta.Teresita St., Barangay Kapitolyo, Pasig M: 0929-605-4258 OPEN: Daily, 9 a.m. – 5 p.m. by appointment.

J&S Surf Shop

U B V

SPECIALTY: Board sports gear with a specialty in hard-to-locate kiteboard and skateboard brands.

J&S carries a wide range of gear for surfing, skateboarding, and kiteboarding enthusiasts. They retail several popular brands as much as hard-to-find brands like Loaded, Landyatchz, Best, Air Rush, and Cabrinha. Stand-up paddleboarders can also check out the available SUPs by Jimmy Lewis and Starboard. Those going for the total look can check out the following apparel and accessory brands: Skull Candy for headphones, hands-free devices, and audio packs; and board shorts, skateboard shoes, bags, caps, and protective gear from C1rca, Globe, and Adio.

PRICES: Cabrinha Kite Switch Blade 10 m P76,538.

PAYMENT: Cash, credit card. WEBSITE: jandssurf.com ADDRESS: 2285 Solidhouse Bldg., Don Chino Roces Ave. (Pasong Tamo), Makati T: 893-5766 OPEN: Daily, 11 a.m. – 8 p.m.

Legend: U=Unique, B=Bargain, V=Variety

Jackass Project Skateshop (online)

U B V

SPECIALTY: Wide assortment and updated stock of skateboards and skateboard parts, skater apparel and accessories.

PRICES: Skateboard decks, P2,300 and up; skateboard shoes, P2,000 and up. Plus shipping.

PAYMENT: Cash, bank deposit. WEBSITE: jackassshop.multiply.com

N.A.P.A.

U B V

SPECIALTY: Funky yet artistic lifestyle items, apparel, and accessories by young and independent Filipino designers.

A motley crew of products has been infected with patriotic fever: triangular purses are emblazoned with the black agimat insignia, and hot-pink prints of the Philippine map are placed sporadically against a white abstract background on a futon's backrest.

PRICES: Accessories like earrings and purses start at P120, shirts at P350, and small to mid-sized home accessories such as lounge lamps and decorative accents at P750.

PAYMENT: Cash. ADDRESS: Shop 7, Cubao Expo, Gen. Romulo Ave., Araneta Center, Cubao, Quezon City T: 440 8807 OPEN: Tue – Sat, 12 nn – 8 p.m.

Pawparazzi

U B V

SPECIALTY: Remarkable range of professional grooming services (bath and blow-dry, nail trim, ear cleaning, oral care, anal sac prophylaxis, pedicure, dental tartar scraping, and de-shedding treatment) plus fur coloring! Non-toxic dyes are used and naturally rinse out after a few washings. Pink poodle? Yes, they can! Pawparazzi also does pet pick-up and drop-off.

PRICES: Full grooming, P350–750 for puppies (1–6 mos), P450–1,000 (adults); fur coloring, P200–1,200, depending on area of coverage (spot or full) and length of coat.

PAYMENT: Cash. WEBSITE: They have a Facebook page ADDRESS: M/L De Dios Bldg., 138 Timog Ave., Brgy. Sacred Heart, Quezon City T: 410-5098 OPEN: Mon–Sat, 10 a.m. – 8 p.m.; Sun, 10 a.m. – 7 p.m.

Paws & Tails

U B V

SPECIALTY: Professional pet grooming and precision styling with results worthy of international show dog competitions.

Paw & Tails is headed by expert groomers certified by the Singapore Kennel Club. Services are customized based on your dog's breed, but the same attention to detail is given regardless (be the dog pedigreed or a mongrel), since the owners and staff are first and foremost animal rights advocates. Their boutique carries all manner of pet grooming supplies, accessories, and "canine couture."

PRICES: Grooming and styling, P400 and up.

PAYMENT: Cash. WEBSITE: pawsandtails.multiply.com ADDRESS: 2316 Karrivin Plaza Bldg. (across Mead Johnson), Don Chino Roces Ave. Ext. (Pasong Tamo Ext.), Brgy. Magallanes, Makati T: 844-9293 M: 0922-880-3340 OPEN: Daily, 9 a.m. – 7 p.m.

Pinoy Petz

U B V

SPECIALTY: Online classifieds for various pets (birds, cats, dogs, exotic animals) and pet needs (accessories, apparel, training, food, etc.)

WEBSITE: pinoypetz.com

Legend: U=Unique, B=Bargain, V=Variety

RAK K-9 Training Academy

U B V

SPECIALTY: Professional one-on-one dog obedience courses in a specialized training facility.

Its Quezon City facility takes care of the dogs' food, lodging, and personal care for the duration of the training, and can house 10 dogs, which is the maximum number of "students" accepted per training period. Each potential "enrollee" is subject to initial assessment before being accepted for training. Owner Gio Marcelo got his certification from a reputable K-9 school in California and does the one-on-one training himself. Boarding for dogs is another service offered—it's basically professional dog-sitting.

PRICES: Basic Obedience, P15,000 (training period of 1 month, with board and lodging). Advanced Obedience, P30,000 (training period of 2 months, with board and lodging). Boarding for dogs, P300 a day, food to be provided by owners.

PAYMENT: Cash. WEBSITE: k9manila.com EMAIL: gio@k9manila.com T: 904 1196 M: 0927-219-6526 OPEN: Mon–Sat, 10 a.m.–6 p.m.

Skate of the Nation

U B V

SPECIALTY: Longboarding decks and accessories. Specialty longboarding brands: Loaded, Earthwing, Gravity, Landyacthz, Pink, Venom, S-One. They also have signature art decks from surfing or skating icons. The owners are more than willing to help beginners pick out the best deck based on skill level and budget. Check their website for board events and competitions.

PRICES: Longboards and decks, P7,000–14,000; trucks, P2,100–4,000; protective gear (helmet, pads, etc.) P1,300–3,000.

PAYMENT: Cash, bank deposit, G-Cash. WEBSITE: skateofthenation .multiply.com EMAIL: skateofthenation@gmail.com ADDRESS: 1 Tomas Morato cor. E. Rodriguez, Quezon City T: 413-7661 OPEN: Mon – Sat, 3 p.m. onward

Stoked, Inc.

U B V

SPECIALTY: Wakeboarding and surfing.

Stoked, Inc. is the local distributor of Billabong, Nixon, VonZipper, Gator, and Birdhouse for skateboards and JS Surfboards for surfboards. The Greenhills branch carries discounted and sale merchandise—with some discontinued brands at up to 70% off. Drop by any branch to book a surf lesson with the Billabong San Juan Surf School (La Union).

PRICES: JS 5'10" Nitro surfboard, P26,500; Gator Gonzales wakeboards, P18,800; Sanuk Sidewalk Surfers, P2,500; boardshorts start at P2,000.

PAYMENT: Cash, credit card. WEBSITE: stokedinc.com.ph EMAIL: customerservice@stokedinc.com.ph ADDRESS: 2/L Power Plant Mall, Rockwell Center, Makati T: 898-1913 OPEN: Daily, 10 a.m. – 8 p.m. See directory for other branches.

Tiendesitas' Pet Village

U B V

SPECIALTY: Exotic pets, premium dog food, pets and pet accessories.

The numerous stalls here often sell the same items, but there are shops that stand out for niche markets. The Unicorn's Den sells only exotic animals such as snakes, sugar gliders, aquatic turtles, and spiders. Doggieland carries premium-grade organic dog and cat food (Acana, Orijen, Canidae, Solid Gold). At the center of Pet Village is Animal Care Vets, for routine check-ups as well as more serious pet concerns. Under the Sea and Other Things sell no aquatic pets, only aquatic accessories.

PRICES: Tarantulas, P1,500; organic dog food, P550 (2.5 kg); toy-dog breeds with papers (e.g., Yorkshire terriers), P30,000.

PAYMENT: Most take only cash; Animal Care Vets takes credit card. ADDRESS: Tiendesitas, Ortigas cor. E. Rodriguez Aves., C-5, Pasig T: 635-6895 (Animal Care Vets) OPEN: Daily, 10 a.m.–9 p.m.

Urban Doggies

U B V

SPECIALTY: Home service professional pet grooming.

Urban Doggies offers home service professional pet grooming in the Muntiparlas (Muntinlupa, Parañaque, Las Piñas) area with a mobile grooming trailer equipped with a full-sized bath tub, warm running water, grooming table, hair dryer, clipper, and its own power supply. Only natural grooming and care products are used on the pets.

PRICES: Grooming with trim and ear cleaning, P450.

PAYMENT: Cash. T: 517-2892 M: 0922-823-4849 OPEN: By appointment.

Eco-Friendly Couriers

Pedala Bike Messengers are bicycle-riding, same-day delivery couriers, many of whom are cyclists and athletes endurance-training for competition.

PRICES: The bikers can either pick up the package for delivery from a client and bring to the designated recipient (one way trip, P70–100) or wait for a reply and return to original sender (round-trip, P120–150). Cash payment is made to the biker upon pick-up or delivery.

EMAIL: pedalabikemessengers@gmail.com M: 0920-698-7777
OPEN: Mon–Fri, daily cut-off for booking orders is 11 a.m.

2Rats (online)

U B **V**

SPECIALTY: Japanese anime toys, collectibles, and videos.

2Rats is an online vendor with shops in different locations. It carries a whole range of anime toys, collectibles, and videos, from slightly used to brand new. Figurines are usually characters from video games like Street Fighter and from shows like Naruto, Chromed Shelled Regios, Junjou Romantica, Gundam, Toradora, Soul Eater, Vampire Knight, and Rideback (the shop also carries DVDs of these shows). There's a smattering of items from Western cult pop as well, such as figurines from Marvel Comics, DC Comics, Vertigo, and movie blockbusters. If you'd rather buy from their outlets, it's best to call to inquire about the availability of the product you want in the branch that you intend to visit.

PRICES: Slightly used action figures (with original packaging, but without weapons and accessories), P150–500; brand new action figures and miniature toys, P800–1,500; limited-edition action figures with stand, weapons, and accessories (like Fate Stay Night Rider), P3,000 and up.

PAYMENT: Cash, bank deposit, G-Cash, PayPal. WEBSITE: 2ratsph.multiply.com T: 643-4534 M: 0917-882-7287 Store locations: Sta. Lucia East, Robinsons East, Makati Cinema Square, Shoppesville Greenhills, Festival Mall Alabang, Eastwood Libis OPEN: Daily, 11 a.m.–8 p.m.

Bloom Service

U B V

SPECIALTY: Fresh Ecuadorian roses. Also delivers.

Ecuadorian roses have substantially larger and more solid buds, their petals are hardier, and their colors are deeper and richer. Since Ecuador grows roses all year, Bloom Service consistently restocks and can easily order a variant for you if it isn't on-hand. Far from the cellophane-wrapped wilted single stems hawked on the streets, or the gaudy airbrushed bouquets in pricey shops, Ecuadorian roses from Bloom Service are plump, healthy, and, despite being ablaze with color, still fresh- and real-looking. The online store also has a limited albeit premium line of Holland tulips. Pre-orders are encouraged since the flowers aren't kept on-hand for too long, making sure that each batch is fresh. Delivery within Makati is free of charge, and there are two venues for pick-up. Call or text for pick-up schedules.

PRICES: Ecuadorian roses, P300 (single long stem with card and grosgrain ribbon tied around stem); P550–2,160 (arranged bouquets from 3 pcs to 1 dozen). Tulips (pink or purple), P250–1,780 (single stem to a dozen).

PAYMENT: Cash. WEBSITE: bloomservice.multiply.com
EMAIL: bloomservice2009@gmail.com PICK-UP POINTS: (Makati) David residence, 4 Cabildo St., Urdaneta Village. M: 0917-810-6274; (Quezon City) Hernandez residence, 4 Rizal St., Ayala Heights Village M: 0917-888-0386

Breathing Space

U B V

SPECIALTY: Novelties and collections like snow globes and other figurines. However, the most coveted piece in the store is one of the original pictures of Tetchie Agbayani for Playboy.

PRICES: Highly variable. Halfway between thrift shop prices and those in upscale art gallery boutiques.

PAYMENT: Cash. WEBSITE: mybreathingspace.multiply.com
ADDRESS: Unit 56, Cubao Expo, Gen. Romulo Ave., Araneta Center, Cubao, Quezon City T: 439-7414, 912-8519 M: 0928-258-2030
OPEN: Mon–Sat, 12 nn–10 p.m.

Collector's Hangout

U B V

SPECIALTY: Retro everything and anything from the '50s; blown-up, black and white photo prints depicting old Manila—from World War II to the '80s.

Goods are carefully handpicked and rescued by store owner and avid vintage collector George Bonsay from old, condemned, or burned-down houses, schools, and buildings. The items on display are in forgivably worn to mint condition. Old soda and liquor bottles with the labels and logos that are still bright and legible are wiped regularly. Laddie magazines from days of yore (think FHM of the '60s—one was called Ginoo), trade paperbacks, and peso and dollar bills no longer in circulation are individually sealed in clear plastic sleeves. Most of the manual cameras and rotary phones still work or are salvageable.

There are regularly held collector swap meets here, too. A trip to Collector's Hangout also proves to be educational for new collectors. George can talk lengthily about each item in his shop as only an impassioned collector can and is very generous with trade secrets he's acquired in the business, such as how to determine if something is priced right, how to tell if certain items are authentic or of a certain period, etc.

PRICES: Black and white photos (approx. 12"X15"), P250 each.

PAYMENT: Cash. ADDRESS: G/L Swapmeet Bldg., 124 Kamuning Rd., Quezon City T: 466-9500 OPEN: Mon–Fri, 10 a.m.–8 p.m.

Dimasalang Flower Market

U B V

SPECIALTY: Widest variety of fresh flowers in the city at wholesale prices.

The Dimasalang Flower Market may be more commonly known as the Dangwa Flower Market, due to its proximity to the Dangwa Bus Terminal, where flowers from the north were originally delivered and unloaded. This is where most retail florists and some importers in Manila get their stock, so one can imagine the variety of flowers available here. Common local flowers are abundant in a plethora of colors. But if you scour through the market's 150 or so stalls, you can find more exotic varieties like lilies, hydrangeas, carnations, marigolds, and even rarer items like pineapple "bonsai" and other genetically tweaked fruit and flower plants. Major importers in the area carry upscale tulips, calla lilies, and cabbage roses. The flower market is open 24/7, though it is generally ideal to buy from 1 a.m. to 3 a.m., when deliveries have just arrived. Flowers that haven't been prepped by the vendors (i.e., trimmed, cleaned) are cheaper. The best deals are past midnight, Fridays, when stocks are at their most abundant and diverse in anticipation of the weekend crowd.

PRICES: A dozen of most flower varieties start at P50 to P150; a dozen for less common types like casablancas, P180–250. Flowers for import are generally 50%–80% cheaper than in commercial shops.

PAYMENT: Cash. ADDRESS: Dimasalang St., Quiapo, Manila
OPEN: 24/7

Dory's Lambanog

U B V

SPECIALTY: Flavored *lambanog* with special native packaging.

Packed under the brand Lambalites, colorful fruit-infused *lambanog* (local coconut vodka) concoctions come in classy looking smoked bottles and labels. Flavors include jackfruit, melon, strawberry, and blackberry. Each bottle even comes with a sticker recipe of recommended cocktail mixes that go well with the chosen flavor of *lambanog*. As a gift item, it can be packaged in native-looking but tasteful *sinamay* (woven fiber) bottle pouches.

PRICES: P300 (750 ml bottle), plus P30 for *sinamay* packaging.

PAYMENT: Cash, credit card. EMAIL: dorys*lambanog*@yahoo.com
M: 0917-938-0344, 0918-489-5828 See directory for retailers.

Druid's Keep

U B V

SPECIALTY: Comic books, graphic novels, manga, and indie local comics.

Hands-on shop owner Felix Cua has an almost encyclopedic knowledge about comic books and can recommend titles that suit your preferences or guide you if you're only beginning to collect. He can source out titles that aren't available on-hand, and as a supporter of both established and independent local comic book artists, he also hosts comic book launchings and signing.

PRICES: New commercial releases, about P700.

PAYMENT: Cash, credit card. ADDRESS: 3/L Gateway Center, Gateway Center, Paseo de Magallanes, EDSA cor. Don Chino Roces Ave. Ext. (Pasong Tamo Ext.), Makati T: 854-5332 OPEN: Tue–Sun, 10 a.m.–8 p.m.

Emil Palomares

U B V

SPECIALTY: Handcarved and handpainted aircraft models made from seasoned, cultured, and kiln-dried timber.

Just email images or diagrams showing three different angles of the aircraft that you want drawn and indicate the scale or length in inches, preferred color scheme or livery, registration number if any, quantity, and other specs. Depending on the intricacy of the piece and volume of your order, your aircraft model can be shipped to you within a week of payment confirmation.

PRICES: Prices vary depending on the size and specs of your order, but Palomares can usually create something according to your budget. A modern fighter jet 12.5" in length and 8.5" in wingspan starts at around P2,700, plus shipping.

PAYMENT: Bank deposit. EMAIL: pinoymodeller@gmail.com M: 0919-260-3384

Enchanted Hearth

U B V

SPECIALTY: Wiccan altar tools, charms, incense, oils, crystals, candles, spell kits, magical body and bath products, potions, and other enchantment products for love, healing, wealth and prosperity, and protection and justice.

Dana Ebright, practicing Wiccan and owner of the shop, also offers services such as counseling, oracle and tarot card reading, past life reading, auric healing, metaphysical healing, chakra alignment, home and business clearing, spells and rituals, and classes and tutorials in Wicca. Readings and counseling can be done over the phone.

PRICES: Love potion, P1,000 (50 ml); luck and prosperity mojo bags and charms, P2,000 (for a set of 7 herbs, seeds, stones, and prosperity symbols, a mini pillow, and a 5 ml bottle of anointing oil); Egyptian wand, P2,000; small voodoo doll, P10,000. Readings and counseling, P3,000 and up a session.

PAYMENT: Cash, bank deposit, Western Union. WEBSITE: ladydanaw.multiply.com EMAIL: lalunaisis@gmail.com, lady.danez@yahoo.com, ladydanahptss@hotmail.com, mysticsandmagick@hotmail.com
ADDRESS: Polaris cor. Felipe Sts. Bel Air, Makati T: 489-5778, 468-8677 M: 0920-801-6373, 0932-686-2505

Fresh Manila

U B V

SPECIALTY: Novelty and designer Japanese toys, collectibles, and limited-edition apparel.

The hip young things behind Fresh Manila are devoted to keeping things new with merchandise ranging from novelty t-shirts (with limited runs) to hard-to-find toys. The store, a haven for toy collectors, is the place for hunters of Devil Robot, Kozik, Uglydoll, and the ever-trendy ToKiDoki. These are not your childhood toys. Not with prices that sometimes go as high as P13,000. Stock is constantly changing and items tend to arrive in very small amounts. Even the self-produced apparel are made in finite amounts with little chance of re-ordering once stock has run out. Fresh Manila also teams up with local artists to promote limited-edition merchandise such as the WeWillDoodle Riki Chair, a foldable sofa bed covered in doodles, created in partnership with Uratex. Another timely item targeted at the local market were the Idol Kho tees, a nod to the early 2009 sex video scandal involving Dr. Hayden Kho.

PRICES: YOD Rubber Keyrings for P592, Ken Men's Tees for P2,431, Idol Kho novelty shirts P850, Doraemon Figurine P13,000.

PAYMENT: Cash, credit card. WEBSITE: freshmanila.com ADDRESS: Unit A, 15/L Strata 2000, F. Ortigas Jr. Rd. (Emerald), Pasig T: 634-2888, 634-7888 ADDRESS 2: DOMANI, 9–10 The Renaissance Hotel, Makati OPEN: Daily, 10 a.m.–7 p.m.

Genshiken

U B V

SPECIALTY: Anime (Japanese animation) and anime specialty products like toys, manga, collectibles, katanas, and cosplay outfits and accessories.

PRICES: Cosplay accessories, P250 and up; figurines, P150–1,500; mini katanas, P2,500 and up.

PAYMENT: Cash. WEBSITE: genshikenanime.multiply.com, tara21shinme.multiply.com ADDRESS: Unit 55, Cubao Expo, Gen. Romulo Ave., Araneta Center, Cubao, Quezon City OPEN: Mon–Sat, 12 nn–8 p.m.

Grand Thrift Shop, The

U B V

SPECIALTY: Old film equipment as home accents.

In flea markets, one usually needs to sift through piles of trash before finding treasure, but not at The Grand Thrift Shop. The store gets all the sorting and cleaning out of the way and leaves nothing but vintage crème de la crème on display. Everything here is worth a fondle, from old cameras and rotary telephones to the Imelda Marcos memorabilia and antique copies of U.S. Playboy. Collectibles from local showbiz are aplenty, like black-and-white photos of Guy and Pip in candid poses, and old copies of fan

Legend: U=Unique, B=Bargain, V=Variety

magazines like Kislap and Orig. The shop is a mandatory stop for offbeat home accents.

PRICES: Antique film equipment, P1,800 and up; rotary phones (that still work), P900; '60s-era typewriters, P2,500; 30-year-old copies of U.S. Playboy, P300 each; black-and-white local celebrity photos, P60–120 each; old fan magazines, P150.

PAYMENT: Cash. ADDRESS: Cubao Expo, General Romulo Ave., Cubao, Quezon City OPEN: Mon–Sat, 12 nn–8 p.m.; Sun, 1 p.m.–7 p.m.

Great Toys Online (online)

U B V

SPECIALTY: Extensive range of American and Japanese toys and collectibles, anime, gashapons (mini figures), action figures, and die-cast, super robots.

Apart from carrying a wide product range, Great Toys Online's products are all genuine. No replicas here. Though in the running with other hobby shops when it comes to updated anime trends, one thing unique to this shop is that it is one of few stores in Manila where one can get "vintage" stuff like Macross, Transformers (the animation!), Voltes V, and Voltron die-cast figures or old school tin lunch boxes. And if they don't have it on-hand, they will source it out for you. Check their online catalogs for advanced orders, and their updated product stock lists for what's available on-hand per branch. Email or text Great Toys for provincial orders.

PRICES: Die-cast Transformer robots/cars, P600–1,200; 1/6th scale action figures with figure stand, complete arsenal of interchangeable and detachable weapons, and detachable costumes and accessories, P6,000 and up.

PAYMENT: Cash, credit card. WEBSITE: greattoysonline.com EMAIL: inquiry@greattoysonline.com M: 0922-852-5320, 0922-516-7550, 0917-820-6666 See directory for retailers.

Hobbes & Landes

U B V

SPECIALTY: Hub for family activities with specialty boardgames, puzzles, card games, and a host of fun, modern, yet analog "thinking" toys.

Kids can hang out at the Try Me station to play board games and do puzzles for free as you look on from the in-store café. With a special focus on family fun and bonding, its products are decidedly "analog" at heart—game cards, board games, puzzles, building blocks like Lego, and a host of other "thinking" toys. But the toys here are no less exciting than their electronic counterparts. Board games feature exciting popular sci-fi themes, puzzles come in standard cardboard to finely crafted variants like metal and fiberglass pieces. The shop also carries consigned items that range from baby's to children's gear. What's more, to ensure that no family member is left out, the store has taken a "pet friendly" stand, offering a pet station with water bowls. Hobbes & Landes has regular workshops, game tournaments, and pet club meet-ups, so check out their website for updates.

PRICES: Kung Fu Kids Desk Collection, P1,200–1,400 for a set.

PAYMENT: Cash, credit card. WEBSITE: hobbesandlandes.com
ADDRESS: Bonifacio High St., Bonifacio Global City, Taguig T: 856-0935, 856-0936 OPEN: Mon–Thu, 11 a.m.–10 p.m.; Fri, 11 a.m.–12 mn; Sat, 10 a.m.–12 mn; Sun, 10 a.m.–10 p.m. See directory for other branches.

Holland Tulips

U B V

SPECIALTY: Wide variety of fresh, weekly flown-in Holland tulips.

One of the largest flower retailers in the country, Holland Tulips flies in a batch of several kinds of fresh tulips from Holland once a week. Choose from classic monochromatic cup-shaped varieties to more exotic kinds like Lily-flowered Tulips (petals point outward), Fringed Tulips (petals have fringes), or Adrem Tulips (petals are closed in at the top, making them look like a large bulbous bud even in full bloom). Holland Tulips also offers a full array of flower arrangements for several occasions using imported floral accessories and other flowers like Dutch roses, carnations, calla lilies, and freesia. You can visit their retail shops or order online.

PRICES: Tulips, P225 (single stem), P2,700 (a dozen, no arrangement), P3,180 (a dozen, with floral arrangement). Mixed-flower bridal bouquet, P3,000–6,000; boutonnieres and corsages, P1,000–1,300.

PAYMENT: Cash, credit card. WEBSITE: hollandtulips.com T: 807-7854, 809-2435 M: 0917-860-7042, 0917-850-8200 OPEN: Daily, 10 a.m. – 8 p.m. See directory for branches.

Indie Art & Brown Label (online)

U B V

SPECIALTY: Pretty and handmade, decorative storage boxes using scrap canvas fabrics, eco-safe paint and ink, recycled paper, and mixed paper fibers. Indie Art & Brown Label doesn't have retailers yet, so check out their website occasionally to get updates on bazaars and other sales venues.

PRICES: P300 for a medium-sized set of 3 boxes.

PAYMENT: Cash. WEBSITE: brownlabel.blogspot.com

Island Rose (online)

U B V

SPECIALTY: Fresh-cut French and Dutch farm-grown roses.

Island Rose prides itself with being the very first nationwide flower delivery service and the first to accept orders online. Products have expanded to include stuffed-toy bears with customized messages on their shirts, boxes of Belgian chocolate truffles and pralines, fruit crates, personalized handcrafted journals, and homeware like room fragrance sets, bath sets, and bed linen sets. They also offer floral services for special occasions.

PRICES: Same-day flower delivery is available in Metro Manila from Monday to Saturday for orders placed before 10 a.m. For the provinces, they offer next-day deliveries. Deliveries start at 11 a.m.

PAYMENT: Cash, credit card. WEBSITE: islandrose.net EMAIL: helpdesk@islandrose.net T: 816-3091 OPEN: Daily, 8 a.m. – 5 p.m.

Jay Cee Kay

U B V

SPECIALTY: Personalized engraved paper paraphernalia.

Jay Cee Kay is one of the few printers left who still do traditional engraving on paper. In business since 1978, it survives in the age of digital technology and do-it-yourself printing because the Windows Copperplate font is no match for a real copperplate. Engraving takes time and is not cheap, so people normally turn to it only on special occasions like weddings. But lately, increasing numbers of businessmen have been going to Jay Cee Kay for their professional needs. Thermo-graving is an option if you want things slightly cheaper, but fussy eyes will notice the difference (the letters are sharper and finer with real engraving). Jay Cee Kay doesn't stop at stationery, business cards, and invitations. They can do virtually anything on paper (greeting cards, recipe cards, menus, baby books, yearbooks, labels, etc.). Just present a sample so they can come up with a quote. Lead time is three weeks.

PRICES: Engraved business cards, P6,400 (200 pcs); engraved letterheads and envelopes, P7,700 (100 pcs). Reprints cost P1,000 less than the price of first printing.

PAYMENT: Cash, check. ADDRESS: San Antonio Arcade, McKinley Rd., Forbes Park, Makati T: 817-6384, 817-6786 OPEN: Mon – Fri, 9 a.m. – 7 p.m.; Sat, 10 a.m. – 5 p.m. See directory for other branches.

King Louis

U B V

SPECIALTY: Imported seedlings, locally grown fresh flowers of all varieties.

King Louis Flowers and Plants supplies fresh flowers from their six-hectare farm in Trinidad Valley, Benguet. With a hidden cabinet of local and international awards, and as a trusted supplier for the Department of Tourism, it has decorated floats in major festivals around the country. The biggest local grower and seller of hydrangeas and poinsettias, King Louis also carries a wide variety of rare flowers like African violets, petunias, and snapdragons. Orders for delivery are accepted.

PRICES: An arrangement of Ecuadorian roses, lilies, carnations, and gerberas, inclusive of vase, P1,500; a bouquet of a dozen fuchsia roses, P800; a pot of hydrangeas, P400–650. Delivery within Metro Manila, P200.

PAYMENT: Cash. EMAIL: kinglouismanila@yahoo.com ADDRESS: Manila Seedling Bank Foundation, EDSA cor. Quezon Ave., Quezon City T: 929-4110 OPEN: Mon–Fri, 7 a.m.–5 p.m.

Knife Land (online)

U B V

SPECIALTY: Wide range of custom knives—from utilitarian and tactical folding and fixed-blade types made from carbon fiber, titanium and titanium carbide to hand-crafted artisan knives and scrimshaw art objects crafted from materials like bone, coral, and stone.

PRICES: Steel pocket utilitarian knives, P1,000 and up; top-of-the-line designer tactical knives like the Warren Thomas titanium line, P25,000 and up; handcrafted custom artisan knives, P12,000–90,000.

PAYMENT: Cash, bank deposit. WEBSITE: knifeland.multiply.com

Lil's Futaba

U B V

SPECIALTY: Extensive range of model kits for tweens and up.

According to avid modelers, this shop has the most extensive and affordable product line of model kits which include vintage fighter and commercial planes; vintage and rally sports cars; as well as 4WD and RC car racing kits. Popular foreign brands carried include Copterx, Cosmo Fuel, GT Hobbies, Hirobo, Italeri, RC Airplane, and Tamiya. All products are made with top quality wood and fiberglass.

PRICES: Helicopter model kit, P14,500; remote control for RC planes and cars, P3,000.

PAYMENT: Cash, credit card. EMAIL: megamall@lilsfutaba.net ADDRESS: Basement, Bldg. A SM Megamall, Mandaluyong T: 633-6358 OPEN: Daily, 10 a.m. – 8 p.m.

Little Cigar Store

U B V

SPECIALTY: One-stop smoke shop offering a full-line of 100% premium hand-rolled (Philippine, Dominican, Cuban) cigars, single malts, smoking accessories, pipe tobacco, and personalized cigars and boxes. Custom orders require a minimum purchase of 25 individually packaged cigars and 50% downpayment.

PRICES: Medium-flavored Cubans, average of P130 per stick; wooden humidors, P1,300–2,700; cigar ring, P98 per 25 cigars; humidor carving and inscription, P240 (first line), P155 (second line); humidor logo engraving, P238–392. Exclusive of delivery.

PAYMENT: Cash, credit card, bank deposit. WEBSITE: littlecigarstore.com ADDRESS: G-4, Bel Air Soho Condominium, 45 Polaris cor. Badajos Sts., Makati T: 897-2113 M: 0918-936-9787 OPEN: Mon–Sat, 10 a.m. – 8 p.m.

Legend: U=Unique, B=Bargain, V=Variety

Mabini Antique Shops

U B V

SPECIALTY: Local cultural antiques such as *santos* and *bul-ols* (rice gods).

Mabini looks just like any rambunctious Manila street nowadays, but during the Spanish era, it was known as La Calle Real, the posh main avenue of the Ermita and Malate residential districts. In modern times, it became the haunt of the "Mabini Masters," most famous of which was the painter Cesar Buenaventura, who had a shop on the street.

Today, moneychangers outnumber the art and antique dealers, but a few shops are surviving. Via Antica has a fine collection of antique *santos* (religious relics) recovered from different parts of the country; Sieva's has old coins, bank notes, medals, stamps, antique jewelry, and excavated porcelain and pottery; Golden Salakot has blue-and-white Chinese porcelain, ceramic jars, and ivory figurines. Gallery Deus at the Padre Faura Center near Mabini has excellent antique *santos* and Philippine tribal art, weapons, and textiles curated by its owner, writer/director Floy Quintos.

PRICES: A tangkil (armlet) made from the tusks of wild boar costs P5,000. Old bracelets made entirely of ivory cost P25,000. Antique *santos* are priced P10,000 and up.

PAYMENT: Cash and check. OPEN: All are open Mon – Sat, 9:30 a.m. – 7 p.m.

Michi Calica Fresh Flowers

U B V

SPECIALTY: Designer flower arrangements, personalized messages, and flower deliveries.

Fashion designer Michi Calica's flair for creating formal wear and wedding gowns was parlayed to flowers when her bridal clients began asking for bouquets to go with their dresses and floral arrangements to decorate the churches they would be wed in. This was good news because the usual flower shops could stand to lose some cheese. Calica's arrangements are so versatile, they can say "I'm Sorry" as well as "I Do." Ordering can be done online from anywhere in the world as long as the delivery address is in the Philippines. If you're ordering flowers to be delivered as a gift, there's an online feature for including a message. For bulk requirements, call the shop for package rates.

PRICES: A bouquet of hydrangeas, P1,850; a dozen red roses, P3,000; a vase of yellow calla lilies inspired by the look of fashion icon Coco Chanel, P7,450.

PAYMENT: Cash, credit card. WEBSITE: flowersexpress.com.ph, michicalica.com EMAIL: info@michicalica.com ADDRESS: Michi Calica Bridal & Home, G/L The Oasis, 169 Aurora Blvd., Quezon City T: 725-7124 M: 0917-897-9759 OPEN: Mon – Sat, 10 a.m. – 6 p.m.

Oriental Rug Auction

U B V

SPECIALTY: Exotic one-of-a-kind Oriental rugs handcrafted by nomadic master artisans from Central Asia, India, and the Middle East. Auctions are organized twice yearly as a fundraising event by In Touch, a non-profit group specializing in telephone-based crisis counseling. Contact In Touch for updates on subsequent auctions.

PRICES: The auction feels more like a sale as prices can be slashed by as much as 70% off the original retail value. Authentic Persian rugs valued at over P300,000 are taken home at less than P150,000.

PAYMENT: Cash, credit card, checks from pre-selected international banks. WEBSITE: www.in-touch.org EMAIL: intouch@i-manila.com.ph ADDRESS: 48 McKinley Rd., North Forbes Park, Makati T: 893-1893, 810-6233 OPEN: Mon – Fri, 9 a.m. – 5 p.m.

SM Kultura Filipino

U B V

SPECIALTY: Largest Filipino lifestyle retail chain carrying quality regional products from all over the Philippines.

Up until the '90s, unless you were willing to troop to Quiapo, souvenirs for tourists and balikbayans were found in Filipiniana sections of department stores. These sections were small and neglected with a limited and unchanging inventory. Mall giant SM, however, recently relaunched its Filipiniana section as Kultura Filipino, which culls regional specialties from handicrafts and delicacies in one roof, and also features an extensive line of contemporary yet distinctly Filipino home accessories and fashion items from local designers. In-store services include money changers, gift-wrapping in special native packaging like *sinamay*, delivery, and online product reservation.

PRICES: Delicacies, P170 (pack of dried mangoes) to P550 (flavored wine made from Philippine wild berries); hand embroidered Spanish fans, P200; bamboo spice rack, P250; handcarved wooden Bul Ol (ancestral pagan gods) 10" figurines, P400; Maria Clara style formal embroidered blouse, P3,500; multicolored sports shirts with Philippine map logo, P500.

PAYMENT: Cash, credit card. WEBSITE: kulturafilipino.com
EMAIL: inquiries@kulturafilipino.com ADDRESS: 2/L Main Mall, Mall of Asia, J. W. Diokno Blvd., Pasay T: 556-0416 to 17 OPEN: Sun–Thu, 10 a.m. – 9 p.m.; Fri/Sat, 10 a.m. – 10 p.m. See directory for other branches.

Sputnik

U B V

SPECIALTY: Mainstream and independent comics, geeky toys and merchandise (i.e., action figures).

Sputnik is the venue for indulging in some geeky love, whatever your budget. It carries mainstream comic titles but also champions the independent comic book artist—both foreign and local. It actively sources for catalogs of non-mainstream comics and graphic novels to be able to provide the best selection possible. Fans will recognize titles by renowned local artists like Gerry Alanguilan, Louie Cordero, and Arnold Arre. Comic newbies need not worry: the people behind the counter are bent on matching each customer with the right title to start with. Recommendations are qualified based on a customer's taste: What does he like to read, watch? (This makes Sputnik the perfect shopping partner for clueless gift-givers who aim to please their comic-loving friends.) Sputnik's passion for the comic world carries on to the merchandise being sold: from action figures to stickers, shirts to journals. People can log on to the website to reserve titles—the shop occasionally even sets up delivery areas or meet-ups for special purchases. On some occasions, Sputnik also transforms into an exhibit space, but follows one simple rule—no traditional art. Shows are likely to feature pop and street culture items like stickers, shirts, and skateboards.

PRICES: About P5,000 for an imported specialty comic book anthology.

PAYMENT: Cash and major cards accepted. WEBSITE: sputnikcomics.com ADDRESS: Shop 60, Cubao Expo, Gen. Romulo Ave., Cubao, Quezon City T: 709-1867 OPEN: Mon–Sat, 2 p.m.–10 p.m.

Video 48

U B V

SPECIALTY: Old hard-to-find movies.

Video killed the radio star, and pirated DVDs killed the video store. So why is Video 48 still around? Because it did something the chain stores failed to do. From the day it opened nearly 20 years ago, V-48 offered something more than plain distribution. It's called curation. The owner, Simon Santos, lives and breathes film, and has the most informed selection of local and Hollywood classics among all the video shops in the metro. Many a young filmmaker's education was nurtured here, and the late greats like Lino Brocka and Chaning Carlos were regulars, as are today's active directors and screenwriters. Some movies at V-48 are for sale, others are for rent, and they come in formats that span the history of home video—Betamax, VHS, Laser Disc, VCD, DVD. If you're looking for particular titles, just ask the staff and they can bring them out for you. Add to that the old movie posters, celebrity autographs, and memorabilia displayed throughout the store, and the sense of nostalgia will make you want to shed cinematic tears. Happy ones, of course.

PRICES: Movies for rent, P60 for 6 days; movies for sale start at P100 (Betamax, VHS, Laser Disc, VCD, DVD). Framed movie posters, P1,500–2,500; comic books, P150–250; celebrity autographs not for sale.

PAYMENT: Cash. WEBSITE: video48blogspot.com ADDRESS: Marisan Bldg. (Mary Santos Artcade), 48 West cor. San Francisco del Monte Aves., Quezon City T: 415-0108, 373-2936 OPEN: Mon–Sat, 10 a.m.–8 p.m.

Village, The

U B V

SPECIALTY: European country-themed home accents and furniture; collectibles and curios that make for whimsical gifts like out-of-print poetry books, French bistro ceramics, and 1960s lamps.

Provincial European prevails in most of the designs, but pieces are reworked with style-forward details. A mahogany Louie chair, for example, is reupholstered in pink, brown, and white Pucci-like swirls. A French-looking provincial birchwood table gets a coat of ultra glossy paint and lush tassels.

PRICES: Louie chair, P12,000; French provincial end table, P9,000; antique edition of The Complete Poetical Works of Percy Bysshe Shelley, P1,200.

PAYMENT: Cash. ADDRESS: Unit 2-C, Valuepoint Bldg., 227 Salcedo St., Legaspi Village, Makati (near cor. Gamboa St.) M: 0917-885-1138 OPEN: By appointment.

Vint

U B V

SPECIALTY: Curated vintage collectibles (trunks, radios, cameras, barber's chairs, car miniatures, limited-edition books) from the U.S. and Germany.

PRICES: Highly variable depending on the rarity of the item and whether or not it still works. Post-WW2 camera that no longer works, P1,500 and up; pre-WW2 German medium-format camera in near-mint condition that works and comes in original leather case, P8,000 and up. 1940s barber's chair, P20,000 and up.

PAYMENT: Cash, credit card. ADDRESS: 2/L A-Venue Mall, Makati Ave., Makati M: 0915-988-1852 OPEN: Daily, 11 a.m. – 7:30 p.m.

Vtoyz Hobby Shop

U B V

SPECIALTY: Fast-food toys like tumblers and drinking straws depicting movie characters; small and cute plastic toy figures from anime and Hollywood sci-fi movies; Coca-Cola toys and memorabilia; and a couple of hentai figurines.

PRICES: Mini figurines and plushies, P150 – 250; 15" plastic and rubber figurines, P600.

PAYMENT: Cash. ADDRESS: 3/L Blue Lane of Shoppesville, Greenhills, San Juan M: 0917-980-2643 OPEN: Daily, 10 a.m. – 8 p.m.

Wonder Toy's Store

U B V

SPECIALTY: Authentic Sylvanian Families and Sanrio collectibles.

Hello Kitty and the rest of the Sanrio gang were such a hit in the '80s to late '90s. But so were the cult Sylvanian Families, toy plush figures that featured woodland creatures. Both Japanese brands, Sanrio and Sylvanian Families gained a lot of collector fans of their miniature accessories, houses, and outfits for their plush characters. As toy trends changed, however, authentic Sanrio and Sylvanian Families became hard to find. Wonder Toys is a small store that's packed with a great collection of rare Sanrio and Sylvanian Families finds, both at regular prices for brand new items and sale prices for those with minimal scratches and defects.

Legend: U = Unique, B = Bargain, V = Variety

PRICES: Small 3-pc Sylvanian Family set, P650.

PAYMENT: Cash, credit card. ADDRESS: 3/L Festival Mall, Corporate Ave. cor. Civic Drive, Filinvest Corporate City, Alabang, Muntinlupa T: 850-4053, 850-4054 OPEN: Daily, 10 a.m. – 8 p.m.

Yash/Kulintangan

U B V

SPECIALTY: Antique Maranao crafts.

Antique shops in Metro Manila carry mostly Spanish colonial and Cordillera tribal pieces liberally mixed with Chinese, Thai, and Balinese. Yash and Kulintangan break the mold by specializing in items of the Maranao, the royal lake people of Mindanao. The Maranao have a long tradition of creating opulent brassware, embroidery, and weaponry that predate the arrival of the Spanish. Yash carries brass ornaments and household items adorned with okkir, the delicate curving patterns that are a trademark Maranao motif. Yash also has heavy wooden chests inlaid with mother-of-pearl, and authentic gongs, daggers, swords, and occasional large wooden sculptures of the mythical *sarimanok*. Kulintangan has a big collection of swords and daggers, some of which have beautiful ivory handles. Both shops offer a taste of life in a sultan's *torogan*, which is every bit as regal as a hacienda home.

PRICES: A hardwood chess table inlaid with mother-of-pearl and chess pieces made from narra and carabao horn, P30,000. Large wooden antique *sarimanok* with ivory beak, P25,000.

PAYMENT: Cash. ADDRESS: Handicraft and Antiques Village, Tiendesitas Frontera Verde, Ugong, Pasig M: 0910-986-8212 (Yash Antique Shop), 0919-6118723 (Kulintangan Antiques) OPEN: Daily, 11 a.m. – 8 p.m.

Book Sale (online)

U B V

SPECIALTY: Bargain-bin commercial books without having to sort through bargain bins. Order online and specify the branch where you want to pick up your order.

PRICES: 50%–70% off SRP (books are mostly used books or old releases).

PAYMENT: Cash. WEBSITE: booksale.com.ph EMAIL: info@booksale.com.ph ADDRESS: Suite 708 7/L Cityland 10 Tower 2, H.V. Dela Costa St., Makati T: 824-0947, 776-0230 OPEN: Daily, 10 a.m.–8 p.m. See directory for other branches.

Bookay Ukay

U B V

SPECIALTY: Bargain-bin quality and rare books, book trading—a book shop by book lovers for book lovers.

The store was put up by a group of self-proclaimed poor and struggling anticorporate nitpicking intellectuals who rummage for treasured rare reads in Recto's dusty book bins or from cultural organizations like Goethe Institute. Find obscure but prized titles by writers from the Beat generation (a.k.a. beatniks), Philosophy books from Hume and Aristotle to The Tao of Pooh, books on offbeat topics like Eastern mysticism and the occult, and contemporary titles (from Sun Tzu's Art of War and Palahniuk's pop cult existentialism to Coelho's inspirational pieces and Murakami's poetic urban tales). You can also sell, swap, and borrow. Check the website for updates; you can also order and purchase online.

PRICES: Used books, P100 and up; new books, P250 and up. Plus shipping.

PAYMENT: Cash, bank deposit, G-Cash. WEBSITE: bookay.multiply.com EMAIL: bookayfriends@yahoo.com ADDRESS: 55 Maginhawa St., U.P. Village, Diliman, Quezon City M: 0905-428-3125 OPEN: Daily, 12 nn–10 p.m.

Bound Bookshop

U B V

SPECIALTY: Curated new and read books at affordable prices.

A couple of journalists put up a small bookshop in 2004 to promote reading through affordable prices (some cheaper than bargain basement books). The selection is sourced and curated by the owners themselves, all well-read and passionate book lovers. As a result, Bound Bookshop is able to offer both new and second-hand personally chosen and high-quality socio-political reads, biographies, children's books, literary treasures, and rare finds. The store now has more than 1,500 titles, 65% of which are second-hand. The shop also hosts poetry readings, book launchings, and art exhibits. Check out their website and get on their mailing list for updates.

PRICES: Second-hand books, P30–50 (for titles like The Shipping News by E. Annie Proulx and Robert Kennedy and His Times by Arthur M. Schlesinger, Jr.); new books start at P130.

PAYMENT: Cash. WEBSITE: boundbooks.net ADDRESS: 105-A Scout Castor St., Barangay Laging Handa, Quezon City OPEN: Daily, 10 a.m.–10 p.m.

Different Bookstore, A

U B V

SPECIALTY: One of the pioneers in alternative modern book releases.

Opening its first outlet in 1994, A Different Bookstore was one of the first independent book stores to offer offbeat selections among literary titles and books that delved into controversial socio-political issues. It now has over 30,000 titles, 90% from the U.S. and the U.K. And despite being a supplier not only to several universities nationwide but to other book retailers, A Different Bookstore deliberately keeps expansion regulated, putting a premium on staff training and customer service in each of its four branches. Check out their website for online book reservations.

PRICES: Trade paperbacks, P250 and up; hardbound, P800 and up. Polemic titles, P1,000 and up.

PAYMENT: Cash, credit card. WEBSITE: adifferentbookstore.com ADDRESS: 2/L, Glorietta 4, Ayala Center, Makati T: 893-5918 OPEN: Daily, 10 a.m. – 8 p.m. See directory for other branches.

Filed! (online)

U B V

SPECIALTY: Funky organizer doodads like multi-compartment folders, portfolio cases, multi-compartment beach totes, and date books.

Filed! takes the mundane folder and gives it small yet transformational improvements: MP3 player pocket, calculator pocket, detachable pencil case, paper sleeves, two big pockets, card holder, post-it pocket, and optional handle attachment. With eye-popping iPod-inspired colors, round corners, and a Velcro latch, Filed! folders easily became a hit for the young and disorganized and now features limited-edition designs. New products include beach totes (with water-resistant pockets for electronics like MP3 players, detachable toiletries pouch, wet clothes bag, and pockets for flip flops) and planners with envelopes and Post-It pages.

PRICES: Folders, P495; beach tote, P695; planner, P400 (5"×7" hardcover and ring-bound cream-colored sheets).

PAYMENT: G-Cash, bank deposit. WEBSITE: filed.multiply.com EMAIL: get.filed@yahoo.com M: 0927-554-3494 See directory for resellers.

Fully Booked

U B V

SPECIALTY: Extensive line of literary titles and premium alternative titles in mainstream categories (lifestyle, children, humanities, etc.), design books, graphic novels, and custom orders.

Definitely no hole-hidey, super book store Fully Booked is the foremost option for premium alternative titles, with over 100,000 titles targeted at diverse interests. For bestsellers, the store usually keeps up with release dates abroad. Each branch also provides a few comfortable reading areas for reading unsealed books without having to purchase them. Notable among these branches is the one at Bonifacio High Street. Housed in a three-story building, the store has a coffee shop at the second floor where book buyers can start reading their purchases with a cuppa joe, and a roof deck for special events like book-launch cocktails. Fully Booked also carries limited-edition figurines, rare CDs, specialty paper products, funky laptop bags, and other collectibles; it is also the exclusive distributor of specialty international jazz, classical music, and new age record labels.

PRICES: Manga, P400 and up; graphic novels, P600–1,500. Music CDs, P450–1,500. Worldwide bestsellers typically cost twice more than the SRP of major book store chains in the U.S.

PAYMENT: Cash, credit card. WEBSITE: fullybookedonline.com EMAIL: fb_fort@fullybookedonline.com ADDRESS: Bldg 6, 902 Bonifacio High St., Bonifacio Global City, Taguig T: 858-7000, 858-7036 to 38 OPEN: Sun-Thu, 10 a.m.–9 p.m.; Fri/Sat, 10 a.m.–10 p.m. See directory for other branches.

Libros Filipinos

U B V

SPECIALTY: Online book store specializing in Philippine books, journals, magazines, videos, music, and CD-ROMs.

Libros Filipinos is the bookshop of Filipinas Heritage Library. It carries an extensive and expertly curated selection of Filipiniana books, journals, magazines, videos, music, and CD-ROMs that cover everything from business management and culture to history and the arts. It also provides unique services such as email capsule reviews of books to help you better choose among their titles. Lectures and book launchings at Filipinas Heritage Library are opportunities for getting autographed copies of the speakers' books; a service called Pirma is for those who wish to obtain autographed copies but can't make it to the lecture or launching.

PRICES: Trade paperbacks, P250 and up; coffee-table books, P1,500 and up; textbooks, P450 and up; DVDs and CD-ROMs, P500 and up.

PAYMENT: Bank deposit. WEBSITE: libros.com.ph EMAIL: librosfilipinos@ filipinaslibrary.org.ph ADDRESS: Filipinas Heritage Library, Nielsen Tower, Makati Ave., Ayala Triangle, Makati T: 892-1801 OPEN: Tue – Sat, 9 a.m. – 6 p.m.

My Bookstore (online)

U B V

SPECIALTY: Over 4,000 titles from the usual bestsellers, graphic novels, and a wide selection of local classic comics (Best of Pupung, Pugad Baboy, Chaka Chronicles). The site also lets customers immediately find out about the availability of items—no more waiting for email replies.

PRICES: Trade paperbacks, 15%–20% cheaper than in major bookstores. Local comics, P118–170.

PAYMENT: Bank deposit, credit card. WEBSITE: www.mybookstore.ph

National Book Store

U B V

SPECIALTY: Extensive range of office supplies, school supplies, text books, and commercial book titles from a retail institution.

National Book Store is the supermarket of book stores. It doesn't carry rare finds, but it does have a complete line of school and office essentials at affordable enough prices that—barring bulk buys—null any savings from inconveniently located bargain areas like Divisoria. Also available are premium branded pens like Montblanc, Lacrosse, and Parker. When you buy any of these pens, National Book Store can have it engraved free of charge. They also accept orders for items they don't have on-hand. They'll source out the item then advise you of the status and price. If you're using your credit card, the product can be posted on their website so you can buy it off there and have it shipped to you. Or you can pay via bank deposit and will be advised when the item is ready for pick-up at your preferred branch.

PRICES: Prices are industry-standard. Designer pens like Montblanc typically go for P2,000 and up.

PAYMENT: Cash, credit card. WEBSITE: nationalbookstore.com EMAIL: info@nationalbookstore.com.ph ADDRESS: Glorietta 5, Ayala Commercial Center, Makati T: 757-0525 to 26 OPEN: Sun-Thu, 10 a.m. – 9 p.m.; Fri/Sat, 10 a.m. – 10 p.m. See directory for other branches.

Office Gateway (online)

U B V

SPECIALTY: Extensive range of office supplies for delivery. Delivery is free for Alabang, Muntinlupa, Parañaque, and Makati. Online orders made by 4 p.m. for these areas are delivered within two days, Monday to Saturday.

PRICES: Orders outside the mentioned areas have a delivery fee of P250 for purchases totaling less than P7,000. For rush deliveries, orders should be worth P10,000 minimum, plus P250 delivery fee. Prices of items follow standard SRPs in-mall major book stores and office supplies stores.

PAYMENT: Cash, credit card. WEBSITE: officegatewayph.com EMAIL: sales@offficegatewayph.com T: 468-9922, 776-3145 OPEN: Delivers Mon – Sat, 8 a.m. – 6 p.m.

Popular Bookstore

U B V

SPECIALTY: Hard-to-find books by Philippine authors.

Once upon a time after World War II, Popular Bookstore stood shoulder-to-shoulder with the biggest book stores in the country. But Popular didn't care about being popular, so it never grew as big as the others. Its founder, Joaquin Po, was jailed in the 1950s for selling Marxist titles. The store's collection of books on Philippine history, literature, and contemporary culture is still the most unconventional mix you can find. Taglish cookbooks for house help exist alongside treatises on the Bangsamoro struggle in Mindanao. If you want to see how the Philippine book scene would look in an ideal world, this is the place to go.

PRICES: Coffeetable books on Philippine art, P2,000 and up; collectors' titles like Si Nora Aunor sa mga Noranian by Nestor de Guzman, P330; Tagalog sex novelettes from LitErotika, P90. Limited-edition foreign titles, P700 and up. The discount section often yields unexpected gems such as an early hardbound edition of Bel Canto for only P395.

PAYMENT: Cash. WEBSITE: popularbkstore.com EMAIL: info@popularbkstore.com ADDRESS: 305 Tomas Morato Ave., Quezon City T: 372-2162 OPEN: Mon–Sat, 10 a.m.–7 p.m.

Power Books

U B V

SPECIALTY: Wide variety of mainstream titles, specialty books, and book-related accessories (book pillows, clip-on-page reading lamps, etc.), as well as kiddie-friendly reading areas, events, and activities.

Power Books was actually the first major book store chain to offer complimentary in-store reading. It also made available to a broad market a wider variety of specialty publications like graphic novels, coffeetable books, and how-to books. Now, despite stiff competition, it thrives by offering value-added services such as book club membership, discount cards, and family-oriented events that foster PARKING love of books among young readers. Many branches have children's sections where kids can plop down anywhere on the colorful foam floor with their shelf pick.

PRICES: Books have standard commercial SRP.

PAYMENT: Cash, credit card. WEBSITE: powerbooks.com.ph EMAIL: ibid@powerbooks.com.ph ADDRESS: 2/L Glorietta 3, Makati T: 757-6428 to 29 OPEN: Daily, 10 a.m.–8 p.m. See directory for other branches.

Solidaridad Bookshop

U B V

SPECIALTY: First-rate Filipiniana and foreign titles selected by a pillar of Philippine literature, F. Sionil Jose.

Novelist and National Artist for Literature F. Sionil Jose put up Solidaridad in 1965 to self-publish his books and create a venue for local writers and artists to find each other. It still fulfills those functions today as a bona fide independent store. Buying books here is almost an act of conscience for those who want to keep the idea of authenticity alive in the world of publishing and retail. Solidaridad's book selections show a lot more judgment. The best output of the country's university presses and local publishing houses are gathered here, along with Indian, African, Russian, and Latin-American literature. English and American authors are well-represented, and one display window is devoted to the owner's own works. It's a writer's bookshop, with the magazine rack laden with copies of The Atlantic, The New York Review of Books, The New Yorker, and local stalwarts the Philippine Free Press and Philippine Graphic.

PRICES: F. Sionil Jose's famous Rosales saga, P150 a volume; limited-edition coffeetable book, P2,000 and up; hard-to-find biographies, P750.

PAYMENT: Cash. ADDRESS: 531 Padre Faura St., Ermita, Manila
T: 523-0870, 525-5038 OPEN: Mon–Sat, 9 a.m.–6 p.m.

Tradewinds Bookstore

U B V

SPECIALTY: Handwritten collections of plays, poetry, fiction, and non-fiction mostly by national artists and local literary luminaries. The specialty shop also carries collectibles for serious coin and stamp collectors.

PRICES: Titles that go for about US$30 in specialty bookshops abroad and online vendors can start at P200 (US$5) here.

PAYMENT: Cash only. ADDRESS: 744 Calle Real del Palacio (Gen. Luna St.), Intramuros, Manila T: 527-2112 to 14 OPEN: Mon–Sat, 10 a.m.–7 p.m.

Acoustic Dimension

U B V

SPECIALTY: Grado headphones, pre-owned and brand new vinyl records, and high-end audio gear.

Apart from Grado, maker of high quality retro-designed headphones and the store's most recognizable brand, are specialty items like audiophile-grade speaker systems and TVs, tube amps, vinyl records that span as wide a range of music genres as major CD stores, and record players for the serious music lover. The store's limited floor area is designed around a sofa where you can spend the rest of the day choosing speakers that are precisely matched to your amplifier—as well as to your design preferences.

PRICES: Grado headphones start at P6,000. Pre-owned vinyl records, P350–550; brand new vinyl records, P2,900 and up. Home theater audio systems easily reach hundreds of thousands.

PAYMENT: Cash, credit card. EMAIL: eric_lim@globelines.com.ph
ADDRESS: 3/L Power Plant Mall (cinema area), Rockwell Center, Makati T: 756-1579 OPEN: Daily, 10 a.m.–8 p.m.

Autoplus Sportzentrium

U B V

SPECIALTY: Car tuning services and diagnostics; the Philippines' first commercial dynamometer (inertial, all wheel drive).

In 1994, Autoplus introduced and popularized premium parts for the car enthusiast. It offered speed-enhancing gear (camshafts, free flow exhaust systems, turbocharger systems) and brands used by premiere professional race teams and drifters (Spoon, Volk Racing, Ray's Engineering, Sard, 5Zigen, HKS Teichi Tsuchiya). In 2001, it introduced the country's first inertial 4-wheel-drive chassis dynamometer, a device that more accurately measures a vehicle's power output without the need to remove the engine.

PRICES: Tune up and oil changes start at about P2,400 with Motul synthetic oil, while dyno tuning services are at an hourly rate of P5,000. Headworks start at P40,000 with other specialized services also offered

Legend: U = Unique, B = Bargain, V = Variety

on a per project basis. Promo periods throughout the year offer as much as 50% off.

PAYMENT: Cash. ADDRESS: 233 EDSA, Mandaluyong T: 726-0399, 726-3066 M: 0922-497-3597 OPEN: Daily, 10 a.m.–7 p.m.

Autotechnika/DTM

U B V

SPECIALTY: Car tuning and diagnostics (axle-type 4-wheel-drive chassis dynamometer) for European luxury cars.

Being only one of the few automotive centers that offer immobilizer key programing and re-programing, Autotechnika/DTM has made a mark by specializing in high-end European vehicle modification, particularly BMWs. Of particular note is the bolt-on supercharger kit from ASA Supercharger, which bumps up the power output of almost any BMW by 40% without the need for further modification. Tuning is done through DTM's in house Dyna-Pack chassis dynamometer, a system that allows accurate measurement and tuning of both 2-wheel and all-wheel drive vehicles with power outputs of up to 1200 horsepower. Being a complete Euro and American specialty auto tuning house, Autotechnika also offers accessories from Hamann, Carlsson, Shrick, Supersprint, Hawk and Gibson exhaust systems. Other specialty services like the Lav'Ramon radiator and cooling system descaling, Transtech transmission oil flushing and replacement, and Carbon Clean combustion chamber, valve, piston cleaning are also offered.

PRICES: Oil change services and diagnostic trouble code scanning starting at P1,500; carbon cleaning starts at P4,000; Lav'Ramon descaling, P2,000.

PAYMENT: Cash, credit card. EMAIL: thefort@autotechnika.com.ph
ADDRESS: Mancor Corp Center, 32nd St., Fort Bonifacio Global City, Taguig T: 856-1882 OPEN: Mon–Sat, 8 a.m.–5 p.m.

Avant

U B V

SPECIALTY: Comprehensive line of mainstream-branded electronics and appliances that you can road-test.

Yes, it's an Abensons in disguise and prices are strictly average. But there are two reasons to visit. First, the expansive floor area means that Avant is home to a remarkable range of gizmos—from mobile phones and Hi-Def TVs to oven toasters. Second, and more importantly, you can actually road-test a large number of the gadgets. Upstairs, you may be even offered popcorn as you lounge around on their sofas and test out their TVs and surround sound systems. All the usual suspects are represented in this store—Sony, Samsung, Canon, Nokia.

PRICES: Standard manufacturer's SRP.

PAYMENT: Cash, credit card. WEBSITE: abenson.com.ph EMAIL: shoponline@abenson.com ADDRESS: 2/L Greenbelt 4, Makati T: 758-2315 to 20 OPEN: Daily, 10 a.m.–8:30 p.m. See directory for other branches.

Ambassador

U B V

SPECIALTY: The latest gadgets on the cheap.

The tiny store is about the size of a walk-in closet—but it's overflowing with all the latest tech, you'll find yourself elbow deep in kids looking at iPods. You will find a complete mix of gear, from Apple MacBooks and digital cameras from Canon, Nikon, and Olympus to audio/visual systems and TVs. Underneath the counter is an assortment of accessories: memory cards, batteries, and whatnot. If you've ever been to tech stores in Hong Kong or Tokyo, where space is small but business is big, you'll feel right at home here.

PRICES: Pre-haggling, prices are at least 10% cheaper than at major retailers.

Legend: U=Unique, B=Bargain, V=Variety

PAYMENT: Cash, credit card. ADDRESS: Shop Number 215, Phase B, 2/L Shangri-La Plaza Mall, EDSA cor. Shaw Blvd., Mandaluyong OPEN: Daily, 10 a.m. – 8:30 p.m. See directory for other branches.

Bang & Olufsen

U B V

SPECIALTY: Hi-tech and sleek home theater systems.

There are good brands, there are premium brands—and then there's Bang & Olufsen (or simply B&O), which caters to the philosophy "Looks good. Sounds good. Expensive beyond belief." More than that however, it creates A/V systems that are truly unique—even iconic. Each product is part aural engineering genius, part sculpture, meant to be a centerpiece whereas other electronic products are often your dirty little secret with wires and cables tucked behind them. Bang & Olufsen are such symbols of prominence, they've made countless appearances in movies. In one of the James Bond installments alone, Tomorrow Never Dies, more than 11 B&O products were given screen time. Schedule a demo of their products by giving them a call.

PRICES: B&O A8 Earphones, P13,500. Full systems easily range in the hundreds of thousands: BeoSound 9000 (the glass-paneled, 6-disc audio system you see in a lot of movies), about P220,000.

PAYMENT: Cash, credit card. EMAIL: bang&olufsengb5@rgoc.com.ph ADDRESS: G/L, Greenbelt 5, Ayala Center, Makati T: 728-8766 OPEN: Daily, 10 a.m. – 8 p.m.

Bose

U B V

SPECIALTY: Relatively affordable premium brand of upscale sound systems and audio accessories.

Bose is one of the few premium audio brands with strong store presence in the country. Their most prominent product line is their home theater series, but they also carry an extensive line of smaller scale items (MP3 player speaker docks, sound-isolating stereo headphones, etc.).

PRICES: Their famed 321 GSX sound system, P103,000; SoundDock iPod speaker dock, P26,000; Quiet Comfort 3 headphones, P24,900.

PAYMENT: Cash, credit card. WEBSITE: bose.com, eleksis.com
EMAIL: wgso@eleksis.com ADDRESS: 3/L Power Plant Mall, Rockwell Center, Makati T: 898-2048 OPEN: Daily, 10 a.m.–9 p.m.
See directory for other branches.

DB Gadgets (online)

U B V

SPECIALTY: Mobile phones and digicams on the cheap.

DB Gadgets claims to be a wholesale distributor for malls, which is why it can offer such low prices, and offers products with manufacturer warranties. Major mobile phone brands are available and up to date with new releases; as are branded point-and-shoot and prosumer digital cameras. The occasional gaming console and the entire iPod clan are also thrown into the mix. Orders are confirmed upon a downpayment of P500 and get to you via agreed pick-up points or shipping.

PRICES: 15%–25% lower than malls and commercial retailer prices.

PAYMENT: Cash, bank deposit. WEBSITE: dbgadgets.multiply.com
EMAIL: dbgadgets@yahoo.com M: 0922-843-2843, 0915-591-7925

Digital Walker

U B V

SPECIALTY: Laptop bags and accessories; iPod cases and accessories.

Roughly half the store is devoted to laptop bags and no matter how big or small your laptop is, you'll find a bag, sleeve, or case for it here. In addition, laptop cooling pads, wireless mice, and designer USB thumb drives are just some of the treasures you'll find if you dig around. Since Digital Walker first gained popularity as a store for iPod accessories, they carry a wide range of headphones and iPod docks as well. JBL, Sennheiser, Jabra, Jamo and Shure are just some of the brands they carry. The depth and range of their products easily outperforms the lineup from authorized Apple resellers. The store also has promo periods offering discounts as much as 50%. Most remarkable about the store, however, is the profuse, almost fanatic, positive buyer feedback about Digital Walker owner Charlie Paw, known for customizing package deals for returning customers and promptly answering queries over the phone or email. For urgent cases like last-minute gift buying, if an item you want is out of stock, Charlie has been known to go as far as making arrangements for another gadget shop (a friend's) to provide the item without nulling any previously agreed-on discounted rates.

PRICES: Standard SRP. Philmug members get 10%–15% discount.

PAYMENT: Cash, credit card. ADDRESS: 3/L V-Mall, Greenhills Shopping Center, Greenhills, San Juan T: 725-5136 OPEN: Daily, 10 a.m.–8:30 p.m. See directory for other branches.

DZ Racing

U B V

SPECIALTY: Wide variety of original and replacement aftermarket parts and optional auto accessories, ABS and PU body kits.

PRICES: Affordable alternatives to original accessories and parts such as the Japanese domestic market (JDM) Type R body parts conversion kit for the 2006–2008 Honda Civic, P32,000; 2009 FD2 front conversion parts for Honda, P21,000. Rates exclusive of labor.

PAYMENT: Cash, credit card. WEBSITE: dzracingphil.multiply.com EMAIL: dz_racing_phil@yahoo.com ADDRESS: 86 Unit 6 Sta Catalina St. cor. Banawe Ave., Quezon City T: 415-5418, 740-6863, 416-0619, 712-4344 OPEN: By appointment.

Emperor/Autokozmetix

U B V

SPECIALTY: Aftermarket car performance parts and services.

Emperor Motorsports is a one-stop shop for all serious motorsports purists and Fast and Furious enthusiasts. With a wide range of original Japanese domestic market (JDM) aftermarket parts—from air intakes, electronics, exhausts, coil overs, forged wheels, and racing seats to weight-reduction modifications—the shop carries brands like HKS, Greddy, BLITZ, Fujitsubo, TEIN, Bride, Rays Engineering, Work, ARC, and Cusco. Indent orders upon special request are also accommodated. Emperor Motorsports also caters to the increasing demand of the exotic-car enthusiast by selling new and pre-owned exotic vehicles. Autokozmetix, on the other hand, offers accessories and aesthetic modifications for locally sourced vehicles, affordable audio set-ups, body kits like Varis and Sym's, and HID conversion kits.

PRICES: Brand new Nissan Skyline GTR-35's, around P7M; Nissan 370Z's, about P3.2M; pre-owned and modified Mitsubishi Lancer Evolution X's, about P2.6M. Autokozmetix tints start at P3,500, audio set-ups start at P15,000.

PAYMENT: Cash, credit card. WEBSITE: emperormotorsports.com EMAIL: emperor_motorsports@yahoo.com ADDRESS: 128 Ortigas Home Depot, Julia Vargas Ave., Pasig T: 706-3755 OPEN: Mon–Sat, 9:30 a.m.–7 p.m.

EYO

U B V

SPECIALTY: Latest gaming consoles and gaming console repair.

One of the troubles of living in a country where software piracy is rampant is that gaming companies, most notably the big three—Nintendo, Microsoft, and Sony—have no official presence here. But if you're looking to buy one of their gaming consoles, EYO's a good bet. One thing that sets this store apart from others in its category is its on-board team of knowledgeable

Legend: U=Unique, B=Bargain, V=Variety

gaming console technicians that offer extensive after-sales services. And when it comes to new releases, EYO is incredibly up to speed. Many of their gaming console packages include unlimited games—that is, you can visit them as much as you want and have as many games changed and/or installed at no extra cost.

PRICES: About 10% lower than major retailers.

PAYMENT: Cash, credit card. ADDRESS: 3/L V-Mall, Greenhills Shopping Center, Greenhills, San Juan T: 724-0755 OPEN: Daily, 10 p.m. –8:30 p.m.

Gilmore

U B V

SPECIALTY: All things PC.

Gilmore refers to an area densely populated by computer stores offering all things computer, monster gaming rigs, and little itty bitty laptops. Clientele is diverse: gamers looking to upgrade their machines, modders looking for interesting components, businessmen in need of office workstations, etc. Though it's legendary among computer-savvy folk, Gilmore is especially useful for those who have their computers repaired at home. A lot of the shops in Gilmore have branches all over Metro Manila, which can serve as reliable sources of affordable yet warrantied and brand new computer systems and parts.

Dominating the Gilmore landscape are PC EXPRESS (PCX) and PC GILMORE. At PCX, most of the space is devoted to their warehouse. The store itself is just a small room. You order your laptop/PC parts in one window, pay in another, wait less than an hour, then go to the store front to claim your purchase fresh from the back room warehouse.

Meanwhile, a latecomer to the computer retail industry, PC GILMORE has managed to establish itself in a crowded marketplace within a relatively short period by addressing three key principles: low prices, knowledgeable service, and reliable warranties. You will be hard pressed to find cheaper prices elsewhere, as PC Gilmore's rates are almost always the least expensive among local retailers. Targeted for the more tech-savvy buyer, they, too, have eschewed a sprawling sales area or a dazzling array of display shelves in their branches, and instead, focused on conversant well-informed staff ready to help, especially with custom-built PCs.

PC Corner

PRICES: New, branded computer desktop packages start at P18,000. Netbooks, P11,000 and up. Branded laptops, P30,000 (Asus) to P99,999 (Macbook Pro). LCD projectors start at P25,000. Game Box Alienware laptop, P99,999.

PAYMENT: Cash. WEBSITE: pccor.com.ph EMAIL: pccor._help@yahoo.com ADDRESS: G/L CGI Bldg., Gilmore Ave. cor. Aurora Blvd. New Manila, Quezon City T: 723-1718 and 37 M: 0917-505-3888, 0917-934-7888, 0908-515-1513, 0908-515-1514 OPEN: Daily, 10 a.m.–8 p.m. See directory for other branches.

PC Express

PRICES: Processors, motherboards, and specialty video cards are at least 15% cheaper than a majority of computer retail chains and computer superstores found in malls.

PAYMENT: Cash. WEBSITE: pcx.com.ph ADDRESS: 23-A Gilmore Ave., New Manila, Quezon City T: 725-8888, 726-5041, 725-4383 OPEN: Daily, 10 a.m.–8 p.m. See directory for other branches.

PC Gilmore

PRICES: Processors, motherboards, and specialty video cards are at least 15% cheaper than a majority of computer retail chains and computer superstores found in malls.

PAYMENT: Cash. WEBSITE: pcgilmore.com.ph EMAIL: main@pcgilmore.com.ph ADDRESS: 3/L, Computer Graphics Bldg., Gilmore Ave., Quezon City T: 721-3496, 726-7628 M: 0922-599-8032 OPEN: Daily, 9 a.m.–7 p.m. See directory for other branches.

The stores' respective websites are quite useful and have a product search function by product type, brand, price, technology, and components. You can also get updates on new arrivals that usually have discounted introductory prices and clearance sales of store display units.

HP Racing

U B V

SPECIALTY: Engine modifications and turbo rebuilding.

HP Racing houses all the essentials of a tuning shop: mechanical works, ECU tuning, fabrications, turbocharger servicing, and racing parts sales all under one roof. It has some of the quickest daily-driven turbocharged cars prowling the streets of Metro Manila. It holds one of the fastest Honda SOHC 1/4-mile records at 11.7 secs, a feat that has encouraged the Philippine auto-performance industry to take risks with the underdog Honda single-cam engine. It has also successfully modified, turbocharged, and tuned a Hyundai 4-cylinder engine to over 300whp levels—on a daily-driven car. Engine swap installation, Honda ECU tuning with "Neptune," bodywork, and painting services are also available.

PRICES: Full synthetic oil changes with Royal Purple oil, P2,800 and up; engine-rebuilding services, P15,000 and up; "starter" turbocharger kits, P95,000 and up.

PAYMENT: Cash. WEBSITE: turbohpracing.multiply.com EMAIL: hp_almotor@yahoo.com ADDRESS: 30-B Don Pepe St., Sto. Domingo, Mandaluyong T: 384-1005 M: 0917-526-6973 OPEN: Mon–Sat, 10 a.m.–5 p.m.

Illusion Lens (online)

U B V

SPECIALTY: Special effects lenses for digital point-and-shoot cameras.

Digital point-and-shooters and certain camera cellphones can now enjoy special-effect and funky lenses formerly available only for digital SLRs and specialty analog cameras like Lomo. Miniature, candy-colored, and plastic-rimmed, the lenses are built more like toys than proper camera accessories, but they do open up some lens options that add "oomph" to minimally featured point-and-shooters. Lens types available are FishEye, 6-Image Mirage, 3-Image Mirage, Starburst, Vignette, Soft Lens, Spark, Polarized, Heart Frame with Green Filter, and Star Frame with Antique Filter.

PRICES: Lens, P200 each.

PAYMENT: Cash, bank deposit. WEBSITE: illusionlens.multiply.com
See directory for resellers.

Infomaxx

U B V

SPECIALTY: Digital cameras and Blu-ray discs.

Apart from carrying both major-brand digital SLR cameras from Nikon and Canon as well as harder-to-find, top-of-the-line models, Infomaxx also has a wide variety of accessories like lenses, flash units, lens filters, camera bags, tripods, and other shutterbug treats. Occasionally, a few odds and ends do appear, like the iPhone 3G which was already on offer when it was only available in the U.S. An assortment of MIDs (Mobile Internet Devices) and laptops has also been known to make an appearance before hitting mainstream stores. In each branch, you'll find a surprisingly extensive collection of Blu-ray discs, including box sets and limited-editions.

PRICES: Single Blu-ray discs, P1,700–2,100; a 5-piece set of Blu-ray discs, P4,800–7,500.

PAYMENT: Cash; credit card for selected items. EMAIL: infomax@pldtdsl.net ADDRESS: SM Cyberzone, 4/L SM Megamall Bldg. B, EDSA cor. Julia Vargas Ave., Brgy. Wack Wack, Mandaluyong T: 914-0000 OPEN: Sun-Thu, 10 a.m.–9 p.m.; Fri/Sat, 10 a.m.–10 p.m. See directory for other branches.

Infonet

U B V

SPECIALTY: Wide selection of new, second-hand, and for-trade-in console and computer games.

If America has stores like Gamestop, which buy and sell used games, the Philippines has Infonet (which, ironically, is right across Datablitz, retailer of full-price brand new games). Sell old games for approximately a third of their original SRP, or buy slightly used games at 50% off—haggling is alive and well here. Trade-ins are also welcome.

PRICES: Around P1,800 for a PS3 game that sold for P3,500 when it was brand new. If you take the trade-in option, you might pay as little as P800. Prices are variable, depending on the popularity of the title as well as the condition of the game.

PAYMENT: Cash. ADDRESS: 3/L V-Mall, Greenhills Shopping Center, Greenhills, San Juan OPEN: Daily, 10 a.m.–8:30 p.m.

L.A. Car Accessories, Tint & Sound Room

U B V

SPECIALTY: Premium car accessories, tinting, and in-car entertainment.

L.A. Cars offers extensive after-market services and products that include Xenon light wiring, head light cleansing, fog lights, car care products, car security systems, alarms, and horns. A notable service is the Laser Light alignment, the first service of its kind in the country, designed to ensure that headlights, high-intensity discharge (HID) lamps, and fog lights are safely and properly aligned. Its in-car entertainment section, Sound

Room, carries a comprehensive range of speakers and sound systems from prestigious (though some obscure) brands like Audiovox, Blaupunkt, JVC, Jensen, Kenwood, Soundstream, Pioneer, Kicker, Rockford Fosgate, JBL, Infinity, DLS, Ryan Audio, JL Audio, Audiobahn, Peerless, Sound Magus, Cerwin Vega, MTX, and MB Quart, with attendant services like iPod interfacing for pre-MP3 car models. It offers clients a chance to road-test different systems without pressure to purchase. A major source of L.A.'s pride stems from its Tint Room, however, a unique temperature-controlled environment that guarantees high-quality and pollution- and dust-free car tint application. It also carries V-Kool, so far the world's best graded tint, used by NASA for space travel and by the U.S. Armed Forces on stealth missions. Clients who want to wait for their cars can enjoy free drinks, ambient electronic music, and free Wi-Fi access at the lounge. More branches are slated to open all over Metro Manila.

PRICES: Xenon lights, P8,500 (includes installation and laser light alignment); complete car sound system package, P50,000 and up; V-Kool Tint, P26,500 for average-sized sedan.

PAYMENT: Cash, credit card. WEBSITE: lacaraccessories.com EMAIL: amrit@lacaraccessories.com ADDRESS: 7280 Mayapis cor. Malugay Sts., San Antonio Village, Makati T: 817-8617, 812-8366, 813-2338 M: 0917-817-8617 OPEN: Mon–Sat, 9:30 a.m. – 7 p.m.; Sunday, 9:30 a.m. – 4 p.m.

LapDance (online)

U B V

SPECIALTY: Fashionable women's laptop bags.

At first glance, LapDance bags look like typical stock in the ladies' bags section of a department store. But as laptop bags, they're a breed trying to break the mold of big-black-and-bulky while still protecting your laptop or netbook. Beyond the colorful synthetic calf or alligator leather exterior of each bag is an interior built with high-density foam padding, non-slip suede lining, and a military-strap sleeve grip. LapDance bags come with a moderate variety of designs, but more importantly, in sizes that can fit netbooks and standard-sized laptops. Product descriptions on the website also include which laptop models perfectly fit each bag.

PRICES: Two-toned man-made calf or alligator leather totes that can fit 12"–13" laptops, P2,500–2,900. Slim unisex backpacks for 15" laptops, P2,295. Shipping within Metro Manila, P200.

PAYMENT: Cash on delivery, credit card, PayPal, bank deposit.
WEBSITE: lapdancetechgear.com EMAIL: info@lapdancetechgear.com
T: 823-2218 M: 0917-534-4181, 0917-326-9057

Listening In Style

U B V

SPECIALTY: Home theater and specialty audio equipment and accessories.

Listening In Style is the place to go whether you're looking for a pair of bookshelf speakers or planning to convert one of your house's rooms into a cinema. The spacious store is crammed with all manner of home entertainment systems—from entry-level Yamaha surround systems to more obscure brands favored by audiophiles, such as Dynaudio, Wilson, Halcro, Acustik-Lab, etc. Supersized televisions are another specialty. Think wall-sized plasma TVs or projectors that would put your local cinema to shame. Listening In Style also carries branded mainstream TV brands, though. The store has a comfortable sala-like, staff-assisted test-driving area where you can enrich your audiophile vocabulary by learning what "warm," "bright," or "tone" means when it comes to sound quality.

PRICES: Home theater systems from mainstream brands like Toshiba start at P45,000 (6-piece speaker set, multimedia player, and 32" TV).

PAYMENT: Cash, credit card. WEBSITE: listeninginstyle.com.ph
EMAIL: jrp@listeninginstyle.com.ph or jrp@avcor.com ADDRESS:
5/L Shangri-La Plaza Mall, EDSA cor. Shaw Blvd., Mandaluyong
T: 632-9785, 632-9345 OPEN: Daily, 11 a.m.–9 p.m.

Lomographic Embassy Manila

U B V

SPECIALTY: Lomo cameras, accessories, and lifestyle items; events and exhibits for Lomo enthusiasts.

Lomography is a style of analog photography that champions the unprocessed spontaneous snapshot in the age of digital cameras and Photoshop. Alternative film processing, oversaturated colors, off-kilter exposure, blurring, and accidentally "artsy" shots are characteristic of the Lomo aesthetic. Lomographic Embassy Manila is probably the most comprehensive retailer in the country of all things Lomo. As part of local design collective Team Manila, it also hosts activities for Lomo hobbyists and pros. Check their website for product and activity updates.

PRICES: Analog cameras can start as low as P2,800; camera packages average at P14,300 (includes camera unit, cable release, Lomographiere hardbound book, two film rolls, batteries, manual, and warranty). Film, P180–350; Diana 20 mm fisheye lens, P2,000; Gorillapod bendable mini tripods, P1,350–2,750; Colorsplash flash, P2,150 (includes hot shoe flash unit, editorial poster, battery, 12 color gel filters, and warranty).

PAYMENT: Cash, credit card. WEBSITE: lomographicembassymanila .com, lomoembassymanila.multiply.com EMAIL: lomography@ teammanila.com ADDRESS: Team Manila Studio, 146-B Jupiter Ave., Makati T: 899-1570 OPEN: Daily, 10 a.m.–7 p.m. See directory for resellers.

Oh Shoot!

U B V

SPECIALTY: Specialty cameras and collectibles for analog photographers.

Carrying more than 30 brands, Oh Shoot! locally distributes the best and most unique toy cameras from around the world. These "toy"cameras are actually film point-and-shooters in whimsical and funky designs and are known for unique analog imagery. The Slim Devil Fat Lens cameras, for example, are a top pick because of their Apple-like sleekness and wide-angle

22mm lens. They produce color-saturated pictures with vignetting and high contrast. The Fuji Instax Cheki cameras, on the other hand, are chunky and round-cornered multicolored Polaroid-type cameras that use cartridge film and produce wallet-sized pictures instantly. The shop also supplies various types of slide and negative film from Provia, Sensia, Elitechrome, and Ektachrome for your chosen analog camera. Though the shop does specialize in film point-and-shooters, it also carries an interesting line of quirky digital cameras, mostly from Japan. One of the most awaited items in their digital line is the Digital Harinezumi camera, a micro point-and-shooter (perfect for spy fantasies) in the shape of a 110mm film roll and popular for its melancholic images. (It also shoots video!) The shop has limited store hours, but it delivers nationwide. Check their website for product updates, online tech help, as well as schedules of photo exhibits that are sometimes held in the shop.

PRICES: Slim Devil Fat Lens camera, P1,600; Fuji Instax Cheki camera, P3,500; Digital Harinezumi camera, P8,200. Most colored and b&w slide or negative films, P180–280 (for a roll of 24 shots); film for the instant-photo Instax, P660 (for a cartridge of 20 shots).

PAYMENT: Cash, bank deposit. WEBSITE: ohshootlomo.multiply.com EMAIL: info@ohshoot.us (for more info), order@ohshoot.us (to order) ADDRESS: Unit GB, Murphy Center, 187 Boni Serrano Rd., Quezon City T: 912-3624 OPEN: Mon–Fri, 1 p.m.–6 p.m.

Ozaki

U B V

SPECIALTY: Innovative screen and body protectors for the iPhone 3G.

Ozaki carries three innovative accessories for the iPhone 3G: iCoat Wardrobe, iCoat Mirror, and iCoat Privacy. iCoat Wardrobe are outer wraps for your iPhone, and each set has five differently colored casings and one colorless casing called iCoat Invisible. These casings protect against scratches and dust without impeding access to ports and controls. iCoat Mirrors are fingerprint-proof screen protectors with a reflective finish that allows you to check whether or not your mascara has run. But when the phone is on and lit, the screen display is just as clear as it would be without the iCoat Mirror. Last but not least is the iCoat Privacy, a screen protector and filter that prevents the screen from being viewed by others outside its 60-degree viewable angle (the protective screen darkens beyond the 60-degree parameter). With non-damaging, anti-smudge , and glare-resistant material, the iCoat Privacy doesn't affect touch screen sensitivity. All three items come with residue-free adhesive backs for easy application and reapplication. Ozaki is exclusively distributed by MSI-ECS Phils., Inc.

PRICES: iCoat Mirror, P690; iCoat Privacy, P870.

PAYMENT: Cash, credit card. WEBSITE: msi-ecs.com.ph EMAIL: marketing@msi-ecs.com.ph ADDRESS: Topy II Bldg., 3 Economia St. Libis, Quezon City T: 688-3180, 688-3181 OPEN: Daily, 10:30 a.m. – 7 p.m.

Punch Drunk Panda (online) U B V

SPECIALTY: Funky laptop sleeves and bags; handmade leather journals.

Punch Drunk Panda's prints no more than 50 pieces per design. Sizes are made for 10, 13, 14, and 15" laptops. A bulk order of at least 50 pieces is required for custom designs or sizes outside this range. There are also DIY kits: blank canvas sleeves and art supplies (multicolored fabric pens, textile paint, acrylic, spray paint) that let you make your own designs. Orders get to you in three days. Any requests for exchange should be made within seven days from delivery/receipt of the item/s, but you'll have to shoulder shipping charges for exchanged items. Punch Drunk Panda also offers travel journals under the brand Muni. These 4.5"×7.5" journals contain 110 ecru pages interspersed with 20 sketches depicting various exotic Philippine locations off the beaten track, with travel details for each location found on the last few pages. The pages are hand-stitched to soft leather covers. Muni journals donate a percentage of their sales to Yabang Pinoy and the Children's Environmental Awareness and Action Foundation.

Legend: U=Unique, B=Bargain, V=Variety

PRICES: Netbook and laptop sleeves start at P700; DIY sleeves, P600–750; Muni travel journal, P795. Sleeve prices are inclusive of matching charger bags, adjustable and detachable straps, and delivery within Metro Manila. Plus shipping for orders outside Manila. Prices are generally around 20% lower than resellers'.

PAYMENT: Bank deposit, G-Cash, PayPal, Western Union. WEBSITE: punchdrunkpanda.multiply.com EMAIL: punchdrunkpanda@gmail.com M: 0917-521-0255, 0917-791-4499 See directory for resellers.

Quiapo's Camera Bargain District

U B V

Even before the advent of digital cameras, Quiapo, especially R. Hidalgo St., has long been the gear Mecca for Filipino photographers. Here you'll find an assortment of cameras and accessories for both hobbyists and professionals, mostly at prices that are about 10% lower than other freestanding retailers and distributors outside malls, and about 15% (sometimes even 20%) lower than mall retailers. Though the area does have a host of legitimate or authorized resellers and distributors, it is still best to verify claims if the item is a local warranty unit by calling the local distributor with the serial number of the item. (See Directory for Canon and Nikon contact info.) There are smaller shops that offer second-hand analog cameras, from double-lensed Yashicas to medium-format Mamiyas. But the collection at any of these shops is much too random and variable that not one shop can claim vintage cameras as a specialty. And most old analog cameras for sale here no longer work or are in dire need of major repair and parts replacement.

QUIAPO PARKING

If you must bring a car, you can park at SM Sta. Cruz found near P.Gomez St., on the west end of Hidalgo. There's also paid parking on C. Palanca, near the flyover. Both parking venues are walking distance to Hidalgo.

The following are stores that are considered by industry professionals as Quiapo's best-stocked and most competitively priced.

Avenue

SPECIALTY: Widest selection of filters, from high-end brands like Tiffen to the more mainstream Hoya, along with filter accessories like 52-63 step-up rings; third-party lenses, the brand Tokina leading the pack; and a moderate line of Pocket Wizard flash and camera triggers and prosumer point-and-shooters.

PRICES: Filters, P800–1,000; multicoated circular polarizers, P2,500 and up. Flash and camera triggers, average of P18,000 a pair. Tokina 11–18 mm f/2.8 wide angle lens, P31,000.

PAYMENT: Cash, credit card. WEBSITE: avphotoinc.com EMAIL: ave.98@info.com.ph, info@avphotoinc.com ADDRESS: 712 R. Hidalgo St., Quiapo, Manila T: 733-5474 OPEN: Daily, 10 a.m.–7 p.m.

Henry's

SPECIALTY: Authorized importer of rare and high-end or specialty accessory brands like Giotto (for ball heads and tripods), Lowepro (for high-performance camera bags), and Tamron Tokina (lenses).

PRICES: Giottos MT8341 Tripod, P13,500; Lowepro Stealth Reporter, D100 AW shoulder camera bag, P4,600.

PAYMENT: Cash, credit card. WEBSITE: henryscameraphoto.com EMAIL: henryscamera@yahoo.com ADDRESS: 310 P. Gomez St., Quiapo, Manila T: 733-7723, 734-5099, 735-7989 OPEN: Daily, 10:30 a.m.–7 p.m.

Mayer's

SPECIALTY: Digital SLRs and accessories; compact cameras.

Don't be thrown off by the store's dilapidated exterior or the proprietor's grouchy disposition. Inside are the latest models in cameras and photography gear at truly competitive prices. If you are canvassing the area, this should be your last stop, as proprietor Mang Ramon will match the lowest price you can find in other shops (if his isn't the lowest already) and maybe even throw in freebie accessories to sweeten the deal. Just don't get on his bad side by haggling and haggling with no serious intent of buying.

PRICES: About 15% or more lower than those of camera shops in Makati, Quezon City, and Greenhills.

PAYMENT: Cash, credit card. ADDRESS: 712 R. Hidalgo St., Quiapo, Manila T: 733-5474 OPEN: Daily, 9:30 a.m. – 5:30 p.m.

YKL Color Lab

SPECIALTY: Negative color films and professional films.

Photography purists have this store for specialty color and black-and-white films that in-mall commercial film labs don't usually have. Specialty color film brands include Velvia, Astia, and the more mainstream, consumer-targeted Sensia; Neopan and Provia for black-and-white films. They also offer colored film processing.

PAYMENT: Cash. WEBSITE: www.yklcolor.com EMAIL: digital_info@yklcolor.com ADDRESS: 302–304 P.Gomez St., Quiapo, Manila T: 488-1758, 743-6601 to 06 OPEN: Daily, 9 a.m. – 6 p.m.

SpeedLab

U B V

SPECIALTY: Automotive aftermarket performance parts and services.

SpeedLab offers everything from basic service checks to full engine, manual and automatic transmission rebuilds. The shop has a spacious 20-work-bay fully enclosed area but is especially proud of its tech: Tru-Line Portable Laser Alignment for accurate wheel alignment, EFI computer systems and diagnostic scan tools, and Dastek Chassis Dyno for full and part throttle dyno tuning. Every aspect of speed performance is addressed here, from power add-ons to customized turbo systems even for late car models. Other areas of performance are also addressed, such as brake and suspension upgrades. SpeedLab also organizes track days for various car clubs and enthusiasts, giving clients the opportunity to experience racing in a safe and controlled environment.

PRICES: Brake and under chassis services starting from P750.

PAYMENT: Cash, credit card. WEBSITE: speedlab.com.ph EMAIL: speedlab@speedlab.com.ph ADDRESS: 871 Quezon Ave., Quezon City T: 376-4648, 376-4651 OPEN: Mon – Sat, 8:30 a.m. – 5:30 p.m.

Velocity Motors

U B V

SPECIALTY: Collision repair, chassis alignment, automotive refinishing/ painting, and race-car body preparation.

Velocity Motors Inc. offers premium diagnostics through its Launch X31 OBD2 Scanner, designed to modernize car electronic and computer systems of any model. Another in its line of modern equipment, the EZ Liner chassis alignment rack and the Genesis Velocity laser chassis measurement system guarantee precision measurement and reversal of even the heaviest collision damage without unduly stressing the vehicle body's metal any further. Being the only shop catering to precision chassis correction and adjustments for various motorsports requirements, the shop boasts in-house technicians that can handle practically any type of automotive service requirement, particularly chassis preparations for race applications. State-of-the-art oven-baked urethane coating and paint finishes are also offered.

PRICES: Chassis alignment analysis starts at P3,500; seam welding for full-blown motorsport car preparation starts at P15,000.

PAYMENT: Cash, credit card. EMAIL: denspeed05@yahoo.com.ph ADDRESS: 369 Shaw Blvd. cor. Nueve de Febrero and Gomezville Rd., Brgy. Addition Hills, Mandaluyong T: 721-2524, 721-2472, 727-9722 OPEN: Daily, 10 a.m. – 8 p.m.

Assad Mini Mart

U B V

SPECIALTY: Tremendous selection of Indian groceries, specialty food items, ingredients, and delicacies like ghee, masala powder, all sorts of lentils, all sorts of flour, rice, bread, dried spices, dried fruit preserves, and kitchen implements like specialty cookware used in Indian kitchens.

PRICES: Spices start at P40 (50 g); snacks like naan and roti, P50 and up a pack; specialty professional cooking kitchenware, P1,000 and up.

PAYMENT: Cash. ADDRESS: Eurocrest Bldg., Jupiter St., Bel Air Village Makati ADDRESS 2: 1268-IJK Midtown Hotel Executive Homes, U.N. Ave., Paco, Manila T: 526-1349, 526-5034.

Big Little Store

U B V

SPECIALTY: Chinese grocery with many items otherwise only found in Binondo; also purportedly has the best fresh lumpia in the city without going all the way to Chinatown.

PRICES: Just about 5% higher than the food stores and groceries at Binondo. Lunch packs with classic homestyle Chinese viands (Soyed Chicken, Kikiam, *Adobo* Egg, Fried or White Chicken, or Lomah), 120 and up (for a set meal of rice, 2 appetizers, and 2 main dishes).

PAYMENT: Cash only. ADDRESS: G/L Gilmore IT Center, 1st St. cor. Gilmore Ave., New Manila, Quezon City T: 723-6881 OPEN: Mon/Wed–Sat, 7:30 a.m.–8 p.m.; Tue, 7:30 a.m.–10 p.m.; Sun, 7:30 a.m.–1:30 p.m.

Bitewise Trading

U B V

SPECIALTY: Hero Great Bites sausages and processed meat products free of artificial coloring, MSG, salitre, and TVP; Australian steaks; all-lean beef burger patties; sliced and spiced ready-to-cook crispy pork jowl.

PRICES: Schublig and frankfurters, P350 a kilo (9–12 pcs); Australian rib eye steak, P600 a kilo (approx. 4 pcs); sliced and spiced ready-to-cook crispy pork jowl, P100 (250 g).

PAYMENT: Cash. WEBSITE: bitewise.multiply.com EMAIL: bitewise@gmail.com ADDRESS: 325 Aries St., Rainbow Village 2, UPS5, Sucat, Parañaque T: 820-7409 M: 0920-857-5357, 0923-566-4666. You can also call to order in advance and pick up your order in the following alternative pick-up points: 218 B. Padilla St., San Juan and 18-09 URCI Townhomes, Real St., Pamplona 3, Las Piñas.

Bohemia Cakes

U B V

SPECIALTY: Custom-made cakes and cupcakes.

Baker Erika Fortunado takes pastries to a whole new level with customized cakes and cupcakes that she makes right in her home kitchen. The accents are all hand-molded and the cakes made from scratch. Her cake designs aren't limited to those in her website's photo galleries, which serve to give potential clients an idea of her range. Clients in the past have asked to create the following designs: an iMac laptop, an old-school Singer sewing machine, and figurines in the likenesses of the celebrants themselves. It's best to discuss what you want and on what scale so she can send you a prototype and a target price range. The art on the these goodies doesn't come at the expense of taste. Cupcake flavors include Milk & Cookies (vanilla cupcake with a cookie dough center, vanilla frosting, and a choco chip cookie top) and Breakfast Cuppie (bacon cupcake with maple frosting and a fondant designed as a sunny-side up). The cakes are often ordered in Orange Rhum, Chocolate, and Vanilla with brown sugar-nut swirl. Orders are ready for pick-up after two weeks.

PRICES: No set prices as each cake involves different amounts of labor but a rough estimate is as follows: six-inch-high cake with toppers P2,500; set of 8 cupcakes with personalized toppers P1,800. Items can be delivered for a minimum purchase of P10,000.

Legend: U=Unique, B=Bargain, V=Variety

PAYMENT: Cash, bank deposit. WEBSITE: bohemiacakes.multiply.com EMAIL: bohemiacakes@yahoo.com ADDRESS: 213 Balayan St., Ayala Alabang Village, Muntinlupa M: 0917-843-0915 OPEN: Pick-up of orders by appointment.

Bouquet de Bonbons

U B V

SPECIALTY: Traditional French bonbon (fruit jam or pulp, nut praline, or chocolate in a thin candy crust). Bonbons Barnier, maker of the original French handcrafted bonbon based in Normandy, still produces the popular confection the traditional way. Their creations are now available in Manila. Those of age can opt for the company's fine collection of liqueur bonbons filled with Cognac, Cointreau, etc.

PRICES: Standard bonbon variants, P200–300 for a pack of about 10 pcs

PAYMENT: Varied, depending on retailer. EMAIL: bouquetdebonbon@hotmail.fr ADDRESS: Distribution office: 117C Doña Soledad Ave., Better Living Subdivision, Parañaque M: 0920-229-1964, 0922-876-3449 See directory for retailers.

Carla & Elaine's (online)

U B V

SPECIALTY: Custom celebration, indulgent desserts and specialty breads.

Sisters Carla Lo-Uy and Elaine Lo are no newcomers to the baking circle. Their flagship store, Carla & Elaine's, marks the culmination of their home baker backgrounds. Previously known as two separate enterprises—Cakes By Carla and Cosmo Bread—the sweet destination houses the specialties the sisters have followings for. Cakes By Carla had specialized on custom celebration cakes like weddings, birthdays, while Cosmo Bread was into desserts and specialty breads. Together, they have come up with an impressive repertoire of baked delights: classic cakes with home-style goodness, American-style goodies such as mango and strawberry shortcakes, decadence, mocha crunch, almond toffee, custom-designed cakes for special occasions, and special items such as maple oatmeal bread, cinnamon raisin flat bread, tuna curry flat bread. Word-of-mouth specialties include Almond Toffee which has almond toffee bits folded in the chocolate mousse, and Decadence, a classic chocolate cake with gooey caramel on top. Similarly, the tasteful details, careful execution, and scrumptious outcome of the specialty custom cakes have rendered many customer raves.

PRICES: Dessert starts at P85 for mini cakes, P350 for junior sizes, and P650 for 9" cakes. For custom cakes, a 6" starts at P850. They accept requests for favorite characters or other made-to-order designs.

PAYMENT: Cash, check for custom cakes. WEBSITE: carlaandelaines.com EMAIL: carla_lo@yahoo.com, sales@carlaandelaines.com ADDRESS: 198 Promenade Bldg., Wilson cor. P. Guevarra Sts., San Juan T: 480-9457 M: 0923-477-1480 OPEN: Mon–Thu/Sun, 10 a.m.–7 p.m.; Fri/Sat, 10 a.m.–8:30 p.m.

Chef's Nook

U B V

SPECIALTY: Extensive line of Thai cooking ingredients; Asian delicacies; and a well edited selection of cooking and baking gear (a lot of which are from specialty imported brands) and artisanal baking ingredients like gourmet French baking chocolate and nuts (all of which are temperature controlled to prolong shelf life and ensure freshness).

PRICES: Artisanal ingredients and imported cooking and baking gear, standard SRP are priced about 10% lower than at most upscale delis and culinary stores.

PAYMENT: Cash. ADDRESS: 220 Pilar St., Addition Hills, Mandaluyong T: 724-5812 OPEN: Mon–Sat, 9 a.m.–5:30 p.m.

Choto Stop

U B V

SPECIALTY: Japanese grocery with almost everything priced at P75.

In the midst of bustling ramen houses and sushi bars, Choto Stop is an almost-everything-at-P75 shop that carries Meiji brand and other Japanese candies, okashirai (snacks), senbei rice snacks, a whole shelf of furikake flavors (dry rice topping flakes), various brands of instant ramen, and shelves of sanma kanzume (canned sardines), soy sauce, sesame-based salad dressings and instant curry mixes. With a well-stocked frozen section that has vacuum-sealed unagi, fresh enoki mushrooms as well as several brands of soba, udon and rice vinegar, Choto Stop is a one-stop-shop for the meticulous cook in pursuit of authentic Japanese ingredients. You'll see a lot of Japanese women shoppers when new deliveries arrive. Fresh vegetables and frozen goods are imported from Japan on a weekly basis. Give the shop a call to find out when delivery schedules are. At the back of the store is a small snack bar specializing in bento box meals. For a quick meal during the afternoons, since most Japanese restaurants within the vicinity are closed between lunch and dinner, try the beef cube bento, as the meat is remarkably tender.

PRICES: Almost everything at P75 a piece for grocery items; specialty items like frozen unagi, P350 (300 g); shiitake mushrooms, P100 a dozen; bento box meals average at P220.

PAYMENT: Cash. ADDRESS: 2277 Chino Roces Ave., San Lorenzo Village, Makati T: 759-5560 OPEN: Daily, 10 a.m. – 10 p.m.

Cocoa Pantry, The

U B V

SPECIALTY: Baking ingredients, supplies, and packaging made especially for newbie bakers, home bakers, and those with small baking businesses.

The Cocoa Pantry carries all the essential ingredients in baking with several choices for each one. Chocolates can come in blocks or in chips, can be dark, bitter, milky, or white. There's flour for bread and for cake, with whole-wheat options, too. Then there's everything that goes between the baking pan bottom and the icing: fruit-flavored filling, nuts, candy sprinkles, dried fruit, glazed fruits, mini marshmallows, sugar confetti, edible fairy dust, crushed chocolate cookies, rolled oats, etc. They have a product line ideal for newbies, carrying items like lightweight molds and fun-shaped cookie cutters. One of their concept products in this line is Recipe In A Jar, which comes with pre-measured ingredients for about four dozen cookies packaged attractively in one container. Another is the Baker's Bowl—a set of ready-to-bake ingredients arranged artistically in a big 26 cm stainless steel mixing bowl, with mitten, spatula, cupcake liners, and ingredients and recipe for Great Moist Chocolate Chip Cupcakes. The shop also offers various packaging products, from kiddie cupcake stands to elegant cupcake cups with scalloped edges. It can also create party giveaways and centerpieces. Best of all, The Cocoa Pantry, though based in Quezon City, now delivers to the South through their pick-up point in Alabang for a minimum purchase order of P500.

PRICES: Recipe In A Jar, P350; Baker's Bowl, P400.

PAYMENT: Cash, bank deposit. WEBSITE: thecocoapantry.multiply.com
EMAIL: thecocoapantry@yahoo.com ADDRESS: 130 Katipunan Rd., Saint Ignatius Village, Quezon City T: 497-6957 OPEN: Mon–Fri, 10 a.m.–4 p.m.; Sat, 10 a.m.–6 p.m.

Conlins Coffee World

U B V

SPECIALTY: Premium luxury coffee grounds/beans and coffee machines.

Originally a coffee roaster, Conlins Coffee World expanded its business and now carries a prestigious selection of imported and premium local coffee beans. They are the exclusive distributor of Bluenotes Coffee, the only single-origin variant of Arabica beans that's locally available. Also available are artisan and designer coffees, the product of original blends created by master roasters, as well as aromatic coffees. For their imported line,

Legend: U =Unique, B =Bargain, V =Variety

they have Brazilian, Sumatran, Malawi, Columbian, Indian, and Ethiopian coffee. Chief of this selection of course is the Arabica Jamaican Blue Mountain blend, known as one of the world's finest and most expensive coffees. They also carry beans that do well as dessert coffee concoctions, such as Viennese coffee; as well as different roasts, from light *Barako* and American medium-light roasts to bolder, smokier Italian and French roasts (commonly used for espresso). Those who want the convenience of instant coffee but the flavor of brewed have a wide selection of coffee pods to choose from (i.e., pre-packaged ground coffee beans in their own filter, to be steeped in hot water, like a tea bag). The coffee machines, mostly from Europe, run the full range from sleek single/double cup coffee makers to industrial-grade machines.

PRICES: Coffee beans (500 g), P180–400 (local designer or artisan coffee), P400–1,000 (imported gourmet coffee), P6,000 (Arabica Jamaican Blue Mountain coffee). Machines range from P5,000 to P15,000 for home models, and go north of P50,000 for industrial-grade models.

PAYMENT: Cash, credit card. WEBSITE: conlinscoffee.com ADDRESS: Conlins Coffee World Inc., 2753 Park Ave., Pasay T: 551-3216, 831-2729 M: 0916-529-4052 OPEN: Daily, 10 a.m.–8 p.m. See directory for other branches.

Country Vegefoods

U B V

SPECIALTY: Vegetarian supplies and ingredients like seitan, soy products, nuts, vegetarian-friendly mixes and sauces, and vegetarian meat, franks, burger, choplets, tapa, and sausage. They have cooked food to go as well as frozen goods for cooking at home. Staff is accommodating and knowledgeable enough to talk to you about what goes into each product.

PRICES: Vegetarian meat substitutes (burger, sausages), P90–180 a kilo.

PAYMENT: Cash. ADDRESS: 161 Luna Mencias St., San Juan T: 724-4379, 726-1692, 723-8614 M: 0906-222-8898 OPEN: Mon–Fri/Sun, 9 a.m.–5:30 p.m.

Dolor's Kakanin

SPECIALTY: Authentic Malabon sticky rice delicacies.

PRICES: Sticky rice cake delicacies come in three traditional bilao sizes classified according to diameter (bilao is a flat and round bamboo tray), P190 (11 inches), P170 (10 inches), and 140 (8 inches).

PAYMENT: Cash. EMAIL: info@dolorskakanin.com ADDRESS: 19 Governor Pascual Ave., Concepcion, Malabon T: 282-0071, 283-5782 OPEN: Mon, 7 a.m. – 3:30 p.m.; Tue – Sun, 7 a.m. – 6:30 p.m.

Good Grains Deutsche Backerei

SPECIALTY: Artisanal breads and baked goods like baguettes, focaccia, ciabatta, sour dough rolls, and pretzels in regular, whole-grain, and multigrain variants. Bromate-free and sparing in the use of sugar and oil.

PRICES: Baguettes, P55 (regular), P17 (small), P5 (mini); sesame rolls, P10; focaccia, P36; ciabatta with sun-dried tomatoes, P8; lemon squares, P29; choco chip muffins, P28; garlic parsley butter spread, P65.

PAYMENT: Cash. ADDRESS: 171 Aguirre Avenue, BF Homes, Parañaque T: 825-8978 M: 0915-868-8752 OPEN: Daily, 6:30 a.m. – 8 p.m.

Happy Cream Puff

SPECIALTY: The most remarkable range of commercial fresh cream puffs, eclairs, and nama choux pastries in the city.

You can go as plain as you want, with nothing more than custard filling in a pastry shell; or you can start with a basic custard-filled puff, have freshly whipped cream added to the filling, have strawberry slices added to the custard and the cream, and have the entire pastry shell coated with chocolate syrup THEN dusted with confectioner's sugar. And you can have this in either a mini or regular-sized puff. Happy Cream Puff pastry shells are baked in a way that makes them crisp outside and slightly dense and doughy inside, like a meatier croissant. What regular patrons love most is that the custard isn't too sweet nor the whipped cream sweetened, so the filling doesn't rival the flavor of other add-ons. Choose from different flavored frostings (caramel, dark chocolate, strawberry sprinkles, cookie, almond crush, etc.) and fruits (strawberry, mango, etc.)

PRICES: Mini puffs per piece, plain, P18; with frosting, P20. Regular sized puffs per piece, plain, P30; with frosting, P40. Nama choux series per piece (with freshly whipped cream, fruit add-on optional), P65–105.

PAYMENT: Cash. WEBSITE: happycreampuff.com ADDRESS: The Zone, 7224 Malugay St. cor Se. Gil Puyat Ave, Bel Air, Makati T: 707-1263 OPEN: Daily, 10 a.m. – 9 p.m. ADDRESS 2: Foodcourt Level, SM Southmall (diagonally across ice skating rink), Las Piñas OPEN: Daily, 10 a.m. – 8 p.m.

Herbana Farms

U B V

SPECIALTY: Organic produce, food items, and ingredients.

Herbana Farms is a four-hectare ecological organic farm more than 50 km south of Manila. It specializes in the production of herbs, organic salad greens, specialty vegetables, free-range chickens, and tilapia aquaculture. It also serves as orientation grounds for those interested in learning about organic and natural farming. Available herbs, either fresh or as a preserve for seasoning, include banaba, bittermelon, garlic, ginger, gotu kola, most tropical, ayurvedic, and Chinese herbs, lagundi, liquid extracts, kelp, neem, noni, oregano, turmeric. Specialty vegetables include various types of lettuces (arugula, sorrel), Asian greens (bokchoy, tatsoi, mizzuna), different types of heirloom tomatoes, Swiss chard, Hawaiian super sweet corn, and Japanese edamame. It offers several types of fresh cut flowers: sunflowers, zinnia, cosmos, echinacea, and Mexican sage. Produce are available in Manila through organic stores and weekend markets.

PRICES: Salad greens, P100 a kilo; specialty greens (arugula, sorrel, mizuna, mibuna, and tatsoi), P150–350 a kilo; specialty vegetables (edamame, cherry radish, supersweet corn, heirloom tomatoes), P20–50 a kilo or bunch; oyster mushrooms, P120 a kilo; potted herbs, P50 and up per pot; cut flowers, P50 and up per bunch.

PAYMENT: Cash. ADDRESS: OPTA Coop Organic Naturally! 69 Esteban Abada St., Loyola Heights, Quezon City. Also available at the following weekend markets: Salcedo Weekend Market, Velasquez Park, Salcedo Village, Makati, 7 a.m. – 2 pm, Saturdays; Eastwood Libis, 8 a.m. – 3 pm, Sundays.

Homemade by Roshan Samtani

U B V

SPECIALTY: Gourmet cupcakes, cookies, and homemade ice cream.

Manila's savviest dinner party hosts are well acquainted with Homemade by Roshan, a source of specialty hard-to-find desserts—all of which are homemade with specially sourced premium ingredients, a hit with dinner guests, food critics, and fellow bakers. Call for orders.

PRICES: Homemade frosted cupcakes with cream filling, P575 per dozen; Ghirardelli Chocolate Chip Cookies, P600 per dozen; Triple Ginger Walnut Biscotti, P500 for 14 pcs; Mango Crepe Samurai, P1,150 (good for 15); homemade gourmet ice cream (Food for the Gods, Ghiradelli Chocolate Chip Cookie with Nutella Swirl, Deep Dark Belgian Chunk Brownie, Slow-roasted Macadamia Nut, and more), P600 per quart. Gift boxes that have an assortment of cupcakes, cookies, and biscotti, P900 (for a dozen) to P1,500 (for a half crate of 56 pcs)

PAYMENT: Cash. WEBSITE: homemadebyroshan.com
ADDRESS: Unit E 154 Alexandra Condominium, 29 Meralco Ave., Pasig T: 631-7786 M: 0917-833-6286

Ingrid's Sweet Haven

U B V

SPECIALTY: Wide variety of essential baking ingredients and hardware for both aspiring bakers and home business bakers—from several types of flour and dried fruit preserves to specialty molds and pastry packaging to pre-mixes and baking books.

PRICES: About 10–15% lower than standard SRP in similar in-mall shops.

PAYMENT: Cash. WEBSITE: ingridsweethaven.com EMAIL: ingrid@ingridsweethaven.com ADDRESS: 363 Dr. Sixto Antonio Ave. cor. Liwayway St., Barangay Caniogan, Pasig T: 641-2561 OPEN: Mon–Sat, 10 a.m.–7 p.m.

Jackfruit

U B V

SPECIALTY: Imported fruits.

Buried in the midst of exclusive Chinese schools in Greenhills, Jackfruit looks nothing more than the usual struggling Chinese store: a little seedy and grimy. Yet inside is an array of fruits imported straight from such countries as the U.S., Japan, Korea, and China. The quality and variety of the fruits rival, if not outdo, that of large grocery chains. The store takes pride in its selection of imported produce including California cherries and baby-fist-sized strawberries grown by Driscoll's in California's Pajaro Valley. Other notable products include their pomelo, grapes, and pears. The store does not have a visible sign, only a glass storefront decorated with Chinese symbols for good luck and prosperity, so be on your guard when on the road. The best way to arrive is to pass through Xavier St. and turn to Gen. S. De Jesus cor. Gen. Vicente Lim. The store will be the set of doors on your right after the first intersection. Limited street parking is available and the area should be avoided from 3 p.m. to 5 p.m. on school days due to the inordinate amount of traffic coming from Xavier School and Immaculate Conception Academy.

PRICES: California cherries, P700 a kilo; California strawberries, P530 a kilo; fresh Chinese lychees, P150 a kilo; seedless U.S. grapes, P200 a kilo.

PAYMENT: Cash. ADDRESS: 332 Gen. S. De Jesus St., San Juan T: 725-1076 OPEN: Daily, 7:30 a.m. – 8:30 p.m.

La Boulangerie de Manille

U B V

SPECIALTY: French sourdough bread and fresh bread made from imported whole wheat and flour for delivery.

The hand-kneaded, brick-oven-baked goodies have no fat, sugar, or preservatives and keep for a week. Delivery to Alabang and Parañaque is free of charge, to Makati is for a minimum purchase of P500. Deliveries are made the same day of ordering or the morning after to ensure just-baked freshness.

PRICES: Semi whole-wheat country farmers bread, P35 per 200 g, P150–185 for a medium and large round; dark rye flour bread, P185 for a large whole loaf; semi whole-wheat rustic leaven bread, P150 (plain), P185 (with dry raisins or black olives and olive oil), P250 (with walnuts).

PAYMENT: Cash. WEBSITE: pamilyas.com/boulangerie
EMAIL: laboulangeriedemanille@yahoo.com T: 807-7463 M: 0916-605-4318

Lartizan Boulangerie Française

U B V

SPECIALTY: French sourdough artisanal breads and almond croissant.

Lartizan makes old-fashioned French sourdough bread and other baked treats like croissants, baguettes, French table buns, muffins, pretzels, and bagels. But it also has items you won't find in commercial bakeshops, such as the lavash, a thin flat bread that's soft and tortilla-like when it's just out of the oven, then crisp and cracker-like after it has cooled. Lavash goes well with cheese, hummus, pâtés, and other spreads and dips. There's six-cereal bread and 100% whole-grain bread for the health-conscious. All goods are baked fresh daily right at the store, with specialty ingredients (like sour dough) flown in from France.

PRICES: Lavash, P60; sourdough rye bread loaf, P90; dessert croissants, P65; quiche, P150 and up.

PAYMENT: Cash, credit card. ADDRESS: Inside Mickey's Deli, 144 Jupiter cor. Orbit Sts., Bel–Air 2 Village, Makati T: 899-6923 OPEN: Daily, 10 a.m.–10 p.m.

Le Cellier Wines

U B V

SPECIALTY: Premium French wines.

Le Cellier is an importer and distributor of fine wines from French regions (Bordelais, Bourgogne, Beaujolais, Vallée du Rhône, Loire Valley, Champagne, and Alsace). Stock is kept in properly temperature-controlled storage, and new wines are added on a regular basis to ensure a rich range—from younger, more accessible varieties that are easy to drink, to rare finds in older vintages for collectors. Le Cellier also offers auxiliary items like modular wine cabinets that simulate a proper cellar's insulation, temperature, humidity, ventilation, and absence of vibration. Le Cellier is one of only two wine distributors in Manila that the French expat community get wine from for events and big occasions.

PRICES: P450–950 a bottle.

PAYMENT: Cash, credit card. WEBSITE: lecellier-wines.com EMAIL: info@lecellier-wines.com ADDRESS: Le Cellier Quality Store, Unit 201 Sunnette Tower, Durban St. cor. Makati Ave., Makati T: 897-1480 OPEN: Mon–Sat, 10 a.m.–6 p.m.

Lung Center Weekend Market

U B V

SPECIALTY: Fresh produce, delicacies, specialty ingredients, organic food.

Every Sunday, early in the mornings, stall owners set up on the grounds of this hospital compound to take part in a thriving weekend market. There are over 100 stalls laid out from one end to the other and the variety can be quite overwhelming. Food from all the regions are represented, savory and sweet. Off to one side are stalls that specialize in fresh produce, seafood and beef. In another section are snacks that can be eaten while walking around. Not for the faint of stomach is the stall from Nueva Ecija, where a man skins lives frogs and sells them by the kilo. This community market has also grown beyond food and showcases dry goods ranging from toys to furniture. Regional products such as woven bags from the South sit side by side with Ikea imports. Also on site are potted flowers, trees (saplings as well as mature plants), and pets (mostly birds). The market has its fair share of regular stalls and patrons but there is the occasional newcomer that brings in something new and interesting.

PRICES: Box of assorted *kakanin* P200; frogs (skinned and gutted), P300 a kilo; Kiat-kiat trees (large), P4,000.

PAYMENT: Cash. ADDRESS: The Lung Center, Quezon City Circle, Quezon City OPEN: Sun, 6 a.m. – 1 p.m.

Machiavelli Chocolatier

U B V

SPECIALTY: Gourmet Eurasian fusion chocolate.

When a food lover succumbs to the delectable charms of chocolate, an adventure in taste begins. Machiavelli Chocolatier is exactly that—an exploration of taste and surprises. Owner and chocolatier Raul Matias, who began offering his chocolate explorations in New York and Orlando, presents Belgian and French gourmet chocolate fused, in a surprisingly pleasant way, with Asian flavors. Favorites include Yema De Manila (a chocolate homage to leche flan), Purple Yam Yum (ube-accented milk chocolate), Guava-Asia (guava paste in dark chocolate), Ivorie Jack (jackfruit purée in dark chocolate), and Negros Crunch (muscovado ganache with crunchy almond and hazelnut gianduja in milk and dark chocolate). These pairings may be hard to imagine but they do breathe new life into refined but jaded palates. Take note, too, of the visual they provide: not only are they placed in lovely boxes, the chocolates themselves also display very stylishly rendered designs.

PRICES: Chocolate, P50–75 a piece; sweet potato, banana, and tortilla chips dipped in chocolate; P260 (the tortilla chips are a must-try—their chocolate dip is sprinkled with chili powder). Customized orders available upon request.

PAYMENT: Cash, credit card. WEBSITE: mach-chocolatier.com EMAIL: contact@mach-chocolatier.com ADDRESS: G/L Essenses Area, Glorietta 4, Makati T: 483-9854 M: 0916-297-8729 OPEN: Sun-Thu, 10 a.m.–9 p.m.; Fri/Sat, 10 a.m.–10 p.m.

Mira Angeles Dips & Dressings

U B V

SPECIALTY: Homemade gourmet dips and salad dressings for pick-up.

PRICES: Cheese Boursin, garlic blended Herbed Cream Cheese, P220; Herbed Cream Cheese With Pistachio, P240; Herbed Cream Cheese With Sun-dried Tomato, P240; Herbed Butter, P200; Cheese Pimiento, P200; Asian Salad Dressing, P200; Strawberry Balsamic Vinaigrette, P220.

PAYMENT: Cash. Pick-up details upon confirmation of orders. EMAIL: mira.angeles@gmail.com M: 0917-527-0913

New Hatchin

U B V

SPECIALTY: Fresh Japanese produce.

Except for the Filipino sales staff, it's all things Japanese once you step into New Hatchin. That would be a problem for non-Japanese readers since all the items, apart from a few, carry labels in pure Japanese. It's a good thing that the sales staff knows most of the items they sell, and they readily help lost customers. Anyway, each item is labelled with its price in peso. You can find in this grocery everything you need to whip up an authentic Japanese meal – from Japanese cooking pans, all the fresh ingredients, to chopsticks. In fact, apart from appliances, if it's Japanese-made or Japanese-grown, it's probably in this grocery: candies and biscuits, fruits and vegetables, seafood, sauces, pet food, Japanese paperbacks, cooking and cleaning utensils, Shiseido cosmetics, school supplies, knives, toiletries, and bottles of chardonnay and Japanese vodka, among others. Because all the items are imported from Japan, prices are steeper than your usual grocery. But this isn't your usual grocery, so that's okay. It apparently takes on another nationality, however, with the bakeshop – Bebe Rouge Patisserie – right by its entrance. Specialties include the Mousse Au Chocolat and its jams in raspberry, cherry, and kiwi.

PRICES: Salmon sashimi, P850 a kilo; Tonkatsu sauce, P150 per 1000 grams; Strawberries, P400 per pack; Japanese knives, from P83 to P730 each; Pocket books in Japanese, P50 each; Sake wine (for drinking), P1,200 per 1.8-liter bottle; Plastic and wooden chopsticks, P92 per pair.

PAYMENT: Cash. EMAIL: hatchin1@pldtdsl.net ADDRESS: 602 Sacred Heart St. cor. Metropolitan Ave., San Antonio Village, Makati T: 897-7207, 890-5038, 890-1649 OPEN: Daily, 8 a.m. – 7 p.m. ADDRESS: Unit 6 Cartimar Plaza, Leveriza St., Cartimar, Pasay T: 833-8905 OPEN: Mon – Sat, 7 a.m. – 5 p.m.; Sun, 7 a.m. – 2 p.m.

Panaderya ni Gng. Bukid

U B V

SPECIALTY: Fresh home-baked goodies that use organic ingredients and their famous "Best Maja Blanca."

Premium products here include whole wheat pandesitos (smaller versions of pandesal, so savory they can be eaten without filling), famous Jewish bread challah and bagels—all of which start baking by batches starting late evening so that they're fresh and ready by the crack of dawn. Panaderya ni Gng. Bukid (a Tagalized name play that literally translates to "Mrs. Fields") doesn't scrimp on ingredients: chocolate chip cookies are studded all the

Legend: U = Unique, B = Bargain, V = Variety

way to the edges, as are raisin loaves. This home bakery also has a good mix of Filipino desserts (maja blanca, cassava cake, leche flan) and cakes (red velvet cake, double-layer chocolate mousse). The maja blanca, neither too sweet nor too runny, is purportedly the best in the city. It is sold out by 9 a.m. at weekend markets. Also available are organic products from the store owner's farm such as organic sugar and organic Ilocos vinegar.

PRICES: Maja blanca, P60 – 300; leche flan, P70.

PAYMENT: Cash. WEBSITE: ginangbukid.blogspot.com EMAIL: ginangbukid@gmail.com ADDRESS: Mazda Compound, Pasong Tamo Ave., San Lorenzo, Makati. Also available in the Salcedo Village Weekend Market on Saturdays and the Lung Center Weekend Market on Sundays. T: 815-4552, 474-2600 M: 0916-286-0900 OPEN: Daily, 6 a.m. – 7 p.m.

Philippine Mountain Coffee

U B V

SPECIALTY: Hand-picked, charcoal-roasted local coffee.

Philippine Mountain Coffee is a small stall at the Delicacies Village in Tiendesitas which offers vacuum-packed coffee beans and grounds in four different blends: Tagaytay's *Barako* (medium), Northern Luzon's Kalinga Gold (strong), Bukidnon's Malaybalay Blend (mild), and Kanlaon Blend from the Visayan region. "Charcoal-roasted" means that the beans reach a very dark roast, giving them a full and smoky flavor, as is the case with Spanish blends, French blends, and beans used for espresso. The stall also has a vat for each of the four blends, ready for serving. Order a cup, perfect with the stall's home-baked pastries, pandesal, and croissants.

PRICES: P130 (150 g); cup of coffee, P50; pastries, P30 – 50 each.

PAYMENT: Cash. ADDRESS: Delicacies Village, Tiendesitas, Libis, Quezon City T: 633-2058 or 59 OPEN: Daily, 10 a.m. – 8 p.m.

Royce

U B V

SPECIALTY: Artisanal "Nama" chocolates from Japan.

From Hokkaido, Japan, Royce has a loyal cult following who hoard boxes of these chocolates and ship them in insulated containers with ice packs. Since its opening in Manila in 2008, it's gained a following among Manila's sweet-toothed as well, being especially frequented for its Nama chocolate. The foremost description of Nama chocolate across the board has always been some version or other of "melt in your mouth goodness." This is because Nama chocolate, used to make other variants in Royce's line like the chocolate potato chips or the liqueur-infused chocolate, is made from fresh chocolate with very high cocoa butter content. The box in which royce chocolates come is in fact insulated to watch against heat and humidity.

PRICES: A box of Nama chocolates (comes in 5 flavors: Au Lait, White, Champagne, Mild Cacao, Bitter), P580 for about 12 pcs.

PAYMENT: Cash. ADDRESS: Playground Section, 3/L Power Plant Mall, Rockwell Drive cor. Estrella St., Makati T: 492-5051 OPEN: Daily, 11 a.m. – 8 p.m. ADDRESS: G/L Greenbelt 5, Legaspi St., Legaspi Village, Makati T: 489-6946 OPEN: Daily, 11 a.m. – 8 p.m.

Salcedo Weekend Market

U B V

SPECIALTY: Hard-to-find ingredients; specialty food items.

The Salcedo Weekend Market is most notable for their rule that each stall must sell something that the others do not offer. So while the number of actual vendors may not be as extensive as that of other markets, the variety of merchandise found here is at a premium. One of the first stalls to welcome customers is the one selling traditional French crepes—its bestseller being the banana crêpes with custard crème. Further down is a stall with no name, selling all sorts of fresh and cooked seafood, including crab meat, grilled tuna belly, spicy chili crabs, deep fried mussels, and Nobashi for tempura. Gourmet's (of the Tagaytay fame) is part of the

Legend: U=Unique, B=Bargain, V=Variety

market, too, selling its signature Arabica coffee and pesto sauce. For people into baking and exotic cooking, Spices and Flavours offers rows and rows of bottles of hard-to-find spices and seasonings such as aromatic vinegar, gourmet dressings and marinades, cardamom, and pink peppercorn. The market is also a treasure trove of organic and vegetarian-friendly produce: organic rice, vegetables (roman lettuce, broccoli, asparagus, tomatoes), exotic fruits in season (mini mangoes, lady papayas), wheatgrass and kefir growing kits, and vegan snacks like Citroment chicharon made of tofu. Stalls selling fresh produce usually get sold out the earliest. People who come late in the morning usually stay until after lunch. For this, the market offers ready-made meals such as Salcedo's Chicken Inasal. Neneng's Batangas Tilapia, paella (Valenciana and Negra), bottles of ready-made meals such as Callos al estilo "Morado" and Ranch style corned beef; a wide choice of meats from Chef Ed Quimson's Delimondo such as schublig, Dutch smoked ham, and other cold cuts; local meats like Cebu *lechon* and roasted cow; Namiyaki Japanese pancakes (that look like small, fat *bibingka*). You can take your meals home or eat at one of the shaded tables. For dessert, try Freshly Baked By Bernice's richly moist banana bread, the frozen brazo de mercedes, and baklava (if you haven't already maxed out your dessert limit with the crepes!). Though the primary purpose of coming to the market is to enjoy the gastronomic feast and edible goods, there is still an impressive selection of dry goods: baskets, native hammocks, Acamani Meat Shop's wooden cooking utensils, bowls, and servers, and anahaw-made baskets and ottomans, among others.

PRICES: Jiro's Cebu *Lechon*, P130 (4 kg); Paella Negra, P3,360 (good for 12); traditional French quiche, P160 a slice; traditional French crêpes, P150; ready-to-eat corned beef, P130 a jar; Japanese pancakes, P15 each; Arabica whole-bean coffee, P270 (500 g); pesto sauce, P160 a bottle; chicken inasal flakes, P200 a pack; Banana bread, P150 (small loaf), P250 (big loaf); Budbud kabog from Dumaguete, P25 each; tofu chicharon, P120; kesong puti, P50; broccoli, P250 a kilo; strawberries, P600 a pack; crab meat, P250 a kilo; pink peppercorn, P598 (25 g); Salcedo's Chicken Inasal with Garlic Rice, P120; wooden salad tossers, P150 a pair; pandan-made ottoman, P1,500.

PAYMENT: Cash. EMAIL: salcedomarket@barangaybelair.ph ADDRESS: Velasquez Park, Salcedo Village, Makati City T: 895-4011, 899-6509, 895-4408 OPEN: Sat, 7 a.m. – 2 p.m.

Sin Kian Heng

U B V

SPECIALTY: Affordable quality glassware, kitchenware, and baking needs.

An institution among savvy home cooks and restaurant employees, Sin Kian Heng continues to boast a remarkable selection of glassware for storage (the kind you see in mid to upscale homeware shops, like rubber cork pop-top jars, cylindrical vases, candy jars, fish bowls, etc.) and serving (many a fine-dine restaurant get some of their glassware and kitchenware here). The kitchenware (both for home and some industrial-grade) is substantially more affordable than those found in commercial centers, and many of them come from reputable manufacturers.

PRICES: Vacuum pop-top storage jars, P50 and up; a semi-pro Kitchen Aid food processor that retails at P25,000 in appliance stores and malls goes for around P18,000 here.

PAYMENT: Cash. ADDRESS: 196–198 C. Palanca Sr. St. (Echague), Quiapo, Manila T: 733-2129, 733-2133, 733-6376 OPEN: Daily, 10 a.m. – 7 p.m.

Sommelier Selection

U B V

SPECIALTY: Hard-to-find French wines.

A major goal of Sommelier Selection, a wine importer and distributor, is to be an authentic and balanced representation of France's wine diversity. They constantly visit the 15 wine-growing regions of France, meet with wine makers, and participate in wine tastings to come up with the best store selection. Theirs is among the widest inventories of French wine in the Philippines, covering nine of the major wine regions (with a special focus on traditional, boutique estates) and about 50 grape varieties. One unique service they offer is Wine Appreciation Classes, which is given every year by in-house oenologist Jérôme Philippon. Topics usually include wine branding vs. wine making, history of wine in France, key elements in wine making, old world vs. new world wines, and wine tasting principles and methodology. Call for inquiries.

PRICES: Everyday selections, P625–920 a bottle; premium selections, north of P1,200 a bottle; Champagne, P3,200–5,100 a bottle.

PAYMENT: Cash, credit card. WEBSITE: sommelierselection.info EMAIL: sommelierselection@mac.com ADDRESS: 2320 Don Chino Ext. (Pasong Tamo Ext.), Magallanes, Makati T: 840-4211 OPEN: By appointment.

Spices 'N Flavours

U B V

SPECIALTY: Extensive selection of both commonly used and exotic, hard-to-find spices and seasoning blends.

Spices 'n Flavours is a fortune of food finds with an unparalleled selection of spices and seasoning blends from the Middle East, Asia, and Europe. One section offers local spices in large drums, while another is dedicated to an organic line which includes vanilla beans from Madagascar, crystallized ginger from the States, and assorted flavorings and extracts perfect for baking. Also found here are loose leaf teas, some of which purportedly have slimming qualities or are good for one's voice. Bestsellers include the frozen food line, artisanal salt and olive oil, and cinnamon stick stirrers encrusted with white or brown sugar.

PRICES: Dried spices and seasoning, P300 (45 g); dried herbs and loose-leaf tea, P100 and up (15 g); artisanal flavored sea salt, P990 (100 g).

PAYMENT: Cash, credit card. ADDRESS: RR-7 Phase 1 St., Market! Market! Fort Bonifacio Global City, Taguig T: 728-9562 OPEN: Daily, 11 a.m.–8 p.m.

Sweet Lorraine

U B V

SPECIALTY: Cupcakes with premium ingredients like French and Danish butter, pure Madagascar vanilla, Sri Lankan cinnamon, organic free-range eggs, Valrhona and Ghirardelli chocolate, and fresh fruit—all for delivery three days upon ordering.

PRICES: P800 and up for a dozen. Minimum of 12 pcs per flavor.

PAYMENT: Cash, PayPal, credit card. WEBSITE: sweetlorrainebakeshop.com M: 0915-116-6303

Taj, The

U B V

SPECIALTY: Indian groceries; remarkable array of specialty food items and ingredients including hard to find spices (cardamom, nutmeg seeds, mustard seeds, fennel, cumin seeds, aromatic bay leaves, potent dried chilli flour), dried fruit preserves, rice, dried and fresh lentils and beans, curry mixes, ready-to-heat naan, roti, and hearty snacks like samosas.

PRICES: Prices for spices start at P40 (50 g).

PAYMENT: Cash. ADDRESS: 1 Guijo cor. Bagtikan Sts., San Antonio Village, Makati T: 890-0558, 757-3992 OPEN: Daily, 9 a.m. – 8 p.m.

Tiong Hwa

U B V

SPECIALTY: Ready-to-eat silk tofu, Wan Ja Shan soy sauce paste.

The shop is a shrine to soya, with a little taho café on one side and a refrigerated wall of tofu and soy milk on the other. There are three kinds of tofu at Tiong Hwa: firm tofu, for when you want your curds crispy fried as with tokwa't baboy; soft tofu, for steaming; and silk tofu, which is ready to eat straight from the package, for soups. Tiong Hwa also sells condiments and food products from Taiwan (where the store owner is originally from) that go very well with tofu, such as salted duck eggs and salted century eggs,

Legend: U=Unique, B=Bargain, V=Variety

and the magical Wan Ja Shan naturally brewed soy sauce paste, which can make even bland vegetables taste like steak without the MSG after-taste. Tiong Hwa's tofu products and soya milk (which comes both sweetened and sugar-free) are all-natural and have no preservatives. They need to be refrigerated within two hours after you buy them, and should be entirely consumed as soon as the package or bottle is opened.

PRICES: Tofu, P40 (400 g); Wan Ja Shan naturally brewed soy sauce paste, P105; soya milk, P42 (half liter), P63 (1 liter).

PAYMENT: Cash. ADDRESS: 3 Cartimar Shopping Plaza, Pasay T: 832-9091 OPEN: Mon – Sat, 6:30 a.m. – 6 p.m.; Sun, 6:30 a.m. – 1 p.m.

Tita Lynn's Flavored Suman

U B V

SPECIALTY: Homemade *suman* infused with natural flavorants like native chocolate, ginger, coconut, and jackfruit.

PRICES: *Suman*, P15 each; native hot chocolate, P25.

PAYMENT: Cash. ADDRESS: Tiendesitas Food Village, Frontera Verde, E. Rodriguez Ave., Pasig. Also available at the Salcedo Weekend Market. OPEN: Daily, 10 a.m. – 8:30 p.m.

Veggie Boutique

U B V

SPECIALTY: Vegetarian supplies, ingredients, barbecue, and party dishes; and vegetarian meat substitutes for corned beef, nuggets, etc. Delivers also.

A home business that offers both local and imported ingredients and other kitchen stock for vegetarian households, Veggie Boutique is especially perfect for those just starting on the no-meat lifestyle with its wide range of flavorful meat substitutes: nuggets, veggie fish steak, veggie ham, veggie corned beef, veggie patis, veggie "chicken powder," and vegetarian barbecue. The home shop also distributes products of other vegetarian delis or restaurants such as Green Wok Deli's Veggie Sisig and Bean-Nuguan (dinuguan made of beans) and eco-bags in various colors and designs by designer manufacturer Name It. Soon to come are their vegetarian party dishes and platters. Veggie Boutique now delivers within Makati for a minimal delivery fee of P50 for orders worth P300–1,000; the fee is waived for orders above P1,000.

PRICES: Barbecue, P50 (4 sticks); veggie sisig, P70 (200 g); bean-nuguan, P60 (250 g); imported items like veggie fish ham, veggie spare ribs, and veggie *chorizo*, P150–230 (200–600 g). Eco bags, P60–90.

PAYMENT: Cash, bank deposit. WEBSITE: veggieboutique.multiply .com EMAIL: veggie_boutique@yahoo.com, ernando@pldtdsl.net ADDRESS: 532 Camia St., Palm Village, Makati T: 896-1215, 216-1665 M: 0917-631-1421 OPEN: Mon–Sat, 10 a.m.–6 p.m.

Village Pantry, The

U B V

SPECIALTY: Neighborhood store with gourmet desserts, organic food items, and home cooked meals.

What sets this apart from your regular neighborhood store is that it has desserts that seem more at place in an upscale bakeshop (Dulcelin's famous mango torte, Sebastian's Ice Cream) and organic fare normally seen only in weekend markets (Goolai salads, sugar-free and fiber-rich cookies, flavored tofu chips, and soy coffee). The Village Pantry also offers tasty home cooked meals at student-friendly prices.

PRICES: Dulcelin mango torte, P600 (whole); Sebastian's ice cream, P250 (pint), P900 (half gallon). Jars of ampalaya or *ubod* atsara from Delisha, P100; bottle of sundried tomatoes, P70.

PAYMENT: Cash. ADDRESS: 23 Fabian dela Rosa cor. Esteban Abada Sts., Loyola Heights, Quezon City T: 433-7481 OPEN: Daily, 9 a.m.–6 p.m.

Legend: U=Unique, B=Bargain, V=Variety

Wei Wang

U B V

SPECIALTY: Chinese convenience store considered a go-to place for essential ingredients when doing quick but authentic Chinese homestyle meals.

PRICES: Just about 10% higher than standard grocery prices for frozen products, authentic Chinese noodles, and Chinese canned goods.

PAYMENT: Cash, credit card. ADDRESS: 223-B Wilson St., Greenhills, San Juan T: 726-1208 OPEN: Daily, 10 a.m. – 8:30 p.m.

Yamazaki

U B V

SPECIALTY: Japanese grocery; hard-to-find Japanese ingredients; has in-store ramen house with affordable bento meals.

Yamazaki Grocery is a treasure trove of authentic spices, condiments and ingredients flown from Japan. The staff is competent in explaining products to customers who can't read Japanese. With daily deliveries, Yamazaki carries a vast array of seasoning pastes such as wasabi, ginger, and radish, tonkatsu sauce, fermented rice seasoning, Japanese grains, instant ramen, chocolates, nori-wrapped crackers, and other dry snacks. Stocks include hard-to-find seasonings like konbu dashi, made of seaweed kelp and said to give Japanese sauces and broths that distinct umami character. Ice cream products are delivered every Saturday and Tuesday, and one fast-moving item is Yukimi Daifuku–mochi-covered ice cream. Yamazaki Grocery also doubles as a ramen house with a slew of impressively priced take-out bento meals and more than 20 ramen flavors with good-for-two portions.

PRICES: Sauces and seasonings, P128–200 per medium sized pack; Japanese grains, P368 a kilo; mochi-covered ice cream (2 pcs), P 91. Ramen (good for 2), P120–180; bento meals, P90–120.

PAYMENT: Cash. ADDRESS: 2277 Fernando St. cor. Don Chino Roces Ave. (Pasong Tamo), Makati T: 893-2163 OPEN: Daily, 8 a.m. – 9:30 p.m.

FOOD SUPPLIERS & THEIR SPECIALTIES

Starters

CHAT PUEO
Chicken Pâté, Spanish *Chorizo*
18 Anchorage St., Merville Park, Parañaque
T: 824-7428

DEM NASSR
Herbed Cheese
32 Narra St., South Forbes Park, Makati
T: 810-7325

GOOLAI
Packed salads
T: 647-1205.

LE CANARD D'OR
Foie Gras Poached in Wine, Escargots
T: 566-8716
M: 0918-926-4671
farah-tolentino.com

MARIELLE SANTOS
Caviar Pie, Caramelized French Brie
T: 722-2234
M: 0917-532-9174

MELISSA'S CAVIAR PIE
T: 852-6971
M: 0910-380-3743

PANJIE TAYAG
Fish Skin Crisps
M: 0917-832-9360

PIA LIM-CASTILLO
Mini Duck Siopao, Homemade Dimsum
266 Narra Ave., South Forbes Park, Makati
T: 729-5413

SUSIE QUIROZ
Caviar Pie
T: 844-0772, 844-6191
M: 0918-909-4115

ZENY
Vegetables, herbs
T: 912-8137, 911-2101

Mains

ALEXIE
Large *Chorizos*
T: 854-4716

ALING TERESITA
Baked Shellfish
4686 Balagtas St., Parañaque
T: 851-2674, 852-5242

ALTERNATIVE FOODS
Wagyu Beef Cheeks
T: 631-7228 to 30
M: 0927-905-2168

BORROMEO
Pancit Luglug
1128 Ideal St., Mandaluyong
T: 724-5053, 724-0358

CELY SESDOYRO
Chicken Relleno
M: 0927-843-2736

DESNUDOS
Chorizo, Chori Burger Patties, Longganisang Hubad
M: 0917-540-9980

DIONNE'S EMPANADA
Empanada, Torta
54 E. 1st Ave, Cubao, Q.C.
T: 725-2681 M: 0919-495-6021

ENTANG CARBALLO
Chicken Puffs
28 Sto. Tomas St., Urdaneta, Makati
T: 810-6535, 810-6532

FELY GUTIERREZ
Beef Tapa
T: 523-6281

FOOD FACTORY
Chicken Longganiza, Nata De Coco Atchara
T: 842-0261, 842-3453

J'S COCHINILLO
Conchinillo (roast suckling pig)
T: 810-8735

MARITESS INGLES/ MEAN ARISTORENAS
Seafood
M: 0916-743-8206

MELTIQUE BEEF TENDERLOIN
T: 913-6933

MELY
Marinated pigeon, ready to fry
T: 819-3862

MERCY CORDOBA
Salmon
25 Pepper St., Valle Verde V, Pasig
T: 634-2893, 635-3152

MGM
Sausage casings and curing mixes
T: 718-4278

MRS. HOWARD'S
Crabstick On Cheesy Onion Bread Sandwich
T: 412-1682

MYRNA
Adobo Pâté On Focaccia
T: 411-1434

NORMA LIMJUCO
Chicken Loaf, Pancit Luglug, Fresh Lumpia, Lasagna Style Spaghetti, Tuna Fettuccine
2328 Onyx St., Makati
T: 895-6813, 891-0860

NOTHING LIKE HOMEMADE
Longganisa Roll
T: 896-0396

OLIVE PUENTESPINA
Marinated Cabrito (young goat's meat), ostrich meat, and local feta, blue, and goat cheeses
M: 0917-700-1205

PEACH BOX, THE
Chicken Pastel, Callos Madrileno, Lengua Champignon
Greenhills Theater Mall
M: 0906-520-7777, 0922-533-3105

PLAZA
Giant Chicharon, Baked Virginia Ham, Boiled Corned Beef
T: 890-8391
M: 0917-718-2200

PRIME BEEF
Locally aged and larded Australian steaks
T: 926-5647, 926-5664

PTC
U.S., Australian, Canadian, and Japanese steak cuts
Tytana Plaza
2150 Velasquez St., Manila
T: 928-9296, 633-5162

PUYEE AVERILLA
Cream Dory
M: 0917-848-5383

f&b, food prep, ingredients

R L GONZALES
Beef Tenderloin
P. Guevarra St., San Juan
T: 745-7402

RARE VEGETABLES
Chard, Kohlrabi, Spaghetti Squash
T: 886-7779

RENI
Spanish *Chorizo*
M: 0917-855-0215

RICKY'S PULLED PORK
Dulcelin 36 Times St., West Triangle, Q.C.
T: 374-2165; 374-2167;
M: 0917-535-2592

ROBERTO AQUINO
Mediterranean Lamb, Steaks With Sauces
T: 279-0556
M: 0906-840-4323

SEIS SABORES
Party Paella
T: 636-2963
M: 0917-521-7500

SOSTANZA
Diet Food Delivery (South Beach, etc.)
T: 439-0603

SUSHI PLATTERS
T: 637-6013

TEMPEH
(Indonesian soybean cakes)
M: 0917-821-3484
T: 929-7790

UMALAG FARMS
Wagyu Beef
T: 373-2316

VICKY GASPAR
Iranian Chicken Curry
42 Margarita St., Magallanes, Makati
T: 851-9303, 852-5356

WAWA LINDA'S
Callos, Christmas Ham
T: 533-0934
M: 0917-326-8807

VIGER'S WAGYU BEEF
T: 816-1034
M: 0922-467-1003

Native Delicacies

AMBER'S PICHI-PICHI
T: 816-1313

ANNIE NOLAN
Molo, Bacolod Lumpia
T: 929-2585

BAILON'S
Bacolod Lumpia
T: 843-6673

BENEVELLE
Organic Coconut Sap Sugar and Syrup
T: 994-2072, 711-1884
www.benevelle.com

CAFE NI JUAN
Coffee catering using 100% Filipino blends
M: 0917-527-7141

CHARLIE'S PRITCHON
(Crisp, chopped lechon with grilled pita, sidings, and sauces.)
T: 921-0405, 921-0415, 426-5501

ELAR'S LECHON
151 Quezon Ave., Sta. Mesa Heights, Q.C.
T: 732-5125

FLAVORED TAHO
M: 0917-814-1200

GENEVIEVE HING
Lechon
M: 0922-858-8080

GLEN
Home-catered Puto Bumbong and Bibingka
T: 911-3978

HEDDI GAN
Mooncake
T: 726-4770, 242-9588

JOSIE ILLESCAS
Baked Empanadas
T: 895-9476
M: 0917-834-7198

LECHON FAMILY
Cebu Lechon
129 N. Domingo St., Q.C.
T: 724-9353, 725-9342, 410-4281

LORING'S LECHON
T: 724-2867

LULU SALVADOR
Pili Candy
T: 776-4118, 730-3019
M: 0920-950-3620, 0917-815-5803

LUMPIANG HUBAD WITH PEANUT SAUCE
T: 633-0205
M: 0920-544-5439, 0920-912-5850

LYNSTER'S LECHON
Lechon in Indonesian or Garlic flavors
M: 0917-897-5966

MANG CARIO
Special Lechon
316 San Roque St., Cabrera, Pasay
T: 816-0839

MARIBEL VAN HOVEN
Budbud Kabog, Suman
T: 807-1636

NINAY
White Kuchinta
M: 0919-242-5081

PIA LIM CASTILLO
Carabao Cream/Milk
266 Narra Ave, South Forbes Park, Makati
T: 729-5413

PORQUITOS
Davao Lechon
M: 0917-704-7303

PUTO BATANGAS
M: 0910-248-2385

PUTO MANAPLA
1797 Dian St., Palanan, Makati T: 833-5843

RECTO OR VIVIAN
Bibingka Malagkit
522 Kamia St., Palm Village, Makati
M: 0919-559-4892, 0921-928-7286

ROBERT AQUINO
Lamb Lechon
M: 0906-840-4323

SAN VICENTE
Sticky rice cakes
T: 044-511-4382

STEPHANIE QUIZON
Mazapan de Pili
111 4th St., New Manila, Q.C.
T: 721-4572
M: 0917-812-9136

STEPHEN CHANCO
Mazapan de Pili
2688 Figueroa St., Pasay
T: 831-9321
M: 0917-540-6355

VINIA
Baked lechon slabs
T: 926-5647
M: 0918-910-4913

WHOLLY COW
Lechon Baka
M: 0917-791-1008, 0917-880-6168

Asian Groceries

ASSAD GROCERY (Indian)
5 Thaddeus Arcade, Gil

Fernando St., Marikina
T: 645-1596

CHINESE SARI-SARI STORE, THE
Aguirre Ave. (Near gate, across Ice Monster), BF Homes, Parañaque

DREAM ASIA DELI (Korean)
7 Amber Square, Escriva Drive, Ortigas Center, Pasig
T: 638-6465
M: 0917-796-4200

EIE KOREAN GROCERY
G/L Oandasan Bldg., 507 Gen. Malvar St., Manila T: 528-4375

FUJI MART (Japanese)
G/L Pasda Mansion, 77 Timog cor. Panay Aves., Q.C.
T: 373-0948, 410-0083
2/L Walter Mart, Don Chino Roces cor. Arnaiz Aves., Makati T: 894-3812
1725 M. Adriatico St., Malate, Manila
T: 525-4270, 523-1186

HANARO MART (Korean, Japanese)
Presidents Ave., BF Homes Phase I, Parañaque
T: 842-3876

KONBINI STORE (Japanese)
57 Connecticut St., Northeast Greenhills, San Juan
T: 722-4263

MANITA (Indian)
Comet St., Bel Air II, Makati
T: 896-1824, 896-2633, 899-9136

METRO GAISANO (Indian)
Basement, Market! Market!, Bonifacio Global City, Taguig
T: 818-6642

PHASE THREE KOREAN JAPANESE GROCERY
Aguirre Ave., BF Homes, Parañaque T: 820-2092

PRINCE INDIAN GROCERY (Indian)
1350 U.N. Ave., Paco, Manila
T: 306-0035

SANMOO KOREAN GROCERY
Centerpoint Bldg., Garnet Rd., Ortigas Center, Pasig

SEOUL SEOUL MART (Japanese, Korean)
Casa Susana, Alabang Town Center, Madrigal Ave., Muntinlupa

SIMRON'S GROCERY (Indian)
1268-E Midtown Executive Homes, U.N. Ave., Paco, Manila
T: 524-8169

SUNDRIS CATERING (Indian)
1465 Oliman St., San Miguel Village, Makati
T: 896-1452, 896-3921

TALWAR GROCERY (Indian)
1268-H Midtown Executive Homes, U. N. Ave., Paco, Manila
T: 536-3062, 536-5031

UNCLE ED'S (Indian)
Unit 101-102
Metropolitan Terraces
Condominium
Kamagong St., Makati
T: 890-7971
1268-G Midtown
Executive Homes, U.N.
Ave., Paco, Manila
T: 521-4579,
523-0266

Desserts

A LA DIANE
Apple Pie With Warm
Butterscotch Sauce,
Banana Caramel Fudge
123 Sto. Domingo St.,
Q.C.
T: 731-1964

ALDO'S DELIGHT
Rum Cake
T: 931-8990
M: 0921-717-0447

ANGE
Frozen Brazo
M: 0917-823-8198

ANGEL'S KITCHEN
Rustic Apple Pie,
Sunburned Lemon Tart
57 Connecticut St.,
North East Greenhills,
San Juan
T: 721-8822, 744 1018
M: 0917-535-2033

ANGELA COLET
Dark Belgian Chocolate
Truffles With Liqueur
T: 931-6680
M: 0917-536-7827

ANN PUNO
Nutty Chocnut Cake
168 San Enrique
St., Ayala Alabang,
Muntinlupa
T: 807-6431, 807 2757

APPLES
Key Lime Pie
M: 0917-8557805

ARLYNE
Belgian Lace Cookies
in White, Dark, Semi
Sweet and Mint
Chocolate
M: 0917-882-0807

BABA IBAZETA
Nono's Chocolate
Oblivion, Dessert
Buffet, Banana
Cream Pie
M: 0917-524-5892

BABY YULO
Turtle Pie, Strawberry
Shortcake, Mocha
Cake, Walnut Peach
Pie, Napoleons
19 Kawayan St., North
Forbes, Makati
T: 810-8078, 812-4961

BEBE ROUGE PATISSERIE
Strawberry Short
Cake, Chocolate
Mousse, Lemon Cake
c/o New Hatchin
Japanese Grocery 7602
Sacred Heart St. cor.
Metropolitan Ave., San
Antonio Village, Makati
T: 897-7207, 890-
5038, 890-1649

BECKY'S KITCHEN
Swiss Chocolate Cake,
Prune Walnut Cake
1061 P. Ocampo, Vito
Cruz cor. Bautista Sts.,
Singalong, Manila
T: 525-1648
Suha St., Valle Verde I,
Pasig
T: 671- 7606

BEEHIVE PASTRIES
Strawberry Shortcake,
Fudgy Espresso Bars
M: 0922-822-2399,
0922-811-1036

BELLY SWEET
Parmesan Chips,

Panna Cotta, Sans Rival, Profiteroles
98, Gate 6, Ecology Village, Dasmariñas Village Side, Makati
M: 0917-851-6600

BENNY
Leche Flan
M: 0918-550-6733

BEST RUM CAKE
T: 826-0552, 727-5013

BETTER THAN SEX ENSAIMADA
111 Cambridge Circle, North Forbes Park, Makati
T: 812-3175, 819-5422
M: 0917-840-1941

BETTY'S SANS RIVAL
101 Sen. M. Cuenco St., Q.C.
T: 712-1733

BORROMEO
Ube Ensaimada, Canonigo (baked meringue with custard and caramel)
1128 Ideal St., Mandaluyong
T: 724-5053, 724-0358

CASTAÑEDA
Cassava Cake
M: 0917-5301213

CHOCOLAT
Kahlua Chocolate/ Bailey's Chocolate/ Native Tablea Ganache Chocolate/Hazelnut Chocolate Cakes
G/L Llanar Bldg., 77 Xavierville Ave., Loyola Heights, Q.C.
T: 928-9304
G/L SM Mall of Asia, North Parking Bldg., Bay Blvd., Bay City, Pasay
T: 556-0188

CHOCOPIX
Personalized, edible "photo cakes"
Unit 101 Eastside Condominium, 77 Malakas St., Barangay Pinyahan, Q.C.
T: 920-5911
chocopixonline.com

CLASSIC CONFECTIONS
Banana Cream Pie, Chocolate Oblivion, Toffee Walnut Bars, Calamansi Bars
4/L West Capitol Drive, Kapitolyo, Pasig
T: 746-2773, 490-7896
M: 0917-524-5892
2/L Greenbelt 5, Makati

CLAUDETTE'S PASTRY DESIGNS
Almond Cake
G/L Easton Place, 118 Valero St., Salcedo Village, Makati
T: 843-3996, 843-3965

CONES
All kinds of ice-cream cones and waffle bowls
M: 0920-9568488

CONTI'S
Turtle Pie, Mango Bravo, Peach and Walnut Torte
T: 842-5265, 772-3040
M: 0917-844-5852, 0922-847-3004

COOKIE JOY'S KITCHEN
Apple Pie, Lemon Butter Cake
24 6th St., New Manila, Q.C.
T: 721-5800
M: 0917-898-4913

COSTA BRAVA
Fruit Cake, Cake with Marshmallow Icing, Caramel Cake, Choco Cake, Nelusco Cake
12 Polaris St.,
Bel Air, Makati
T: 896-1267, 896-6872

CUERVA BAKESHOP
Honey Cake, Mango Torte, Mango Cake
2/L Petron Dasmariñas, EDSA cor. Arnaiz Ave. (Pasay Road), Makati
T: 844-0966
Hidalgo St., San Lorenzo Village, Makati
T: 817-0200, 817-6286

CUPCAKES BY SONJA
Nutter Butter Cookies, Elvis, Red Velvet Cupcakes
G/L Serendra, Bonifacio Global City, Taguig
T: 856-0308

DÈLIZE
Baked Cheesecake, Pavlova, Concorde, Pistachio Sans Rival, Apple Cake with Caramel Pecan Sauce
33 Sunrise Drive, Cubao, Q.C.
T: 497-8811, 721-7022
M: 0922-826-2673

DENTELLE AU CHOCOLAT LES CHOCOLATIERES
Chocolate Lace Cookies In Dark, Milk, Mint, or White Chocolate
891 Katarungan St., Plainview, Mandaluyong
T: 719 4476

DESSERT DU JOUR
Gateau De Crepe, Cheesecake, Tres Leches Cake, Peanut Butter Cookies
Unit 1913 Alpha Salcedo Condominium, 124 H. V. De La Costa Rd., Salcedo Village, Makati
M: 0917-811-6272, 0917-803-6272

DIMPY CAMARA
Frozen Brazo de Mercedes, Chocolate Cake with Caramel Sauce, Choco Banana
1243 Acacia St., Dasmariñas Village, Makati
T: 843-8086

DOREN TAYAG
White salad (macapuno, kaong, and buco strips) and pastillas cheesecake, decadent chocolate cake with caramel sauce
T: 372-2740
M: 0917-531-2712

DULCELIN
Mango Torte, Callebaut Chocolate Ganache Cake, Chocolate Decadent Cake with Caramel
36 Times St., Q.C.
T: 374-2165
M: 0917-535-2592

ELEANOR GALANG
Butter Cake, Ensaimada
833 Harvard Rd., Wack Wack, Mandaluyong
T: 725-1218, 725-2481

EMPIRE
Macarons
T: 467-1995
M: 0917-886-1190

ERIC ANGELES
Cocoa Loco, Choco Fondue Cake
T: 817 3189
M: 0917-890-3189

ESTRELLE'S CARAMEL CAKE
T: 3722965

FE GUARIN OF CORAZONS
Halo-Halo, Mochi, Carabao's Milk Maja
M: 0917-896-3960

FORTUNE LEDESMA
Chocolate Cake
T: 844-3663

FRANK'S
Carabao Milk Pastillas De Leche, Cashew Polvoron
T: 823-1601, 822-2407
M: 0917-537-3512

FUDGY BONBONS
Super Moist Mini Cupcakes
T: 633-1513

GINA'S MINI TIRAMISU
T: 811-6702
M: 0922-882-8836

GINNY ABELA
Lemon Torte
T: 852-5341
M: 0917-847-2549

GERALD GAN
Cheesecake
cusineroge.blogspot.com

GOODIES N' SWEETS
Banoffee, Lemon Torte, Decadent Chocolate Cake, Tiramisu
108 Carpark Bldg., Greenhills, San Juan
T: 722-8740

GOOEY TOFFEE BARS
T: 525-1648, 671-7606

HEALTISNACKS FOOD
Tropical fruit roll-ups (flavors: mango-dalandan, mango, mango-*piña*)
T: 818-9492
M: 0908-748-9665
www.graciasfoods.com

HOUSE OF SILVANAS
T: 890-8493, 895-3492, 823-4160

INDULGENCE DELI CAFÉ
Death by Chocolate, Pili Yema, Indulgence Torte, Brownie Cheesecake, White Chocolate Cheesecake
116 Perea St., Legaspi Village, Makati
T: 830-0541

IYA'S JUMBO PASTILLAS
Stall 18 J & C Fruits, Market! Market!, Bonifacio Global City, Taguig T: 729-0325

JANVY SPECIALTY CAKES & PASTRIES
Sans Rival
Stall 7 Delicacies Area, Tiendesitas, Frontera Verde, Pasig
M: 0917-857-3564

JILL SANDIQUE
Pistachio Sans Rival
T: 721-7022

JO ESCUETA
Sans Rival, Russian Tea Cookies
T: 921- 9593

JOCONDE CAKES AND PASTRIES
Chocolate Decadence, Honey Crunch Cake
M: 0917-848-6656

JON-JON'S CHRISTMAS BREAD
M: 0915-904-5771

JONAH'S MINIATURE CREAM PUFFS
T: 724-2125

KAREN'S KITCHEN
Better Than Sex Chocolate Cake (choco ganache cake with dulce de leche, whipped cream, and choco shards), White Choco Sans Rival, Banana Cream Pie
428 Adalla St., Palm Village, Makati
karenskitchen.com.ph
T: 898-2280
M: 0917-539-4968

LENI MATTI
Fruit Cake
T: 925-1514
M: 0917-343-0837

LICOR DE CREMA CATALANA
(creamy custard Spanish dessert)
M: 0917-521-7500

LISA LORENZO UY
Date Bars
46 Limasawa St., Magallanes Village, Makati T: 852-7798, 852-5486

LIVY BRIONES
Food for the Gods
T: 372-2740
M: 0917-975-7330

MABANTA TOCINO DEL CIELOS
Spanish for "bacon of heaven," egg yolk custard
M: 0917-846-1952

MAGIC KITCHEN
Triple Hazelnut Mousse, White Velvet Symphony
17 Penelope Lane, Acropolis, Libis, Q.C.
T: 637-8002
or c/o Chef's Nook, 220 Pilar St., Addition Hills, Mandaluyong
T: 724-5812

MARICEL CUNANAN
Mini Ensaimada, Date Walnut Bars.
44 Jasmin St., Valle Verde II, Pasig
T: 631-0798

MARTA MATUTE DESIGNER CAKES
M: 0917-840-9984

MARY ANN RODRIGUEZ
Chocolate Covered Polvoron
20-B Gilmore Townhomes, New Manila, Q.C.
T: 721-3639
M: 0920-243-1321

MELISSA LIM
Chocolate Carrot Cake
T: 911-2329

MIGGY SARMIENTO
Jumbo Pastillas
M: 0917-527-4192

MR. LU
Moon Cake
T: 525-2720

MRS. FIELD'S GIANT COOKIE CAKES
T: 844-1241

MRS. LIEW
Butter Cake
T: 896-6872, 896-1267

NELLIE'S PASTILLAS
Carabao Milk Pastillas
3777 Aster St., Sun Valley Subd., Parañaque
T: 823-1265

NORMA LIMJUCO
Mango Icebox Cake, Chocolate Fudge Cake, Orange Cupcakes
2328 Onyx St., Makati
T: 895-6813, 891-0860

NORMA PALANCA
Profiteroles
404 P. Guevarra St., San Juan
T: 724-2125

PAISLEY PASTRY
Chocolate Fudge Cake, Carrot Cake, Crinkles
T: 850-9917
M: 0920-928-0528

PARK AVE. DESSERTS
Mango Napoleon, Tahitian Vanilla Crème Brûlée, Macaroons
Unit C Zamora St., Pasay T: 834-6636

PASTELLERIA MALLORCA
Tarta de Madrid (dense traditional cake from Madrid), Milhojas (puff pastry with cream and fruit filling), Argellanas (similar to our local otap), Palillos de Milan (thin crisp pastry, like biscuit sheets), Croquembouche (traditional French wedding cake made of several layers of cream puffs that form a tall heap), Gateau San Honore (French round cake made of caramel-dipped cream puffs attached side by side), Tocino del Cielo (classic Spanish custard made of egg yolks)
18 Sct. Fuentebella, Q.C.
T: 373-2789 to 90

PASTRY BIN
Carrot Walnut Cake
T: 712-2676, 413-4996
M: 0917-812-2676

PASTRY QITCHEN
Strawberry/Peach/Mango Shortcake, Carrot Cake with Cream Cheese
45 10th St., Rolling Hills, New Manila Q.C. T: 721-5360
M: 0917-831-2238, 0917-880-8004
qitchen.blogspot.com
qkitchen.multiply.com

PATTYCAKE
Sans Rival Chips (cashew meringue wafer chips with buttercream dip), Baklava
17 V. Lim cor. Dagohoy Sts., Ayala Heights, Q.C.
T: 951-7351/52
M: 0917-857-9990
28 Sto. Tomas St., Urdaneta, Makati
T: 810-653

PIECE OF CAKE
Mini Tier Cakes, Cupcake Tower (26 flavors), Rum-Soaked Figs and Walnut Cupcakes with Salted Caramel Buttercream, Blueberry and White Chocolate, Vanilla and Strawberry Buttercream, Chai Masala with White Chocolate Buttercream
T: 383-9204

PINK CHOCOLATE
Chocolate Crinkles, Molten Lava Cake
T: 952-6468, 952-6515
M: 0917-847-2253

PIXIE SEVILLA
Dulce De Leche
T: 723-2776

POLLY GARILAO
Sans Rival, Pavlova, Double Chocolate Cake With Walnuts, Chocolate Cake With Peaches And Cream,

Mango Torte, Brown Derby Chocolate Cake, Bread Pudding With Spanish Cream Sauce
66 Madrid St., Merville Park, Parañaque
T: 824-7619

POLVOROTTI
Polvoron in Chocolate Crunch, Cookies and Cream, Coffee, Chocolate Peanut Butter flavors
T: 721-7639

PURE COW'S MILK ICE CREAM
25 flavors, among them Pastillas de Ube, Brazo de Mercedes, New York Cheesecake, Chocolate Crinkles, Dulce Gatas, Pastillas Tostado and de Leche, Atis
M: 0929-683-4350

PURPLE OVEN
Banoffee Pie, Chocolate Cappuccino Cake, Dome Cake, Cashew Sans Rival, Oreo/BlueberrY/New York Cheesecake, White Chocolate Sans Rival, Food For The Gods
63 St. Peter St., Oranbo, Pasig
T: 631-4221, 910-1363 to 65

ROSE
Maja Pandan
T: 810-7533

ROSELYN TIANGCO
Banana Toffee Pie
T: 812-0908
M: 0917-894-7477

SAINT MARY DAIRY
Fresh Carabao's Milk, Low-Fat Yogurt, Low-Fat Pastillas
T: 823-2835
M: 0917-204-1952

SALTINE
Bread Pudding, Lemon Squares
M: 0918-811-8088, 0919-895-8603

SAN JACINTO
Fried Milk
T: 671-5942

SANDRA
Lace Cookies from Cebu
M: 0917-855-5502

SANDY'S
Classic Butter/Orange Butter/Lemon Butter Rum Cake
18 Executive Homes, Kaimito St., Valle Verde I, Pasig
T: 671-1089

SEBASTIAN'S ICE CREAM
M: 0917-464-3397

SHORTCRUST
Belgian Truffle Cake, Pandan Cake
Academy One Bldg. 293 A. Aguirre cor. Gov. Santos Aves., BF Homes Parañaque
T: 820-5406
M: 0918-900-2799
peachyjuban.com

SUCRÉE
Caramela, Melania Meringue, Oreo Cheesecake, Orange Rum Bundt Cake
19 Sct. Borromeo, Q.C.
T: 415-0943
M: 0922-878-2733

SUNNY BAKE SHOP
Mango Tart, Vienna Shortbread Wafers, Toffee Sans Rival
33 Molave St., Valle Verde III, Pasig
T: 633-3410, 631-0307

SWEET BELLA
Limoncello Pie, Hazelnut Crunch, Strawberry Charlotte, Dessert Buffet
1730 Banyan St., Dasmariñas Village, Makati T: 844-0680
M: 0928-502-5027
sweetbelladesserts.com

SWEET LIFE, THE
Frozen Brazo de Mercedes, Choco Lust
75 Amorsolo St., San Lorenzo Village, Makati
T: 815-0188, 401-2609
thesweetlife.multiply.com

SYMPHONY SWEETS
Almond Sans Rival, Mud Pie Icebox Cake, Turtle Pie Icebox Cake
7302 Cypress St., Marcelo Green Village, Bicutan, Parañaque
T: 823-5235
M: 0922-808-5639

TARTA DE MADRID
Traditional Madrid cake
T: 373-2789

TASTE TEMPTATION
Amandee (roasted almonds, hazelnuts, and macadamias in dark choco and sugar dust)
T: 272-5504
M: 0917-577-0362, 0917-866-2238
tastetemptation.blogdrive.com

TAZA PLATITO
Dulce De Leche Cake, Tsokolate Cake, Caramel Espresso Crunch,
12-A Sct. Tobias cor. Fr. Martinez Sts., Q.C.

TEANO ALCALA
Pastillas
18 Lions Road, Mandaluyong
T: 531-0045 to 46

TENDER TRAP
Macadamia Rum Cake, Parmesan Ensaimadas
681 Lee St., Mandaluyong
T: 722-9844
M: 0917-530-1936

THERESE DABAO
Bailey's Choco Roll, Limoncello Pound Cake, Limoncello Mousse
M: 0917-538-8025

TIA OPE
Tortitas, Chocolate Cupcakes
T: 895-8576, 896-7265

TIPPI
Lemon Squares
M: 0918-8118088

TRACEY TUASON
Fudgey Chocolate Cake With Caramel Sauce
21 Stella St., Bel Air III, Makati
T: 896-0396

TRUFFLE
Stuffed Mochi
T: 727-1229

VANILLA BEAN CAFÉ
Turtle Cake
G/L Adamson Center Bldg., 121 Leviste St., Salcedo Village, Makati
T: 812-7974

WENDY
Decadent Choco Cake
M: 0917-810-6414

Lunch-Outs & Light Bites

From cheap eats to decadent digs, these places bring back the joy of dining to what has become the most hurried meal of the day: lunch.

Spots for lazy weekend brunches and merienda cena also make the list.

LEGEND U B A

U - UNIQUE pertains to places with innovative cuisine, a rare specialty, or a concept that makes the place more than just your usual restaurant.
B - BARGAIN shows how budget-friendly can still be delicious.
A - AUTHENTIC refers to restaurants that stay faithful to the flavors and preparation styles of the cultural dishes they specialize in.

8065 Bagnet

U B A

SPECIALTY: Five new spins on the Filipino-Ilocano classic *bagnet* (deep-fried pork meat and crackling): *kare-kare*, *sisig*, spicy *ginataan*, curry, and *binagoongan*.

PRICES: *Bagnet* rice meals start at P100, à la carte *bagnet* starts at P180.

PAYMENT: Cash. WEBSITE: Has a Facebook account. ADDRESS: 8065 Estrella St., San Antonio Village, Makati T: 508-1807 OPEN: Mon-Sat, 11 a.m.–1 a.m.

Adarna Food & Culture

U B A

SPECIALTY: Filipino (Historical, regional and heirloom dishes)

The menu at Adarna heralds an exploration of dishes which stem from Filipino culinary traditions. This can be attributed to chef and part-owner Giney Villar's extensive research based on the accounts of old family cooks, families with culinary heritage, and old Filipino cookbooks. The experience at Adarna goes beyond taste: from the furniture to the memorabilia to the function rooms themes of carnival queens and matinee idols of yore, Adarna clearly showcases a pride in Filipino history. The food echoes this sentiment. In most cases, organic ingredients are used and sourced locally to stay faithful to original recipes and traditional cooking. House specialties include the Sulu *Piassok* from Mindanao, beef cooked slowly in smoked coconut cream and ten spices; Batanes Yellow Rice cooked with turmeric, garlic and some pork; a twist on Bicol Express), served stuffed finger chilis with pork and shrimps in coconut sauce, and the Pork *Humba*, which hails from Leyte, succulent *liempo* with banana blossoms, black beans, shallots, and a thick, sweet sauce. Besides these main dishes, recommended too are *Kesong Puti* and *Langka* Fry—fried pieces of Bulacan carabao cheese (*kesong puti*) filled with home-sweetened *langka* (jackfruit) dipped in mango cream sauce, Ang Morena chilled flan with coffee, served with some cashew nuts served in a Carnival coupe as it used to be decades ago, and

Felicidad!, a highly refreshing cold drink made from eggs, cream, milk, rum and vanilla taken from a family recipe.

PRICES: Regional specialties like Pork *Humba*, P185; Bicol Express, P284; and Sulu *Piassok*, P304—all good for 2. Seasoned rice like the Batanes Yellow Rice, P130—good for 2 to 3. Desserts easily fall under P100.

PAYMENT: Cash, credit card. WEBSITE: adarnafoodandculture.multiply.com EMAIL: adarnafoodandculture@yahoo.com ADDRESS: 119 Kalayaan Avenue, Diliman, Quezon City T: 926-8712 M: 0917-9618113 OPEN: Mon – Sat, 11:30 a.m. – 10:30 p.m.

Al Moud U B A

SPECIALTY: Homestyle Indian, Arabian, and Maranao halal specialties. Must-try is the chicken kabsa (Arabic for "rice dish")—roasted chicken with homemade chilli tomato relish on a bed of aromatic rice, both seasoned and spiced with ingredients reminiscent of chicken kabsa served homestyle in Saudi Arabia.

Like most *carinderia*-type eateries, Al Moud, which has less than 10 tables, has an open, nondescript facade without so much as a restaurant sign. Found in the Muslim quarter of Quiapo, it is within walking distance to the Golden Mosque and its surrounding Islamic shops. You can do away with directions, though. Just make a beeline for the huge rotisserie with a long queue of take-out customers.

Also available are other halal items like samosa, spring rolls, filo, noodles, and roti—they even have halal "fast food" like burgers and spaghetti.

PRICES: Chicken kabsa (with ¼ chicken), less than P100. Short orders, P50 and below.

PAYMENT: Cash. ADDRESS: 827 Globo de Oro Street, Quiapo, Manila T: 488-5006

Ambos Mundos

U B A

SPECIALTY: Old-world Spanish-Filipino classics from the oldest existing restaurant in the country. Meaning "both worlds" in Spanish, Ambos Mundos may serve dishes that should technically be categorized as Spanish, or at least Hispanized Filipino food. But to many Pinoys, the dishes here ring of Sunday family lunches and homegrown favorites like *kare-kare*, morcon, paella, *sinigang*, afritada, and many more—all in a setting that makes up for in character and homeyness what it lacks in renovation and refurbishing.

PRICES: Main dishes start at P150, portions good for 2 to 3.

PAYMENT: Cash. ADDRESS: 750-752 Florentino Torres St., Sta Cruz, Manila T: 734-1160 OPEN: Daily, 11 a.m. – 3 p.m.

Annabelle Yuchengco

U B A

SPECIALTY: Privately catered Japanese kaiseki and Chinese homestyle lauriat (must-try: Chinese spaghetti, Noodles with Glazed Pork Belly, Sharksfin Soup, Fried Milk with Kani, Tamago Dofu with Pumpkin Purée, and Avocado Mousse)

Businesswoman, chef, and hostess extraordinaire Annabelle Yuchengco has converted her home into a unique hybrid of an eatery: fine-dine food with the relaxed intimacy reminiscent of dinner parties at a friend's house. Depending on the menu, Bella uses authentic Chinese or Japanese décor for her place settings, such as lacquer place mats and Imari porcelain plates for her Japanese dishes.

PRICES: P1,600 – 1,900 per head; no corkage. Minimum 12 people, maximum 14 people. Softdrinks, coffee, and tea are included in the meal.

PAYMENT: Cash. (Checks for regulars.) ADDRESS: 408 Bougainvilla St., Ayala Alabang Village, Muntinlupa T: 805-6011, 889-8323 OPEN: Lunch and/or dinner, strictly by reservation (two weeks notice).

Assad Café

U B A

SPECIALTY: Authentic homestyle Pakistani and Indian cooking. Must-tries include the Spicy Chicken and Mutton Curry (the mutton is tender and the curry bothers little with taming itself for sensitive non-Indian palates), Shrimp Masala, freshly baked naan bread, and supersized samosas with tamarind chutney. Main dishes are served with a choice of white rice, chapati rice, or basmati rice—all drizzled with ghee (clarified butter). Different lassi flavors, though unlisted, are available. Just ask.

PRICES: About P200 per person can squeeze in an appetizer, a main dish, and a lassi drink. ADDRESS: 1268-D Midtown Executive Homes, U.N Ave., Paco, Manila T: 521-4996 OPEN: Mon–Sat, 11 a.m.–9 p.m.

BBQ

U B A

SPECIALTY: Korean-style fried chicken

BBQ—Best of the Best Quality—is a Korean franchise that spans close to 4,000 restaurants in 37 countries. According to their flyer, BBQ is "the world's most delicious chicken and healthy food." The "healthy" intimation comes from their use of extra virgin olive oil to fry their chicken. A must-try is the Rice Syrup Chicken, covered in a slightly sweet glaze that's lighter than honey, and the Spicy Chicken, which is red and sassy. Kids are fond of the Original Chicken because of the satisfying ratio of skin to crunch. Indeed, BBQ chicken is tasty because of its audible, surround-sound crunch, the juicy meat, and the glaze that pools at the bottom of the foil, perfect for cleaning up and licking off. Each order comes with a small pack of pickled radish that's awash in vinegary fumes. Once you get over the smell, the radish is a thoughtful counter to the chicken.

PRICES: Rice Syrup Chicken and Spicy Chicken, P650 for 16 pcs; Original Chicken, P600 for 8 pcs.

PAYMENT: Cash. ADDRESS: Jupiter St., Barangay Bel Air, Makati T: 896-7799 M: 0917-7310999 OPEN: Daily, 10 a.m.–10 p.m.

Bagoong Club Resto

U B A

SPECIALTY: Filipino (Wide variety of *bagoong*-infused dishes)

Classic Filipino dinner table staples are given a flavorful face lift by incorporating *bagoong* as a main flavorant. *Bagoong* Club chooses from six types of *bagoong* to infuse in the dishes, each one carrying another ingredient to yield a distinct flavor (coconut milk, herbs, chili, etc.). The resulting experiments are dishes that are all at once excitingly new and comfortably familiar. The success of the dishes comes from *Bagoong* Club's discerning use of their star ingredient, adding it mindfully to tweak flavors, not overshadow them.

Of course, not all dishes have *bagoong*. Gathering regional specialties from all over the Philippines, *Bagoong* Club Resto does *bagoong*-free twists on other classics. Bacolod's Chicken *Inasal* is deboned and herb-stuffed; and Ilocos's crunchy *bagnet* is used for the Spanish classic *menudo.*

Converted from an old Spanish house, *Bagoong* Club Resto is casual yet polished. Perfect for both romantic midday meals and *barkada* lunches.

PRICES: *Bulalo sa Monggo*, P225; *Menudong Bagnet*, P230; *Bagoong* Sampler, P100 for all 6 *bagoong* variants.

PAYMENT: Cash, credit card. WEBSITE: *bagoong*club.multiply.com ADDRESS: 122 Sct. Dr. Lazcano, Sacred Heart T: 929-0544, 929-5450 OPEN: Daily, 11 a.m.–3 p.m. for lunch, 6 p.m.–11 p.m. for dinner.

Blissful Belly

U B A

SPECIALTY: Filipino homestyle vegan.

The food is served cafeteria-style with about four to five standard viands to choose from. those who've brought meat-eaters here usually get the veggie barbecue for them, since it purportedly passes off well as the original pork version. But it is ironically the dishes that don't try to be like meat that meat eaters end up liking—straightforward veggie dishes like *pakbet* (veggies sautéed in fermented tofu paste), *kare-kare* (veggies cooked with peanut sauce), and *ginataang kalabasa at sitaw* (squash and strong beans in coconut milk). Even the *bagoong* used for the *kare-kare* and in the pinakbet is vegetarian, a less salty version made from tofu. Everything is cooked just right, with no synthetic seasoning and minimal salt, if at all, and the vegetables, though mostly swimming in some sort of sauce, are never overcooked. Viands are served with red, nutty rice. All the drinks are made from scratch, with the tamarind iced tea as the stellar of the bunch. Dark, sweet, and tangy yet refreshing, the brew is made with real sampaloc.

The people behind Blissful Belly are health care professionals (one of them is an oncologist) and wholistic health advocates who've gone on exposure trips to India and who cater to providing the dietary requirements of cancer patients. Come early during lunch; it can get easily filled, mostly by students.

PRICES: P120 for a set meal of rice and 2 viands.

PAYMENT: Cash. ADDRESS: Unit 215, Llanar Bldg., 77 Xavierville Ave., Loyola Heights, Quezon City T: 920-3487 OPEN: Daily, 9 a.m. – 8 p.m.

Bread Bag Pandesal Bar, The

U B A

SPECIALTY: Hearty *pandesal* snacks and meals (open-faced *pandesal* topped with popular Filipino viands). The *pandesal* is baked in a traditional pugon (clay) oven.

Each *pandesal* meal comes with camote chips and different seasonings and dips, from garlic-mayo to balsamic vinegar. Among the hearty open-faced favorites are *Adobo* Flakes with *Kesong Puti* and the Pan Ala Cubana (with the requisite fried egg and banana). For typical Pinoy breakfast fare, there is the ever familiar Corned Beef Sandwich with egg and onions. Vegetarians can get the *Kesong Puti* with Pesto on Grilled Tomato sandwich. Perfect with these are the strong *barako* coffee and native hot choco from Davao.

PRICES: Hearty open-faced sandwiches start at P120. Minimum purchase of P500 for delivery.

PAYMENT: Cash. ADDRESS: Unit 20A/21A Ortigas Home Depot, Julia Vargas Ave., Pasig T: 703-7784 OPEN: Mon–Thu, 7 a.m.–1 a.m.; Fri/Sat, 7 a.m.–3 a.m; Sun, 7 a.m.–12 m.n.

Café Juanita

U B A

SPECIALTY: Filipino

With antique furnishings, old china ware, ornate chandeliers, lanterns, and tapestries, as well as an assortment of Spanish, Chinese, American and Filipiñana bric a brac, Café Juanita possesses an endearingly gaudy charm. And the food is just as nuanced. Café Juanita is best known for the little innovative touches it whips up to update classic Filipino dishes. The Two-Way Pork *Adobo* Ribs, for example, elevates the mundane version served at home to almost gourmet status by using the most tender pork cuts and parts, then slow-cooking them in a soy-sauce and vinegar reduction. It's served topped with a nest of *adobo* flakes on a bed of sauce with the same consistency as honey, much different from the soupy rendition most Filipinos are used to. Items on the menu that look like fusion dishes are really just a reconfiguration of ingredients and presentation. The fried pork belly in *Bagnet* Salad, for example, is topped with a bed of chopped fresh tomatoes with *bagoong* Balayan (anchovy sauce) as dressing. It looks alien compared to the bare-faced pork pieces traditionally served in Ilocos, from where *bagnet* hails. But then it is also in Ilocos that *bagnet* is dipped in *bagoong* with, you guessed it, chopped tomatoes.

PRICES: Catfish Mango Salad, P189; Two-way Pork *Adobo* Ribs, P396; Fried Lapu-Lapu with Tamarind Sauce, P499; *Kare-Kare* ni Juanita, P483.

PAYMENT: Cash, credit card. EMAIL: cafejuanita@yahoo.com
ADDRESS: United St. cor. West Capitol Drive, Brgy. Kapitolyo, Pasig T: 632-0357 M: 0916-554-8107 OPEN: Daily, 9 a.m.–8 p.m. ADDRESS 2: Burgos Circle, Bonifacio Global City, Taguig City T: 403-1952

Caruz

SPECIALTY: Filipino "gourmet *carinderia*" homestyle dishes.

The 25-year-old Caruz in Pasig is one *carinderia* that "made it big," attracting professionals, office employees, even the occasional foodie. It offers myriad Filipino classics such as *Bopis*, *Ginataang Kuhol,* and *Pinapaitang Baka*—all prepared with bigger portions and more ingredients like herbs and spices than your average *turo-turo*, and a genuine homestyle care that makes you feel like you're eating at a family kitchen instead of a point-and-plate quick-serve roadside eatery. The place now has an air-conditioned dining section, but dishes have stayed at coin-purse prices. Busiest time is lunch (no, they do not take reservations).

PRICES: *Ginataang* Hipon P90; *Ginataang Kuhol*, P55; *Bopis*, P50; *Pinapaitang Baka*, P60; Shrimp Ukoy, P40; *Inihaw na Liempo*, P60; *Ensaladang Talong*, P60; *Lechon Kawali*, P70; *Humba*, P65.

PAYMENT: Cash. ADDRESS: 220 Hillcrest Drive, Barangay Oranbo, Pasig
T: 671-5277 M: 0918-5233368 OPEN: Mon–Sat, 6 a.m.–11 p.m.;
Sundays, open until 2 p.m.

Dezato Café

SPECIALTY: Japanese mochi balls, mochi ice cream, and potato chocolate chips

Dezato Café is a home-based dessert enterprise turned cozy restaurant-café known for its specialty mochi balls, a Japanese dessert of dense and sticky balls with a filling inside. Mochi balls are rare in Manila, and Dezato owner Maria Gorre has perfected her own special recipe, attempting multiple times before conferring them to have the right consistency. It takes a little longer to serve upon ordering as every mochi ball is hand-rolled and freshly-made. The balls come in a range of flavors such as the chocolate-filled variety (milk chocolate, dark chocolate, white chocolate with walnuts, white chocolate with green tea, milk chocolate with peanut butter and chocolate truffle balls) as well as fruity-flavored mochi balls. Ice cream filled mochi are also available mango, green tea, strawberry, chocolate, and coffee flavors. Free Wi-Fi available. Delivers to nearby locations.

PRICES: Mochi, P35 (per pc); mochi ice cream, P175 (6 pcs).

PAYMENT: Cash. WEBSITE: dezato.com, dezato.multiply.com EMAIL: dezato_mochi@yahoo.com, mariagorre@gmail.com ADDRESS: 100 Hemady Street, New Manila, Quezon City T: 727-1229 OPEN: Daily, 12 nn–12 mn

---

F-Word Restaurant

U B A

SPECIALTY: Innovative Filipino fusion

F-word Restaurant is a high-concept eatery that easily lures the adventurous diner with never-heard-of yet alluringly named dishes. Interiors are accented by a wall featuring intense paintings inspired by New York ghetto murals. The fusion here is more about tweaking classic Pinoy items rather than making dishes from different cuisines. The twists in ingredients and preparation seem studied. Most of them even make sense. The lettuce in the *sisig*, for example, is a good foil to each greasy, porky spoonful and helps avoid flavor fatigue. The Black Calamares uses squid ink batter, reinforcing the squid's sea flavor. The raspberry coulis and the cream cheese in the Durian Cheesecake subdues the fruit's pungency with a blanket of tartness, sweetness, and creaminess, leaving just enough durian "essence" to invigorate what is usually a staid dessert. Some of the tweaks, though, are a stretch even for the dining hippie. The smoothest squash purée just won't make the cut as a carbonara cream sauce alternative, for instance. Confident in their flavors, however, salt, pepper, and chili are the only condiments served on the table. If you don't like how a dish is done, you can have it sent back to the kitchen until it is served to your liking. The best way to enjoy F-Word is to go there in groups, since a huge part of the fun is sampling all the strange and interesting dishes off one another's plates. Speaking of groups, a small selection of F-Word's specialty appetizers and entrées is available for to-go party trays, which come in three sizes: good for 8–10, 12–15, and 18–20. Just allow at least an hour for preparation.

PRICES: Appetizers, P150–250; pastas and sandwiches, P200-380; fish and meat entrées, P250–500; desserts, P160–210. Appetizer party tray, P800–1,000 (good for 8–10).

PAYMENT: Cash, credit card. WEBSITE: fwordresto.multiply.com
ADDRESS: G/L 109 F&M Lopez Bldg, C. Palanca St., Legaspi Village, Makati T: 813-0475 M: 0922-777-5142 OPEN: Mon–Fri, 12 nn–1 a.m.; Sat, 6 p.m.–1 a.m.

Ghazal

U B A

SPECIALTY: Homestyle Middle Eastern and Indian halal specialties. This Muslim-owned eatery is a hidden haven of delicious and authentic fare like aromatic rice dishes with roasted seafood and chicken, tandoor-baked meat and seafood specialties, home-made yogurt, Arabian bread, lamb mince, and kebab.

PRICES: Around P150 and up for a specialty meal and a lassi.

PAYMENT: Cash. ADDRESS: 1551 A. Mabini Street, Ermita, Manila

Haiku

U B A

SPECIALTY: Japanese (Must-try: Spicy Tuna Sashimi, Haiku Salad, Haiku Style Tuna Sashimi)

Haiku exchanges Tokyo-style fluorescent-lit interiors and for a romantic bistro setting alongside authentic Japanese fare. The restaurant flies in locally spawned bluefin tuna (favored for its lean meat) a few times a week, making it the star ingredient in many of their house specials. Each scarlet piece from this choice fish is firm and has that subtle cool and sweet briny taste characteristic of fresh catch. Those who aren't as comfortable with raw fish can try out the Haiku–Style Tuna Sashimi: lean tuna slivers seared in hot sesame oil, ginger, onion leeks, and garlic. Haiku also offers a range of lunch set meals or "teishoku" of tempura, teppanyaki, and assorted sushi, all of which include sashimi, miso soup, salad, rice and dessert.

PRICES: House special tuna sashimi dishes, P160–280 per serving; teishoku lunch special, P350 per set.

PAYMENT: Cash, credit card. ADDRESS: 2/L, Greenbelt 3, Ayala Center, Makati T: 757-4597 OPEN: Mon–Fri, 11 a.m.–2:30 p.m., 5:30 p.m.–11 p.m.; Sat/Sun, 11 a.m.–3 p.m., 5:30 p.m.–12 mn.

Hana

U B A

CUISINE Japanese (SPECIALTY: steak dishes and authentic takoyaki balls)

Set in the Japanese garden plaza of Little Tokyo in Makati and built as a narrow dining lay-out that seats around 25, Hana resembles a typical Tokyo eatery. Operating for only a year, it has earned a following of foreign and local diners who wish to enjoy a good yet affordable steak menu any time of the day. A popular choice is the Cubic Steak, 130 grams of US Beef cut into cubes set with miso soup and rice. The staff also recommends the Terriyaki Chicken meal, Tonkatsu, and Sukiyaki Plate. Albeit not in the menu, customers can ask the restaurant's Filipino and Japanese chefs to prepare a sumptuous sushi and sashimi lunch. Sample the Maguro Sushi and Shake Sushi and cap the meal with a bottle of warm or cold sake for a gustatory treat. This is also one of very few places that serve authentic Takoyaki balls. Grilled by a Japanese chef in the afternoon, the Takoyaki balls here are golf-ball-sized (twice the size of those at groceries and mom-an-pop Takoyaki stands). They use real real diced octopus, freshly chopped green onions, and pickled minced ginger as filling. They're then drizzled with homemade okonomiyaki sauce, ponzu, Japanese mayonnaise, seaweed powder, and bonito flakes. Don't expect Takoyaki balls here to be gourmet fare, they are what they: street food. But having them here is the closest you'll get to what they taste like from an Osaka sidewalk vendor.

PRICES: Beef, pork, and chicken meals, P200–290 (good for one, with rice and small vegetable side dish); Maguro and Shake Sushi dishes, P430 per order; warm or cold sake, P200 per bottle; Takoyaki balls, P100 (for 6 golf-ball-sized pieces).

PAYMENT: Cash, credit card. ADDRESS: Unit 1, Little Tokyo, 2277 Don Chino Roces Ave. (Pasong Tamo)T: 339-3855 OPEN: Daily, 11 a.m.–11 p.m.

Harbor View

U B A

SPECIALTY: Filipino (seafood)

Locals may find Harbor View prices slightly higher compared to seafood-market-style offerings nearby (referred to by locals as "dampa"). But what this place lacks in low prices, it makes up for with a view and sophisticated food preparations you won't find in its cheaper counterparts. Built on a jetty overlooking the water, Harbor View offers a picturesque panorama of Manila Bay. The restaurant has its own tanks from where you can select live crabs, lobsters, prawns, and some of their premium fish, ensuring next to just-caught freshness. And whereas most dampa eateries stick to basic sautée-grill-steam-or-stew, Harbor View can prepare your seafood using restaurant-grade sauces and marinades with a much wider variety of culinary styles (Chinese, Japanese, Spanish, etc.). House specials include King Prawns in Crab Roe, Deep-fried Drunken Shrimps, Chinese-style Steamed Grouper, and Live Seafood in Chili Butter and X.O. Sauce. While its menu's choice of appetizers, soups, salads, and meat dishes far exceed what you would expect from a seafood restaurant (they serve Whole Baby Back Ribs, *Crispy Pata*, and *Kare-Kare*!), it's best to stick to what they do best: seafood. The place is found in an area where trash disposal is vigilantly managed, so it offers a rare spot of the bay that's bereft of garbage indiscriminately tossed in the water and its attendant stench. Call it Manila's modest version of San Francisco's Fisherman's Wharf, Harbor View is just the place to bring balikbayans and foreign guests who are willing to trade in cheap for the chance to enjoy a bayside sunset with their meal.

PRICES: P300 per head.

PAYMENT: Cash, credit card. WEBSITE: www.harborview-manila.com ADDRESS: South Boulevard, near Quirino Grandstand, Rizal Park, Manila T: 524-1532, 523-2019 OPEN: Daily, 11 a.m. – 12 mn.

Hatsu Hana Tei

U B A

SPECIALTY: Japanese (must try: Battera Hako Sushi)

Across Little Tokyo, Hatsu Hana Tei is a secret shared by a few Japanese and Filipino sushi aficionados. Filled mostly by Japanese diners, the restaurant is best known for the Battera Hako Sushi, a kind of sushi which originated in Osaka and isn't available in other Japanese restaurants, even upscale ones. Engineered in reverse, the seafood and rice are pressed into a rectangular wooden mold (hako, notice those defined edges) that has first been soaked in water. The mold is then brushed with tezu, a weak solution of water, rice vinegar and salt; think sushi vinegar but less potent. The fish is placed at the bottom of the hako, then the rice. The mackerel might come of as a bit too fishy-tasting for some, but its freshness is impeccable.

PRICES: Battera Hako Sushi, P280; sashimi platters with multiple fish variants start at P370.

PAYMENT: Cash, credit card. ADDRESS: 2/L Herald Suites, Don Chino Roces Ave. (Pasong Tamo)(Pasong Tamo), Makati T: 759-6388, 759-3814 OPEN: Daily, 11 a.m. – 2:30 p.m., 5:30 p.m. – 10 p.m.

Inagiku

U B A

SPECIALTY: Japanese (Must-try: weekend buffet and Abalone Steak)

Inagiku's weekend lunch buffet features not-quite-the-usual Japanese fare and unique sushi concoctions. Kick off the meal with Wakame Seaweed, Vinegared Shrimps, and Smoked Salmon followed by Inagiku Salad. Seafood lovers can partake of a large selection of fresh maguro (tuna), shake (salmon), tako (octopus), uni (sea urchin), or ika (squid) sushi. Inagiku has a spacious teppanyaki area whipping up delectable slices of griddle-cooked steak, gindara and lapu–lapu, combined with assorted vegetables as well as a section for soba, udon, and sukiyaki bowls. For other days of the week, Inagiku features notable à la carte dishes such as Aburi (lightly grilled sushi), Abalone Steak, and Gindara Pepper Steak.

PRICES: Weekend lunch buffet, P1,738.10; weekday lunch specials Aburi and Abalone Steak, P1,300 per order, good for 2.

PAYMENT: Cash, credit card. ADDRESS: Mezzanine Level, Makati Shangri La Hotel T: 813-8888 OPEN: Daily, 11:30 a.m.–2:30 p.m., 6 p.m.–10:30 p.m.

Jakarta Inn & Restaurant

U B A

SPECIALTY: Traditional and contemporary Indonesian halal delicacies. Must-tries include the slow-cooked and spice-marinated beef rendang, the various savory fried rice specialties, the aromatic oxtail consommé, and the traditionally prepared satays. Probably only here can you find classic Lontong (pressed rice cut into cakes and served cold or at room temperature with mains like curries, satays, and meat dishes with sauce).

PRICES: Around P200 and up for a specialty meal.

PAYMENT: Cash, credit card. ADDRESS: 2082 Benitez near cor. San Andres St., Malate, Manila T: 521-1416 OPEN: Mon–Sat, 11 a.m.–2 p.m., 6 p.m.–11 p.m.

JT's Manukan

U B A

SPECIALTY: Authentic chicken *inasal*

JT stands for Joel Torre, the actor. And JT's Manukan is his way of sharing with Metro Manila folk his hometown's famous chicken *inasal* (grilled chicken dish originating from Bacolod that's marinated in vinegar, salt, garlic, and atchuete oil). Because all of JT's chefs and servers hail from Bacolod as well, the chicken *inasal* they serve is bona fide Ilonggo and served with garlic rice, garlic chips, and chicken oil drippings (which you drizzle over the rice). Not to be missed, too, are JT's *Kansi* (beef shank and marrow cooked in a spicy and sour stew that's flavored with uses a fruit indigenous to Bacolod) and *Isol* (grilled chicken bottom). There's nothing pretentious about JT's Manukan, with long plain tables and wooden benches. While its Gilmore branch is open to all the elements, the Malugay (Makati) and Greenhills branches have air-conditioned areas for sensitive lungs. A plus: Joel Torre often stops by his restaurants and, unless he's in the middle of a meal, rarely refuses a photo op.

PRICES: Chicken *inasal*, P88 per stick; *Isol* P50 per stick, *Kansi* P110; extra garlic chips, P17; extra chicken oil, P15; leche flan P95.

PAYMENT: Cash. ADDRESS: The Zone, 7224 Malugay St. Cor. Sen. Gil Puyat Ave. (Buendia), Bel Air, Makati T: 813-0106 ADDRESS 2: 4 Granada cor. Valencia St., New Manila, Quezon Cty T: 721-9025 ADDRESS 3: The Courtyard Bldg., 26 Sgt. Esguerra St., Bgy. South Triangle, Quezon City T: 928-8085 OPEN: Daily, 11:30 a.m.–2 a.m. (for all branches).

KKK Food Revolution

U B A

SPECIALTY: Modernized yet nonetheless authentic regional Filipino specialties.

Think of KKK Food Revolution as the modern-day Barrio Fiesta—it's a conveniently located eatery for bringing tourists who want to sample Filipino food, it's got history etched on its name and wall art (a mural of national hero Jose Rizal eating with his revolutionary buds) to serve as instant conversation pieces, and yet it's affordable enough for Pinoys to make it a gastronomic haunt when they want Pinoy fare that reminds them of grandma's cooking (albeit with some gourmet tweaks). Must-tries here include the *Sinigang na Lechon* Soup, *Adobo ni Jake Espesyal* (with crunchy *adobo* flakes and fried bananas), the *Kanin ng KKK* (fried garlic rice tossed with crunchy grilled pork *liempo* bits, egg, and onion leaves). Value meals are available Mon–Thu, 10 a.m.–11 a.m., 2 p.m.–5 p.m.

A bit of trivia: Though it would be fitting for the resto's name to allude to the Philippine revolutionary movement of the same acronym (Kataas-taasang, Kagalang-galangang Katipunan ng mga Anak ng Bayan—which in English is "High and Honorable Society of the Children of the Nation"), KKK in this case was based more on location than history. The KKK of the first branch, which was on West Avenue, stood for *Kainan sa Kalye Kanluran* (literally Eatery on West Avenue); while in the coastal commercial complex of Mall of Asia, KKK stands *Kainan Katabi ng Karagatan* (literally Eatery by the Sea)

PRICES: Value meals, P98–128; but an à la carte meal would start at about P250 per person for rice, a shared main dish (since most dishes are good for 2–3), a drink, and a dessert.

PAYMENT: Cash, credit card. WEBSITE: Facebook ADDRESS: 74 West Ave., Quezon City T: 371-9099 ADDRESS 2: G/L Entertainment Wing, SM Mall of Asia, Pasay T: 556-0755 ADDRESS 3: 3/L Midtown Wing, Robinsons Place, Malate, Manila T: 567-2186 OPEN: Daily, 2 p.m.–2 a.m. (all branches)

Kanin Club

U B A

SPECIALTY: Filipino comfort food with a twist (must-try: Crispy Dinuguan)

Kanin Club has almost single-handedly built its reputation on one dish: Crispy *Dinuguan*. Practically an oxymoron, this much-maligned Filipino dish that's been relegated to Fear Factor status, is a (soft) blood stew made of pig parts. The Crispy *Dinuguan* hews to the original in terms of consistency (saucy) and color (midnight black), and then skews off into its own tangent. The expected softness is replaced with the unexpected crunch of *lechong* kawali (pan-fried pork belly with skin intact) crashing through the mouth, leaving in its wake a vinegary zing. At once crispy-chewy, it's a dish that, on first taste, can provoke you to let loose a string of fluorescent expletives. Most dishes are great for two people with admirable appetites. Nibblers need not apply. The winsome ambience nods to the classiest of our Filipino heritage. Stained glass windows, hardwood chairs and tables, capiz accents, and paintings of provincial scenes with—thankfully—nary a banana leaf or *barong*-clad waiter to be found. For dessert, the *turon*, a pair of fritters as thick as a child's forearm, is stuffed with *ube* jam, *macapuno* strips, red beans, and *saba* bananas garnished with a scoop of *queso* ice cream. There goes another string of fluorescent expletives.

PRICES: Crispy *Dinuguan*, P261; *turon*, P135; extra ice cream, P53.

PAYMENT: Cash. ADDRESS: Westgate Alabang, Filinvest Corporate City, Alabang, Muntinlupa T: 771-1400 OPEN: Daily, 11 a.m.–11 p.m.
ADDRESS 2: G/L AyalaLand-UP TechnoHub, Commonwealth Avenue, Brgy. U.P. Campus, Quezon City OPEN: Daily, 11 a.m.–11 p.m.

Kashmir

U B A

SPECIALTY: Indian, Malaysian, Arabian

Probably the oldest Indian fine-dining restaurant in Manila, Kashmir has managed to thrive amidst Manila's fickle dining landscape on a steady clientele of businessmen, expats, and families looking to enjoy Indian fare somewhere that readily portends authenticity at first glance. As with authentic Kashmiri cooking, mutton is the restaurant's most notable dish. Usually a challenge to cook since it is older, tougher, and more aggressive in flavor than lamb, mutton is understandably hit-and-miss in most places that serve it. But at Kashmir, cooked in six ways, the mutton is a consistent top-performer—it is neither tough and chewy nor overcooked to the point of disintegration and loss of that distinct "mutton-y" taste. Whether cooked in a richly spiced herb gravy, or with basic garlic, onion, and ginger in a copper kettle over low fire, the mutton remains the star of the dish, with other ingredients serving only to enhance rather than disguise its flavor. The restaurant also has a deli function, something not a lot of diners know. You can buy jars of spices, to-go meals, and ready-to-cook versions of their specialties.

PRICES: Mutton dishes, P420 (good for 2); specialty savory rice dishes, P200–500 (good for 3). To-go and ready-to-cook dishes: Indian bread, P40 per pack of 3 to 4 pcs.; microwaveable meals like lamb curry and palak paneer, P90–140 per order (good for 1); cook-at-home tikka, tandoori, kebabs, and samosas, P100–150 per box. Party trays need to be ordered at least 24 hours in advance.

PAYMENT: Cash, credit card. WEBSITE: www.kashmirmanila.com ADDRESS: 523 Merchant Center Bldg., Padre Faura near cor. Adriatico St., Ermita, Manila T: 524-6851, 523-1521 ADDRESS: Festejo Bldg. 816 Arnaiz Ave. (Pasay Rd.), Makati T: 844-4924 OPEN: Daily, 11 a.m.–11 p.m.

Kikufuji

U B A

SPECIALTY: Japanese (SPECIALTY: variety of set lunches, especially the lunch-time teishoku and donburi)

Made popular by its lunch menus, Kikufuji has become a favorite of both local yuppies and foreign patrons. Diners have the option of eating at the large sushi bar, regular tables, or non-smoking or smoking tatami rooms. Some of the notable lunch offerings include an Ebi Tempura set, fresh servings of Chirashidon, Unidon, Shake Ikura Don, Magurodon, and Nigiri Sushi. Teishoku and donburi meals are served with rice, miso soup, small saucers of salad, seaweed, and fried tuna.

PRICES: Ebi Tempura set, P269; Chirashidon, P386; Unidon, P342; Shake Ikura Don, P440; Magurodon, P352; Nigiri Sushi, P335.

PAYMENT: Cash, credit card. ADDRESS: 2277 Pasong Tamo, Makati T: 893-7319, 893-6131 OPEN: Mon–Fri, 11:30 a.m.–1:30 p.m., 5:30 p.m.–10:30 p.m.; Sat/Sun, 11:30 a.m.–1:30 p.m., 5 p.m.–10 p.m.

King One

U B A

SPECIALTY: Eat all you can rotary shabu-shabu

King One puts a fresh spin on Manila's worn-out eat-all-you-can craze with the hot pot—a domain of Asian cuisine that is relatively unexploited and usually pricey at the few places that have it. Take your pick from six flavors for your soup base (Plain, Spicy Szechuan, Satay, Century Egg Wansui, Korean Kimchi, and Hong Kong Curry), then get ready to "compose" your own hearty concoction from about 90 ingredients (noodles, seafood, meat, veggies, and garnishing) for cooking in your hot pot. You can tick off your ingredients from a list and give it to your waiter, or you can just pick them right off the rotary conveyor belt. Topselling ingredients are the dumplings, mozzarella balls, fish balls, squid balls, lobster balls, beef balls, US-grade beef strips (sliced in front of you), scallops, shrimp, oysters, kani, golden mushrooms, prawns, lamb, fried bean curd, tofu, and fresh bamboo shells. Two complimentary side dishes of the day are served with your hot pot. King One is a come-as-you-are type of place, and you'll find big groups of young Chinese and Korean diner. Hot pots are best enjoyed with the whole family or your *barkada*.

PRICES: Eat all you can hot pot, P449 for lunch.

PAYMENT: Cash. ADDRESS: M2-A Lower Level, Hobbies Of Asia, Pasay
T: 556-1370, 556-1827 OPEN: Daily, 11 a.m.–10 p.m.

La Cocina De Tita Moning

U B A

SPECIALTY: Spanish-influenced traditional Filipino cuisine using family heirloom recipes; fine dining in a 1930s Art Deco ancestral home.

Meals at this by-reservation-only restaurant are served with antique tableware and include a tour of the house. The house itself is a time capsule, with art work by grand masters like Hidalgo and period furniture from the 1930s. It is ironically the menu that hints at a bit of innovation, listing items like pastas and lamb alongside more traditional Fil-Hispanic fare like paella and canonigo. There are abut 15 heirloom dishes to choose from in the lunch menu, which is different yet from the dinner menu. Each meal consists of about seven courses. They can even serve afternoon tea and a spread of choices for merienda. For lunch, must-tries include the lengua cooked in white wine, the baked lapu-lapu, and the paella. For dessert, it is the simple yet rich, buttery, and delicately flavored bread pudding that's become a crowd favorite.

Needless to say, La Cocina is not a place for that casual, walk-in lunch. It's more fitting for big groups on special occasions, a romantic date, or meals out when hosting a tourist.

PRICES: About P1,750 per head. Corkage is P300 per 750 ml bottle.

PAYMENT: Cash, checks (payable to La Cocina de Tita Moning), major credit cards. WEBSITE: www.lacocinadetitamoning.com EMAIL: talktous@lacocinadetitamoning.com ADDRESS: 315 San Rafael St., San Miguel District, Manila T: 734-2146, 734-2141; F: 734-2141 M: 0918-6551040 OPEN: Lunch and/or dinner. Strictly by reservation, at least 24 hours notice (for reservation and choice of menu).

Likha Diwa sa Gulod

U B A

SPECIALTY: Filipino-inspired vegetarian food

Like its quiet ambience, Gulod's location is so unobtrusive that you'd most certainly miss it if you didn't know where it is. The lot is right behind a gaggle of public jeepneys whose drivers have unofficially turned Gulod's frontage into their terminal. Inside the property, a little pond welcomes customers into this haven for pesco vegetarians, artists, NGO workers, as well as students and faculty from UP Diliman. In this place, there are no pork, chicken, or beef dishes around. They serve only organic brown rice with dishes of vegetables, tofu, veggie meat, and seafood. Meat-eaters aren't turned away, though. The dishes are scrumptious enough for non-vegans to appreciate, too—their *Pusitsig* (*sisig* using not pork but squid) is as good as the real thing; their *Daing na Bangus* with salted egg is perfect with its juice and salty tang; the organic coffee hits the spot after a meal. The desserts aren't exactly as healthy as the main dishes, but that's a small price to pay. Try the Choco Banana Dessert after a run around UP's sunken garden or a wall-climbing session in nearby Power Up wall-climbing gym to keep the guilt away. Cementing Gulod's Bohemian vibe is the artwork on its walls and an area with low tables where customers can dine on the floor amid big cushions. Gulod makes being healthy so easy.

PRICES: Vegetarian *Afritada* meal (includes *calamansi* juice and organic brown rice), P75; Vegetarian *Kare-Kare* (includes organic brown rice and vegetarian *bagoong*), P100; Plain Yoghurt Shake, P60; Cheesesticks, P80.

PAYMENT: Cash. ADDRESS: 1 Lot J. Francisco St., Bgy. Krus na Ligas, UP Diliman, Quezon City T: 925-5522 OPEN: Mon–Sat, 10 a.m.–10 p.m.

Makansutra Asian Food Village

U B A

SPECIALTY: Singaporean inspired hawker center food in a foodcourt setting.

The food court of sorts houses a spacious kitchen at the center from which mostly Singaporean-themed specialties, along with Filipino-, Malaysian-, Thai-, Indian-themed are prepared and served through a total of 14 food stations. While it would be wishful thinking to expect each station to serve honest-to-goodness authentic specialties, the place is still worth a visit if only for the availability of multiple regional specialties—Thailand's crispy egg rice with spicy pork or spicy basil chicken, Indonesia's popular satays, Singapore's Hainanese Chicken Rice, or Malaysia's coconut rice with fried chicken and seafood sambal, perhaps—all in one roof. Makansutra's all-Pinoy staff were trained by a few Singaporean street food master cooks, so while food quality won't be the same as that of a standalone Thai or Indian specialty resto, it more than sates general Asian food cravings and provides a good enough deal given the price points.

The tremendous amount of choices can send you into a panic, so unless you're planning to zero in on just one food station, it's best to go around all 14 of them before deciding and lining up to order. Also, if you're dining as a group, finalize your order as a group and assign different people to the different stations from which you plan to order to maximize time efficiency (and most of all keep the food warm).

PRICES: Main dishes, usually with rice, are typically P90–150 (some are good to share for 2 people).

PAYMENT: Cash. ADDRESS: 2/L Manila Ocean Park, Quirino Grandstand, Manila OPEN: Daily, 11 a.m.–9 p.m.

Malate Tea House

U B A

SPECIALTY: Chinese delicacies. Must-tries include the much vaunted beef hofan (purportedly one of the best in the city), Imelda fish head in noodles (steeped in specialty spices and herbs, then slow cooked over low fire for two hours), and fried kingfish with chili sauce.

PRICES: The specialties usually come in group portions, starting at P250 (good for 4) and P550 (good for 10). Solo rice combo meals, about P85 and up. Set menus for big groups (at least 12 people), P3,200 and up.

PAYMENT: Cash. ADDRESS: 728 Gen. Malvar St., Malate, Manila T: 384-3892, 384-0080 (delivers within area) OPEN: Daily, 10:30 a.m.–2 p.m., 5:30 p.m.–11 p.m.

Mien San

U B A

SPECIALTY: Authentic Taiwanese

Though deeply rooted in Chinese cooking, Taiwanese food has its own deviations and unique qualities. Mien San's Taiwanese migrant owner would be glad to explain the nuances and recommend dishes, but she's usually busy in the kitchen. House special appetizer Tofu With Century Egg, for example, is a block of silken tofu and century egg wedges on a bed of sweet soy paste and sesame oil, chopped chives, mustard leaves, garlic, nuts, spring onion, and brown sugar—all mundane-sounding ingredients. But once in your mouth, they're a motley crew of flavors and textures—silken, crunchy, savory, organically sweet, nutty, cool, and garlicky—all in one perfect bite. Noodles are a cornerstone of Taiwanese cooking, a classic sample of which would be the heady, rust-colored Hot and Sour Soup, seasoned with cane vinegar, lemon grass, anise stars, and chili and generously filled with chopped veggies, strips of beef, tripe, gizzard, and home-made pulled noodles. A new batch of dimsum is made every day, and if you're accustomed to what mediocre dimsum is like, you can tell why Mien San's dimsum is fresh. The filling loosely spills into your mouth, the vegetables are crisp and still have their color, and the wrapper is a translucent ivory shell that's tender but not chewy. There is a high volume of old Chinese couples and Chinese locals that keeps the place bustling even on a late weeknight. Ambience-wise, interiors are white-washed and nondescript. When doing lunch at Mien San, call first and ask about available parking. The store front can park five cars during the day; more slots open up at night as adjacent shops close. Mien San dishes are MSG-free.

PRICES: Dimsum, P60 and up for an order of 6 to 8 pcs.; tofu with Century Egg, P110; savory rice for 2–3, P120 and up; meat/seafood/chicken main dishes, good for sharing, P150 and up.

PAYMENT: Cash. ADDRESS: 36 Villa Ortigas, Granada St., New Manila, Quezon City T: 721-5794 OPEN: Daily, 11 a.m.–11 p.m.

Min Sok

U B A

SPECIALTY: Authentic homestyle Korean

There isn't exactly a dearth of Korean restaurants in the city, but only a few will meet Korean expats' approval for authenticity. One of them is Min Sok, found in what has been coined Koreatown (the area of little streets behind Rockwell). The place is unadorned and nondescript; Seeing the individual table grills, however, fuels anticipation for the elaborate meal ahead. Here, you can find out how familiar items like kimchi, bibimbap, japchae, beef stew, and Korean BBQ taste when they're prepared the traditional way. Grilled dishes can come ready to eat, or you can grill them yourself. Most impressive about the place is its platter of sidings and sauces—they could comprise an elaborate tasting menu just by themselves! Min Sok's sidings platter features the usual lettuce (which you fill with rice, meat, sidings, and roll before taking a bite), garlic (perfect to grill with your meat), bean sprouts, kimchi, fish cakes, cucumber, flavorants for your grilled meat, and other spoon-sized portions of delicacies in their own exotic marinades and pickled sauces. Best of all, the platter comes bottomless as long as you order a grilled meat dish.

PRICES: A platter of grilled meat, P250 (for pork) to P350 (for beef spare ribs); Korean noodles like Japchae, P200–250; a la carte set of sidings, P300 (medium) or P500 (large); exotic Korean delicacies like Spicy Chicken Stew or the Kimchi Braised Mackerel, P300–800; a bottle (around 250 ml) of Korean rice wine and other liquors, P280–380. All entrées good for at least 2 people.

PAYMENT: Cash. ADDRESS: 5655 Don Pedro St., Poblacion, Makati T: 897-6799 M: 0917-525-6150 OPEN: Daily, 11 a.m.–11 p.m.

Nanbentei of Tokyo

U B A

SPECIALTY: Japanese traditional yakitori

Yakitori is a way of roasting bite-sized pieces of meat or vegetables that has its roots with the Dutch who settled in Nagasaki during the Edo Period. Nanbentei, a 10 year-old yakitori bistro, continues this legacy with a wide selection of skewered pork, beef, chicken, seafood, and vegetable yakitori. Lunch specials consist of a 7-piece Yakitori set meal with soup, rice, and dessert. A platter truly worth sharing is the Bestseller, a 21-stick medley of aspara maki, tebasaki, pork garlic yaki, shiso maki, negima, corn and poteto maki. Add to that a side order of Onigiri, grilled triangular rice balls stuffed with pickled plum, salmon, or bonito flakes wrapped in nori, and you can have a very satisfying traditional yakitori meal.

PRICES: Yakitori, P65–315 for 2 sticks per order; Yakitori set meal, P445; 21-stick Bestseller, P785; Onigiri, P135.

PAYMENT: Cash, credit card. ADDRESS: 3/L Greenbelt 3, Ayala Center T: 896-9847 OPEN: Sun/Mon–Thu, 11:30 a.m.–2:30 p.m., 6 p.m.–11:30 p.m.; Fri/Sat, 11:30 a.m.–2:30 p.m., 6 p.m.–12:30 p.m.

Nanohana

U B A

SPECIALTY: Japanese (must-try: Haru Maki and their 17 kinds of tempura)

Nanohana is home to a slew of tempura dishes such as Chikuwa Tempura (rice cake), Uni Tempura (sea urchin), and Gobou Kakiage (a white fleshy root that tastes best when cooked with oil). Foreign and local executives flock to the place for the teishoku (set meal) lunch specials which consist of rice, miso soup, salad, the day's appetizer, fresh fruit, and a drink, with a choice of main dishes like Nigiri Sushi, Chirashi Sashimi, or Sukiyaki. Nanohana also serves its own version of spicy tuna roll as Haru Maki, tuna wrapped in rice paper stuffed with lettuce, cucumber, and spicy sauce. Meat aficionados can choose Wagyu Chahan and Wagyu Sirloin Steak. The restaurant imports almost all their seafood, including exotic varieties like Fugu (blowfish), served as a set of sashimi and nabemono (steamboat). Seasonal delicacies are available during the winter months when Ankimono, boiled seasonal angler fish mixed in sweet ponzu sauce, is available. Easily overlooked in the bustling street of Valero and situated behind lush bamboo trees, Nanohana offers indulgent lunches amidst a serene ambience.

PRICES: Chikuwa Tempura (5 pieces per serving), P200; Uni Tempura (3 pieces/serving), P280; and Gobou Kakiage (5 pieces per order), P200; Haru Maki (spicy tuna roll), P315; Wagyu Chahan P350; Wagyu Sirloin Steak, P2,800 for 180 grams; Ankimono, P380. Lunch teishoku or set meals, P425.

PAYMENT: Cash, credit card. ADDRESS: 3/L Milky Way Building, 900 Pasay Rd., Makati T: 843-4285, 812-2913 OPEN: Daily, 11:30 a.m.–2:30 p.m., 5:30 p.m.–10 p.m.

New Bombay

U B A

SPECIALTY: Authentic homestyle Indian

What started out as a quaint eatery, owned by an Indian family and run by its matriarch, has enjoyed enough success over the years to expand with branches in more commercially viable addresses. Many regulars who have tried the newer, "jazzed-up" branches, however, find themselves coming back to the original canteen-like branch (now redecorated, too) for their fix of authentic, affordable Indian food (though prices have risen considerably since its salad days). Maybe it's the Sto. Niño next to the Vishnu statuette in the dining area that lends a kitsch appeal diners find endearing. Or maybe it's that personal care with which the middle-aged, motherly proprietress prepares the dishes that customers find amiss in the other spruced-up branches. Just as she did in the first ever branch, the owner still shuffles back and forth between the kitchen to mind the stove and the dining area to ask customers how they liked their food, like a warm hostess doting on house guests. In any case, New Bombay Canteen continues to please despite the bells and whistles. The place is packed during lunch time and people do have to wait a bit for their orders because no shortcuts are taken in New Bombay Canteen's kitchen. The naan, though buttery, isn't greasy and is made fresh by batches several times a day. In fact, that is one prevailing trait at New Bombay Canteen: none of its dishes have that oily sheen you find in sub-par Indian eateries. The samosas, being a standard appetizer, is prepared with as much attention as the pricier main dishes. The meat dishes are tender, and the vegetables are firm. Familiar-sounding items like curry, masala, tandoor, and tikka are rightly seasoned for the Indian palate, not compromised impostors to curry favor with the uninitiated. But the place cares just as much for the diner, so special requests like holding back on a certain spice for specific dietary needs are accommodated. Making the best of an Indian meal means knowing which dishes go well together. Don't hesitate ask the owner for her recommendations.

PRICES: Samosas, P70; Saffron Rice (basmati yellow rice mixed in dried fruits), P150; Chicken Tikka Masala, P170; Mutton Roghan Josh (cooked with ground almonds, tomato puree, Indian cream), P170; Chicken Tandoor, P160.

PAYMENT: Cash. ADDRESS: G/L Sagittarius Bldg., H.V. Dela Costa St., Salcedo Village, Makati T: 819-2892, 893-7506 OPEN: Daily, 9 a.m. – 11 p.m.

Oboda *Adobo*

U B A

SPECIALTY: Sixteen different kinds of *adobo* such as *Adobong Macho* (beef brisket *adobo*), *Bikolanong Adobo* (*adobo* with *gata*), and *Nagbabagang Adobo with Banana Q* served with sunny side up, *atchara*, *bulalo* soup, sweet potato fries, and your choice of coconut rice, red rice, or garlic rice. The vibe of the place is very laidback-surfer, and everything—even the *atchara*—is 100% local and 100% made from scratch.

PRICES: *Adobo* meals average at around P160.

PAYMENT: Cash. ADDRESS: 227 Katipunan Ave. Ext., Quezon City OPEN: Daily, 2 p.m. – 2 a.m.

Pino

U B A

SPECIALTY: Reinvented Filipino delicacies.

Chef-owned Pino specializes in dishes that, though considered fusion, eschew the curse of the term by fusing established flavors, most of which are still distinctly Some amped-up old-time favorites include the *Kare-Kare*ng *Bagnet*, Red Wine *Adobong Tadyang* (ribs), and the Crispy Tenderloin *Tapsilog*. The flavors are such that, you know you're eating something new and trendy, yet there's that prevalent element—be it the nutty sauce of the *kare-kare* or the garlicky tang of the fried rice in the tapsilog—that harks to Sunday brunches at your lola's house. A more overseas item they have is a dessert called Chunky Choco Tempura, made of two big Kit Kat chocolate logs deep-fried in tempura batter and served à la mode. On paper, it sounds a bit much even to a textbook sweet tooth. On your plate, yes, it is sickeningly sweet and shiny with oil...and shamelessly, inexplicably good.

PRICES: *Kare-Kareng Bagnet*, P245; Red Wine *Adobong Tadyang*, P180; Crispy Tenderloin *Tapsilog*, P200; Chunky Choco Tempura, P125.

PAYMENT: Cash. ADDRESS: 39 Malingap St., Teacher's Village, Quezon City T: 441-1773 OPEN: Daily, 10 a.m. – 2 p.m.

Queens Crystal Garden

U B A

SPECIALTY: Indian, vegetarian, vegetarian options.

Queens Crystal Garden features predominantly Indian and some Indonesian, Malaysian, Singaporean, and Asian Fusion dishes in its menu. With an Indian owner and an Indonesian chef at the helm, whatever is dubbed "spicy" doesn't hold back. Tandoori dishes are cooked in traditional earthen cylindrical ovens (i.e., tandoor ovens) and have that unique savory tang. Halal diners needn't worry about making special requests, as Queens doesn't serve pork or beef (the kitchen is partly staffed with Moslem chefs). Vegetarians and vegans, on the other hand, have generous pickings since nearly 40% of the menu is vegetarian; for the most part of the remaining 60%, vegetarian versions can be ordered. Those new to Indian food will have to rely on purported house specials when the owner, who usually engages customers about the history and nuances of each dish, is away.

Indonesian must-tries include the Paneer Makhaniwala (cottage cheese cubes cooked in a rich stew of tomatoes, butter, cream, and chili), Mutton Vindaloo (lamb with a spice and vinegar marinade, cooked with a piquant masala paste), and the Prawn Biryani (Basmati rice and prawns seasoned with chili, cilantro, garlic, ginger, turmeric, and cumin). Indonesia's Nasi Goreng Crab (fried rice with flavorful accents from tamarind, garlic, ginger, and shrimp paste) and Chicken Satay and Singapore's Chili Crab are favorites in the menu's non-Indian half. All in all, Queens can't really compete with those quaint holes-in-the-wall that have endeared themselves to serious foodies, but then again nor does it want to. What it offers is the luxury of choice, accessibility, and a place to bring special guests or hold big dinners, all without making big compromises with the food—proving perhaps that there's enough epicurean love to go around.

PRICES: At least P700 per person for a 3-course meal.

PAYMENT: Cash, credit card. ADDRESS: 146-B Jupiter St., Makati T: 895-1316 OPEN: Daily, 11 a.m.–10 p.m.

Sabroso

U B A

SPECIALTY: Traditional Visayan-style *lechon*. Interiors are *carinderia*-like and the chalkboard menu doesn't offer much in terms of cooking styles, other viands, or sidings. It's very singular in purpose, but what an awesome purpose that is: to serve honest-to-goodness *lechon* using free-range native pigs for lean and truly flavorful meat (to put that gravy-like liver sauce—or "*sarsa*"—that comes with most restaurant-served *liempo* and *lechon kawali* would be, at least for most Visayans, profanity).

PRICES: *Lechon* meal, P120 (rice, soup, single serving of chopped *lechon*, and one glass of lemongrass iced tea). Orders for pick-up and delivery are accepted: P550 per kilo; P3,000 for a whole *lechon*.

PAYMENT: Cash. WEBSITE: lechonsabroso.multiply.com ADDRESS: E. Rodriguez cor. T. Morato Aves., Quezon City T: 515-8259, 515-8253, 357-0659 M: 0920-910-0841, 0922-841-6220 OPEN: Daily, 8:30 a.m.–6:3- p.m.

Sango

U B A

SPECIALTY: Japanese burgers

From their mayonnaise, seaweed shreds, plum sauce, chili powder to rice grains, Sango uses only Japanese imported ingredients to come up with 25 distinct flavors for their 25 burgers. Bestsellers are the Yakiniku Rice Burger, made of very tender and juicy beef strips with lettuce stuffed in rice patties; and Master Burger, a sandwich layered with tomato, mayonnaise, beef patty, and a tangy, sloppy meat sauce. And even if you don't need a trip to the comfort room, check it out anyway: it has Japan's modern electronic toilet with multi-purpose buttons. The staff is remarkably cheerful make time to create origami pieces to place on take-out bags and food trays. Interiors are clean, bright, and linear in design. But they're given a fun punch of Japanese pop culture with the variety shows shown on the eateries flat screen TVs.

PRICES: Specialty burgers, P62–195; Yakiniku Rice Burger and Master Burger, P109; donburi, P222.

PAYMENT: Cash, credit card. ADDRESS: G/L Creekside Mall, Amorsolo Corner Herrera Sts., Legaspi Village T: 830-0391, 889-4445
OPEN: Daily, 9 a.m.–11 p.m.

Sate Café

U B A

SPECIALTY: Home cooked dishes from Mindanao, Java, Sulawesi, Sumatra, Singapore, and Malaysia.

Sate carries a lot of dishes one expects to find in Malaysian and Singaporean themed eateries. You have your Beef Rendang, Kaya Toast with Boiled Eggs, and several Goreng variants. But they also have interesting dishes that, ironically, turn out to be regional specialties in the Philippines. *Satti,* small morsels of grilled, skewered meat served with sticky rice swimming in a sweet-spicy sauce, is a hawker-stall breakfast staple in Zamboanga; while the Rice Pretzel with Native Chocolate is a sweet treat from Samar.

PRICES: Grilled regional specials, P150 and up; a wide range of mains fall under P100 such as the Satti (P35), Beef Rendang (P80), and Fish Sate in Lemon Grass (50).

PAYMENT: Cash. WEBSITE: profiles.friendster.com/allsate ADDRESS: 101 Sterten Place, 116 Maginhawa St., Teacher's Village, Quezon City T: 436-8398, 396-2660 M: 0922-888-2013 OPEN: Sun–Thu, 8 a.m.–11 p.m.; Fri, 7 a.m.–6 p.m.

Serenitea Cha Kitchen

U B A

SPECIALTY: Tea boutique with extensive choices of hot and cold, freshly brewed tea beverages using only authentic ingredients from Taiwan (no synthetic flavored powders and pre mixes).

Serenitea is a warm and friendly tea salon with its own custom-built tea brewing machine. Their teas come in many choices and in many flavors—from hot fruit-infused teas and iced teas, milk teas, and tea with frosting to iced blends with tapioca pearls and smoothies. Each beverage comes in three levels of sweetness. If you can't quite pin down a drink of your choice from their menu, you can have them custom-spec your own drink. Light snacks like peppered sweet corn, tofu, and chicken chops are available.

PRICES: Hot teas, P50–70; iced blended teas start at P75; light snacks average at P50.

PAYMENT: Cash. WEBSITE: serenitea.multiply.com, Facebook ADDRESS: G&L Bldg, J. Abad Santos cor. V. Cruz Sts., Little Baguio, San Juan T: 379-4166 OPEN: Mon–Sat, 12 nn–10 p.m.; Sun, 12 nn–10 p.m. ADDRESS 2: 268 Aguirre Ave., BF Homes Parañaque T: 794-3288 OPEN: Mon–Thu, 11 a.m.–9 p.m.; Fri/Sat, 11 a.m.–10 p.m.; Sun, 1 p.m.–9 p.m. ADDRESS 3: 74B N. Roxas St., Banawe, Quezon City T: 238-2545 OPEN: Mon–Sat, 10 a.m.–8 p.m.; Sun, 10:30 a.m.–7:30 p.m.

Seryna

U B A

SPECIALTY: Japanese winter menu

One of the finer ways to appreciate Japanese cuisine is in the taste and preparation of its raw delicacies. With 80% of its ingredients shipped from Japan, Seryna boasts fresh imported seafood with sushi and sashimi platters like Santen Mori, a combination of squid, tuna, and salmon; Goten Mori, which is essentially Santen Mori plus octopus and yellowtail; and Nanaten Mori, which is Goten Mori plus Hawaiian yellowtail and halibut. The Sashimi Tokomori features an all-imported shellfish platter of cockle, arctic surf clam, red clam, spot prawns, and bluefin tuna belly. Even rarer delicacies are featured for the winter menu, available from October to February, with a curious order of Fish Testicles blanched in sweet ponzu sauce; large, juicy, melt-in-your-mouth Fresh Oysters in 7-inch shells; and the giant yet flavorful Hokkaido Crab. Seryna's dark wooden interiors, stone flooring, and subdued lighting set a very inviting mood for its many Japanese patrons who usually take their meals with a bottle of sake.

PRICES: Santen Mori, P335; Goten Mori, P505; Nanaten Mori, P730; Sashimi Tokomori, P2,100; Fish Testicles blanched in sweet ponzu sauce, P1,200–1,700; Fresh Oysters in 7-inch shells, P700 per shell.

PAYMENT: Cash, credit card. ADDRESS: 2277 Fernando St., Little Tokyo, Pasong Tamo Ext., Makati T: 894-3855 OPEN: Mon–Sat, 11:30 a.m.–2 p.m., 6 p.m.–11 p.m.; Sun, 11:30 a.m.–2 p.m., 5:30 p.m.–10:30 p.m.

Shinjuku

U B A

SPECIALTY: Japanese (SPECIALTY: 26 ramen flavors)

Shinjuku, one on the older ramen houses in Manila, offers a large selection of miso- and soy-based ramen. People of varying appetites can avail of servings in regular and large ramen bowls, the latter resembling the size of a small basin. The Karakuchi Negi Ramen is a medley of noodles and spicy miso broth, togarashi, ground pork and leeks. Something kinder on the palate is the Mabo Tofu Ramen, a thick mildly spiced soy broth mixed with ground meat, minced vegetables, and very soft tofu. Those who want heavier dishes have a moderate range of rice meals to choose from, the crowd favorite being the Chicken Curry Rice, breaded chicken simmered in a dark brown curry. With interiors that say "come as you are," Shinjuku is a relaxing and casual place for a hearty snack.

PRICES: Karakuchi Negi Ramen, P255/P345; Mabo Tofu Ramen P245/P340; Chicken Curry Rice, P300.

PAYMENT: Cash, credit card. ADDRESS: 2277 Chino Roces Ave., Makati T: 819-1242, 710-3589 OPEN: Daily, 10 a.m.–1 a.m.

Shokuji

U B A

SPECIALTY: Traditional Japanese dishes

Shokuji has witnessed the boom of Salcedo Village since the early 90's and has been a favorite of foreign and local businessmen. For lunch sets, there's the unusually tender Beef Yakiniku or Ebi Tempura rice toppings, and heartier bento meals featuring fish, meat, eggs, vegetables, pickled fruit, and rice. Shokuji is basically a place for restaurant-grade homestyle Japanese dishes.

PRICES: Yakiniku Donburi, P205; Tempura Teishoku, P 220; bento meals, P390.

PAYMENT: Cash, credit card. ADDRESS: G/L LPL Center, 130 San Agustin Rd., Salcedo Village, Makati T: 812-9235 OPEN: Mon–Fri, 11:30 a.m.–1:30 p.m., 5:30 p.m.–10:30 p.m.

Singapore Chicken Rice

U B A

SPECIALTY: Popular Singapore dishes like Hainanese Chicken Rice, Satay, Laksa, Curry, Nasi Lemak, Mee Goreng, and Kaya Toast. They may not be "kopi tiam at Bencoleen Road" authentic, but they deliver! For many office folk who subsist on fast-food for its convenience and affordability, Singapore Chicken Rice is a much welcome reprieve. Pair your meal with their

their Dinosaur Chocolate Shake, a cold choco smoothie generously heaped with Milo, truly a nostalgic comfort drink.

PRICES: Value meals can go south of P70; minimum of P300 for delivery. (Delivers around Cubao.)

PAYMENT: Cash. ADDRESS: 51 Shopwise Arcade, Gen. Roxas Ave., Araneta Center, Cubao, Quezon City T: 440-3888 OPEN: Daily, 7 a.m. – 12 mn.

Su Zhou

U B A

SPECIALTY: Homestyle Chinese-Taiwanese cooking.

Try authentic Xiao Long Pao, succulent soup dimsum that will have you dribbling at the mouth if you don't take the whole piece in one bite. Another bestseller is the Tofu with Century Egg and Pork Floss. The cooking is homey but truly flavorful and carefully prepared in Su Zhou. They use premium grade dinorado rice for their fried rice, for instance. And somehow, though frying is textbook for this kind of cuisine, Su Zhou manages to whip up savory fried rice, crunchy spare ribs, and other oil-cooked dishes that don't feel greasy or sickening on the palate despite their golden fried glory. Proof of just-made freshness. Not to be missed, too, is its diverse range of savory noodle soups that range from spicy, smoky, and piquant to savory yet delicately flavored. Ready-to-steam frozen packs of their specialty dimsum are available for take out.

PRICES: Typically P150 and up per person.

PAYMENT: Cash. ADDRESS: Mabini cor. Araullo Sts., San Juan T: 721-6105 (delivers) OPEN: Daily, 11 a.m. – 12 mn.

Tao Yuan

U B A

SPECIALTY: Purportedly the place to go for the best Singaporean food in town. Authentic and truly exquisite Singaporean and Malaysian delicacies under the culinary expertise of a Malaysian-born, Singaporean-bred chef import. Most popular of the dishes among Pinoys is the Hainanese Chicken Rice. Taking hours to prepare and cook, Hainanese Chicken Rice here has a limit of two orders per day. So call and pre-order if you plan on having this well-loved chicken dish. For the indulgent and adventurous, try the Peking Duck Served Three Ways (roasted, fried with garlic and chili, and ground).

Street parking runs out fast. You can park at Robinsons Place, about a 10-minute walk to the Tao Yuan, or at Pan Pacific Hotel (just have your parking slip validated at an Adriatico Square establishment).

PRICES: Portions here are for group sharing, so items are prices as such. Peking Duck Served Three Ways, P850 (whole); Hainanese Rice,

PAYMENT: Cash, credit card. ADDRESS: 508-512 Gen. Malvar cor. A. Mabini St., Malate, Manila T: 522-7009 to 10 M: 0917-819-1372, 0908-569-6739. OPEN: Daily, 11 a.m. – 3 p.m., 6 p.m. – 12 mn. Reservations are highly recommended, especially on weekends.

Thai Dara Bangkok Street Food

U B A

SPECIALTY: Thai comfort food.

Despite the name, Thai Dara Bangkok Street Food doesn't pretend to be Manila's answer to hawker stalls in Bangkok, but their flavors are well within the vicinity of Thai cuisine and do more than well in a pinch to quickly sate a craving for Thai favorites like pad thai, Thai-style pomelo salad, chicken pandan, curry (green, yellow, and red), or tom yum. The Tom Yum Gai is spicy and made with fresh lemongrass and kaffir leaves, and the curries are home made. They even use authentic Thai serving ware, show Thai TV shows and concerts on their mounted flatscreen, and have framed art work depicting Thai dancers lining their walls.

PRICES: Hearty soups, P200 and up; main dishes, P150 average; specialty beverages like milk tea, P45. Portions are good for 2.

PAYMENT: Cash. ADDRESS: Gilmore Ave. (Granada St.) cor. Valencia St., Quezon City T: 568-0651 M: 0918-365-4250 OPEN: Mon–Sat, 11 a.m.–10 p.m.

Thai Patio

U B A

SPECIALTY: Authentic Thai

Thai Patio is a gem amidst a wasteland of bad to mediocre Thai eateries abundant in the city. Barring hotel restaurants, Thai Patio, part of an international chain (with franchises in Taipei, London, and Hollywood) and staffed with Thai chefs, is one of the few that serve the real deal. Unlike the sweet, oily, and red-tinged versions in most purportedly Thai eateries, for instance, the Pad Thai here is light-bodied with a piquant yet fresh flavor from the right balance of tamarind, chives, Thai fish sauce (much less salty and pungent than our local patis), and chili—just like those sold from carts in Bangkok's food markets. Also here will you discover that real Tom Yum tastes nothing like *sinigang*. As with the Pad Thai, the Tom Yum is a testament to Thai Patio's faithfulness to authentic Thai ingredients and strict regard for freshness—it uses kaffir lime leaves as its souring agent, succulent straw mushrooms (whereas sub-par restaurants use canned button mushrooms), minced lemongrass leaves, chopped cilantro, and firm prawns that still have their seawater sweetness. Lesser known but exquisite delicacies include the Green Mango Salad with Softshell Crab (a luxe upgrade from the more common green mango salad with deep-fried catfish), the Grilled Tiger Prawns in Chili, Lemongrass, and Fresh Mint Sauce, and the ferociously spicy Red Curry Lamb with Peanut. Located in posh Greenbelt 5, this upscale eatery marries restrained Thai decor with ultra modern touches like sleek acrylic furniture befitting a Philippe Starck catalog. Needless to say, expect Greenbelt 5 prices. It's packed on weekends, so call for reservations.

PRICES: Soups like the tom yum, P300 and up; seafood or meat main courses, P500 and up; appetizers and noodles, P250 and up. Servings are good for 1. Expect to pay around P750 per head.

PAYMENT: Cash, credit card. ADDRESS: G/L Greenbelt 5, Ayala Center, Makati T: 729-0742, 729-0650 OPEN: Daily, 11 a.m. – 10 p.m.

Thuk Thai

U B A

SPECIALTY: Popular Thai dishes on the cheap. And they deliver!

PRICES: P180 and up per person for a meal; minimum order of P250 for delivery.

PAYMENT: Cash. WEBSITE: abbondanzarestaurant.multiply.com ADDRESS: G/L North Tower, Rockwell Business Center, Ortigas Ave., Pasig T: 470-8485 M: 0917-800-8485 OPEN: Mon – Sat, 11 a.m. – 10 p.m.

Tsumura

U B A

SPECIALTY: Upscale authentic Japanese cuisine. Must-tries: premium-grade imported sashimi and bento box lunch specials

Owned by master sushi chef Masamichi Tsumura, Tsumura Sushi Bar and Restaurant caters the main cornerstone of Japanese cooking: ingredients have to be fresh enough and of premium enough quality to shine with minimal seasoning. Only here can one find fresh-off-the-boat Otoro, sashimi made from the dense, delicately flavored, and buttery belly loin of bluefin tuna, one of the most expensive ingredients in Japanese cuisine.

The bento box lunch sets are nothing to scoff at. Impressive and intimidating in size, the sheer variety of food offered in one box is inspiring. Beautiful to look at, the Japanese aesthetic is one to meditate on: perfectly rolled cylinders of short grain rice, just-cooked nuggets of succulent beef, seafood cooked in an ethereally light batter, truly deserving of the name "tempura," tamago (egg) rolls, a slab of unagi (freshwater eel) glistening with teriyaki sauce.

Beef Usuyaki, one of the most popular dishes at the restaurant, is made of thin slices of beef rolled around a most succulent combination of garlic, enoki mushrooms, and the fat that has been trimmed from the aforementioned beef slices. Every bite brings forth a gush of fat immersed in beef juices, the salty-sweet water from the mushrooms, the mellow flavor and smoothness of the garlic slivers. This is as juicy as any good meat can hope to be.

PRICES: Otoro sashimi, P400 per piece; bento box lunch specials, P700–1,000; Beef Usuyaki, P500.

PAYMENT: Cash, credit card. ADDRESS: 2/L 88 Corporate Plaza, Sedeño cor. Valero Sts., Salcedo Village, Makati T: 887-4848, 887-4850 OPEN: Daily, 11 a.m.–2:30 p.m., 5:30 p.m.–10:30 p.m.

Ukokkei Ramen Ron

U B A

SPECIALTY: Authentic Japanese specialty ramen, fresh tamago, mainstream Japanese dishes with a twist.

At this quaint eatery, ramen isn't something to warm the tummy as you wait for your "real" orders. Here, ramen is the main dish. The crown jewel. So much so that, barring a limited number of other house specials, the menu eschews standard Japanese items like sashimi and sushi. Cooked by a Japanese ramen chef with made-from-scratch stock and special wheat noodles imported from Japan, each deliberately composed bowl is served scalding hot and glistens with a thin film of flavored oil on the surface. Ukokkei's ramen comes in three soup bases: shia (salt), shoyu (soy sauce), and miso. Of the three, the miso-based ramen is the crowd favorite. It's savory, tangy, nutty, predominantly lively in flavor with a subtly sweet hint towards the end. The shoyu is a close second, appreciated by those who like it earthy, with its own blend of savory-sweet and agreeably moldy yet subtle finish to keep the palate eager for the next spoonful. The noodles are firm to the bite and the toppings are relatively the same for all three variants (thinly sliced pieces of seared pork, vegetables that still have their crisp, leeks, shiitake mushrooms, bean sprouts), save for a few tweaks (some add butter

Legend: U=Unique, B=Bargain, A=Authenticity

ed corn). All-vegetable ramen options are available, as are ramen lunch sets (a typical set would have ramen, some rice variant like curry rice, a side-dish viand like gyoza, and salad). Take-out orders or having leftovers to-go is absolutely not allowed. As long as you're getting ramen from Ukokkei, you either get it at its best and freshest or you don't get it at all.

PRICES: Ramen, P300–390 per solo order, P520–700 for group portions; lunch sets, P380.

PAYMENT: Cash, credit card. ADDRESS: G/L Tesoro Building, 822 A. Arnaiz Ave. (Pasay Rd.), Makati T: 856-4588 OPEN: Daily, 11 a.m.–11 p.m.

You Jie Xiao Chao Chinese Food

U B A

SPECIALTY: Authentic Chinese Hunan homestyle cooking (similar to spicy Szechuan cuisine).

A true word-of-mouth place, this modest sized eatery doesn't even have a sign on its front door. Owned and managed by a Chinese couple, the place serves authentic Hunan homestyle specialties, characteristically earthy and spicy.

It does away with English translations altogether in its menu. Instead, it has a photo of the dish, and ordering for non-Chinese speakers becomes an affair of point-and-gesture—adding a bit more to the authenticity of the place. Your bill also comes in Chinese characters (barring the price), so just ask for assistance from one of the waiters.

Try house specials that you won't find elsewhere, such as the hot pots (variants come in chicken, seafood, eel, duck, and pork innards), the spicy stir-fried meat dishes (beware: "spicy" is serious business here, don't expect a gratuitous sprinkling of dried chili flakes), the Chinese Pancake (make with egg batter and diced veggies and seafood), the Gong-bao Chicken (tender chopped chicken with nuts), and the Spicy Tofu.

PRICES: Eat all you can rice, P20; main dishes (good for 3), P200 and up.

PAYMENT: Cash. ADDRESS: 6404 Camia St., Guadalupe Viejo, Makati. From EDSA Southbound, turn right on Estrella St. and right on Amapola St. The first street after that is Camia St., turn left there and keep a hawkeye for the house number (white facade with white grill gate). M: 0915-425-2972, 0927-787-6999 OPEN: Daily, 11 a.m. – 10 p.m. (no reservations).

Zensho

U B A

SPECIALTY: Eat all you can lunch buffet prepared a la carte style. You order from the buffet menu, and the dishes are prepped and cooked only upon ordering. You can order in halves, as well! The buffet menu is nothing to be scoffed at, as it includes a good part of the resto's more "premium" items like the oyster teppanyaki, salmon sushi, etc. The surprisingly tender beef yakiniku and seafood fried rice are notable standouts in terms of flavor, exceeding what you'd expect from an eat-all-you-can. Watch as your Japanese steaks are grilled and flipped over before your eyes on the open teppan island counter.

PRICES: Lunch buffet, P385 per person.

PAYMENT: Cash, credit card. ADDRESS: 168 Tomas Morato cor. Roces Aves., Quezon City T: 929-1069 OPEN: Daily, 11 a.m. – 2:30 p.m., 6 p.m. – 11 p.m.

Abbondanza

U B A

SPECIALTY: Casual canteen-style Italian.

Italian, even when it's fine-dining, is quite friendly. In Abbondanza, it's downright buddy-next-door. The abundance of choices is no small matter, however. Their pizzas and pastas alone can boast a diversity in ingredients found only in upscale Italian eateries (eggs, artichoke, mussels, blue cheese, porcini mushrooms) and little practical innovations paralleled by none: you can order a netted dough to keep pizza crisp outside but doughy inside.

PRICES: "Group special" 27" pizzas, P900 and up. Standard pizzas (12-inch), P300 and up. Pastas, P150 and up (portions usually good for 2).

PAYMENT: Cash. WEBSITE: abbondanzarestaurant.multiply.com ADDRESS: G/L The Crescent Condominium, Amethyst Drive, Ortigas T: 633-6336 (delivers within their area), 986-3012 OPEN: Daily, 11 a.m.–10 p.m.

Alexa's Deli

U B A

SPECIALTY: Dine-in deli with a relatively wide range of French, Italian, and Australian wines, several types of cheese, and European coffee.

Interiors that look like an Ikea showroom and the glass display of cold cuts, cheeses, and wine are reminiscent of modern European and New York deli cafés—casual but sleek. Skip the meals like pastas and rice combos and stick to the cold cuts, cheese platters, and deli sandwiches for consistently good chow time at Alexa's. Also get a load of the free Wi-Fi!

The place also retails imported specialty food items and drinks from France, Italy, Germany, United States, United Kingdom, Australia, Spain, Chile, and Argentina.

PRICES: Deli sandwiches start at P150, European coffees start, cheeses start at P150 (100 g), European coffee starts at P75 per cup.

PAYMENT: Cash, credit card. WEBSITE: alexasdeli.com ADDRESS: G/L, Classical Condominium, 112 H.V. Dela Costa St., Salcedo Village, Makati T: 813-7097, 813-4218 OPEN: Daily, 7 a.m. – 10 p.m.

Amalia's

U B A

SPECIALTY: Wide variety of classic Spanish comfort food and notably flavor-packed paella with Amalia Jocson, former executive chef of legendary restaurant Mingoy's, at the helm.

The place is no Iberian deli and looks more like a quaint, cottage-like neighborhood joint (because it is!), but the high number of lunching señoras who arrive in chauffeur-driven German cars is a good enough street cred meter. Be sure to try the smoky *Chorizo* Bilbao, the garlicky Paella Marinara (with the requisite "*tutong*" at the bottom), and any of the specialty chicken dishes.

PRICES: Paella, P440 (good for 3); appetizers, P110–245; specialty chicken dishes, P245 and up.

PAYMENT: Cash. ADDRESS: 67 Aguirre Ave., BF Homes, Phase 1, Parañaque T: 850-3123, 842-2182 OPEN: Daily, 11 a.m. – 2 p.m., 5:30 p.m. – 10 p.m.

Apartment 1B

U B A

SPECIALTY: All-day gourmet breakfast and brunch.

Literally an apartment unit in one of Makati's high-rise condos, Apartment 1B is a welcome relief from the concrete jungle with its homey interiors and "gourmetized" comfort food. Open as early as 7 a.m., they offer breakfast dishes as simple as a bowl of old fashioned oatmeal (110 pesos) to something as loaded and hearty as the Three-Egg Omelet with Smoked Bacon, Canadian Ham, Maple Sausage, and Smoked Salmon (420 pesos). Apartment 1B's Eggs Benedict, a breakfast icon, is one of the best that can be had in the city—the eggs are poached to perfection, the spinach is fresh, the muffins slightly crusty on the outside and tender inside, the Hollandaise sauce buttery and just subtly piquant, and the Canadian ham savory, a little toasted, and smokey. Another variant has smoked salmon instead of Canadian ham. This is also probably the only place in Manila that serves traditional homestyle meatloaf. Almost an inch thick, it's made fresh every day and served with buttered veggies, garlic mashed potatoes, and a generous amount of rich, homemade gravy. Non-breakfast entrées like the Grilled Pork Chops with Homemade Apple Sauce and Potato-corn Gratin, or a manly meat and 'tatoes combo that uses U.S. Certified Angus Rib eye, continue to exemplify the gourmet comfort food theme. Although the place can seat over 60 people, expect to wait for a table during lunch time if you don't have a reservation. Turnovers tend to be quick, though, since most people are rushing back to work.

PRICES: 3-Egg Omelet with Smoked Bacon, Canadian Ham, Maple Sausage, and Smoked Salmon, P420; Eggs Benedict with Canadian Ham and Spinach, P320; Eggs Benedict with Smoked Salmon and Spinach, P470; Grilled Pork Chops with Homemade Apple Sauce and Potato-corn Gratin, P490; Meatloaf, P420; Angus Rib Eye with Fries, P1,340.

PAYMENT: Cash, credit card. WEBSITE: www.apartment1b.com EMAIL: apartment_1b@yahoo.com ADDRESS: G/L Unit 1-B 132 L.P. Leviste cor. Sedeño St., Salcedo Village, Makati T: 703-5494 OPEN: Mon–Thu, 7 a.m.–11 p.m.; Fri/Sat, 7 a.m.–12 mn.

Aubergine Restaurant Patisserie

U B A

SPECIALTY: Modern French Continental dining.

The much vaunted Aubergine Restaurant and Patisserie is one fine-dining joint where discriminate gourmands, both local and expat, put no reservations on how the food is well worth the hefty prices. (It made it to the Miele Guide Top 20 Restaurants in Asia.) Staff service and food quality have been said to hold a candle to fine-dining restaurants abroad. A practicum lab of sorts for affiliate culinary school ISCAHM, where culinary interns get to work with veteran executive chefs and an experienced kitchen crew, Aubergine serves French continental fare that includes both traditional delicacies like melted french brie, pan-seared duck foie gras, and French duck confit, as well as contemporary items like Australian beef carpaccio, Caesar salad with cointreau, and roasted Wagyu beef with foie gras. Plating and presentation are top-notch, without compromising portions—plus, you can eat everything on the plate, no such thing here as bland but pretty garnish.

Parking is available below 32nd and Fifth Building, behind HSBC; there's an open parking lot across Bridgestone Tires Building.

PRICES: A set menus, P1,350 (3-course) to P1,950 (7-course); à la carte main dishes start at P590.

PAYMENT: Cash, credit card. WEBSITE: aubergine.ph EMAIL: dine@aubergine.ph ADDRESS: 2/L32nd and 5th Bldg., 5th Ave. cor. 32nd St., Fort Bonifacio, Taguig T:856-9888 OPEN: Daily, 11 a.m.–2:30 p.m., 6 p.m.–10 p.m.

Aussie Café & Resto

U B A

SPECIALTY: Aussie–style ribs and grilled meats.

For Filipinos, Australia is usually about the vast outback or surfing its indigo waters. Food isn't the first thing that comes to mind. Aussie Café & Resto, however, is striving to change all that with its wide selection of surf and turf cuisine that includes different kinds of steaks such as sirloin and tenderloin, as well as light seafood dishes such as fish and chips and fried calamari. The palate magnet that will surely entice local appetite is Chef Bernie's Mouthwatering Ribs—two hefty slabs of meat that have been slathered in sweet marinade and then served with a tangy barbecue sauce. The tender meat literally falls off the bone and melts in the mouth. Not shunning its pescetarian customers, the restaurant also serves flavorful seafood. Most of the ingredients, such as lamb, steaks, and even coffee are imported from

Australia. The restaurant also offers Australian Victoria Bitter Beer, a robust beer that goes well with grilled meat.

PRICES: Tenderloin Steak, P995 (225 g), P1,300 (300 g); Chef Bernie's Mouthwatering Ribs, P395 (single); Australian Lambchops, P695 (225 g); Manly Surf and Turf, P745 (225 g); Australian Victoria Bitter Beer, P130.

PAYMENT: Cash, credit card. WEBSITE: aussiecafe.multiply.com EMAIL: celine.choa@gmail.com ADDRESS: BCG Group Center, Block 27 Lot 2B, Filinvest, Alabang (beside South Supermarket), Muntinlupa T: 659-2658 M: 0917-630-8800 OPEN: Daily, 7 a.m.–10 p.m.

Banapple Pies and Cheesecakes

U B A

SPECIALTY: Bakery café with bed-and-breakfast style comfort food, cakes, and pies.

Banapple is the kind of place borne from home-bred culinary talent and a passion for food and cooking. The unpretentious and warm, cottage-like interiors are matched by an equally homey menu of pastas, hearty sandwiches, savory and dessert pies, and cakes—the kind of scrumptious home-made fare that's perfect for a lazy Sunday brunch.

The earliest crowd favorites are the all-day breakfast items—fried seasoned rice, a main dish like country ham or *chorizo* (or salpicao or bacon), with creamy parsley eggs. After that are the pastas, with good old Carbonara and an appetizingly gooey Cheesy Baked Penne topping the list. If you're looking for all manner of cheesecake (from the traditional blueberry to the more experimental Snickers), Banapple has more than enough. The most stellar in their ensemble cast of pies and cakes, however, is still THE pie that was there from the very beginning: their banoffee pie, a multilayer of buttery graham crust, caramel cream filling, tender chunks of just-right ripe bananas, whipped cream, and semi-sweet dark chocolate shavings.

Portions are ample, cake slices are hefty, and the place is packed for lunch and dinner. Chef school students can be seen at breakfast time in the first Katipunan branch.

PRICES: A meal (main, dessert, and drink) typically starts at P250.

PAYMENT: Cash, credit card. ADDRESS: 225 Katipunan Ave., Blue Ridge, Quezon City T: 439-2675 ADDRESS 2: 206 Katipunan Ave., Blue Ridge, Quezon City T: 438-2675 ADDRESS 3: 2/L, IL Terrazzo Mall, IL Terrazzo Mall, 35 Tomas Morato Ave. cor. Scout Madriñan St., Quezon City T: 413-2675 OPEN (ALL BRANCHES): Daily, 7 a.m. – 11 p.m.

Bizu

U B A

SPECIALTY: French-style pastries, macaroons, and an authentic Victorian-era, English afternoon tea set from 3 p.m. to 5:30 p.m. every day.

Bizu's afternoon tea service is comprised of exquisitely prepared savory and sweet bites like scones, petit sandwiches, hors d' oeuvres, petite gateaux (small cakes reminiscent of those rectangular miniature cakes in hotel buffets), lemon tarts, macaron de paris, and chocolate truffles served on a three-tiered tray alongside your choice of tea.

PRICES: Afternoon tea, P575 (good for 2 to 3).

PAYMENT: Cash, credit card. WEBSITE: bizupatisserie.com ADDRESS: G/L Greenbelt 2, Ayala Center, Makati ADDRESS 2: Promenade, Greenhills Shopping Center, San Juan T: 724-2498, 726-2496 ADDRESS 3: 3/L Glorietta 4, Ayala Center, Makati T: 757-2086 ADDRESS 4: G/L Corte Delas Palmas, Alabang Town Center, Muntinlupa T: 809-2498, 772-1917/18 OPEN: Daily, 7 a.m. – 1 a.m.

Bona Coffee

U B A

SPECIALTY: Low-sugar, low-fat, and low-cal flavorful dessert coffee concoctions and baked goods.

Bona's coffees may look like typical coffee boutique fare, but they use 100% Philippine grown beans (from arabica of highlands like Benguet, Kalinga, and Baguio to robusta from Batangas and Bukidnon) that are locally roasted, and are rich, well-bodied, never bitter, and have warm caramel undertones. Apart from local coffee love, Bona boasts yummy guilt-free coffee concoctions. Best thing is that their drinks and food don't seem to sacrifice flavor for cutting back on the bad stuff. In short, you can still taste the chocolate, the whipped cream, and the milk in their coffee smoothies; and you can still feel the buttery moisture in their muffins. The West Gate branch has free Wi-Fi and is open 24 hours.

PRICES: Hot specialty coffee brews, P75 and up; iced dessert coffees, P120 and up; hearty sandwiches, P150 and up; muffins, P60 and up.

PAYMENT: Cash, credit card. WEBSITE: bonacoffeecompany.com
ADDRESS: Unit E Banco Filipino Bldg., Elizalde St., BF Commercial Plaza, Parañaque T: 772-0427 OPEN: Daily, 7 a.m.–1 a.m. ADDRESS 2: G/L The Serenity Place, Westgate Center, Filinvest Corporate City, Alabang, Muntinlupa T: 771-2385 OPEN: Daily, 7 a.m.–1 a.m.

Brasserie Boheme

U B A

SPECIALTY: Predominantly French, Spanish, and Continental cuisine, with a smattering of "Europeanized" local dishes.

Brasserie Boheme is the laid-back, less old-world progeny of The Gustavian, a fine dining institution in Cebu made famous by its homemade European sausages, artisan breads, and gourmet creations of awarded chef and saucier Robert Lilja. Despite the name, however, it is more upscale than a brasserie and more chi-chi than it is Bohemian. Nonetheless, it can pack quite a crowd because of the daily set menus, which, at P390 for a salad or soup, a main dish, and dessert, is about the best deal there is among similarly upscale restaurants in Manila. The choices for the set menu are anything but paltry: Cream of Tomato Soup or Provencale Tomato Salad, Beef Bourguignon for main dish (there's also always a vegetarian option), and Mango Crepe suzette with Fresh Cream for dessert. The set menu changes every month.

PRICES: P390 for a set meal of soup or salad, main dish, and dessert. Light main dishes like pasta typically start at P240; heavier fare like steaks start at P600.

PAYMENT: Cash, credit card. WEBSITE: aussiecafe.multiply.com EMAIL: celine.choa@gmail.com ADDRESS: BCG Group Center, Block 27 Lot 2B Filinvest Corporate City, Alabang (beside South Supermarket), Muntinlupa T: 659-2658 M: 0917-630-8800 OPEN: Daily, 7 a.m. – 10 p.m

---

Bulan

U B A

SPECIALTY: Mixed European

Tucked in Little Baguio, a small, nondescript neighborhood in San Juan, lies Bulan (Ilocano for "moon"), a restaurant-cum-museum that allows guests to experience a totally different dining experience. A colorful, refurbished church door with intricate carvings welcome visitors into an old three-level mansion filled to its stone walls and high, cathedral ceiling with exquisite Asian art and furniture. Each piece of furniture is well though-out: green and blue chandeliers from India provide a romantic setting for quiet dinners; a cozy hardwood bar with ebony and bone inlays highlights the center of the restaurant's ground floor, and even the customized dragon bathroom doors from Tibet are art pieces in themselves. A strong contrast to the Asian-inspired interiors is Bulan's Continental cuisine, which features typical European fare such as lamb and schnitzel, but given a slightly different twist by owner and Master Chef Tony Aguilar. Favorites include Roma (grilled orange-flavored fillet mignon in marsala sauce), Crystal's Flamre (linguine with three different kinds of mushrooms blended with blue cheese and served with sour cream), and Achilles (grilled lamb marinated in herbs and oranges, served with Ratatouille). The less adventurous may opt to try Bulan's Ham and Cheese or Hamburger sandwiches. The former is given a healthy side of Jalapeño French fries, while the burgers come with coleslaw and regular fries. All art displayed in Bulan (and even most of the furniture) are for sale, so it's best to bring a checkbook or extra cash, if you want to bring part of Bulan home with you.

PRICES: Expect to spend at least P1,000 per head for dinner and drinks, with pasta ranging from P395 to P595, and main courses from P650 to P880.

PAYMENT: Cash, credit card. ADDRESS: 3 Gen. de Jesus St. (near cor. J. Abad Santos St.) Little Baguio, San Juan T: 725-8496 OPEN: Reservations only; lunch and dinner

Caffé Caruso

U B A

SPECIALTY: Authentic Italian homestyle cooking using top-tier and ingredients to ensure faithfulness of flavor.

The pastas are made from scratch, the pizzas are done to perfection from a traditional wood-fired oven, and dishes are heirloom and regional specialties that go way beyond the ubiquitous carbonara—all from an open kitchen that lends confidence and credibility. It is recommended for first-timers to order Caruso's sampler dishes where there are three of a kind in one appetizer or in one pasta dish.

PRICES: Set menus for lunch start at P890 for your choice of antipasti, pizza, and pasta.

PAYMENT: Cash, credit card. ADDRESS: 210 Nicanor Garcia St., Bel Air II, Makati T: 895-8790, 895-2451 OPEN: Daily, 11 a.m.–2 p.m., 6 p.m.–10 p.m.

Charlie's

U B A

SPECIALTY: Black angus burger and fish-and-chips.

A small eatery in Kapitolyo that shares space with a carwash, Charlie's started out as a hole-hidey but savagely grew in popularity by word of mouth alone that it had to extend the dining area with outside tables, the line at the order counter was long and slow-moving, and you had to be ready to wait 30 minutes to get something as pedestrian as a burger. But then, what a burger—salt-and-pepper-rubbed black angus beef ground upon ordering and molded into massive, compact, and juicy patties. It isn't overseasoned and it doesn't suffer from condiment overload—i.e., you can enjoy it without the whole thing disintegrating into a putrid soggy mess. It's served open-face on a black sesame seed bun that nicely toasted, doughy, and tastes a bit like sour dough bread. The attendant lettuce, onions, and tomato have a just-sliced freshness to them. The fries on the side, seasoned only with salt and pepper, are from real potatoes huge enough to be Idaho-grown. They use cream dory for the fish and chips, and you can see the fish meat through the batter, which is always a sign of good batter-fish proportion. Sidings and condiments include jalapeño pieces, kosher dill pickle strips, veggie sticks with blue cheese, and real malt vinegar for the fish and chips.

PRICES: Black angus burger with fires, P250; philly cheesesteak with fries, P280; foreign beers, average of P180 per bottle; desserts start at P160.

PAYMENT: Cash. ADDRESS: 16 East Capitol Drive, Bo. Kapitolyo, Pasig
T: 635-4857 OPEN: Daily, 11 a.m.–2 a.m.

Chateau Europe

U B A

SPECIALTY: German deli restaurant and watering hole

Chateau Europe Restaurant and Deli (maybe the official name, what it says on the receipt). Specializes in German sausages, bread, and beer (I had a taste of Oettinger—very nice fruity malty stuff). Though I'd recommend this place more as a deli from which to buy supplies than a restaurant. The lapu-lapu, in their Fish and Chips, for instance, though moist, crisp, and savory, is ruined by the pre-cooked frozen French fries that supposedly account for the "Chips." That's always been a pet peeve of mine, fake anything served along authentic items or served in a place that prides itself for its authenticity. Plus there's not much as far as ambience is concerned (it actually looks like a provincial seafood resto with fluorescent lighting, rattan chairs, concrete floors, and green checkered tables). The outdoor dining area (aka smoking area) feels a bit muggy and has a small but palpable mosquito population (negligible for normal folk, nightmare for mosquito magnets—like myself; something about people who smell a certain way being more mosquito-attractive). though during World Cup season and other major European sporting events, the place becomes a lively convergence of expats and local sports fans because they show these events via widescreen live telecast satellite TV.

PRICES: The German dishes don't go over P200 (servings good for 1); German beers don't go over P100.

PAYMENT: Cash. ADDRESS: 142 Elizalde St., BF Homes T: 801-6369
OPEN: Daily, 8 a.m.–1 a.m.

Chesa Bianca Swiss Restaurant

U B A

SPECIALTY: Swiss homestyle cooking and delicacies.

Chesa Bianca boasts truly authentic Swiss fare with ingredients prepared or flown in fresh on a regular basis. (It also helps that it's right next to a prominent deli, a food and wine importer, and a sausage and cold cuts manufacturer.) They have lunch specials whose menu changes weekly, and a relatively wide selection of wines by the glass. A lunch set menu can consist of a Cheese Toast "Malakoff" with Pickles as appetizer; a "Wallisser" Chicken Escalopes with Raclette and Tomatoes, Stuffed Zucchini, and Buttered Tagliatelle as main dish; and your choice of coffee, cappuccino, espresso, or tea.

They also have specialty sandwiches hearty enough to be either a light lunch or heavy merienda. Choose from their Salami Milano, Forest Ham, Grilled Ham with Gruyère Cheese sandwiches. Or go all out with their

Chesa Bianca Cheeseburger: Swiss beef burger, Gruyère cheese, bacon, and caramelized onions and tomatoes.

PRICES: Set lunch menu, P695. Specialty sandwiches, P185–230. Chesa Bianca Cheeseburger, P490. Wine by the glass, P165–220.

PAYMENT: Cash, credit card. WEBSITE: chesabianca.com.ph ADDRESS: 7431 Yakal St., San Antonio Village, Makati T: 815-1359, 893-1573 OPEN: Daily, 11 a.m.–11 p.m.

Cocina Juan

U B A

SPECIALTY: Central American style hearty comfort food in a cozy rustic art gallery environment.

Cocina Juan is the inspired brainchild of its owner's impassioned travels to Latin America. The menu offers far more choices than burritos and quesadillas (it has those, too), including both regional delicacies and "Latinized" contemporary dishes (think crisp chili fingers instead of fries as siding for their burgers). A must-try is the Sofrito Cream Dory Specials, huge tender slabs of cream dory double-wrapped in foil with sofrito (minced herbs and other aromatic ingredients slow-cooked in olive oil) then charcoal-grilled. For dessert, get the Crema Con Chocolate, three flavors of ice cream with grape fruit bits, chocolate, and fried tortilla. Their iced tea, which you can get by carafe, is made from pre-steeped tea bags, and come in flavors like rooibos and chamomile, with honey as sweetener.

PRICES: Burrito specials, pizzas, and quesadillas average at P150 and are good for 2 people. Sofrito Specials, P200 and up.

PAYMENT: Cash. WEBSITE: Facebook ADDRESS: 100 Maginhawa St., Teacher's Village, Quezon City T: 434-3911 OPEN: Mon–Sat, 11 a.m.–11 p.m.

Eflav Ice Creamery

U B A

SPECIALTY: Unique ice cream flavors like beer, Yakult, wasabi, Bailey's, and Tequila Rose. (The liquor flavors have real, though minimal, liquor content. Minors can't order them.)

PRICES: P40–70 per ice cream scoop, P10 per ice cream topping.

PAYMENT: Cash. EMAIL: elfav.pergola@yahoo.com ADDRESS: 2/L Pergola Mall, Aguirre Ave. corner Elsie Gaches St., Phase 1, BF Homes, Parañaque T: 659-3025 OPEN: Daily, 11:30 a.m.–9 p.m.

Elbert's Steak Room

U B A

SPECIALTY: Steaks prepared European and American style

Elbert's Steak Room can fit only a maximum of 42 people. It has a small bar, a cigar room, and a private room that can accommodate 10 people. There is neither a restaurant signage on the door nor anywhere in the building. Located on the third floor of a building, they only have a red sliding door to mark their existence. Upon entering, you are greeted with elegant warm, wooden interiors, hefty one-leg tables (no more bumping your leg), leather couches, and voluptuous seating. They only serve USDA Prime beef, the highest level in the grading system of the USDA, with the Rib Eye Prime and the Super Prime as the chef's personal steak favorites. These steaks are brought in from the U.S. chilled, not frozen. Only chilled steaks allow one to determine accurately how fresh they are and how long they've been aged. They have a Prime Rib Lunch, a set menu featuring a salad of Tagaytay greens with Asian ginger vinaigrette, soup of the day, USDA Choice Prime Rib slow-roasted bone-on and served with truffled mashed potatoes, dessert, and coffee or tea. Choice of cuts include the Queen's Cut (1/2 to 3/4 of an inch thick), English Cut (3 thin slices), and King's Cut (3/4 to 1 inch thick). Standard set lunches are available, consisting of your choice of soup or salad, then meat choices in the form of either a sandwich (Philadelphia cheese steak, house burger, roast beef) or a rice meal of salpicao or beef stroganoff. A crowd favorite seems to be the roast beef sandwich, which is sukiyaki-cut slow-roasted USDA choice ribeye served open-faced on a half ciabatta, smothered with a mushroom gravy, with pommes frites on the side.

PRICES: Set lunch, P550; Prime Rib Lunch, P1,200 (Queen's Cut), P1,400 (English Cut), P1,600 (King's Cut).

PAYMENT: Cash, credit card. WEBSITE: www.steakroom.com EMAIL: info@steakroom.com ADDRESS: 3/L Sagittarius Bldg. III, 111 H. V. Dela Costa St., Salcedo Village, Makati T: 339-3363 OPEN: Mon–Fri, 11:30 a.m.–2:30, 6:30 p.m.–9:30 p.m. (kitchen closes); Sat, 6:30 p.m.–9:30 p.m. (kitchen closes). Closed on Sundays except special holidays or on special request.

Enchanté

U B A

SPECIALTY: Authentic country-style French fine-dining.

Chef Jessie Sincioco of Le Souffle fame put up Enchanté late 2009. After only a few months of growing pains in the kitchen and food, this new addition to Ortigas eateries quickly won over many discriminate diners and has earned the stamp of approval and authenticity of French expats as well. Signature Le Souffle crowd favorites such as the Pan-fried Goose Liver, steaks, and lamb dishes are on the menu, as are classics with innovative touches. House specials include savory and dessert soufflés, Trio of Goose Liver, Roast chilled U.S. Black Angus Striploin, and sinful desserts like Dark Chocolate Macadamia Nut Slice, Grand Marnier Crepe, and Meringue Island with Crème Anglaise.

PRICES: A light lunch will set you back from P500 to P1,000.

ADDRESS: 3/L Oakwood Joy Nostalg Center, 17 ADB Ave., Ortigas Center, Pasig T: 425-2650 M: 0918-563-7541, 0928-524-8481 OPEN: Daily, 11 a.m.–10 p.m.

Good Burger

U B A

SPECIALTY: Flavorful vegetarian and lean chicken burgers.

The chicken burgers are made of ground lean chicken without extenders, and the veggie burgers use wheat and soy. Toppings are where you can go crazy. Have a Persian Burger by adding sautéed onions and peppers and garlic aioli sauce, a BLT by adding bacon bits, and an Herb Delite with fresh torn basil leaves and crumble cottage cheese. Or make your own concoction picking individual add-ons. Your burgers come in either wheat or white bread buns, and in sizes ranging from small to large.

PRICES: For menu burgers, P75 and up for small, P85 and up for medium, P100 and up for large. Individual toppings start at P18.

PAYMENT: Cash. WEBSITE: Has a Facebook page. ADDRESS: One Kennedy Place, Annapolis St. cor. Ortigas Ave., Greenhills, San Juan T: 723-4663 (delivers) ADDRESS 2: 106 E. Rodriguez Jr. Ave., C5, Pasig T: 671-4242 ADDRESS 3: 10 East Capitol Drive, Kapitolyo, Pasig T: 636-4663 ADDRESS 4: 162 Maginhawa St., Sikatuna Village, Quezon City T: 435-4663 ALL BRANCHES OPEN: Daily, 10 a.m.–8 p.m.

Goodles

U B A

SPECIALTY: Pasta to-go. Goodles serves pasta dishes like Garlic Shrimp and *Chorizo*, Chicken Vodka, Mediterranean Tuna, and other exciting flavors that go beyond the usual pesto with your choice of noodles (linguine, spaghetti, farfalle, etc.)—all read to-go in eco-friendly coated cardboard tubs.

PRICES: P120 and up.

PAYMENT: Cash. WEBSITE: Has a Facebook page. ADDRESS: 4/L Robinsons Galleria (near Movieworld), EDSA cor. Ortigas Ave., Quezon City OPEN: Daily, 10 a.m.–8 p.m.

I'm Angus Steak House

U B A

SPECIALTY: Continental. Various preparations of U.S. certified Angus steak (grilled, chilled, fresh, etc.) and other premium gourmet meat and seafood dishes like Steak Tartare and Duroc Pork Chop (a.k.a. The black angus of pork).

Owned by the same group behind gourmet delicatessen Säntis I'm Angus Steak House extends the same freshness and quality in its premium grade fresh meats and steaks (of which there is a dearth among local meat suppliers). Inside, it is spacious, minimalist but classy. There's even an open chef kitchen, which, when interpreted as"We're confident about our food, take a look! We have nothing to hide!," is always a telltale of good things to come. On your plate, I'm Angus is relaxed gourmet—the meat is flown fresh from A-grade sources around the world, and you're offered a bevy of gourmet sauces like a béarnaise and wine reductions (though you could also go au jus). Asking for gravy is almost criminal.

PRICES: Executive lunch (Angus Summer Salad with spring onion, cream cheese roulade, greens, and apple vinaigrette; Blackened Salmon Unilateral with potato risotto; and coffee or tea), P765.

PAYMENT: Cash, credit card. WEBSITE: werdenberg.com/im_angus ADDRESS: 7431 Yakal St., San Antonio Village, Makati T: 892-6206 OPEN: Mon–Sat, 11 a.m.–3 p.m., 5 p.m.–11 p.m.

Je Suis Gourmand

U B A

SPECIALTY: French

Je Suis Gourmand was one of the first fine-dining restaurants in Bonifacio Global City (more commonly referred to as "The Fort") and isn't even located in the district's commercially packed area—it shares a sparsely populated block with just one other fine-dining place, Bistro Filipino. It definitely lacks the posh and polish of the newer places and, apart from changing the white cartolina table covers and fresh-flower centerpieces, has eschewed any major changes to its original minimalist, deli-like interiors. But it enjoys a loyal following among true epicures and French expats looking to dine on no-frills, honest-to-goodness classic French fare that is consistent in quality, flavor, and freshness. House specials include the homemade duck foie gras with greens and toasts, roasted Chilean seabass, and braised lamb shank. If you have a favorite that's no longer on the menu, the chef can still prepare it for you. The most popular "secret" is the duck foie gras pan-seared in a honey-balsamic reduction. Portions are more substantial here than in many upscale restaurants in its category, making Je Suis Gourmand that rare eatery that is truly gourmet fine-dining yet explicitly value for money. The pan-seared foie gras, for instance, arrives in 3/4-inch slices and is 4 pieces per order—that's thicker and more pieces than you'll see in other restaurants offering similarly priced foie gras preparations. Je Suis Gourmand also has frequently varying 3-course lunch specials and a take-out listing with bottled sauces, tapenades, and other delicacies used in the dishes.

PRICES: Main courses average at P600; foie gras, P650 (with salad and toasts, good for 2–3), P880 (pan-seared in honey-balsamic reduction, good for 2–3); 3-course lunch special, P990; bottled take-out items, P250 and up.

PAYMENT: Cash, credit card. ADDRESS: G/L, Net One Center, Bonifacio Global City, Taguig T: 815-8801 OPEN: Mon–Sat, 10 a.m.–10 p.m.

Kitchen of Cakes and Coffee

U B A

SPECIALTY: Warm cottage-like coffee shop offering all-day breakfast and brunch specials like French Toast with Poached Pancakes with Country Sausages on the cheap. Comfort food mains like pastas and hearty sandwiches also available. For dessert, a must is the Chocolate Decadent cake.

PRICES: About P130 for a big brunch set which would include French toast, 2 eggs, bacon, farmer's ham, and coffee.

PAYMENT: Cash. ADDRESS: 258-A, Tomas Morato Ave., Quezon City T: 412-3358 OPEN: Daily, 9 a.m. – 12 mn.

Kitchen's Best Home Patisserie

U B A

SPECIALTY: Artisanal homebaked cakes and pastries.

Have the French-Mediterranean Banana Toffee Pie, Lemon Torte, Plaisir Sucré (multilayered hazelnut meringue, chocolate ganache, chocolate crème chantilly, praline, and chocolate sheets), White Chocolate Macadamia Brittle Cheesecake, Sablés (sandy-textured biscuits in butter or Parmesan), Sablé Florentines (shortbread topped with a honey-candy topping and sliced almonds), or Lace Crisps (disk-shaped cookies that are sticky-chewy) amidst cupcake-colored doll house interiors.

PRICES: Specialty cakes, P200 and up per slice. Expect to spend around P500 for a hearty afternoon meal like a sandwich, a drink, and a slice of cake.

PAYMENT: Cash, credit card. WEBSITE: Has a Facebook page. EMAIL: martian@destiny.net ADDRESS: Unit 5B Bldg. B, Karrivin Plaza, 2316 Don Chino Roces Ext. (Pasong Tamo Ext.), Makati T: 381-8518, 843-3847, 812-0911, 812-0908 M: 0917-896-6248 OPEN: Daily, 10 a.m. – 8 p.m.

La Tienda

U B A

SPECIALTY: Authentic, traditional Spanish under an executive chef who hails from San Sebastian (northern part of Spain, considered Spain's food capital).

For true-blue no-frills paella, La Tienda's Vegetable Paella with Basmati Rice is a notable standout among the many versions found in the city. Unlike most paellas, this one is delicately seasoned and isn't bombarded with a hundred ingredients ("sahog") and flavorants to a point where it tastes like neither of whatever's in it. The Vongole Pasta, is another no-frills dish that shines because of fresh caught clams and artisanal first-press extra virgin olive oil. A signature trait across all dishes here is the simplicity of preparation and cooking style paired with fresh, A-grade imported ingredients. The result is an aromatic spread feels, smells, and tastes like a deli meal somewhere in San Sebastian, Spain, right before siesta.

PRICES: Set lunch special, P800 and up. Appetizers, P250–650; main course, P400 and up; dessert, P180–250; side dishes (pomme frites, rice pilaf, etc.), P100 and up.

PAYMENT: Cash, credit card. ADDRESS: 43 Polaris St., Bel Air III, Makati T: 890-4123, 895-1651 OPEN: Daily, 7:30 a.m.–3 p.m., 5:30 p.m.–11 p.m.

Le Bistro Vert

U B A

SPECIALTY: "Sustainable" continental bistro-style food.

Le Bistro hinges its entire operation and menu on the principal of environmental and economic sustainability, offering food products that support earth-friendly initiatives and sourcing them locally to support local farmers and local livelihoods or cottage industries that produce artisanal food specialties.

Under the hands-on management of Michelin-trained Chef Sau del Rosario, who has worked in prominent kitchens in France and different parts of Asia, Le Bistro Vert—or LVB—is on a mission to prove that delicious can be equally healthy and socially conscious through signature dishes like Sagada Orange Salad, Tagaytay Farmed Vegetable Lasagna, Walnut and Herb-crusted Sole Fillet, and Prawn Avocado & Prosciutto and Four-cheese Malagos Sandwich, as well as locally grown premium coffee and tea blends. Smack dab in the middle of Makati's business district, LVB provides a sanctuary past its doors from the rat race outside, with teal and white interiors bedecked with bamboo-themed prints—the visual equivalent of a chilled tropical fruit slush. Behind the restaurant is a modest-sized garden providing many of the fresh herbs that the chefs use in the dishes.

PRICES: All-day standard continental and Filipino breakfast menu, P150 and up; salads and appetizers, P125–275; main course, P195–275.

PAYMENT: Cash, credit card. WEBSITE: lebistro.ph EMAIL: lebistro .frsr@gmail.com ADDRESS: Streetside Fraser Place Tower, Valero St., Salcedo Village, Makati T: 403-1841 Mon–Fri, 7 a.m.–10 p.m.; Sat, 7 a.m.–3 p.m.

Lu

U B A

SPECIALTY: Modern Mediterranean.

Typical Mediterranean eateries in the past conjure images of campy island-themed patterns and tangerine color schemes. Lu's minimalist white interiors instantly bode a dining experience beyond the usual hummus-and-pita. In fact, random glances at menu items make you wonder, "Where's the Mediterranean?" But it is there, that Mediterranean anchor point, in the garnish, the marinade, or the cooking style, and in traditional items like wraps, dips, and kebabs. Lu is simply unafraid to venture out and about, which explains specialties like Crispy Prawn and Shiitake Spring Rolls, Truffle Mac 'N' Cheese and 5 Cheeses, and the Mexican Steak Frites (hanger steak with caramelized onions and melted cheese). And whether you're wolfing down something more familiar (Lamb Shank with Minted Yoghurt, Veggie and Feta Wrap with Hummus) or trying out radical fare that may have to be tagged as "fusion," Lu succeeds in driving home the bottom line: Is it any good? Here, it's oftentimes a "yes" on both counts. For long, lazy lunches, do pair your meal with one of their specialty frozen cocktails. Bestseller is the Diablo, a fun and flirty mojito spin-off with citrusy and herbal hints, served in a huge goblet.

PRICES: Appetizers average at about P185; hearty sandwiches and wraps average at P280; meat and seafood mains average at about P500 and are good to share for 2 to 4. Specialty cocktails, P180 and up.

PAYMENT: Cash, credit card. ADDRESS: G/L, Joya Bldg., Joya Drive, Rockwell, Makati T: 403-3991 M: 0915-246-8420 OPEN: Daily, 11 a.m. – 3p.m., 6 p.m. – 10 p.m. (1 a.m. on Fri/Sat).

Malcolm's Place

U B A

SPECIALTY: Mixed Continental.

A bright corner in Salcedo Village is home to one delicious Wagyu Cheesesteak served with large potato wedges and an aioli dip. With deep orange interiors and steel linear dividers, Malcolm's is a cozy hang out for afternoon tea or dinner. Be sure to make reservations for lunch as it is packed most days. Two of their mouth-watering offerings are Salmon Says, a cream-based pasta with smoked salmon and capers; and La Mancha, a *chorizo* sandwich made with choice bread and Manchego cheese plated with a generous portion of potato wedges and vinaigrette side salad. Because Malcolm's is known for wagyu beef, the Rib–Eye Steak is worth the price—a hefty portion of melt-in-your-mouth steak with a siding of rice, mashed potatoes, creamed spinach, creamed corn or coleslaw. Savory dishes, excellent service and great location make Malcolm's one extraordinary find. Has free Wi-Fi.

PRICES: Wagyu Cheesesteak savory sandwich, P350; Rib–eye Steak with sidings, P450/20 g.

PAYMENT: Cash, credit card. ADDRESS: 108 H.V. Dela Costa and Tordesillas Sts., Salcedo Village, Makati T: 844-0000 OPEN: Mon–Fri, 8 a.m. – 11 p.m.; Sat/Sun, 9 a.m. – 11 p.m.

Masseto

U B A

SPECIALTY: Modern Italian fine dining.

With nothing but a red M emblem resembling a wax seal marking its entrance. Masseto is a posh hole-hidey that has gained quite a lunch following that easily rivals the crowd it primarily drew as a wine bar at night. Looking at the interiors alone—lounge ambience with big plush leather and suede arm chairs alongside marble-top tables—you immediately know you're going to spend. Ironically, however, the menu, though filled with artisanal ingredients and food specialties, foils all that luxe by doing away with exotic foreign names and is rather plainspoken in its list of dishes: "Crispy Duck Leg, Roasted Potatoes," for instance, is already both name and description.

Everything is made in-house and from scratch, from appetizers to desserts, with ingredients flown in from their places of origin in dishes where they matter. Portions are typical of fine dining (i.e., not big), but they serve to highlight the sublime quality found in each relished morsel. A serving of Ravioli with Olive Butter and Fresh Ricotta probably comes up to less than 12 fork-fulls. But each ravioli piece is packed generously that it breaks open upon every bite, releasing gobs of premium fresh ricotta and artisanal olive butter. The Tripe, Lamb Sausage, and Bone Marrow Crust, an appetizer that barely comes up to half the height of the bowl it's in, is proof of Masseto's best efforts in all its dishes, be it a meager siding or a main, and that scrimping is unheard of here. Named after one of Italy's signature wines, the restaurant takes pride in its wine list, a carefully studied selection vaunted by discriminate oenologists in the city, with choices meant to be paired with certain items on the menu.

PRICES: Ravioli with Olive Butter and Ricotta, P320; Tripe, Lamb Sausage, and Bone Marrow Crust, P440; meat and seafood main dishes, P520 and up; dessert, P200 and up; specialty wine, P300 and up per glass.

PAYMENT: Cash, credit card. ADDRESS: 108 H.V. Dela Costa and Tordesillas Sts., Salcedo Village, Makati T: 844-0000 OPEN: Mon–Fri, 8 a.m.–11 p.m.; Sat/Sun, 9 a.m.–11 p.m.

Myron's Place

U B A

SPECIALTY: Gourmet continental brunch; six varieties of Eggs Benedict—Traditional (poached eggs over English muffins with Hollandaise sauce, and ham or bacon), Florentine (with sautéed spinach instead of ham), Vegetarian, Southwestern (ingredients substituted with chipotle or southwester Hollandaise, Monterey Jack cheese, Canadian bacon, cilantro, salsa, sour cream, and soft flour tortillas instead of muffins), Irish (uses corned beef hash instead of ham), and Salmon.

Breaking the predominantly Western menu is the Pinoy Big Breakfast, serving garlic rice, side salad, two eggs, and your choice of US Angus tapa, chicken and lamb *adobo*, boneless chicken leg and thigh tocino, or daing na bangus. Completing these fantastic brunch items are brunch cocktails (Mimosa, Bellini, and Kir Royale) and the more traditional hot chocolate—dark cocoa with peanut butter for criminal bittersweet goodness.

PRICES: About P500 per person for brunch and a drink.

PAYMENT: Cash, credit card. ADDRESS: G/L Power Plant Mall, Rockwell Drive cor. Estrella St., Makati T: 728-9898 OPEN: Daily, 11 a.m.–12 mn.

Peanut Butter Company

U B A

SPECIALTY: Savory and dessert peanut butter dishes.

Peanut Butter Company or PBCo., with tagline "Spreading life's simple comforts," is the first peanut butter restaurant in the Philippines. A fun, little store, it offers sandwiches (hot ones and riffs on the classic pb&j), pastas, and specials that use peanut butter as more than just a spread. Here, peanut butter is an enhancement instead of a distraction. To wit: a smear is spread with a sparing hand of the Chili peanut butter, an accent to the Chili Fried Chicken Sandwich. The ensuing heat and sweet is a foil to the super crunchy chicken breast fillet. The Cold Asian Noodles, a refreshing summer dish, has the sesame peanut butter as its base coating. Aside from the chili and sesame, there are 10 more different peanut butter incarnations: creamy, crunchy, curry, dark chocolate, green tea, cinnamon, white chocolate, sun-dried tomato, butter, and cardamom.

There are, however, other dishes that require some stretches of the imagination. The Crunchy Sardine Jelly Sandwich is a mishmash of crunchy peanut butter, sardines, and grape (!) jelly—only for the gutsy. On the other hand, peanut butter is neither a star nor a support but a garnish in the BBQ Wings (chili peanut butter glaze) or the Fish n' Chips (peanut-cucumber dip).

Nevertheless, Peanut Butter Company (PBCo.) is a tremendous and admirably courageous concept that fulfills the desires of people whose hearts pitter-patter for peanut butter. We say tremendous and courageous because it's a ballsy move to open a single concept store in the Philippines. (Filipinos adore variety even though most of us end up choosing the same thing over and over again.) Think back to the one-food kiosks/establishments of the past, the subsequent copycats, and the withdrawal into obscurity or demise of the weaker ones. Though there are single-concept establishments that are thriving, and PBCo. should be one of them.

PRICES: A jar of specialty and flavored peanut butter, P210 (590 g)—you can even ask for a taste (or two or three) of the butters you like before buying! Hearty sandwiches, P130 and up.

PAYMENT: Cash. ADDRESS: 2/L SM City North EDSA, North Ave. cor. EDSA, Quezon City T: 401-3826 OPEN: Daily, 10 a.m.–8 p.m.

Poco Deli

U B A

SPECIALTY: Cold cuts and sausages from prominent saucier and resto-deli Mickey's, natural frozen yogurt, and a modest selection of mostly New World wines (with a few Old World specialties like German Riesling), and a smattering of Belgian and German beers.

Seating at most 25, Poco Deli is a quaint but cheerful hole in the wall that hits the spot when you're looking for gourmet on a budget. They carry specialty cold cuts, sausages, and cheeses from Mickey's that you can buy frozen or order off their menu as pica platters. Apart from that are a couple of pasta dishes, deli sandwiches, and homespun rice meals with a twist (e.g., Callos with Bacon Rice).

This little deli is also the only place, apart from weekend markets, where you can get Dave's Natural Frozen Yoghurt, which comes in some eight flavors and two sizes (cup and pint). The yogurt is free of any fancy toppings and lets you revel in its just-like-ice-cream creamy goodness. More fuss is given to the flavors: you can barely taste the piquant trait of yogurt in their Intense Chocolate, while Wildberry tastes like milky fruit instead of a simplistic mix of sour and saccharine.

Free Wi-Fi until 5 p.m.

PRICES: Sausage and cheese platters, P230 and up (good for 2–3); hearty deli sandwiches served with all-natural potato chips, P180 and up; pizzas, P175 and up; yogurt, P80 for a cup.

PAYMENT: Cash, credit card. WEBSITE: Has a Facebook account. EMAIL: poco.deli@gmail.com, joydeleon@gmail.com ADDRESS: 21 East Kapitol Drive, Kapitolyo, Pasig T: 664-0519 M: 0928-558-4874 OPEN: Daily, 10 a.m.–10 p.m.

Purple Feet

U B A

SPECIALTY: Freestyle Continental

Purple Feet is decidedly unfussy in ambience and almost utilitarian in décor. Guests are surrounded by crates of wine and sit on wooden tables and chairs; wine choices are listed on pillars. A purveyor of freestyle cooking, the chef invites diners to let their culinary imaginations fly. The chalkboard menu lists raw materials that the chefs can work on: prime cuts of beef, pork, poultry, rabbit, and ostrich, and seafood. After choosing from the list, you specify your preferred preparation and flavor. The chefs can purportedly handle cuisines from Indian to Spanish. Weekend kitchen warriors will relish the idea, those who don't putter with pots and pans might be terrified. The chef is used to such fearful indecisiveness, though, and readily talks to the diner, making recommendations gleaned from the conversation. One thing that makes this "choose your own meal adventure" worth the gamble is Purple Feet's masterful handling of top-tier ingredients. You also have the option of leaving your meal to the chef, indulging any of his self-concocted recipes. One such dish would be *laing* stuffed in pork tenderloin, roll it up, and topped with uni butter. It doesn't sound so impressive, but the dish comes awash in the delicious aromas. The smokiness of the *laing* works well with the uni butter (which is whipped butter, uni, foie gras, and truffle oil); and every bite of pork tenderloin is juicy. When at Purple Feet, it is best to talk directly to a chef when mulling over what to eat, not to the servers. Chefs obviously give more enlightened food choices instead of a server who recites things by rote. Purple Feet is about a way of eating that is intelligent and inspired, dishes are true to their flavors with unexpected seasonings that evoke both surprise and pleasure.

PRICES: Expect to pay at least P1,000 per person for a 3-course meal, and at least P1,400 if you have a glass of wine with it.

PAYMENT: Cash, credit card. ADDRESS: 217 Nicanor Garcia St. (Reposo St.), Bel Air, Makati T: 897-3220, 897-8167 OPEN: Mon–Sat, 10:30 a.m.–2 p.m., 5:30 p.m.–10 p.m.

Qizia Café

U B A

SPECIALTY: Extensive breakfast and lunch menu of neighborhood coffee-shop staples like pastas and sandwiches with more culinary thought put into them than their more big-time, multinational counterparts.

They use fresh, torn basil leaves in their pastas; their cheesecakes, baked and dense, use fresh blueberries—just small touches that make all the difference from this little café that could. The astonishingly pocket-friendly prices help much, of course.

PRICES: Pastas, P105 and up; dessert coffee smoothies, P85 and up; Tacos, P85 (regular), P160 (large); lunch sets, P150 and up.

PAYMENT: Cash. ADDRESS: SDS Medical Center Compound, Katipunan Ext. cor Pio del Pilar St., Concepcion II, Marikina T: 489-0760 OPEN: Daily, 8 a.m.–12 mn.

Restaurant Ciçou

U B A

SPECIALTY: French-Mediterranean gourmet.

From its gilded interiors, fancy plating, and menu, Ciçou is undeniably fine-dining. During the day, though, when it is awash in sunlight, the intimidating eatery becomes warm and welcoming yet no less refined. Here one can have a leisurely chef-made lunch before easing back into Makati's bedlam. They have two- to three-course set lunches featuring hearty, down-to-earth French bistro items like cream-based soups or warm savory salads, plated entrées that are "sets"in themselves (e.g., Parmentier of Lamb and Shiitake Confit—seasoned, cooked in its own fat, and prepared with potatoes—Lamb Pie, and Rosemary Sauce), and traditional homey desserts like the Galette des Rois (a flat, flaky, buttery cake filled with almond cream). The à la carte menu is a mouthwatering list of both classics (onion soup, foie gras, duck, and lamb) and innovations (e.g., prawn bisque with sea urchin flan). There's also a list of the chef's suggestions, as well as an 8-course tasting menu with choice à la carte picks (sardines, duck liver, prawns, salmon, beef, and a dessert). Ciçou also boasts made-from-scratch ice cream and sherbet, and the use of organic, first-press raw muscovado sugar (purportedly found in no other restaurant).

PRICES: Set lunch menu, P650 (2-course), P850 (3-course); 8-course tasting menu, P1,500. Corkage is waived for a minimum purchase of P2,000 net.

PAYMENT: Cash, credit card. ADDRESS: G/L Hotel Celeste, San Lorenzo Drive cor. Arnaiz St. (Pasay Rd.), Makati CONTACT: T: 889-6728, 887-8080 loc. 2 OPEN: Daily, 6 a.m. – 10 a.m. (breakfast buffet), 12 nn – 2 p.m., 6 p.m. – 10 p.m.

Ristras

U B A

SPECIALTY: A wide variety of made from scratch burritos using only fresh (as in nothing from a jar or can) and prepped slow-cooked ingredients.

The burritos are no mean feat for the modest of appetite. They're huge and jampacked with your choice of cilantro-lime or *chorizo* brown rice, pinto or vegetarian black beans, red or green chilis, meat, salsa, corn salsa, guacamole, cheese, sour cream, and lettuce. Service and ambience are fast-food style, though, so it's perfect for the dine-and-dash lunch crowd. Have your burrito with a virgin margarita slushy or a lemon grass lemonade.

PRICES: Burrito, P290; Nine Layer Dip and Nachos, P355; virgin/non-virgin margarita, P90.

PAYMENT: Cash. ADDRESS: J. Abad Santos cor. Lopez Jaena, San Juan T: 748-7519 (delivers) OPEN: Daily, 11 a.m. – 11:30 p.m.

Sala

U B A

SPECIALTY: European fine dining with a changing menu determined by what's fresh and in season.

Seating 30 to 40, Sala is one of Manila's most upscale restaurants. They do, however, carry two-and three-course executive lunches from Monday to Friday with a menu that changes every week. You can have Imam Bayildi (a Turkish delicacy of aubergines stuffed with onion, garlic, and tomatoes baked in olive oil) generously sprinkled with goat's cheese and roast pepper salsa as a salad, followed by a seared zatar-crusted tuna steak with fennel hash, roasted tomatoes, and lemon saffron dressing. Dessert can be a simple but elegant creamy pavlova with fresh, ripe strawberries. They also have a tasting menu that let's you try out a little of everything on their à la carte menu for 1,800 pesos. The same is true for their wines, where you can have a portion of their recommended pairing of wines for each course. Servers don't hover about but are right there when you need something.

PRICES: Executive lunch, P790 (2-course), P980 (3-course); tasting menu, P1,800. For à la carte meals, expect your bill to rise above P1,000 per head if you're having wine.

PAYMENT: Cash, credit card. WEBSITE: www.salarestaurant.com EMAIL: info@salarestaurant.com ADDRESS: Podium Level, Locsin Bldg., 6752 Ayala Ave. cor. Makati Ave., Makati T: 750-1555, 893-0242 OPEN: Mon–Fri, 11 a.m.–2 p.m., 6 p.m.–11 p.m.; Sat/Sun, 6 p.m.–11 p.m.

Sala Bistro

U B A

SPECIALTY: Upscale European.

From the same proprietors of posh and upscale restaurants Sala and People's Palace, Sala Bistro has a less fine-dining and cozier vibe, while retaining the lofty standards of the other two restaurants in its own menu.

One can get a gourmet sandwich for a light meal or get the Express Lunch special for something hearty. You can have a salami, roast chicken, or roast beef sandwich—all accessible choices that get royal treatment in Sala Bistro's kitchen. The chicken sandwich, for instance, is made with lean chicken breast roasted with paprika and served with tarragon-infused mayonnaise, greens, and alfalfa sprouts on sourdough bread. Their Express Lunch is a three-course set menu that changes every day. A sample menu would have something like pumpkin, sage, and pancetta soup with Parmesan crostini for starters, crispy skin salmon fillet with sweet pepperonata and herbed courgette for the entrée, and bread and butter pudding with rum and raisin ice cream for lunch. On weekends there's a gastronomic brunch menu that puts the spotlight on organic eggs. Take them scrambled with salmon and dill, or as an omelette with forest ham, sautéed spinach, and Gruyère. There's also bacon and minute steak made with pan-seared Australian beef fillet.

The owners, with more than 10 years of experience in the restaurant business, put up the bistro so they could offer hotel-grade food without the hotel prices. Ingredients are freshly sourced and almost everything is made in-house. Check out the website for menu updates.

PRICES: 3-course express lunch, P690; 2-course weekend brunch, P690; 2-course weekend brunch with bottomless sparkling wine served either plain, with cassis, or with fresh peach or orange juice, P1,280.

PAYMENT: Cash, credit card. WEBSITE: salabistro.com ADDRESS: G/L Garden side, Greenbelt 3, Ayala Center, Makati T: 729-4888 OPEN: Daily, 11 a.m. – 11 p.m. Express lunch available Mon – Fri, 11:30 a.m. – 2:30 p.m.; weekend brunch available Sat/Sun, 11 a.m. – 2 p.m.

Sophia's

U B A

SPECIALTY: Family-style Mediterranean dishes.

Go for the meat specialties, all slow-cooked and whose heaviness in flavor is offset with piquant seasonings like red wine reductions, lime-infused butter, and a host of herbs and spices. Most of all, however, you must not leave without trying the Spanakopita ("spinach pie"): delicately crisp and buttery phyllo pockets stuffed generously with creamy clots of fresh feta cheese and sautéed spinach, served on a bed of crisp salad greens drizzled with a light vinaigrette. It's just an appetizer, but it delivers a gourmetgasmic punch that can outshine some of the mains.

PRICES: Spanakopita, P365 (8 pcs); lamb delicacies, P550 and up. About P500 a head for a light appetizer, light entrée (like pasta), and drink.

PAYMENT: Cash, credit card. WEBSITE: sophiasmediterranean.com ADDRESS: West Gate, Filinvest, Alabang, Muntinlupa T: 771-7717 OPEN: Daily, 11 a.m. – 2 p.m., 6 p.m. – 11 p.m.

Legend: U=Unique, B=Bargain, A=Authenticity

TJ's

U B A

SPECIALTY: Tex-Mex dishes.

A definite must-try is the Baja Fish Taco, a lightly battered log of white fish smothered in fresh and crisp seasoned minced veggies and wrapped in a crisp golden tortilla shell. (The tacos are usually served in a soft tortilla shell, tell them you'd like your shell fried—huge lips-smacking difference!). Priced at under P100, it's the best taco deal in town.

PRICES: Tacos, P85 (regular), P160 (large); lunch sets, P150 and up.

PAYMENT: Cash. ADDRESS: City Golf Compound, Julia Vargas Ave., Pasig OPEN: Daily, 11 a.m. – 11 p.m.

Tomatokick

U B A

SPECIALTY: Mom-and-pop Italian.

Regulars come here for purse-friendly comfort food such as the T-bone steak (which threatens to spill over, occupying 3/4 of the plate) and the pita-thin pizzas. The pastas, though cheap, come in your preferred spaghetti, fettuccine, or penne. Apart from the comfy food and prices, the place itself, along a residential strip of home-based eateries, exudes a vibe that is neither pretentious nor shabby. It's your typical neighborhood hangout, where the area's cult-cool youth get their grub.

PRICES: T-bone steak, P160; pasta, P100 – 140.

PAYMENT: Cash. WEBSITE: tomatokick.multiply.com, also has a Facebook page. EMAIL: paolobernaldo@yahoo.com ADDRESS: 55 Maginhawa St., U.P. Village, Quezon City T: 489-5503 M: 0927-9624174 OPEN: Mon – Thu, 11 a.m. – 12 mn; Fri – Sun, 11 a.m. – 2 a.m.

Astralis

U B A

SPECIALTY: European and Asian fine dining.

The Astralis menu is a collaboration of Manila Diamond Hotel's different chefs where new dishes sparkle among selected bestsellers from the hotel's fine dining outlets.

For starters, try the Baked Camembert in phyllo pastry. Hot and oozing from its delicate cocoon, it's presented like a Pollock painting: dollops of red tomato jam, green pesto, and pink peppercorns dot the canvas.

A salad doesn't make a meal, but the curiously named Our GM's Favorite Salad probably could. It consists of sautéed portobello mushrooms and greens tossed into a crispy Parmesan basket. From the side, slices of Laguna buffalo cheese beckon beside cherry tomatoes dribbled with grape seed oil. Not to be outdone, the entrées are no less compelling: the Grilled US Angus Prime Rib, for instance, comes with delectable marrow.

The menu's inimitable dish, however, is the runny but luxurious Parisian Scrambled Eggs with Foie Gras and Toast. It will take every iota of willpower to stop yourself from grabbing a ladle instead of politely scooping the heavenly fluff with a teaspoon.

PRICES: Phyllo Pastry, P340; Our GM's Favorite Salad, P290; Parisian Scrambled Eggs with Foie Gras and Toast, P480.

PAYMENT: Cash, credit card. ADDRESS: Astralis, Lopez Drive, Power Plant Mall, Rockwell, Makati T: 703-2688 OPEN: Daily, 11 a.m. – 10 p.m.

Bistro Filipino

U B A

SPECIALTY: Filipino with continental touches

Back in the early 2000s, one of a foodie's most guarded secrets was the address of a private Makati home where chef Rolando Laudico catered intimate dinners or romantic dates with unique fine-dining fusion fare served to you at his garden gazebo. As demand grew, Laudico ended his

Legend: U=Unique, B=Bargain, A=Authenticity

home business to put up Bistro Filipino, a public arena showcasing culinary inventions such as the well-received *Adobo* Overload (sticky rice stuffed with chicken *adobo* and topped with seared fresh foie gras, fried *adobo* flakes, and *adobong kangkong*), or the playfully presented *Ubod* Spring Roll (crisp cone-shaped rolls with *chorizo*, prawns, heart of palm, and a spicy fermented vinegar sorbet—served in individual shot glasses on a tiered metal stand). But managing a restaurant can take its toll on the consistency of the food served, to say nothing of how fusion is rife with hits and misses. Despite a few hiccups in this area, Bistro Filipino has by far shown the most innovation in terms taking Filipino dishes out of comfort-food realms that it's almost criminal not to try. And what remains consistent, is that the dishes, though inventive, are thought out and still employ old-school made-from-scratch cooking wherever they can (e.g., the peanut sauce for the *Kare-Kare* is made from freshly ground peanuts, not unsweetened peanut butter). Try out the set lunch menu (Mon–Fri) and the set brunch menu (weekends) to try out a majority of Bistro Filipino's offerings and home in on what you end up liking.

PRICES: Lunch and brunch set menus, P700 and up.

PAYMENT: Cash, credit card. WEBSITE: EMAIL: ADDRESS: G/L, Net 2 Bldg., 3rd Ave., The Fort, Bonifacio Global City, Taguig T: 856-0634, 856-0541 OPEN: Daily, 11 a.m.–3 p.m., 6 p.m.–11 p.m.

Canteen At Trilogy

U B A

SPECIALTY: Light meals and deli sandwiches using continental food preparation and local premium ingredients.

Must-tries include the Fish and Tofu with Red Curry, Miso Glazed Mahi-Mahi, Mango Ice Box with Tapioca, Tonkatsu Burger with Camote Chips, Pasta with Shrimp and Green Mango, and homemade Choc Nut Ice Cream. Continental brunch (Eggs Ben, French Toast, etc.) is available all day, 10 a.m.–5 p.m. As in-store cafe of Trilogy Boutique, Canteen lets you do some shopping while waiting for your order.

PRICES: P250 and up for an appetizer, main, and drink.

PAYMENT: Cash, credit card. WEBSITE: thetrilogyboutique.com, twitter.com/trilogyboutique; they also have a Facebook page. EMAIL: trilogyboutique@gmail.com ADDRESS: 110 Alvion Center, Rada St., Legaspi Village, Makati T: 328- 1071 OPEN: Mon–Fri, 11 a.m.–8 p.m.; Sat/Sun, 10 a.m.–5 p.m.

Chi's Oven Baked Kitchen

U B A

SPECIALTY: Italian–Filipino fusion (Oven-baked pizzas, *lechon* pugon).

Save for the checkered table cloth, this restaurant has all the typical accouterments of an authentic Italian cantinetta: an authentic wood-fired oven prominently displayed at the far end, a fresco, old wrought-iron chandeliers, brick-lined wall accents, and huge dark wooden tables. But the menu was made for the Filipino palate. If you're looking for traditional fare, this is not the place. But if you're up for something unexplored, make sure to get their oven-baked must-tries like the Puchon (pugon-baked *lechon*). Filipinized pizzas feature one topped with *adobo* flakes and another topped with *balut*—and by "*balut*" we do mean the entire thing, not just the yellow penoy part. They don't use duck eggs older than 18 days, so the *balut* embryo is tender, generously seasoned with garlic, and free of soggy hair-like feathers and "mature" parts found in older *balut*. For *balut* eaters, this is a savory street. For non-fans, this is could be a more acceptable entry into the *balut* eating world. Even the specialty dessert comes in the form of a pizza: chocolate topped with white chocolate shavings all in one molten disc.

PRICES: Main courses such as the pastas and pizzas average at P250–325; the roast meat dishes at P350. Servings are good for 3 people.

PAYMENT: Cash, credit card. WEBSITE: brickovenkitchen.multiply.com ADDRESS: Unit 105, 209 Aguirre Ave., BF Homes T: 820-7210 M: 0917-926-0555, 0917-897-1117 OPEN: Tue–Thu, Sun, 11 a.m.–11 p.m.; Sat, 11 a.m.–12 nn.

Gourmet's Palate

SPECIALTY: Delicious and affordable comfort food like burgers, tacos, and other fast-food items given a generous dose of kitchen TLC.

The name is a bit misleading. If you're looking for foie gras, look elsewhere. But if you're looking for a quick but well-prepared hearty snack or meal at a friendly neighborhood joint, this is definitely the place. Dimsum and steaks find themselves side by side on the menu, but the crowning glory is the charbroiled burgers, of which there are more than 10 diverse concoctions—from blue cheese toppings to Latin-inspired chilis to wasabi!

PRICES: Specialty burgers, P72 and up; tacos, P38; sizzlers (porterhouse steak, chicken teriyaki, sisig with egg), P67 and up.

PAYMENT: Cash. ADDRESS: 168 Tomas Morato cor. Roces Aves., Quezon City T: 929-1069 OPEN: Daily, 11 a.m.–2:30 p.m., 6 p.m.–11 p.m.

Greens Café and Restaurant

SPECIALTY: 100% lacto vegetarian dishes (no meat, no fish, no eggs) that span both continental fare like pasta primavera and shepherd's pie and downright Pinoy grub like relleno and sisig. Parking is typical of the area (i.e., scant), but the vibe is homey and an unpretentious kind of artsy.

PRICES: Appetizers average at P80 (good to share); pastas, P80 and up; hearty main dishes, P130 and up; combo platters, P105.

PAYMENT: Cash. WEBSITE: Facebook, Twitter ADDRESS: 92 Sct. Castor St., Quezon City T: 415-4796 OPEN: Mon–Sat, 11 a.m.–10 p.m.; Sun, 12 nn–9 p.m.

Museum Café

SPECIALTY: Mixed Continental and Asian; Sunday jazz brunch.

Museum Café or M Café belongs to that rare breed of hip establishments with substantiated hype, owing mainly to their success at mixing and matching Western and Asian fare in one menu without falling out of grace with discriminating foodies. And from crowded cocktail lounge with DJ-spun music at night, M Café transforms into a bright, wholesome family brunch place on weekends, the scent of waffles and Eggs Ben easing out hangovers from the night before.

The weekend brunch spread has a tremendous range of choices for both the culinary adventurer (Honey Duck Rolls with Hoisin-Lime Sauce and Mint, Smoked Bangus and Quesong Puti on Tagaytay Greens) and the traditionalist (eggs benedict, and waffles dusted with cinnamon, drizzled with real maple syrup, and topped with heaping clouds of fresh whipped cream and coarsely chopped walnuts). In between are several choices in smoked meats, cold cuts, breakfast steaks, salad, pasta, freshly baked bread, cheeses, and bubbly breakfast cocktails like Mimosas (Champagne with fresh orange juice), Bellinis (sparkling Italian wine with peach purée), and any of their signature tropical margaritas (try the lemongrass flavor!). On Sundays, brunch is given some sass with a live jazz trio, while complimentary art activities are organized to keep the kids entertained.

PRICES: Brunch buffet, P888 (adults), P488 (age 12 and below).

PAYMENT: Cash, credit card. ADDRESS: G/L Greenbelt 4 (across Ayala Museum), Ayala Center, Makati Ave., Makati T: 757-6000, 757-3000 OPEN: Daily, 10 a.m.–8 p.m.; weekend brunch, 10 a.m.–3 p.m.

Ninyo Fusion Cuisine

U B A

SPECIALTY: French–Japanese fusion cuisine with an evolving menu.

Ninyo's origins provide an insightful perspective: as the family's historical home, filled with personal furniture and souvenirs from travels, a restaurant visit becomes very much like a visit in a friend's house for an inviting, delectable meal wrapped in an air of nostalgia. Or it can very much be the personal touch that transforms a place into a lovely venue: outside, a gazebo

Legend: U=Unique, B=Bargain, A=Authenticity

awaits cozy meals, intimate dates, even romantic proposals. Upstairs, newly-renovated second floor showcases a wine lounge. Experienced or beginning sommeliers can choose from a vast selection to pair with a meal, indulge in for a nightcap, or for an evening of wine-tasting. At Ninyo, co-owner and chef Niño Lauz prepares weekly menus that feature the fusion of refined simplicity that marks Japanese cuisine and the sophisticated complexity of French fare. This coming together of taste and technique is the starting point of Ninyo's offerings. One might be drawn to Duck Leg Confit served with edamame risi bisi, Char-grilled Tiger Prawns in spicy red bell pepper sauce with Japanese paella and buttered edamame, or Char-grilled US Hanging Steak Salad with yuzu infused Sesame Thai Chili dressing. It can be the Wasabi Fried Oysters with citrus mayo dressing, the Baked Unagi with Pan Seared Foie Gras, or the Honey Glazed Grilled Salmon with Dalandan Miso that catches the eye. When dining at Ninyo, call for a reservation, especially on weekends.

PRICES: Salads and appetizers average at P300, mains at P500. A gustation may be a good idea if the choices overwhelm. For a little over P1,000, enjoy a recommended selection to appreciate at your own pace.

PAYMENT: Cash, credit card. WEBSITE: www.ninyo.ph
EMAIL: ninyofusion@gmail.com ADDRESS: 66 E. Abada St., Loyola Heights, Quezon City T: 426-0301 M: 0917-5385813 OPEN: Daily, 11 a.m.–2 p.m., 6 p.m.–10 p.m.

Van Gogh is Bipolar (VGIB)

U B A

SPECIALTY: Organic, mood-enhancing "left-brained" food.

Van Gogh Is Bipolar—or VGIB—is really more of a dinner place, though it can accommodate people for lunch if you call at least a day ahead. It has no visible signage from the road. Located in a compound, the only telltale sign of its existence is a stretched T-shirt painted with the eatery's name and mounted by the front door. You are greeted by a table spread of assorted teapots from which you can pick to hold your tea or hot chocolate. While waiting for your order, browse the bookshelf for an interesting read or pick up a magnifying glass and browse stamp-sized nudes. You can also pick up a marker or a screw driver and write, doodle, or etch on certain walls, chairs, and tables designated for free expression.

The café is the home and living art space of artist, filmmaker, and travel photographer Jetro B. Rafael. Clinically diagnosed to be bipolar himself, he eschews traditional medicine and advocates organic and mood-altering food that regulates "happiness" hormones like serotonin and dopamine in the menu. He doesn't use salt but manages to create truly flavorful dishes with ingredients you'd never think to put together but make sense. The Godfather I, for example, is truly al dente spinach pasta sautéed in virgin olive oil, garlic, onions, and red tomato with freshly sautéed cabbage and salted egg. His own blend of spices and herbs are added to the mix to give it a delicate kick similar to that of cilantro and a little fresh cayenne. If the menu daunts you, Jetro can whip up something personalized and more within your comfort zone.

The food is slow-cooked and the place isn't staffed like a restaurant, so be a little patient with your order and with some self-serve features. Don't forget to leave your shoes by the door when you enter (the place is still someone's home off operating hours).

PRICES: Pasta specials start at P155 (solo) and P405 (group); meat and fish entrées start at P200 (solo) and P350 (group). Solo servings can feed up to 2, group servings good for 3 to 4.

PAYMENT: Cash. WEBSITE: Has a Facebook page. EMAIL: vangoghisbipolar@gmail.com ADDRESS: 154 Maginhawa St., Sikatuna Village, Quezon City (in a compound fronted by Redbucks eatery) T: 394-0188 M: 0929-163-8592, 0922-824-3051 to 52 OPEN: Daily except Tue, 5 p.m.–12:30 a.m. Lunch by reservation.

Recreation & Activities

Take up a new skill, rediscover an old one, get a little cultured, or just try something beyond the usual. There's something in here for all ages.

LEGEND

H A C W

H - HISTORY/HERITAGE Museums or activities about Philippine history, culture, or heritage.
A - ART Museums, galleries, and institutions exhibiting art work. Exhibited art works are usually for sale.
C - CHANGING EXHIBITS/EVENTS/ACTIVITIES Galleries, museums, and institutions with changing exhibits or events scheduled throughout the year.
W - WITH WORKSHOPS/CLASSES

Y U V W

Y - YEAR-ROUND Activities/events available year-round.
U - UNIQUE Hard to find specialty activities/events/workshop.
V - VARIETY Has a good mix of activities/events/workshops for varying levels and interests.
W - WITH WORKSHOPS/CLASSES

U B V / U B V W

U - UNIQUE Hard to find or novel workshop/activity.
B - BUDGET Pocket-friendly rates/fees/tuition.
V - VARIETY Has a good mix of activities/events/workshops for varying levels and interests.
W - WITH WORKSHOPS/CLASSES

Alliance Française De Manille (AFM)

H A C W

SPECIALTY: French language learning and cultural center.

AFM fosters an active cultural exchange between Filipinos and French through French language classes, translation services, a library, a French restaurant, an art gallery, weekly French film screenings, and events like fashion shows, art exhibits, book fairs, and wine and food tasting. These events are especially anticipated during French Spring in Manila, an annual celebration spanning three months (April–June) tightly booked with additional workshops and events. AFM members enjoy free use of AFM's facilities, discounts on language classes and in the restaurant, and updates about upcoming events. However, you don't have to be a member to attend any of the events and activities.

PRICES: Membership fee, P900. Basic French language classes, P2,600 (12 hours) to P4,990 (48 hours). Film viewings are free of charge and are on a first-come, first-served basis.

PAYMENT: Cash. WEBSITE: alliance.ph EMAIL: info@alliance.ph ADDRESS: 209 Nicanor Garcia St. (Reposo), Bel Air II, Makati T: 895-7585, 895-7441 OPEN: Mon–Sat, 9 a.m.–6 p.m.

Art 19B

H A C W

SPECIALTY: Modern art from young local talent and a good selection of paintings from national artists.

With old-fashioned hardwood floor boards and semi-industrial bay windows, this split-level gallery fits Cubao Expo's indie atmosphere. Though the place does exhibit the works of budding local talent and hosts yoga sessions and other activities deemed "new age" by the traditional art buyer, it seals its credibility as a serious art house with its collection of early works by local grand masters and national artists such as Joya and Legaspi.

PRICES: A budding artist's work can go for P10,000 and up. National artists' paintings are typically in the 6 figures.

PAYMENT: Cash. WEBSITE: art19b.multiply.com EMAIL: art19b@gmail.com ADDRESS: Shop 14-B, Cubao Expo, Gen. Romulo Ave., Araneta Center, Cubao, Quezon City T: 494-4886 M: 0928-5214348, 0928-5214349, 0920-906-5650 OPEN: Mon–Sat, 12 nn–8 p.m.

Artist-Run Independent Art Space

H A C W

SPECIALTY: Avant-garde art by upstarts and the talented but unknown.

Though eluded by fame, unsung visual, mixed-media, and installation artist Bobby Nuestro is a name known well by discriminating art collectors. He founded this art space 2005 with a special motivation to support the talented but anonymous, the creatively avant-garde but obscure.

PRICES: Works exhibited go for P5,000 and up.

PAYMENT: Cash. EMAIL: arias10122@yahoo.com ADDRESS: 210 LRI Design Plaza, Nicanor Garcia St. (Reposo), Makati T: 895-9837 M: 0917-4772660 OPEN: Mon–Sat, 10 a.m.–8 p.m.

Asian Food Museum

H A C W

SPECIALTY: Vignette exhibits depicting popular Asian dishes, their history, and trivia, as well as interesting facets of food culture and traditions in different Asian countries. Certain exhibits have kid-friendly interactive games using chopsticks, street food carts, and touch screen graphics.

PRICES: Free admission.

ADDRESS: Manila Ocean Park, behind the Quirino Grandstand, Luneta, Manila T: 567-7777 OPEN: Daily, 11 a.m.–9 p.m.

Legend: H=History/Heritage, A=Art C=Changing exhibits/events/activities, W=With workshops/classes

Ateneo Art Gallery

H A C W

SPECIALTY: First museum in the country dedicated to the collection, display, and interpretation of modern Philippine art.

It houses around 500 post-war works (paintings, prints, drawings, sculptures, photographs, and posters), over 200 of which were donated by late art scholar and Ateneo teacher Fernando Zóbel de Ayala. Its 300-piece collection of over 300 etchings, engravings, woodcuts, lithographs, and other media by artists both local (Sansó, Amorsolo, Manansala, Ocampo, Magsaysay-Ho, Luz, Legaspi, Abueva, Ang Kiukok) and international (Rembrandt, Goya, Delacroix, Toulouse-Lautrec, Picasso), spanning the Renaissance to the present, has been cited by critics both here and abroad as arguably one of the finest in Southeast Asia. As the gallery can only hold a limited number of visitors, large groups should schedule their visit ahead of time. The gallery is wheelchair-accessible and can make arrangements for other needs.

PRICES: Free admission; free group tours by appointment.

WEBSITE: gallery.ateneo.edu ADDRESS: G/L Rizal Library Bldg., Ateneo de Manila University, Katipunan Rd., Loyola Heights, Quezon City T: 426-6488, 426-6001 loc. 4160. OPEN: Mon–Fri, 8 a.m.–5 pm; Sat, 8 a.m.–12 nn.

Avellana Art Gallery

H A C W

SPECIALTY: Contemporary fine art.

Located in a genteel, colonial-era neighborhood dotted with trees, Avellana Art Gallery is safely cocooned from the outer bedlam that is Pasay City. From the outside, it looks like a house; and inside, despite standing amidst hung abstracts, it still feels like a house—inviting, comfortable, and bereft of the "Do not touch!" atmosphere in typical major art galleries. The owner-curated gallery mostly features abstract expressionist work by young and budding talent. Reinforcing its home-gallery format are its breakfast exhibit launches where guests view new works over classic comfort breakfast food like hot pandesal, cottage cheese, and tapa with sparkling wine.

PRICES: P20,000 and up for paintings.

PAYMENT: Cash, check. ADDRESS: A-19 2680 F.B. Harrison St., Pasay T: 833-8357 OPEN: Mon–Sat, 10 a.m.–7 p.m.

Ayala Museum

H A C W

SPECIALTY: Extensive historical and iconographic collection.

Established in the 1950s, this prominent institution boasts a handmade 60-piece diorama section on Philippine history, a gallery of watercraft miniatures, archaeological and cultural minority artifacts, 19th-century art work, paintings of local grand masters Juan Luna and Fernando Amorsolo, 18th- to 19th-century ethnic wear, and Chinese and Southeast Asian trade ceramics that date back to more than a millennium. The vast four-level art space houses regularly changing collections of contemporary art works, from oil abstracts to architectural sculptures to elaborate cinematic set and costume design vignettes. An in-house gift shop carries art-themed paper products, fashion accessories, books, and multimedia. Individual audio-guide devices are available for certain exhibits. The museum also holds a broad range of events that promote public awareness of contemporary art and foster art appreciation and creativity in children.

PRICES: Admission for G/L to 3/L, P150 (adults), P75 (kids, students, senior citizens); G/L to 4/L, P225 (adults), P125 (kids above age 8, senior citizens). Children age 8 and below are not allowed on 4/L galleries due to the delicate installations in the area.

PAYMENT: Cash. WEBSITE: ayalamuseum.com EMAIL: museum_inquiry@ayalamuseum.org ADDRESS: Makati Ave. cor. De La Rosa St., Greenbelt Park, Ayala Center, Makati T: 757-7117 to 21 loc. 25 or 35, 757-3589 OPEN: Tue–Fri, 9 a.m.–7 p.m.; Sat/Sun, 10 a.m.–6 p.m.

Bahay Tsinoy Museum

H A C W

SPECIALTY: The only in-depth exhibit of Filipino–Chinese culture and heritage; stunning life-like dioramas and historical artifacts.

Bahay Tsinoy is one of the most well-kept and maintained exhibits with helpful and informative tour guides. Here you will learn about little-known parts of Filipino-Chinese history, the many locations of Chinatown before its current location, the first Chinese merchants and business people in the Philippines, and Tsinoy icons and heroes through its exhibit of photographs, books, paintings, and ceramic collections.

PRICES: Admission, P100 (adults), P60 (children and students).

PAYMENT: Cash. WEBSITE: bahaytsinoy.org EMAIL: info@bahaytsinoy.org ADDRESS: Kaisa-Angelo King Heritage Center, 32 Anda cor. Cabildo Sts., Intramuros, Manila T: 527-6083, 526-6796 OPEN: Tue–Sun, 1 p.m.–5 p.m.

Carlos Celdran Walking Tours

H A C W

SPECIALTY: Walking tours of Old Manila.

The inimitable, energetic, and engaging street docent that is Carlos Celdran has managed to make the hip and young interested in—even fork cash over for—Philippine history. His walking tours, aside from being practical and informative explorations of the city for expats and tourists, have become the stuff of quirky daytime dates, *barkada* weekend jaunts, foodie exploits, and photographer walkabouts among locals. Celdran's walking tours cover different parts of old Manila and home in on different themes of Philippine history—pre-Hispanic and Spanish-era architecture through a leisurely walk in Intramuros, the beginnings of a Filipino-Chinese subculture via a Binondo stroll, and contemporary history like the Martial Law years and the Philippines in the '70s. What makes Celdran's walking tours engaging is Celdran himself, who, without compromising accuracy or propriety, uses humor and trivia to spice up what could easily become a boring history lecture. Almost all the walking tours have a food stop or two at eateries that contribute to the theme of the tour (merienda at an old Filipino-Spanish café for the Intramuros tour, dimsum at a legendary hole-hidey in Chinatown for the Binondo tour, etc.), as well as shopping stops for souvenirs and curios you can't find in malls. Check out the website for updates on tours and schedules.

PRICES: Typically P900 (adult) and P450 (students) for a half-day tour, inclusive of transfers and food. Should you not find tour dates that fit your schedule, notify Carlos three (3) weeks in advance, and he can open up a public tour on your preferred date at the regular tour rate.

WEBSITE: celdrantours.blogspot.com EMAIL: celdrantours@hotmail.com
ADDRESS: Unit 24, North Syquia Apartments, 1991 MH del Pilar, Malate, Manila T: 484 4945 M: 0920- 909-2021.

Casa Manila

H A C W

SPECIALTY: Colonial-period ilustrado lifestyle museum.

Found inside Intramuros, across San Agustin Church, lifestyle museum Casa Manila is a reconstructed Spanish 1800s house that recreates the colonial-period lifestyle of a typical ilustrado (upper class) family through a carefully

Other Tour Guides Recommended By Carlos Celdran

MABUHAY GUIDES
The Blue Badge-trained Mabuhay Guides of the Department of Tourism are perfect for touring around dignitaries and visitors of distinction. They are young, fun, street smart, and are the kind of people you would want to hang out with anyway.
M: 0920-947-9024

GREG DORRIS
Tall American (easy to spot when walking through crowded areas). Also has a book of archival photos of Old Manila like Carlos, Carlos's official alternate.
gahdorris@hotmail.com
M: 0916-766-9170

ARMANDO HILDAWA
One of the smartest tour guides in town, if not THE smartest. Also does Corregidor.
M: 0916-494-0623

TERRY QUITEVIS
Veteran tour guide of Manila. The standard to beat.
M: 0917-891-1182

VITO HERNANDEZ
Smart dude from University of the Philippines. Really really nice guy. Knowledgeable in history, sociology, and geology. It's like hanging out with a college buddy.
M: 0916- 634-9649

OLIVIER BORTEN
Frenchman with extensive knowledge on fun in Manila. Speaks English and some Filipino.
M: 0919-516-4631

PATRICK TUDANCA
Speaks German.
M: 0917-526-6786

MELA METHARUN
Great Spanish guide.
M: 0926-666-9908

WILLIE SALAMANCA
Veteran Spanish tour guide.
M: 0919-556-5571

Above info is an excerpt from the sidebar "Other Guides and Agencies," celdrantours.blogspot.com curated selection of 17th to 20th century furniture, antiques, and art pieces from China, Europe, and the Middle East. Notable period pieces include a four-post ebony bed with canopy, crystal chandeliers, Ming dynasty vases, Persian rugs, a harp, Victorian walls, Castillan-inspired high ceilings and wide hardwood floor boards, and capiz windows. It was typical for the first floor of houses in colonial-era Manila to be rented out to shopkeepers. In Casa Manila, there are shops at the ground floor that carry antiques, art objects, and souvenirs.

PRICES: Admission, P75 (adults), P50 (children, students, teachers, and senior citizens with respective I.D.s, guests with disability).

PAYMENT: Cash. ADDRESS: General Luna St., Manila T: 527-4084 OPEN: Tue–Sun, 9 a.m.–6 p.m.

Daniel W. Tantoco, Jr. Collection

H A C W

SPECIALTY: Around 600 rare excavated Philippine pottery and Southeast Asian ceramics dating back as early as 200 B.C. and 11th century A.D. Artifacts valued at over P1 million by the National Museum.

PRICES: Free admission.

ADDRESS: De La Salle University Library Bldg., De La Salle University, Taft Ave., Manila T: 250-4611 OPEN: Mon–Fri, 8 a.m.–5 p.m., by appointment.

Drawing Room, The

H A C W

SPECIALTY: Fine art on paper by established contemporary Filipino artists.

Founded in 1998, The Drawing Room primarily features high-quality works on paper. Its maiden exhibit showcased works from the country's premiere draftsmen—Ben Cabrerra, J. Elizalde Navarro, Kiko Escora, and

Marcel Antonio. Having established itself as a respected venue for art on paper, The Drawing Room soon included paintings, mixed media, and high-concept installations. The gallery hosts monthly exhibits, and the feel and theme of each one being contingent on the featured artist. Motivated to expose local artists internationally, the gallery regularly participates in art fairs abroad and exhibits in around Asia and the U.S.

PRICES: Works typically start at the mid 5-figure range.

PAYMENT: Cash, check. WEBSITE: drawingroomgallery.com EMAIL: drawings@pldtdsl.net ADDRESS: G/L Metrostar Bldg., 1007 Metropolitan Ave., Makati T: 897-6990, 897-7877 OPEN: Mon–Sat, 10 a.m.–8 p.m.

Filipinas Heritage Library H A C W

SPECIALTY: Workshops and research resource on Philippine art and culture.

Once the site of Philippine Airlines' maiden voyage on March 1941, the Filipinas Heritage Library (FHL) now stands in the middle of the Ayala Triangle—between the old Nielsen Airport runways, Ayala Avenue and Paseo de Roxas, and Makati Avenue. The FHL, originally conceived as a research library, focuses on conserving, collecting, and making available to the public materials on Philippine art, culture, and history. It offers an extensive collection of Filipiniana resources and photo library of daily Filipino life as far back as the 15th century. It also holds regular workshops on various topics such as features writing, public speaking, theater performance, art and art appreciation, and photography (from basic to underwater), and food styling by guest speakers and instructors considered esteemed practitioners in their respective crafts. A section of the FHL called the Alcove Perspective is home to a special collection of photography-related books, magazines, and other publications. Email to be included in their mailing list and in the loop about events and workshop schedules.

PRICES: Workshop fees vary but usually cost P2,500 and up. Early reservations may entitle some to as much as a 10% discount.

PAYMENT: Cash, credit card, or Globe Globe G-Cash. WEBSITE: (For workshops) filipinaslibrary.org.ph/featuredevents.asp, (for an online catalog of Filipiniana resources) librarylink.org.ph, (for an online catalog of Filipiniana images) retrato.com.ph EMAIL: (For inquiries on the workshops) fhl_inquiry@ayalafoundation.org, (for questions on the library) asklibrarian@filipinaslibrary.org.ph ADDRESS: Makati Avenue, Ayala Triangle T: 892-1801; F: 892-1810 OPEN: Tue–Sat, 9 a.m.–6 p.m.

Finale Art File

H A C W

SPECIALTY: Local cutting-edge art.

Running for more than 25 years, Finale Art File has retained its original occupant's warehouse look. Converted from a brandy bond store, this 450 sqm space serves as a playground for contemporary artists. Find yourself engulfed in hyperrealist works, like a Louie Cordero sculpture (giant flayed head with drooped eyeball and exposed brain matter in fuchsia, tangerine, and neon green). Finale Art File has three exhibit spaces dominated by the Tall Gallery. On the second level lies the aptly named Upstairs Gallery, and the Video Room. This triumvirate of space conspires to bring new exhibits a month from some of the country's most prominent names in contemporary art. Finale is also equipped with a library and a large storeroom to accommodate several artists' portfolios of works. Guards can direct you to available parking within the area or near the gallery.

PRICES:Art works range from P3,500 for paper works to millions for a master painter's work.

PAYMENT: Cash, credit card, check. WEBSITE: finaleartfile.com EMAIL: info@finaleartfile.com ADDRESS: Warehouse 17, La Fuerza Compound (Gate 1), Chino Roces Ave. (Pasong Tamo), Makati T: 813-2310, 812-5034 OPEN: Mon–Sat, 10 a.m.–7 p.m.

Galerie Joaquin

H A C W

SPECIALTY: Wide spectrum of notable art pieces from both grand masters and exceptionally talented upstarts; active lineup of exhibits, lectures, painting sessions, and art workshops.

The two-storey glass structure is a warm yet polished place where buyers can carefully mull over their selected art pieces. The gallery has also tapped into international opportunities and markets for its artists and exhibitions, showcasing premiere Filipino works.

PRICES: Works of established artists average at the mid 5-figure range.

PAYMENT: Cash, credit card, check. WEBSITE: galeriejoaquin.com EMAIL: info@galeriejoaquin.com ADDRESS: 371 P. Guevarra St. cor. Montessori Lane, Addition Hills, San Juan T: 723-9253, 723-9418 OPEN: Mon–Sat, 10 a.m.–8 p.m. See directory for subsidiary galleries.

Galleria Duemila

H A C W

SPECIALTY: This grande dame of galleries in Manila occupies a rarified space in local art history as the oldest running gallery in the country (with over 15,000 fully documented pieces) and by continuing to promote the best of Filipino modern art.

The gallery has two large exhibition spaces, proportionally spacious storage, and a documentation area. Higher ceilings and a huge garden allow for cocktails during the launch of big sculptures and installations, performances, and video shows. The gallery also maintains a collection of rare art books of Filipino and foreign artists and important art films. The best time to see the gallery is during its openings, so sign up for their monthly invitations by emailing them. Parking is limited to about 20 cars in their lot, but the guards can direct you to nearby parking.

PRICES: Artwork prices vary greatly beginning at P5,000 for a drawing or a print.

PAYMENT: Cash, credit card, check, money transfer. Installment options are also available. WEBSITE: galleriaduemila.com EMAIL: duemila@mydestiny.net ADDRESS: 210 Loring St., Pasay T: 831-9990, 833-9815 OPEN: Mon – Sat, 9 a.m. – 6 p.m.

Gallery Big

H A C W

SPECIALTY: The first and only gallery in the country specializing in huge artworks by renowned masters and noteworthy emerging artists, offering these art works at the lowest acquisition cost.

Art-related services include fine art pawn brokerage, mural and fresco rendition, artwork cleaning/restoration, art appraisal and authentication, art consultation and presentation, framing, and professional handling and transport. Check out their website to get updates on annual "Big Sales."

PRICES: Masters' paintings measuring over two feet in width and height average at about P200,000.

PAYMENT: Cash, check. Term payments for large purchases are available. WEBSITE: gallerybig.com EMAIL: info@gallerybig.com ADDRESS: 2/L LRI Design Plaza, 210 Nicanor Garcia St. (Reposo), Bel Air, Makati T: 895-4516 M: 0917-880-8787 OPEN: Mon – Sat, 10 a.m. – 7 p.m.

Hiraya Gallery

H A C W

SPECIALTY: Contemporary art from young local and new talent.

PRICES: You can get a print or drawing for below P10,000, though paintings have a wide price range, from low five-figures and up.

PAYMENT: Cash. WEBSITE: hiraya.com EMAIL: hiraya@info.com.ph ADDRESS: 530 United Nations Ave., Ermita, Manila T: 523-3331 OPEN: Mon – Sat, 9 a.m. – 5 p.m.

Ivan Man Dy Walking Tours

H A C W

SPECIALTY: Walking tours of Intramuros, Chinatown, San Miguel, the chinese cemetery and an architectural tour of the FEU campus.

Another celebrated street docent is Ivan Dy, whose half-day anecdotal tours give history lessons a vibrant spin and show a glimpse of four centuries' worth of history through museums, churches and colonial houses, past plazas, cobbles, ruins, bulwarks and even tombstones. Most anticipated among the tours, however, is his Chinatown walking tour, where people "nibble" their way through the Chinese quarter with food stops in the area's best kept culinary secrets, from a 16th century Baroque cathedral all the way to the last stop that is the Chinese shrine. Apart from chowing down on Chinese delicacies, you get to take a peek at a traditional chocolate factory, listen to enthralling immigrant stories, and watch how an authentic Hokkien-style spring roll is made.

For those who'd rather roll on pavement than pound it, there's the Halo-Halo Special, a half-day whirlwind experience of a car tour combining three tours: Intramuros, Chinatown, and the bargaining central that is Quiapo.

The tours also have an optional fine-dine lunch or dinner at the Legarda mansion, a well-preserved pre-war 1930's just a stone throw's away from Malacañang Palace. Customized and private tours are accommodated. They also train applicants who wan to be part of their team of tour guides. Check out the website and their Facebook page for tour schedules and updates.

PRICES: Typically P950 per person (for half-day tour inclusive of food).

PAYMENT: Bank deposit. WEBSITE: oldmanilawalks.com EMAIL: fun@oldmanilawalks.com T: 711-3823 M: 0917-329-1622

Japan Foundation Manila

H A C W

SPECIALTY: Japan language learning and cultural center.

Japan Foundation Manila (JFM) fosters an active cultural exchange through language courses and cultural activities. It has Japanese language classes for multiple levels, translation services, and a library. JFM also offers fellowship grants and more competitive programs designed for postgraduate students, experienced researchers, and cultural specialists, aspiring teachers of the Japanese language, librarians, and curators. The library, which is open to the public, holds books, newspapers, magazines, and multimedia on Japan, Japanese studies, and Nihongo. Come July, when the Philippines-Japan Friendship Month is celebrated, a packed line-up of activities and cultural events is scheduled in Manila as well as other provinces such as Baguio, Cebu, and Davao. There's a film festival, silent film features, concerts featuring Japanese imports, contemporary Japanese art exhibits, a touring mobile manga library, a dance festival, performance arts workshops facilitated by Japanese artists, and a J-Pop Anime singing competition. Membership is not required and you can get updates on upcoming events and activities through their website or their Facebook page.

PRICES: Japanese language courses, P2,000 (24 hours) to P7,000 (64 hours).

PAYMENT: Cash. ADDRESS: 12/L Pacific Star Bldg., Sen. Gil Puyat (Buendia) cor. Makati Aves., Makati T: 811-6155 to 58 OPEN: Mon–Fri, 9 a.m.–5 p.m.

Jeepney Tours

H A C W

SPECIALTY: Various cultural, heritage, shopping, and culinary tour packages in Manila aboard the iconic Philippine jeepney—a convenient way to show foreign guests around without having to worry about driving and the itinerary.

The jeepneys used in these tours are clean, air-conditioned, and custom-fitted with videoke equipment, can fit 20 passengers comfortably, and come with a cooler for drinks and a tour facilitator. Daytime tours within the city are the Intramuros Culture Heritage Tour, the Intramuros Golf Tour, and the Spa and Shopping Spree. The Intramuros Culture Heritage Tour includes a running tour of commercial complexes like SM Mall of Asia and Harbour Square within the CCP Complex, and visits to the Rizal Park, the Light and Sound Museum (life-sized light and sound diorama gallery in Intramuros on Philippine history—from pre-historic Philippines and Spanish colonization to conversion to Christianity and independence from the Americans), the San Agustin Church and Museum, Fort Santiago, Mananzan Handicrafts for souvenir shopping, and Barbara's for a buffet lunch. The tour lasts five hours. The Intramuros Golf Tour includes a running tour of commercial complexes and a game of golf at Club Intramuros, a relatively short course (par 66 with a length of 4,326 yards) made interesting by water hazards and out-of-bounds. It can be played in about two hours. Another golf tour is at the Bermuda-planted, all-weather, nine-hole Philippine Army Golf Course, also playable in two hours.

PRICES: Intramuros Heritage Tour, P2,500 a person (inclusive of tour facilitator pick-up and drop-off services at partner hotels, Light and Sound Museum entrance fee, buffet lunch, Fort Santiago entrance fee, tour of Intramuros, bottled water or soda). Golf Tour, P6,000 a person (inclusive of tour facilitator, pick up and drop off services at partner hotels, golf trainor, golf rental kit, and caddy).

PAYMENT: Cash. WEBSITE: jeepneytours.com EMAIL: info@jeepneytours.com (email reservations must be done at least days in advance) T: 638-6644, 994-6636.

Kaida Gallery

H A C W

SPECIALTY: Paintings, sculptures, graphic art, and installation pieces from upcoming talent, especially young local female artists.

A substantial amount of artworks shows a socio-political bent, depicting locally deep-seated issues such as women's struggles and poverty through acrylic on canvas, sculpted marble, or mixed media; other works are abstract and non-representational.

PRICES: Artwork prices vary, depending on the collection, but there are still paintings priced below P10,000.

PAYMENT: Cash, check. EMAIL: info@kaidagallery.com ADDRESS: 2/L GFO Bldg., 122 Kamuning Rd., Diliman, Quezon City T: 414-4777 M: 0928-505-7285 OPEN: Daily, 10 a.m.–8 p.m.

Kulay Diwa Gallery

H A C W

SPECIALTY: Extensive collection of contemporary art (performance, sculpture, conceptual, graffiti/street art, abstracts, drawing, painting, video-art, installation, mixed-media, digital) by upcoming and established artists from the Philippines and Southeast Asia.

PRICES: Highly variable, depending on collection and artist.

PAYMENT: Cash, check. WEBSITE: kulay-diwa.com EMAIL: bobbit@kulay-diwa.com ADDRESS: 25 Lopez Avenue, Lopez Village, Sucat, Parañaque T: 826-0574, 425-2647 OPEN: By appointment only.

Lopez Museum

H A C W

SPECIALTY: Ancient maps, books, newspapers and letters, as well as famous art works from renowned artists.

Founded almost 50 years ago and built from the personal acquisitions of post-World War II industrialist Eugenio Lopez, Sr., this pleasant museum located in the Ortigas Center business district is a wonderful way to spend a long lunch hour or a quiet Saturday. Tour the exhibits with a knowledgeable docent provided by the museum, who will discuss the highlights and answer all your questions. Spend a leisurely hour or so to see the highlights, and then come back again and spend even more time to learn the rich history of the Philippines while browsing through the library full of hand written letters from national heroes, original newspapers over 100 years old, rare books and antique maps. In all, the library houses some 16,000 Filipianiana titles by 12,000 authors including Antonio de Morga's Sucesos de las Islas Filipinas (with notes by Jose Rizal, published in 1890), as well as 93 letters by Rizal to his parents, siblings, and other relatives. Photographs from the early Spanish-American up to the Martial Law can also be found within their collection. Join a group for an interesting lecture by contemporary authors who share your interest in history to fully experience all that this museum has to offer. Semi-annual special exhibits make this a place you will want to visit more than once. The museum holds a small permanent exhibit by famed 19th century Filipino artists Juan Luna and Felix Resurreccion Hidalgo, along with locally excavated pottery dating from 14th and 15th century Asian trade routes. This may also be the perfect place to take a school group and spark their interest in learning more about Philippine history. Only paid parking is available nearby.

PRICES: Admittance (inclusive of library access), P100 (adults), P80 (college and high school students with I.D.), P60 (grade school students with I.D.).

PAYMENT: Cash. WEBSITE: lopezmuseum.org.ph, pezseum.blogspot.com
EMAIL: admin@lopez-museum.org ADDRESS: G/L Benpres Building, Exchange Rd. cor. Meralco Ave., Ortigas Center T: 631-2417 OPEN: Mon–Sat, 8 a.m.–5 pm.

Manila Contemporary

H A C W

SPECIALTY: Southeast Asian contemporary art.

Manila Contemporary focuses on crossing art influences to develop a wider collector base by exhibiting the works of noted Southeast Asian artists alongside local talent. Each month, these group exhibitions boast of a healthy mix of local and foreign artists. Not only is the local viewing public treated to a taste of regional artwork, local artists also have a chance to exhibit in other of Manila Contemporary owner's galleries around the region. While multiple exhibits can become a miasma of themes and media, there's more than enough proverbial "breathing space" to go around in this high-ceiling, 300 sqm minimalist cavern. Art openings are always well attended, with guests milling about, wine glass in hand.

PRICES: Prices for artworks vary depending on the dimension of the work and career of the artist. Small student works may begin at P12,000, while a young artist's 7'×9' work may start at P480,000.

PAYMENT: Cash, credit card. Installment plans can also be negotiated. WEBSITE: manilacontemporary.com EMAIL: manilacontemporary3@gmail.com ADDRESS: Whitespace 2314, Don Chino Roces Ave. Ext. (Pasong Tamo Ext.) T: 844-7328 OPEN: Tue–Sat, 11 a.m.–7p.m.; Sun, 11 a.m.–4 p.m.

Manuel Quezon Shrine

H A C W

SPECIALTY: Tribute shrine to former Philippine President Manuel L. Quezon, best known for establishing the Commonwealth government.

The tallest edifice in all of Quezon City, the shrine is located at the heart of an 27-hectare elliptical park, the surrounding road referred to as the Quezon City Circle. It houses not only relics, memorabilia, and personal effects of the former president but his remains as well, encased in a bronze casket.

PRICES: Free admission.

ADDRESS: Elliptical Rd., Quezon City T: 297-4420 OPEN: Daily, 8 a.m.–5 p.m.

Metropolitan Museum

H A C W

SPECIALTY: Pre-colonial heritage collections, local grand masters, and well-curated contemporary collections by artists here and abroad.

The Metropolitan Museum of Art is reputedly one of the most well-curated modern and contemporary museums in the city. Despite its prominence in the art circle, however, the museum has always prided itself with its "Art for All" advocacy, which it supports through frequent exhibit openings featuring diverse themes, traveling exhibits, interactive stations, and educational activities. Its permanent exhibit features the Philippine Central Bank's collection of 8th- to 13th-century classical Philippine goldwork (decorative items, ritual artifacts), revealing a prosperous pre-colonial Philippines. Equally impressive are the 8th- to 13th-century pre-colonial pottery (homeware, ritual aids, burial vessels); locally crafted religious images and icons; and paintings by Philippine grand masters Felix Hidalgo and Juan Luna. Its changing exhibits feature rich and diverse pieces by renowned artists from the country and abroad that nevertheless reflect Philippine history and society—from preserved antiquated ternos worn by ilustrado ladies during Spanish times to figurative works by Indian artists. Past events and activities include workshops on bag-making out of recycled materials, art therapy, and guided walking tours that pay homage to national artists. The museum has tour packages for groups of 50 and above. A guided tour of the Museum may also be arranged for groups of 50 and below. Call or fill out the online booking form to book group visits.

PRICES: Admission, P100.

PAYMENT: Cash. Cash. WEBSITE: metmuseum.ph EMAIL: info@metmuseum.ph ADDRESS: Bangko Sentral ng Pilipinas Complex, Roxas Blvd., Manila T: 521-1517, 536-1566, 523-0613 OPEN: Mon–Sat, 9 a.m.–6 p.m. The Gold and Pottery Exhibits (permanent) are open Mon–Fri until 4:30 p.m.

Museum of Filipino Culture

H A C W

SPECIALTY: Ilustrado lifestyle museum.

Museum of Filipino culture was the first ever lifestyle museum in the country, featuring traditional wear, tools, furniture, religious icons, and other artifacts typical in ilustrado (privileged class) homes during Spanish times. Nayong Pilipino's "Bahay Tisa" (chalk house) serves as the museum's backroom repository, housing very finely crafted local antiques.

PRICES: Free admission.

ADDRESS: Central Bank Mint Building, East Ave., Quezon City T: 922-2191 OPEN: Mon–Fri, 9 a.m.–4 p.m.

Museum Foundation

H A C W

SPECIALTY: Online bulletin board of major art/cultural activities and events.

The Museum Foundation of the Philippines, a membership and volunteer organization affiliated with the National Museum, aims to raise awareness and appreciation for art and culture through organizing cultural tours and activities, art workshops, and museum appreciation programs for kids, and mostly by posting updates and schedules of events, activities, workshops, and exhibit launches in major museums apart from the National Museum. The foundation has interesting in-house activities, too. One was a three-hour, air-conditioned Pasig River Cruise on a waterborne path through Manila, Makati, Mandaluyong, Pasig and Marikina, with merienda at Malacañang Park. Another was a metal sculpture workshop about creating art from junk material and useless spare parts. Check out the website or join the mailing list to keep tabs on upcoming activities, workshops, and events.

PRICES: In-house day tours start at P800 a person; workshops start at P2,500 (member) to P2,700 (non-member) a person.

PAYMENT: Usually cash, but variable, depending on establishment. WEBSITE: museumfoundationph.org EMAIL: inquiry@museumfoundationph.org ADDRESS: G/L Museum of the Filipino People, Finance Rd., Manila T: 404-2685, 722-9073 M: 0928-503-9392 OPEN: Mon–Fri, 9 a.m.–5 p.m.

National Museum

Ⓗ Ⓐ Ⓒ Ⓦ

SPECIALTY: The country's official repository of prized ethnographic, anthropological, and archaeological artifacts as well as art works from local grand mansters.

When speaking of the National Museum, one actually refers to two American colonial style buildings along Agrifina Circle in Rizal Park—the Museum of the Filipino People (former Finance Building) and the National Art Gallery (former Legislative Building).

The Museum of the Filipino People holds an astounding collection of anthropological and archeological artifacts, most notable of which are the recovered Spanish galleons like the San Diego (used to fight off Dutch pirates in 1600) and its precious Chinese porcelain cargo, excavated Ming Dynasty porcelain and antique jars from China, Cambodia, Viet Nam, and Siam, and astounding ethnographic relics such as the Neolitihic Manunggul burial jar depicted on the current 1,000-peso bill. The collection dates as far as 20,000 years back, its number of artifacts almost reaching a million.

To have an exhaustive experience of the exhibits, take any of the museum tours given by museum senior consultant and docent John Silva. His tours are filled with such engaging historical accounts and back stories behind the collections, and everything is delivered with eloquence and contagious passion, a far cry from the usual cordon tours with ushers who lifelessly narrate the museum's inventory from rote.

Across the road, the National Art Gallery houses Juan Luna's Spolarium—what the Mona Lisa is to the Louvre, or The Kiss to the Belvedere. The

13'x23' painting depicts dead, bloodied gladiators being dragged off the arena and blood-thirsty spectators awaiting the next skirmish; a woman is crouched, grieving over a corpse. The painting was an allegorical piece on Spanish cruelty to Filipinos, and it won first prize in Spain's Exposición Nacional de Bellas Artes in 1884. The rest of National Gallery of Art's space is allocated to the 3,000-piece collection spanning centuries of paintings and sculptures from the nation's most iconic names , as well as capsule exhibits scheduled throughout the year.

PRICES: Admission, P100 (Museum of the Filipino People), P70 (National Art Gallery), P150 (all-day pass to both). Admission is free on Sundays. Museum tours are available Wednesday to Saturday.

PAYMENT: Cash. WEBSITE: nationalmuseum.gov.ph, johnsilva.blogspot.com (National Museum tour guide) EMAIL: jsilva79@mac.com (National Museum tour guide) ADDRESS: Agrifina Circle, Rizal Park, Manila T: 527 0278 OPEN: Wed–Sun, 10 a.m.–4:30 p.m.

Nova Gallery

H A C W

SPECIALTY: Modern "socio-realist" works by both upcoming and established local talent.

PRICES: Free admission. Prices of paintings highly variable depending on collection and artist, but typically start at the mid 5-figure range.

PAYMENT: Cash, check. EMAIL: gallerynova@gmail.com ADDRESS: Warehouse 12 A La Fuerza Plaza Compound, 2241 Don Chino Roces Ave., Makati T: 392-7797 M: 0922-800-6927 OPEN: Tue–Sat, 11 a.m.–7 p.m.

Pablo Gallery

H A C W

SPECIALTY: Alternative art space for local contemporary artwork.

Legend: H=History/Heritage, A=Art C=Changing exhibits/events/activities, W=With workshops/classes

Indulgent of both experimental art and non-mainstream music, Pablo Gallery owners confess to being open to radical proposals. Heavy Hitterz, a collective of over 80 lowbrow and graffiti artists based in San Francisco, descended upon their walls and turned them into modern murals. For Valentine's, artist couples showcased collaborative artworks in Pablo Cubao. Pablo has also been a venue for album launchings, treating the denizens of Cubao X to a night of music and revelry. Bands such as the dance-punk inspired Pedicab, neo-soulful Chillitees, and indie rockers Taken by Cars have all added a dash of their own good vibrations into the space. On the second floor is NAPA—Not Another Play Area—a retail store run by the Pablo gallerists, showcasing novelty knick-knack designed by Manila's edgy graphic artists and costing north of P100. This year, Pablo Gallery opened another branch catering to mid-career and international artists. Located at the more upscale Fort Bonifacio, gallery owners Osie Tiangco and Yo Garcia let the second branch play elder brother to Pablo Cubao—it's toned down, slightly more serious, but still ready for a good time.

PRICES: Art pieces at the Cubao branch range from P300 to P5,000 for small works, while larger ones sell for P8,000 to P25,000 depending on the artist. Art pieces at the Fort Bonifacio branch start at P20,000.

PAYMENT: Cash, check. Term payments for large purchases may be arranged. WEBSITE: pablogalleries.com EMAIL: cubao@pablogalleries.com, fort@pablogalleries.com ADDRESS: Shop 7 Cubao Expo, Gen. Romulo Ave., Araneta Center, Cubao, Quezon City T: 440-8807 OPEN: Tue–Sat, 12 nn–8 p.m. ADDRESS 2: Unit C–11 South of Market Condominium, Fort Bonifacio Global City, Taguig T: 986-3887 OPEN: Tue–Sat, 2 p.m.–8 p.m.

Pateros Day Trip

H A C W

SPECIALTY: Multi-way *balut* (unhatched duck egg) and duck meat, alfombra slippers.

Next to its slick neighbor Taguig, Pateros may seem like the sticks. But it has its own unique draw. Going there is like a trip to the province without leaving Metro Manila. The name Pateros is compounded from "pato" (duck) and "sapatos" (shoes), the two items that comprise the municipality's main trade. Drop by Andoy's Best, makers of the popular bottled *balut* (unhatched duck egg) sold in supermarkets. Here you can buy *balut* cooked or raw. Then, head on to Dos Hermanas for duck. At this restaurant, you can have duck, duck's egg, and everything in between cooked in a variety of ways—fried or kaldereta (sautéed and simmered in a rich, tomato-based sauce). Servings here are good for two to three. Your last stop should be Hannakuchichi's for alfombra slippers, traditional ornate slippers with cushioned "velvet-carpeted" insoles which have been around since the 1940s. Past 3 p.m., *balut* vendors will be bringing out abnoy—abnormal *balut* whose embryo failed to form, but still good for all the cooking styles done on "normal" *balut*.

PRICES: Fresh *balut*, P96 a dozen; bottled *balut* in brine, afritada, or kaldereta flavors, P70 a bottle (there are two *baluts* in each bottle); fried itik (duckling) at Dos Hermanas, P190.

PAYMENT: Cash. ANDOY'S BEST ADDRESS: 11 M. Lozada, Brgy. Sto. Rosario, Pateros T: 640-7120 OPEN: Daily, 8 a.m. – 5 p.m.
DOS HERMANAS ADDRESS: B. Morcilla St., Brgy. Poblacion, Pateros T: 642-5840 OPEN: Daily, 8 a.m. – 1 a.m. HANNAKUCHICHI'S ADDRESS: 117 M. Almeda St., Pateros T: 642-3826 OPEN: Daily, 9 a.m. – 6 p.m.

Philippine Army Museum and Library

H A C W

SPECIALTY: Records, documentations, and artifacts that preserves stories about the Philippine army.

The Philippine Army Museum and Library (PAML), located southwest of the Philippine Army headquarters in Fort, is a replication of the old facility that used to be located at MacArthur Avenue corner Memorial Road. This relatively young museum houses a collection of antique World War II weapons, artillery, scorpion tanks, and various English and American armored vehicles that kids can climb, as well as captured ammunition and weapons of the New People's Army (NPA). With interactive multimedia features, the museum is a virtual time capsule of all things military.

PRICES: Admission, P5 (public), P2 (military personnel), free for retired military.

PAYMENT: Cash. ADDRESS: McArthur Drive, Fort Bonifacio, Makati T: 815-2899 OPEN: Mon–Fri, 8 a.m.–4 p.m. Open on weekends only for organized tours or by special arrangement.

Philippine Museum of Ethnology

H A C W

SPECIALTY: Artifacts from Philippine ethnic minorities.

One of Nayong Pilipino's museums, this one showcases cultural artifacts, ethnic wear, indigenous musical instruments, and traditional crafts that reflect the multiple cultures that have resulted from the Philippines' archipelagic nature. The museum also occasionally holds culturally themed workshops, such as how to play the Ifugao nose flute, or how to properly wrap yourself in a sarong as a T'boli tribeswoman would.

PRICES: Admission to Nayong Pilipino (inclusive of all museums and features inside), P30 (adults), P20 (children). Parking, P30.

PAYMENT: Cash. ADDRESS: Nayong Pilipino, NAIA Rd., Pasay T: 831-0128, 832-3760 to 63, 831-0303, 831-0328 to 29 OPEN: Daily, 8 a.m.–6 p.m.

Ramon Magsaysay Memorabilia

H A C W

SPECIALTY: Commemorative 300,000-piece collection featuring the private writings, photos, scrapbooks, books, pamphlets, art objects, tapes, and news clippings of former Philippine President Ramon Magsaysay, a well-loved statesman also most known as the "people's president."

PRICES: Free admission.

ADDRESS: Ramon Magsaysay Centre, Roxas Blvd., Manila T: 521-3166 loc. 139 OPEN: Mon – Fri, 8 a.m. – 12 nn, 1 p.m. – 5 p.m.

San Agustin Museum

H A C W

SPECIALTY: Spanish-era ecclesiastical art and architecture.

Found inside the San Agustin Church monastery, this museum houses Spanish colonial-era art and regalia featuring the history of the Agustinian friars and monastery in the Philippines, huge religious oil paintings, a crypt storing the remains of relevant historical figures, the room where Spanish forces surrendered to the Americans, and a 1600s choir loft hand-carved from molave.

PRICES: Admission, P100.

PAYMENT: Cash. ADDRESS: 2/L San Agustin Monastery, Gen. Luna cor. Real Sts., Intramuros, Manila T: 526-6794, 527-4060, 527-4060 to 61 OPEN: Daily, 9 a.m. – 12 nn, 1 p.m. – 5 p.m.

Shoe Museum

H A C W

SPECIALTY: Extensive shoe collection of prominent Philippine personalities.

The 10-year-old museum is internationally known for housing the most popular size-8.5 shoes in world history—those of legendary former Philippine First Lady Imelda Marcos. Imelda's shoes range from stilettos and knee-high boots to strappy flats and furry bedroom slippers, from couture labels such as Dior to local brands like Maro. However, you won't find among her 800 pairs those rumored diamond-encrusted and gold-plated heels that figure prominently in Imelda shoe lore. What the museum does have is a growing shoe collection from other equally prominent figures such as past Philippine Presidents Ferdinand Marcos, Fidel Ramos, Ramon Magsaysay, and Manuel Roxas, prima ballerina Liza Macuja-Elizalde, and the late Jaime Cardinal Sin. In its own glass shelf space alongside Imelda's shoe arsenal, are two pairs that were donned by the late President Cory Aquino, known most for her role in the 1986 downfall of the Marcos regime. Irony never looked as good.

PRICES: Free admission.

ADDRESS: J. P. Rizal St., Sta. Elena, Marikina T: 646-1634, 646-2360
OPEN: Mon–Fri, 10 a.m.–7 p.m.

Silverlens Lab

H A C W

SPECIALTY: Avant garde local art.

As the equally sleek but offbeat younger sister of museum-grade photography art space Silverlens Gallery, SLab ventures past photography to accommodate diverse modern art works. It has exhibited works by some of the country's edgiest young creatives, featuring diverse media—from abstract diptychs to video and performance pieces, from graphite drawings to sculptural art worn as clothing. SLab has two galleries: the main gallery for major exhibits and the cozier 20Square for smaller shows, projects, and consignments. New works are launched every two to three weeks, with artist talks given monthly. Email them to join their mailing list and keep tabs on SLab activities.

PRICES: Artist talks are usually free of charge. Exhibited artworks typically go for P15,000 and up.

PAYMENT: Cash, credit card, check. WEBSITE: slab.silverlensphoto.com EMAIL: manage@silverlensphoto.com ADDRESS: 2/L YMC Building 1, 2320 Don chino Roces Ave. Ext. (Pasong Tamo Ext.), Makati T: 816-0044 M: 0905-265-0873 OPEN: Mon–Fri, 10 a.m.–7 p.m.; Fri, 1 p.m.–6 p.m.

Tin-Aw Gallery

H A C W

SPECIALTY: Modern expressionist work.

Though Tin-aw manages a few multiawarded senior artists, it predominantly features upcoming artists whose works are decidedly fresh, young, idealistic, if not a bit raw, and rife with social commentary. Paintings depict parodies of iconographs; while delicate perfume bottles containing the stench of a polluted Pasig river become a social statement about commercial frivolity. Here, you will find neither still-life flowers nor geometric abstracts. Tin-aw's modern expressionist pieces are a breath of fresh air for those who need their art to say what it means.

PRICES: Prints (6"×6"), P5,000 and up; paintings, P12,000 and up.

PAYMENT: Cash, check, term payments for large purchases. WEBSITE: tin-aw.com, tinawartgallery.multiply.com EMAIL: info@tin-aw.com ADDRESS: UG/L Somerset Olympia Bldg., Makati Ave., Makati T: 892-7522 OPEN: Mon–Sat, 10 a.m.–6 p.m.

UST Museum

H A C W

SPECIALTY: Zoological and botanical specimens indigenous to the Philippines (some endangered, others extinct); Spanish-era ecclesiastical and liturgical art; and artifacts from different Philippine tribes.

The 1,500,000-piece collection, covering both exhibited items and those in storage, make UST's collection the largest in the Far East.

PRICES: Free admission.

ADDRESS: 2/L Main Bldg., University of Sto. Tomas, España, Manila T: 731-3101 loc. 269 or 327 OPEN: Mon, 8 a.m.–12 nn; Tue–Fri, 2 p.m.–5 p.m.

Whitebox Studio

H A C W

SPECIALTY: Modern art work (from geometric abstracts to the macabre) by young and upcoming local talent, painting workshops. Also sells art supplies.

PRICES: Medium-sized painting (15"x15") averages at P10,000.

PAYMENT: Cash. WEBSITE: whiteboxstudio.multiply.com EMAIL: whitebox_studio@yahoo.com ADDRESS: Stall 59 Romulo Ave., Araneta Center, Cubao, Quezon City T: 437-3839 OPEN: Mon–Sat, 2 p.m.–9 p.m.

Yuchengco Museum

H A C W

SPECIALTY: Filipino and Chinese antiques; classic and contemporary art.

The Yuchengco Museum initially housed the personal art collection of prominent ambassador and industrialist Alfonso T. Yuchengco. Today, its primary goal is to foster awareness and appreciation of Filipino–Chinese fine art. The museum's Masters Gallery is a shrine of works by three of the most revered names in local visual art: Juan Luna, Fernando Amorsolo, and Carlos "Botong" Francisco; while pieces in the Corporate Collection come from Yuchengco Group of Companies executive offices, mostly from renowned Filipino modernists and national artists. Yuchengco Museum's most regularly updated collections are the themed series of art works:

Sino-Filipino Expressions, which highlights creative expressions by notable Chinese Filipinos; Bridging Cultures, which brings in both contemporary and traditional art works and crafts from abroad; and Design as Art, Art as Design, which features items originally created with utilitarian purpose, but whose designs elevate them into art object. The museum also has training courses on curating, workshops on traditional Chinese brush painting, internship programs, etc.

PRICES: Admission, P100 (adults), P50 (students age 15 and up), P25 (kids below 15, senior citizens). Group discounts for 10 people and up given advanced booking. Parking, P40 for first 2 hours; valet service is free.

PAYMENT: Cash. WEBSITE: yuchengcomuseum.org EMAIL: info@yuchengcomuseum.org ADDRESS: Courtyard of RCBC Plaza, Corner Ayala and Sen. Gil J. Puyat Aves. T: 889-1234, 887-5144 OPEN: Mon–Sat, 10 a.m.–6 p.m.; closed on holidays.

ACTS Dance and Fitness

Y U V W

SPECIALTY: Up to date street dance workshops

With classes in street dance, jazz funk, and break dance taught by practicing dancers, A Company of Three Strands (ACTS) dance workshops are worth the trip to EDSA. Geared more towards teenagers and young professionals, classes are taught by dancers who have come from competitive collegiate dance groups like Miriam College's Company of One and Ateneo de Manila's Company of Ateneo Dancers. Instructors also have affiliations with local dance groups such as Stylettos and Cross Effects. Unlike workshops that offer classes taught by middle-aged men and women predominantly geared towards health and fitness, ACTS workshops are meant for aspiring dance pros. Affiliated with other dance studios, the ACTS instructors are also able to teach in other venues around the metro. Classes in ballet, fitness, and martial arts are also offered for children and adults.

PRICES: Most street dance classes start at P3,500 for 12 sessions, while a special promo rate at P5,500 for 24 sessions is also available.

PAYMENT: Tuition payments may be made via cash or through Bank of the Philippine Islands (BPI) bank deposits. WEBSITE: actsworkshops.net EMAIL: ellaine@actsworkshops.net, jane@actsworkshops.net ADDRESS: Unit B Mezzanine Level G.A. Tower, 1 Boni EDSA T: 719–4062 M: 0917-7028277, 0922-8243762 OPEN: Mon–Sat, 8 a.m.–9 p.m.

Airdance Company

Y U V W

SPECIALTY: Innovative form of contemporary dance that incorporates aerial suspension into the choreography.

Developed in the 1960s, aerial dance or air dance is a modern type dance with influences from gymnastics and circus aerial routines. But as opposed to flying trapeze and other aerial acts in circuses, air dance is low flying, its choreography providing interaction between suspended and floor dancers.

Most of all, it still fundamentally looks like a dance, not an exhibition. Established in 2001 and staffed by a group of young professional dancers from different dance backgrounds, the company is the first to bring airdance to the country, offering both year-round and summer classes. To learn airdance, however, one must become a member of the company or go through screening since the airdance classes require prior dance experience and advanced training. But the company also has basic to intermediate classes on other contemporary dances like Jazz, Break dance, Street or Hip Hop, Ballroom, and Contemporary (also known locally as "interpretative dance"). You can start off with these and pursue airdance as you develop further as a dancer. Another interesting class is their kiddie program called Kids' Movement. Open to ages 5 to 10, it's an informal, exploratory class that uses some steps from ballet, some from hip hop, and some from jazz for movement, coordination, and creativity exercises like follow the leader, mirroring, and improvisation. Rather than developing technical dance skills, Kids' Movement is meant to be a fun way to teach kids how to be comfortable in dance and movement in general, express themselves confidently, follow instructions, and be a team player.

PRICES: Airdance, P300 a 3-hour class; other dances, P400 a 1.5-hour class.

PAYMENT: Cash. WEBSITE: airdance.com.ph EMAIL: airdance_ph@yahoo.com ADDRESS: 36E West Ave., Quezon City M: 0916-3566693 OPEN: Airdance classes, Mon–Fri, 3 p.m.–6 p.m.; other dances, usually twice a week, 6 p.m.–7:30 p.m. Call for schedule updates.

Ateneo Blue Repertory

Y U V W

SPECIALTY: High-quality amateur musical theater.

Described by noted theater critic Gibbs Cadiz of Philippine Daily Inquirer as "a campus theater group that's become known for harnessing the energy and enthusiasm of young people for musical theater," Ateneo Blue

Repertory has come a long way from the resurrected student organization back in 2001.These days, Ateneo Blue Repertory has become a source of young talent and a breeding ground for future professional theater actors. Get a glimpse of great talent and take in a little culture by catching their shows at inexpensive prices. By training students in the different demands of theater and working with established professionals like Chari Arespacochaga, Robbie Guevara, and Felix Rivera, young students from different schools (not just Ateneo) learn the passion and dedication it takes to stage a great musical play. Over the years, this student-run organization has staged musicals such as “Footloose,” “Sweet Charity,” Disney's “High School Musical,” and “The 25th Annual Putnam County Spelling Bee.” Lately, it has even ventured into more gritty themes such as forbidden love and homosexuality in “Bare,” a rock musical, which received the 2001 Los Angeles Ovation Awards for Best Musical and Best Original Score. As the organization approaches adulthood on its 17th year, theater lovers can only expect even better shows season after season.

PRICES: Tickets are start at P200 each. For updates on upcoming shows, auditions, and projects, sign up for their e-group on groups.yahoo.com/groups/bluerepnews.

PAYMENT: Cash. WEBSITE: groups.yahoo.com/groups/bluerepnews EMAIL: bluerepnews-owner@yahoogroups.com ADDRESS: Ateneo de Manila University, Katipunan Ave., Loyola Heights T: 426-6001 loc. 5050 OPEN: Mon–Fri, 9 a.m.–4:30 p.m.

Bateria Brigada

Y U V W

SPECIALTY: Bateria Brigada is a Filipino group of extremely talented musicians with a shared passion for Samba and Brazilian music. The group plays Samba, but they also draw from a lot of other music such as Hip-Hop, Drum n Bass, Reggae, 2Step and indigenous Filipino rhythms. You can get updates about their gigs online. Or better yet, drop by every Wednesday, 4:30 p.m., at U.P. sunken garden, where they hold free practices and you can learn Brazilian drum playing or simply jam with them. For more formal lessons, though, email or give them a call.

WEBSITE: bateriabrigada.multiply.com, Facebook. EMAIL: bateria_brigada@yahoo.com M: 0917-520-8674

Center for Pop

Y U V W

SPECIALTY: Extensive as well as short-course classes on contemporary ("pop") singing and stage performance with practicum "exams" a culminating recital for the full pop singing program (five levels); specialty workshops on belting, modulation, and techniques for reaching high notes for aspiring pros and videoke pop singing for hobbyists and amateurs. Center for Pop Music alumni include

PRICES: About P9,000 and up for the full pop singing program, 18 2-hour sessions.

PAYMENT: Cash. WEBSITE: centerforpopmusic.com EMAIL: info@centerforpopmusic.com, center4_pop@yahoo.com ADDRESS: 73 Ermin Garcia St., Cubao, Quezon City T: 727-5293, 414-7081, 415-8352 OPEN: Please call for schedule inquiries and the branch nearest you (has 25 branches nationwide).

Centra de Danza Flamenca

Y U V W

SPECIALTY: Children's and beginners' to advanced flamenco classes and Andaluzia Bellydance classes headed by Clara Ramona, a Filipina dancer, choreographer, and producer classically trained in the U.S. and Spain in dance, dance pedagogy, and choreography.

PRICES: One-time registration fee, P1,000. About P3,500 for 10 classes or P700 per class.

PAYMENT: Cash. WEBSITE: clara.group.ph EMAIL: info@clararamona.com ADDRESS: 5917 Algier St. (parallel to Rockwell Drive/Kalayaan Ave.), Poblacion, Makati T: 899-1346 M: 0915-434-5789 OPEN: Mon–Sat, 9 a.m.–5 p.m.

Cinema One Originals

Y U V W

SPECIALTY: Film fest showcasing five original independent Filipino film that have been awarded budgets to make their winning screenplay into a movie.

Submission of hard-copy screenplay entries start at the beginning of each year. Emailed, faxed, and soft-copy entries will not be considered. Entries may include character and story development, as well as proposed production timelines. Five finalists are chosen by a panel of judges and each one is awarded P1M to produce their film. Screenings of the finalists' films and award ceremonies take place by the last quarter of the year. Screenings are held at Robinsons Galleria and Robinsons Place Cinema One theaters.

PRICES: Standard movie ticket prices.

PAYMENT: Cash. ADDRESS: 8/L ELJ Communications Center, Lopez Drive, Quezon City, Mon–Fri, 9 a.m.–5 p.m. Submission deadline is usually on the last week of February.

Cinemanila/Machinima

Y U V W

SPECIALTY: Biggest international film festival with almost 100 independent and art house pieces from about 30 countries over a span of 10 days; edgy feature films and digital shorts from budding local talent.

Established in 1999, the Cinemanila International Film Festival strives to uplift local movie-watching culture and nurture young Filipino directors by featuring over 80 films comprised of independent movies from the

Philippines and other parts of Southeast Asia and the most recent international art-house offerings from alternative yet prestigious film festivals abroad like Cannes (France), Berlin (Germany), Rotterdam (Netherlands), Sundance (U.S.), Venice (Italy), Locarno (Switzerland), and Pusan (South Korea). Like most film festivals, the final night of screening features the festival's awardees for different categories like Best Short Film, Best Feature Film, Best Director, Best Actor, etc. Awards are also given to best Southeast Asian short and feature films and best Filipino digital films. A new component of the Cinemanila is the Cinemanila Machinima, coined from the term "machine-animation" or "machine-cinema." Machinima pieces are digital shorts and music videos are made from clips, avatars, maps, locations, and other elements of popular video games like Grand Theft Auto and World of Warcraft—basically, DIY animation. Awards for Machinima are also given during the Cinemanila Film Fest. The Cinemanila International Film Fest's new home is in Bonifacio Global City, with cinema screenings at Serendra, Market! Market!, Fully Booked U-View, and open fields installed with video walls during the film fest. Tickets are available at the Cinemanila office and screening venues. Call, email, or check website for updates on other ticketing outlets.

PRICES: Regular admission, P120, with 10%–20% discounted rates for students and senior citizens; premiere screenings, P200; screenings attended by Cinemanila guest of honor, P250; gold tickets, inclusive of 8 film screenings and attendance in event with Cinemanila gust of honor, P950. Cinemanila gusts of honor in the past have included screenwriter Paul Schrader (Taxi Driver) and director Quentin Tarantino (Pulp Fiction, Inglourious Basterds).

PAYMENT: Cash. WEBSITE: cinemanila.org, cinemanilamachinima.org
EMAIL: cinemanila@gmail.com, cinemanila.machinima@gmail.com
ADDRESS: Unit 4A, 4/F, ABBA Bldg., 5756 Kalayaan Ave., Pinagkaisahan, Makati T: 392-7935 OPEN: Mon–Fri, 9 a.m.–5 p.m. (Cinemanila office). Screenings usually start at noon.

Fundacion Centro Flamenco

Y U V W

SPECIALTY: Children's and beginners' to advanced flamenco classes given by clasically trained and professionally performing instructors, some of whom have been trained in Spain.

PRICES: About P3,500 for 8 classes.

PAYMENT: Cash. WEBSITE: centroflamencophil.com
EMAIL: contact@centroflamencophil.com ADDRESS: 5/L SJG Bldg., 8463 Rockwell Drive (Kalayaan Ave.) cor. Don Pedro St., Makati T: 359-8761 M: 0917-810-2063 OPEN: Mon – Sat, 9 a.m. – 5 p.m. Beginners' classes are usually in the afternoon.

Gantimpala Theater

Y U V W

SPECIALTY: Independent drama company specializing in classic Filipino plays, original Filipino plays, and translated foreign work; musical theater workshops for ages 13 and up.

The 32-year-old Gantimpala Theater Foundation (GTF) is an independent drama company housed inside Luneta Park's Open Air Auditorium. It is known for its annual production of four classic Filipino period plays: Ibong Adarna, Florante at Laura, Kanser (Noli Me Tangere), and El Filibusterismo. Apart from these, the company also does plays based on works of national artists for literature and theater as well as translated English classics such as Rome and Juliet, as well as musicals that feature original songs and scoring. GTF, a theater company that aims to nurture theater arts beyond Manila's cultured set, goes on provincial tours and holds free plays at the Luneta. Despite a conscious move to veer from more commercial ventures such as restaging Broadway or West End hits, GTF is a well respected institution, with nationally recognized industry heavyweights comprising the company's actors, playwrights, and directors. GTF's summer workshops integrate drama, music, and dance, and culminate with a recital usually held at the Open Air Auditorium.

PRICES: Summer workshop, P5,000 for 18 to 24 4-hour sessions.

PAYMENT: Cash. WEBSITE: gantimpalatheater.multiply.com EMAIL: gantimpalatheater@yahoo.com ADDRESS: Rehearsal Hall, Open Air Auditorium, Luneta Park, Roxas Blvd., Manila T: 528-0603, 536-5860 M: 0921-5286308 OPEN: Classes are usually MWF, 1 p.m. – 5 p.m.

Groove Dance Studio

Y U V W

SPECIALTY: Beginner and advanced classes and workshops on street dance, break dance, and a fusion of jazz and street styles taught and managed by seasoned choreographers and performers from the Philippine National HipHop Team, UP StreetDance Club, Manoeuvres, and the Philippine Street Dance Team which has joined street dance festivals around Asia.

PRICES: Classes are about P250 a session (1.5-hours); around P3,500 for unlimited attendance in 2 months' worth of summer dance workshops.

PAYMENT: Cash. WEBSITE: groovecentralstudio.multiply.com EMAIL: groovecentralstudio@yahoo.com ADDRESS: 4/L Manna II Bldg, V. Luna St., Quezon City T: 906-1330 M: 0927-876-1270

Hip Dance Studio

Y U V W

SPECIALTY: Beginners' and intermediate classes in hip-hop, bellydancing, jazz, ballroom, break dance, and flamenco taught by active dance professionals from performing groups like Manouvers (Gary V's official backup dancers) and Bodyworx.

PRICES: Typically P2,000 for 8 1-hr. sessions.

PAYMENT: Cash. EMAIL: johngym2006@yahoo.com ADDRESS: 19 Dao St., Project 3, Quezon City T: 435-5006, 911-0125 M: 0920-7829359, 0906-3507708. OPEN: Mon–Fri, classes start 5 p.m. and up; Sat/Sun, classes start 10 a.m. and up. Please call for details on schedules.

House of Dance

Y U V W

SPECIALTY: Beginners' and intermediate classes in ballet, jazz, street dance, tap dance, contemporary dance, break dance for kids and adults; international cultural dances like the hula, flamenco, Tahitian, and belly dancing for teens, adults, and those vying for certification as dance instructors. Students have the opportunity to participate in yearend recitals.

A by-invitation dance company, House of Dance is one of the Philippine affiliates of the International Dance Organization. As such, they occasionally fly in guest dance instructors for collaborative concerts and specialty workshops in both modern and cultural dances from Russia, Taiwan, Korea, and Japan.

PRICES: Typically P2,200 for 12 1.5-hour sessions.

PAYMENT: Cash. WEBSITE: houseofdance.ph EMAIL: info@houseofdance.ph, mirellaclarete@houseofdance.ph ADDRESS: #11 V. Salumbides St., BF Homes, Quezon City T: 931-6276 M: 0926-7174004, 0921-8439046 OPEN: Mon–Fri, 9 a.m.–5 p.m. Dance classes, usually one to two hours, are on MWF and S, 5 p.m. and up. Saturday classes start at 10 a.m. Please call for schedule details.

New Voice Company

Y U V W

SPECIALTY: Acting and theater workshops for both beginners and those pursuing a profession in theater; modern pieces like musicals, straight plays, parodies, comedies, and satires with contemporary social and gender-issue themes.

New Voice Company (NVC) was founded in 1994 by theater vet Monique Wilson who, apart from performing lead roles in West End, is also an alumna of the London Academy of Music and Dramatic Arts and a teacher at London's Royal Academy of Dramatic Arts. NVC has gained recognition both here and the rest of Asia for mounting socially and politically charged productions that, despite a modern Western feel and treatment, deal with universal and sometimes even risqué topics like women's rights, sexuality, gender inequality, sexual harassment, homosexuality, and poverty, oppression and violence against women. Among past productions are fairytale satire Into the Woods, dark romantic dramedy and musical Aspects of Love, and episodic off-Broadway piece Vagina Monologues. Those with theater experience or looking to pursue a profession in theater can look into NVC's Actor's Studio which offers year-long professional training on theater performance, direction, production, technical management, and experimental theater. For kids and aspirants, NVC has annual summer workshops on musical theater and acting and improvisation using the Stanislavski–Uta Hagen devised approach (a.k.a. Method acting, practitioners of which include critically acclaimed actors like Jennifer Jason Leigh, James Dean, Charlize Theron, Robert de Niro, Marilyn Monroe, Al Pacino, Ellen Burstyn, and Daniel Day Lewis). This includes exercises and devices like sense memory, physical and psychological actions, animal work, and character development, as well as theater games like designed to develop trust in your fellow actor, confidence, concentration, creativity, and imagination. All workshop teachers are practicing professionals with formal theater training. Workshops take place at the NVC Actor's Studio; shows and productions are usually staged at the RCBC Plaza Theater in Makati. Call, email, or check the website for show schedules.

PRICES: P700 (balcony) to P1,200 and up (orchestra center).

PAYMENT: Cash. WEBSITE: newvoicecompany.com EMAIL: nvc@pldtdsl.net ADDRESS: NVC Actor's Studio, 8020 Tanguile St., San Antonio Village, Makati T: 896-5497, 896-6695, 899-0630. Tickets are also available at all Ticketworld outlets; T: 891-9999; ticketworld.com.ph

---

Pelicola.TV

Y U V W

SPECIALTY: Pinoy Internet TV with a strong indie bent.

Think of YouTube, then take out the open-source video sharing component (i.e., anyone can post a video). Next, take out any show you've seen on regular TV and the brand of commercial appeal and pop sensibility present in noontime variety shows and local primetime programing. Add HD-captured all-original local work spanning music videos, live studio sessions, short films, and lifestyle shows, then factor in downloadability. Do the math. That's Pelicola.TV

ADMISSION/PRICES: No subscription or download fees. All you have to do is register. WEBSITE: pelicola.tv

EMAIL: contact@pelicola.tv T: 638-5487 M: 0917-620-5103

PETA

Y U V W

SPECIALTY: Socially provocative Filipino productions; theater arts summer workshops.

PETA—Philippine Educational Theater Association has long been reputed to be the serious Filipino artiste's theater group with its socially provocative productions and highly literary material. And though the company has produced lighter fare as of late, the nature of its workshops remain faithful to PETA's gravitas. The company's workshops run the entire spectrum from basic theater for kids and teens to theater as a medium for advocacy. They also provide training in all aspects of theater production, such as playwriting, directing, production design, and lighting. Basic theater workshops for kids ages 5 to 12 are designed to develop a child's experience with music, movement and dance, puppetry, storytelling, story and character interpretation, drama improvisation, poetry, and writing with the use of games and activities that stimulate imagination and self-confidence. Workshops for teens offer further fine-tuning of emotional internalization, the intricacies of modern and traditional theater, as well as stage production. Courses for college-aged teens and adults start branching off to different specializations: Creative Musical Theater, Creative Dance Theater, Production Design, Playwriting, Directing, and Lighting. Advanced courses with a more pedagogical approach such as Theater for Advocacy, Theater and Therapy, and Gender Sensitivity are designed for those who foresee a career in theater. The workshops can take anywhere from 5 to 19 sessions and are usually scheduled in the evenings or weekends from April to May and from October to November. Children's and teens' courses typically last four hours a session; weekend sessions can take the entire day for specialized teen's courses such as stage production. Participants graduate with a recital at the end of each course.

PRICES: Basic theater summer courses (12–20 sessions) for kids and teens range from P6,000 to P7,500.

PAYMENT: Cash, check. WEBSITE: petatheater.com EMAIL: mpr@petatheater.com, peta@petatheater.com ADDRESS: 5 Eymard Drive, Brgy. Kristong Hari, New Manila, Quezon City T: 725-6244, 410-1418, 410-0821; F: 722-6911, 410-0821 M: 0917-5138698 OPEN: Call or email for confirmation of workshop schedules.

Philippine Opera Center Ⓨ Ⓤ Ⓥ Ⓦ

SPECIALTY: The only opera company in the country with regular opera productions; opera vocal training for both amateurs and practicing classical singers.

Founded in 1999 and managed by professional classical singers who perform here and abroad, the Philippine Opera Company (POC) is the only opera company in the country with regular opera productions. Past shows have included "lighter" fare such as "Tribute to Pavarotti"as well as full-length productions such as Puccini's La Boheme. POC has a performing arts school that offers classes on vocal techniques not just for opera and classical singing but also for other genres such as pop, music theater, jazz, and standards; creative but relaxed music and movement classes for toddlers to tweens; masterclass programs by veteran opera singers for those with classical singing backgrounds; and classical programs for piano, guitar, and violin playing. Students get to participate in a culminating recital at the end of a program.

PRICES: Voice lessons, P2,650 (class of 4) to P3,650 (1-on-1) for 5 1-hour sessions; music instrument lessons, P3,650 for 5 1-hour sessions; music and movement for kids to teens, P5,700 for 5 2-hour sessions.

PAYMENT: Cash. WEBSITE: philippineoperacompany.com EMAIL: phil_opera_co@yahoo.com ADDRESS: 15 Garcia Villa St., San Lorenzo Village, Makati T: 892-8786 OPEN: Call, email, or check out the website not just for class schedules but also for updates on their upcoming shows.

Repertory Philippines

Y U V W

SPECIALTY: Professionally produced English plays, Broadway and West End hit musicals, Shakespearean works, and dramas every weekend from an institution in Philippine theater. Also offers extensive summer theater and musical workshops.

TICKET PRICES: P300–700 for season plays; P900–1,350 for a subscription good for three season plays; P250–350 for off-season plays.

PAYMENT: Cash, credit card accepted. WEBSITE: For tickets and Ticket World outlets: ticketworld.com.ph Repertory Philippines: repertory.ph. EMAIL: info@repertory-philippines.com ADDRESS: C2-A Bldg. C, Karrivin Plaza, 2316 Pasong Tamo Extension, Makati T: 887-0710, Onstage, (for ticket and show inquiries) OPEN: Plays usually run Mon–Fri, 10:30 a.m., 1:30 p.m., and 4:30 p.m. (sometimes with additional matinees on the weekend) at OnStage, 2/L Greenbelt 1, Ayala Center, Makati.

Tanghalang Pilipino

Y U V W

SPECIALTY: Socially provocative, original Filipino plays; acting workshops on creative dramatics and musical theater for children and teens, workshops on performance techniques and stage production management for ages 18 and up.

Tanghalang Pilipino is the resident drama company of the Cultural Center of the Philippines (CCP), and specializes in producing socially relevant work mostly through original Filipino plays and translated foreign work. It's children's and teen's workshops use games, storytelling techniques, movement, music, writing, and masks forms of expression. Teen theater workshops also offer script analysis and voice for theater apart from acting. Students stage a recital at the end of the workshop at no less than the Cultural Center of the Philippines, and enjoy the opportunity to be invited to audition or perform in the regular season of Tanghalang Pilipino. The workshop recitals and Tanghalang Pilipino plays, usually attended by talent scouts and industry experts, are a good jump-off point for those looking to pursue theater professionally.

PRICES: Around P5,500 and up for 16 half-day sessions.

PAYMENT: Cash. WEBSITE: You can learn more about Tanghalang Pilipino from the CCP website culturalcenter.gov.ph, sub-menu Programs–Resident Companies. EMAIL: ccptanghalan@yahoo.com ADDRESS: Tanghalang Huseng Batute (Studio Theater), Cultural Center of the Philippines, Roxas Blvd., Pasay T: 832-1125 loc. 1620 and 1621, 832-3661.

Trumpets

Y U V W

SPECIALTY: Professionally mounted family-oriented musicals and extensive vocal and theater performance training programs by Asia's first professional gospel theater group

Trumpets has gained local renown for its energetic and full-production musicals like The Little Mermaid, The Lion, The Witch, and the Wardrobe, and Joseph the Dreamer. It manages to feature works that are fun, funky, and family-friendly without going saccharine (The Little Mermaid, for instance, eschewed Disney's version for the original Hans Christian Andersen story—not as trite a happy ending, but uplifting nonetheless). Apart from its plays, the company has also become known for a comprehensive range of workshops for children, beginners, hobbyists, and aspiring theater pros. There are year-round courses on acting, musical theater, singing, and street dancing for ages 4 and up; and courses designed especially for adults such as modeling, public speaking and hosting, and Destress Express, a fun videoke singing course with integrated voice lessons for grown-ups who just need some creative outlet after work. Year-round training programs usually run thrice a week, with a culminating recital. Call, email, or check out the website to get updates on course schedules and details on any of their upcoming plays.

PRICES: Rates start at P4,500 for 10 1-hour sessions.

PAYMENT: Cash. WEBSITE: trumpetsplayshop.com EMAIL: playshoppers@gmail.com ADDRESS: 5/L Shangri-la Plaza Mall, Shaw Blvd. cor. EDSA, Mandaluyong T: 636-2842, 635-4478, 631-7252.

U.P. Music Summer Program

Y U V W

SPECIALTY: Widest range of musical instrument classes

The UP College of Music is reputed as one of the best music conservatories in the country, and attendant to that is an extensive teaching staff with diverse musical expertise. Future guitarists, pianists, sax players, and cellists are made and bred here—as are those of more exotic musical persuasions who aspire to learn the Filipino kulintang, the Japanese koto, or even the Indonesian angklung and gamelan.

PRICES: Individual lessons start at P5,490 for 14 half-hour classes; cluster classes with 4 students start at P5,490 for 14 1-hour classes; ensemble classes with 5 to 6 students start at P4,650 for 14 1-hour classes.

PAYMENT: Cash. WEBSITE: upd.edu.ph/music T: 981-8500 loc. 2628, 926-0024 OPEN: Call for confirmation of class schedules or inquiries regarding availability of programs outside of summer.

U.P. Madrigal Summer Program

Y U V W

SPECIALTY: One-on-one classical voice instruction on vocalization, proper singing techniques, and repertoire interpretation by alumni of the U.P. Madrigal Singers, a multi-awarded choir both here and abroad that was established by the University of the Philippines. Though workshops mostly take place during summer, you may call to inquire about other individual training arrangements and schedules.

PRICES: P6,000 for 12 to 16 sessions, 45 minutes a session.

PAYMENT: Cash. WEBSITE: philippinemadrigalsingers.com, upms.multiply.com EMAIL: artsinthecity.info@gmail.com, info@philippinemadrigalsingers.com, upms2000@yahoo.com ADDRESS: College of Music, University of the Philippines, Diliman, Quezon City M: 0915-510-0049.

AICA

U B V

SPECIALTY: Culinary programs and diploma courses for all levels (from weekend kitchen warrior to aspiring professional chef).

Put up by accomplished chefs returning from the U.S., Europe, the Middle East, and Australia, AICA— Academy for International Culinary Arts—offers a wide range of training programs, from recreational culinary courses like Fundamentals of Professional Cooking for serious enthusiasts and summer cooking workshops for kids, to diploma programs for those contemplating a career in the food business. For the professional and diploma courses, AICA boasts a 14:1 student-teacher ratio in their classrooms and 100% hands-on training in commercial-grade kitchen facilities. Each diploma course, typically completed between 3 and 12 months, also includes restaurant simulation and immersion programs. Other specialty training programs include food styling, bartending and cocktail mixing, front of house service, catering, and specialty baking and pastry making.

PRICES: Diploma courses, P90,000–235,000.

PAYMENT: Cash, post-dated check. WEBSITE: aicaculinary.com EMAIL: info@aicaculinary.com ADDRESS: Suite 207 Skyway Twin Towers, 351 Capt. Henry Javier St., Pasig T: 672-2271.

Brainfood Workshops

U B V

SPECIALTY: Broad range of communication workshops and seminars on basic communication skills, speech writing and public speaking, visual literacy, training for trainers, fiction writing, book and magazine illustration, comic book writing and illustration.

The workshops and seminars are given in modules, and the modules are customized based on the target students' needs. The major themes are Basic Communication Skills (written and oral communication in English;

writing memos, reports, and resumes; report preparation delivery), Speech Writing and Public Speaking. Designed (speech writing, speech delivery, public speaking, presentation skills, basic office communication, basic customer communication), Training the Trainers (how to effectively present and conduct training for your own in-house teams), Visual Literacy (study of symbols, aesthetics, communicating through design), Fiction Writing (play writing, short story writing, horror, humor, science fiction, fantasy), Book and Magazine Illustration (plus portfolio building and ability to critique works), Comic Book Writing and Illustration (idea generation, plotting, script writing, penciling, inking, digital coloring, lettering, design). Venues and schedules are highly variable, so email or check out website for updates and details. .

PRICES: Typically P500–P1,000 per 3-hour to half-day workshop.

PAYMENT: Cash only. WEBSITE: munimunistories.com EMAIL: brainfood@gmail.com

---

CCA Kitchen

U B V

SPECIALTY: Short courses such as Cuisines of the World, Entertaining at Home, Healthy cooking, Wine Appreciation, Food and Wine Pairing and Baking Classes; and Professional Continuing Education courses like Restaurant Tours, Chocolate Course, and Master Chef Series.

Apart from an extensive program of various culinary courses are food-related workshops on food photography, food styling, and food writing. Hard-to-find culinary tools and ingredients, kits for kids, and kitchen apparel like chef's jackets and aprons and rare cookbooks are available at the school's Culinary Store.

PRICES: Two-year culinary diploma degree, P250,000 and up per year. Short recreational culinary courses for non-professionals, P7,800 and up for 5 half-day sessions.

PAYMENT: Cash, credit card. WEBSITE: cca-manila.com EMAIL: cca_kitchen@cca-manila.com ADDRESS: 3/L Eastwood Mall, Eastwood City, E. Rodriguez, Jr. Ave., Bagumbayan, Quezon City T: 470-3500 KATIPUNAN MAIN CAMPUS EMAIL: marketing@cca-manila.com ADDRESS: 287 Katipunan Ave. Loyola Heights, Quezon City T: 994-2520/30/40, 426-4840 to 41.

Chinese Culinary Arts Center

U B V

SPECIALTY: Culinary workshops on authentic Chinese food cooking and preparation by Hong Kong-based Cantonese executive chef who teaches in Chinese (translated into English by his wife).

RATES/PRICES: P1,000–1,500 per class.

PAYMENT: Cash. EMAIL: chineseculinary@ymail.com ADDRESS: 2130 M. H. Del Pilar St., Malate, Manila T: 525-2720, 530-2053.

Designed By Words

U B V

SPECIALTY: Various workshops such as Feature Writing, Writing About Art, Writing Better Descriptions, and Travel Writing.

The Designed by Words Writers Workshop was conceived with the beginning writers in mind. We are a small group of writers and editors who love writing, literature and reading and aim to help others appreciate and practice all three. We are full time writers and part-time teachers. Foremost, we offer recreational writing classes only—which means, you take the class as a hobby the way you enroll yourself in a yoga, flower arranging or cupcake-making class. Classes usually run as a one half-day session or two sessions/meetings. They also have themed creative writing classes and special courses, depending on availability of the course materials and lecturers. Our students should be 21 years old and older since we offer adult education classes. We are geared towards people who are interested to write but did not take up or did not have access to writing/journalism courses way back in college. So young professionals, mid-career, retirees, teachers, homemakers and the like are very much welcome to attend. Workshop venues are variable, so check out the website for schedule and venue updates. Also on the website are news about mini-writing contests, writing prompts, call for submissions to their blog, alumni discounts and free classes, book launches, writing tips, and more.

PRICES: Half-day workshop, P900–P1,500. Early bird discount of 10% for classes with two sessions.

PAYMENT: Bank deposit. They do not accept payments on the day of the class. WEBSITE: designedbywords.wordpress.com EMAIL: dbw .workshops@gmail.com

---

Dialogues @ Starbucks

Ⓤ Ⓑ Ⓥ

SPECIALTY: Organized open discussions and small performances—basically the art of the themed pagtatambay (hanging out).

Starbucks manages to put a cultural twist to their frothy frap landscape with these hour-long early-evening open discussions about a wide range of topics, from living with HIV in the Philippines to desserts, from online businesses to art and doodling. These informal talks usually have a guest speaker considered to be, if not an expert, then either a practitioner or someone with first-hand experience with regard to the topic of the day. Dialogues are not all talk, though. Jamming sessions have taken place, from freestyle percussion with Paul Zialcita to Chopin on live violin by Berlin-schooled Macky Chua. Whether you're there to listen, talk, or do both, the laid-back vibe at Dialogues are very much like hanging out at the home of your *barkada*. Dialogues take place in various Starbucks branches. Email or check out their Facebook page for updates on branch location, topics, and schedules.

PRICES: Admission is free, and you're not required to buy coffee.

WEBSITE: Look for Dialogues @ Starbucks on Facebook. EMAIL: csr@rustancoffee.ph OPEN: The talks usually start at 6:30p.m.

Enderun Extension

U B V

SPECIALTY: Hands-on culinary short courses and seminars on basic to more complex food handling and preparation, wine appreciation, food styling and photography, and baking and professional pastry making.

A subsidiary of Enderun Colleges, Enderun Extension offers supplemental and auxiliary courses to the college's bachelor's degree program of international hospitality management, business administration, and entrepreneurship course. Foodies and weekend kitchen warriors can choose from several of Enderun Extension's short courses such as Culinary Foundation, Pastry and Baking, Food Styling and Photography, and specialized one-day workshops on culinary niches (cupcakes, dimsum, plating, wine appreciation, etc.).

Culinary Foundation is for those who have a more than rudimentary knowledge of food and the kitchen. It's designed to provide you with the skills and knowledge necessary to becoming a chef, whether recreational or professional. Culinary Foundation comes in two certificate short courses. There are five sessions for each course, and each session is comprised of an hour of lecture, two hours demonstration, and three hours of hands-on application.

The first Culinary Foundation course teaches you how to handle, prepare, select, process, and store a variety of ingredients—from vegetables, grains, and poultry to meat, fish, and seafood. By the end of the course you'll have learned knife skills for proper deboning, cutting, and shelling and a host of culinary terminologies and theories all put to practical application with kitchen work and standard international recipes. The second course takes off from the first and goes deeper into cooking. Here one learns how to make different kinds of stocks and sauces, how and when to use various dry-heat cooking methods (roasting, grilling, baking, pot roasting, and gratinate) as well as wet cooking methods (pot roasting, boiling, simmering, poaching, steaming, blanching, glazing, stewing, braising). This program is more hands-on intensive and each session ends with doing several recipes.

The Pastry and Baking program also has a basic and an advanced course, each with five sessions. The basic course familiarizes you with baking ingredients, preparation, implements, and equipment. Each session ends with hands-on exercises through recipes of biscuits and cookies, custards, cream pastries, pies, tarts, and cakes. The advanced course delves into the more complex world of baking bread, "professionalized" desserts like petit fours (those miniature confections you find in hotel dessert trays and carts), and professional dessert plating.

The three-day Food Styling & Photography workshop has renowned industry experts like TV commercial food stylists, food print ad photographers, and food TV commercial directors at the program's helm. The course familiarizes you with commercial food photography and current trends in both editorial and advertising media. Held in a studio with camera and lights, the workshop teaches you techniques used by pros when it comes to plating, composition, and food-friendly angles and lighting. By the end of the course, you'll learn the secrets to producing photogenic roasted meat and poultry, fluffy creams and soups, multilayered burgers, and steaming hot as well as chilled beverages.

One-day seminars, lasting from four to six hours, delve into specialized topics like dimsum-making, food plating, and wine appreciation.

All programs are held in Enderun Extension's Ortigas campus, whose interiors look like that of a hotel, where classrooms have wireless Internet connection and kitchen labs are installed with live audio and visual feed for better communication of instructions by the chef instructors to the students.

PRICES: Certificate courses, which take from three to five days of lecture, demo, and hands-on application, average from P18,500–P25,000; one-day seminars, P1,500–P3,600.

PAYMENT: Cash, checks. WEBSITE: www.enderunextension.com EMAIL: extensioncourses@enderuncolleges.com ADDRESS: 2/L Wynsum Corporate Plaza, 22 F. Ortigas Jr. Rd., Ortigas Center, Pasig T: 638-5555.

FPPF Photography Workshop

U B V

SPECIALTY: Basic to advanced photography workshops.

The FPPF—Federation OF Philippine Photographers Foundation—also holds regular monthly workshops, with over 2,000 photographers graduated since 1993 (many of whom have turned pro and won in national and international contests). The FPPF workshops are ideal for serious amateurs, would-be professional photographers, P.R./advertising/publication staff, hobbyists and home snapshooters.

The FPPF also holds advanced and specialty photography workshops such as Digital Darkroom, Wedding Photography Workshop, International Cruise Ship Photography, Large Format Black and White Photography, Lightroom for Photographers, and Studio Lighting Fundamentals.

On request, the FPPF occasionally holds photo workshops for employees of private and public institutions. Workshops may be designed to the specific needs of an organization, such as police work, publication work, company documentation, etc. The FPPF also organizes orientations and training sessions for out-of-school youth, senior citizens, barangay vocational programs, and staff training. These activities may include photo exhibitions and audio-visual presentations.

PRICES: Basic photography workshops, P3,500 and up for 8 sessions.

PAYMENT: Cash. WEBSITE: photoworldmanila.com ADDRESS: 302-Annex, FEMII Bldg., Aduana St., Intramuros, Manila T: 524-7576

Garage, The

U B V

SPECIALTY: Hands-on multimedia workshops on web design, animation, graphic design, digital photography, and digital film making and hands-on technology training on the use of a variety of image editors, video editors, animation software, and graphic design software (Adobe After Effects, Adobe Photoshop, Flash, Premiere, Dreamweaver).

Housing two training rooms and a editing suites for students' use, The Garage, the creative technologies training arm of the Jesuit Communications Center, was set up primarily to provide non-government organization employees with modern media skills and tools at reasonable fees—but workshops and classes are open to all. The teaching staff are comprised of industry experts who have received training in prestigious schools abroad such as the New York Film Academy and practitioners who are actively thriving in their respective fields (e.g., Flash animators, music video directors, art directors of major design firms). Here, though some sessions do take place in classrooms, a more hands-on approach is used and each student is given the requisite equipment (editing suite for film students, computer/laptop for graphic design students, in-house studio and lights for photography students, etc.).

Weekday classes are usually held after office hours, like 7p.m.–10p.m. Call or email for confirmation of schedule

PRICES: Workshops and short courses, P4,000–P6,000 for an average of 6 nonconsecutive days, about 3 hours a day.

PAYMENT: Cash, check. WEBSITE: jescom.ph/garage EMAIL: garage@jescom.ph, garagejct@yahoo.com ADDRESS: Seminary Drive cor. Arrupe Rd., Ateneo De Manila University, Loyola Heights, Quezon City T: 426-5971 to 72 loc. 125

ISCAHM

U B V

SPECIALTY: Extensive diploma programs for culinary arts and hotel management, as well as specialty short courses on continental and Asian cooking, desserts, baking, and pastry making.

Owned and run by professionals in the hotel and restaurant management industry, ISCAHM— International School for Culinary Arts and Hotel Management—boasts a professionals program that produces chefs equipped with skills and knowledge needed beyond the kitchen through classroom and hands-on modules. They award internships to senior students at the prominent French fine-dining restaurant Aubergine, where the students work alongside veteran executive chefs and an experienced kitchen crew as their practicum. If the food at the much lauded restaurant is any indication of what goes on in ISCAHM classes, then the teachers at this culinary institute must be doing something right.

For kitchen warriors who aren't pursuing careers as chef but do aspire to learn more than the usual, there are a couple of interesting specialty courses: Flavors of Asia (three-month course covering Indonesian, Malaysian, Singaporean, Thai, Japanese, Chinese, Vietnamese, Korean, Indian, Cambodian, Persian, Lebanese, and Greek cuisine, including an comprehensive introduction to the herbs and spices prominent in each); Pralines (three-session-hands-on course on gourmet chocolate presentation, students learn to make 15 kinds of pralines, from pralines in truffle shells to hand-rolled pipe pralines). Basic workshops also cover the fundamentals of culinary arts, baking, and pastry making.

PRICES: One-year diploma courses, P300,000 and up for the year; 3-month short courses, P25,000 and up.

PAYMENT: Cash, check. WEBSITE: iscahm.com EMAIL: sales@iscahm.com ADDRESS: 4/L FBR Bldg, Katipunan Ave., Quezon City T: 926-8888, 920-1481

Jo Avila Photography Workshop

U B V

SPECIALTY: Photography workshops on basic theories and principles, composition techniques, basic studio lighting and flash photography, basic photoshop, basic color management, guerilla shooting techniques, and basic to advanced food styling and food photography. Jo Avila has an active professional practice, with extensive experience doing print work and events. Students can use analog SLR cameras for the basic classes. Only digital SLR cameras can be used for advanced classes.

PRICES: Workshop modules, P4,000–6,000. Workshops usually take 5 sessions and include homework. There are special rates for crash-course classes, though, that compress all the workshop components into two whole-day sessions.

PAYMENT: Cash, bank deposit. WEBSITE: web.mac.com/misterkodaker EMAIL: pinakamagalingako@gmail.com ADDRESS: Unit 114, Gold Bldg., 15 Annapolis St., Greenhills, San Juan M: 0917-530-5133.

Komikon

U B V

SPECIALTY: Annual Philippine Komiks Convention and local comics awards, contests, and activities.

Philippine Komiks Convention (Komikon) is an annual event that gathers comic book artists, publishers, and enthusiasts in the country. Since its founding, it has always been held at the Bahay ng Alumni in UP Diliman. The convention aims to promote the work of Filipino komiks artists and raise appreciation for the art of comics in general. In addition to guest speakers, exhibits and art contests, the convention features various sponsor booths selling comics (local and foreign), comic-related merchandise, and original artwork. There is also the "Indie Tiangge," where independent or amateur comic artists can sell their own self-printed comics and merchandise.

PRICES: Comics sold during the Komikon are variably priced, but entrance fee is typically P50–P80.

PAYMENT: Cash. WEBSITE: komikon.org EMAIL: komikon@gmail.com ADDRESS: There are two main venues for the convention: UP Bahay ng Alumni, UP Diliman, Quezon City; and Megatrade Hall, 5th Level, Bldg. B, SM Megamall, Mandaluyong. Email or check website for venue and schedule updates.

Learning List

U B V

SPECIALTY: An online bulletin board of current and upcoming workshops and seminars, covering a tremendous range of topics and themes: Accessories Animation, Art, Arts and Crafts, Blogging, Business Seminars, Cartoons Seminar, Comics Seminar and workshops, corporate workshops, Feng Shui Seminar, marketing Workshop, Photography Workshop, publishing Seminars, public Speaking Workshops, speech Workshops, Stocks Workshops, storytelling, stress Management Workshops, Time Management Workshops, Web Development Seminars, Wine appreciation Workshops, Writing Workshops.

PRICES: Highly variable depending on workshops and workshop organizer.

PAYMENT: Variable depending on workshop organizer, but usually cash and bank deposit. WEBSITE: learninglist.blogspot.com

---

Mad Dog Motorcycle Club

U B V

SPECIALTY: Club for Harley Davidson riders, large bore cruisers, and road hog weekend warriors.

You can easily distinguish an MDMC convoy from other bike clubs because of the Harleys, the leather jackets, and a substantial portion of mestizos among the riders. There's just a palpable sense of gravitas and seniority you don't find in other bike clubs. But far from their stereotyped counterparts on American TV, the Mad Dogs here are anything but goons—in fact, a lot of them are esteemed corporate honchos, most are family men. MDMC is a bike club with diverse personalities that share a common passion for free-spirited riding. They've had a number of provincial weekend rides as well as organized fund-raising rides for charity.

Mad Dog memberships are by invitation only, where an existing member typically sponsors a prospective candidate. But there are things you can do to earn points from scratch. One is to just get to know the Mad Dogs first and foremost, hang around their patch holders and clubhouse to get a better idea about the club and the people in it. Second, and most obvious, is you have to own a 400cc (or larger) bike; the minimum engine displacement standard must be met before being considered as prospect. Though it isn't the required ride, Harley Davidson has come to be a bike that most members prefer due to the legendary brand's speed, agility, quality, reliability, weight, and reputation as being the best motorcycle manufacturer. Ultimately, however, it'll be you, the biker, and not your bike, that determines whether or not you're in. Prospects serve a minimum six-month probation period in which certain tasks are fulfilled—intent is to get to know the club members and have a good time while doing it. After successfully passing probation, full members are obligated to get the club tattoo on his shoulder as a sign of dedication to the club and brotherhood of MDMC. Each tattoo is numbered and is strictly for members only. About 180 tattoos have been issued to date since 2007.

WEBSITE: mdmc.com.ph ADDRESS: MDMC Clubhouse (adjoined with Handlebar Bar & Grill) 31 Polaris St., Bel Air, Makati City OPEN: Mon–Thu, 3 p.m. onward; Fri–Sun, 11 a.m. onward. Sometimes closed for members-only events.

Minnie Puno Cooking Lessons

U B V

SPECIALTY: Basic Thai and Vietnamese cooking classes.

The Thai cooking classes usually cover basic principles and ingredients, plus a culminating hands-on activity where students prepare dishes at least two startersandonemaincourse(ForThai:chickensataywithcucumbersalad,Thai spring rolls, seafood combination with fresh chilies and basil; for Vietnamese: fresh Vietnamese spring rolls, green papaya salad, lemon grass chicken beef pho). The classes, held at Minnie Puno's residence, are followed by a merienda session serving the dishes that were prepared during class. Each class often requires at least 6 students, so gather friends to make a class and call or email for schedule and class updates.

PRICES: P1,200 per person for 4 Saturday afternoon sessions.

PAYMENT: Cash. WEBSITE: minniepuno.multiply.com EMAIL: minniepuno@yahoo.com ADDRESS: 535 Talisay St., Ayala Alabang Village, Muntinlupa M: 0917-838-2559

Negoskwela

U B V

SPECIALTY: Exhaustive range of crafts and livelihood workshops and training sessions on arts and crafts, business skills, food preparation, culinary arts, fashion arts, and chemical and industrial processes. Check website or call for class schedules and updates.

RATES/PRICES: Training ranges typically from P1,500 to P3,800 for hands-on sessions and materials.

PAYMENT: Cash. WEBSITE: negoskwela.blogspot.com T: 433-0637, 497-4163, 924-5111 M: 0920-905-8940, 0917-831-4477

Quezon City Dog Walkers

U B V

SPECIALTY: Scheduled dog-walking events at different in-city scenic routes and locations, organized dog treks and hikes, and other activities for dog lovers and their quad-ped buddies. Check website or email them for updates, guidelines, and a host of info for both new and seasoned dog owners.

PRICES: There are usually no fees to join the activities, just a list of what to bring and prepare for both you and your dog especially on treks and other whole-day activities.

WEBSITE: qcdogwalkers.blogspot.com EMAIL: qcdogwalkers@gmail.com

---

RC Philippines

U B V

SPECIALTY: Website about radio or remote controlled model plane flying, car driving, and boat sailing. The website is a trove of resources for all things RC, from specialty shops to RC venues, events, and clubs.

WEBSITE: rcphilippines.com

School of Fashion and the Arts (SOFA)

U B V

SPECIALTY: Courses on fashion, styling, sewing, and makeup to diploma courses on fashion and marketing, clothing technology, and fashion design.

The School of Fashion and the Arts offers a wide range of fashion courses from degree programs to workshops. One of its short courses is the Personal Styling Module, a basic three-day seminar on the fundamentals of makeup, hair styling, and fashion styling for both TV and photo shoots. More comprehensive courses on styling include the Fashion Overview and Summer Styling Course, which take place over a course of four whole-day sessions, have styling kits, and have more hands-on sessions with culmination projects. Diploma courses include year-long modules designed for those who really want in on the fashion industry. These courses include all aspects of fashion, from fundamentals and styling to purchasing and merchandising.

All instructors are practicing professionals regarded highly in their respective fields of expertise and additionally looked upon as today's generation of avant garde trendsetters.

PRICES: Short courses, P8,000–15,000.

PAYMENT: Cash, check. WEBSITE: www.sofamanila.multiply.com, http://www.sofamanila.com EMAIL: info@sofamanila.com ADDRESS: 55 Paseo de Roxas Ave. Makati T: 892-8807

School Of Spa

U B V

SPECIALTY: Massage courses on professional Reflexology, Traditional Thai Massage, Shiatsu, Foot Spa, and Aromatherapy Massage. Call for class schedule and updates.

RATES/PRICES: P6,500 for a basic 15-hour training course, inclusive of training materials and certificate.

PAYMENT: Cash (to be paid in full before start of the course).

WEBSITE: sanctuariospa.com ADDRESS: 1826 Jorge Bacobo St., Malate, Manila T: 450-1127

Sentro Ng Kaalamang Yaman

U B V

SPECIALTY: Workshops on crafts ideal for home businesses and livelihoods (perfume making, candle making, fruit preservation, gift packaging, herbal soap making, sausage making, styro sculpture making, stone crafting, hair cutting, etc.).

PRICES: Workshops, P2,500–4,000.

PAYMENT: Cash. ADDRESS: 38 San Pedro Bautista St., Frisco, Quezon City T: 373-1887, 415-1662 M: 0919-247-7074

Sir Nicolay's Photography 101

U B V

SPECIALTY: Multilevel digital photography workshops like basic digital photography, natural photo editing & web publishing, portraits 101, still life and landscape photography, advanced editing: raw and HDR, black and white digital photography, and outdoor/street photography. Workshops are held at the U.P. Diliman campus. Check websites for schedules, updates, and special promos.

RATES/PRICES: P1,000–1,250 for a 3-hour session. Usually 15% off for bank deposit pre-workshop payments.

PAYMENT: Cash, bank deposit. WEBSITE: sirnicolay.blogspot.com
EMAIL: sirnicolay@gmail.com

UFO Creativity Workshops

SPECIALTY: Extensive range of workshops on various creative disciplines: filmmaking, standup comedy, cinematography, writing, painting, masterclass in acting, dancing, etc. The workshops are facilitated by practicing industry professionals, and training programs come in various formats—from standard workshops to apprenticeship-style. Check website for schedules and updates.

RATES/PRICES: Workshops consisting of 15 sessions typically start at P5,000; apprenticeship-style training, about P12,000.

PAYMENT: Cash. WEBSITE: ufoworkshops.wordpress.com, also has a Facebook page. EMAIL: ufoworkshops2010@gmail.com ADDRESS: 85 Araullo cor. Balagtas Sts., Brgy. Addition Hills, San Juan T: 509-2792 M: 0926-712-1419

Ark of Avilon

U B V W

SPECIALTY: A zoo in a city, and the first indoor zoo in the country.

Everybody who's ever been to this zoo says only one thing: It's like stepping aboard Noah's Ark. The sister zoo of Avilon Zoo in Rizal, the Ark is home to various exotic animals such as tigers, pumas, orangutans, tortoises, fish, birds, sun bears, lions, crocodiles, peafowls, among others. The walk through the Animal Channel section is a refresher's course on wildlife and biology in general. Here, animals are allowed to interact with visitors, but with extra precaution, of course. For your little ones, a trip to the Ark of Avilon Zoo is much like watching National Geographic for Kids and Animal Planet at the same time—and more. They can pet the eagles, feed the rabbits, ride a donkey, and watch chameleons change color before their eyes. On the other hand, there are the not-so-familiar animal friends, such as the Palawan Hornbill, Luzon Tarictic Hornbill, Egyptian Goose, White Carabao, Victoria Crown Pigeon, or the Helmeted Guineafowl, and more animal names even parents have never heard of—or seen—before. While catching your breath and resting after an educational walk, you can let your kids off to play at the playground or join in some Avilon art activities. Avail of souvenirs to take home from the Ark Sentiments Souvenir Shop, to make your zoo visit more memorable.

PRICES: P250 a person; for kids not taller than their ticketing counter, only P200; free for babies.

PAYMENT: Cash. WEBSITE: arkavilonzoo.weebly.com/ ADDRESS: Ortigas Ave. Extension cor. C5, Pasig City OPEN: Mon–Fri, 9 a.m.–6p.m.; Sat/Sun/holidays, 10 a.m.–7:30 p.m.

Baking Workshop, The

U B V W

SPECIALTY: Year-round baking classes for kids as young as age 3 and the entire family. They also offer themed baking classes (mom–daughter, father–son, siblings, etc.) and baking birthday parties.

PRICES: P4,500 for 5 sessions totaling 10 hrs.

PAYMENT: Cash. WEBSITE: thebakingworkshop.com, thebakingworkshop.multiply.com EMAIL: thebakingworkshop@gmail.com, thebakingworkshop@yahoo.com ADDRESS: Unit 104 G/L AIC Gold Tower, F. Ortigas Jr. Rd., Ortigas, Pasig T: 703-2048 M: 0922-845-7621 OPEN: Classes are held daily, 9 a.m. – 12 nn, 1 p.m. – 4 p.m., and 5:30 p.m. – 8:30 p.m.

Coach E Basketball Clinic

U B V **W**

SPECIALTY: Headed by International Basketball Academy (IBA) president Xavy Nunag, Coach E Basketball clinics boast a 1:5 teacher-student ratio, purportedly the lowest in Asia. It has three personalized and scientific modules focusing on fundamentals and shot training.

PRICES: P8,500 for 1 module (16 sessions or 2 months totaling 32 hrs).

PAYMENT: Cash. WEBSITE: coach-e.com/ EMAIL: iba_phil@yahoo.com ADDRESS: Clinics are currently held in the following venues: Xavier School, San Juan; Club650, Libis, Quezon City; The Zone, Makati; San Beda Alabang, Muntinlupa; EDSA Shangri-La. T: 631-1195 M: 0921-7562639. Call these numbers for class schedules and updates during office hours, Mon – Fri. For EDSA Shangri-La classes, call 633-8888 local 2902 or 2906 and look for Rey Fabricante or Gie Cenar.

Fun Ranch Tiendesitas

U B **V** W

SPECIALTY: A one-stop hub of child-friendly rides, activity areas, restaurants, a pediatric spa, gym for parents, and mini-golf course for tots

Fun Ranch houses a number of independent establishments where you can dine, play, and relax as a family. There's the Big Red Barn, a play area with a child-friendly menu; Active Fun, with a carousel and other classic amusement park rides; Little Lamb, with spa services geared especially for kids and toddlers; and Kinetica, with training and workout programs for kids age seven and up. Even during weekdays, families flock to Fun Ranch for some art and exploration activities at the Sea and Learn Development Center.

PRICES: Free admission; tickets/tokens for the rides, P5–50.

PAYMENT: Cash. WEBSITE: funranch.com ADDRESS: Frontera Verde, Ortigas Ave., Pasig T: 396-5237, 396-5290 OPEN: Mon–Fri, 12 nn–9 p.m.; Sat/Sun, 10 a.m.–10 p.m.

Hobbes and Landes Free Board Game Play

U B V W

SPECIALTY: The Try Me section at Hobbes and Landes stores offers newly released boardgames and puzzles that kids and families can spend afternoons playing for free. For a minimum purchase of P200, one can also register for the store-sponsored Board Game Olympics, usually held every Friday and Saturday.

Visit any Hobbes and Landes store (except the Promenade branch) and check out their Try Me section, where you can road-test board games and brainteasers free of charge. Once you've mastered those, you can register for the Hobbes and Landes Board Game Olympics with a minimum purchase of P200. The tournaments are held Fridays and Saturdays until mid-May at their stores in Bonifacio High Street, Greenbelt 5, and Power Plant Mall.

WEBSITE: hobbesandlandes.com ADDRESS: See directory for Hobbes and Landes store locations. T: 632-1440 OPEN: Daily, 11 a.m.–10 p.m.

Kids Ahoy!

U B V W

SPECIALTY: After-school creative play and age-appropriate activities and talks on civic-minded topics.

Kids Ahoy! Is an after-school creative play center that advocates non-traditional educational activities and fun games through playdates, enrichment classes in arts, and community activities that develop social consciousness among kids at an early age. Special themed classes include arts and crafts, music, theater, drama, baking, cooking, reading, writing, photography, videography, outdoor activities like orienteering and camping, speech, and dance. What makes Kids Ahoy! stand out, though, are age-appropriate activities and talks designed to help kids learn about more "grown-up" but nevertheless important issues like house chores, citizenship, environmental conservation, and bullying.

PRICES: P1,500 a month for 16 hours of playtime and in-house activities; 15% discount on special classes and workshops.

PAYMENT: Cash, bank deposit, Globe G-Cash. WEBSITE: kidsahoy.multiply.com, kidsahoyshop.com EMAIL: kidsahoy@yahoo.com ADDRESS: 56 Lantana cor. New York Sts., Cubao, Quezon City T: 473-7896 M: 0920-517-8127

La Mesa Eco Park

U B V W

SPECIALTY: A 33-hectare public park located right outside the natural boundaries of the La Mesa Watershed, equipped with facilities for various outdoor activities (fitness and mountain bike trail, fishing lagoon, salt water and chlorine-free pool, eco museum, butterfly trail and hatchery, mini golf course, picnic grounds, boating lagoon, and camping grounds).

PRICES: Admission, P50. Use of swimming pool: P80 (adult), P40 (child). Use of boat, P100 per group of 4. Fishing, rod rental, P20. Wall climbing and rappelling, P50. Paintball: P350 (50 bullets), gear rental included.

Admission to Butterfly Trail and Hatchery, P30. Cabana rental, P500 (whole day) for a maximum of 15 people

PAYMENT: Cash. WEBSITE: lamesaecopark.com EMAIL: lamesaecopark@abs-cbn.com ADDRESS: La Mesa Dam Compound, Greater Lagro, Quezon City T: 430-4051 OPEN: Mon–Fri, 7 a.m.–6 p.m.; Sat/Sun, 7 a.m.–5 p.m.

Little Lambs

U B V W

SPECIALTY: Spa and salon services specially for kids.

Little Lamb's Pediatric Wellness Place is a spa, salon, and clinic that caters to the pediatric age group. Interiors are colorful and whimsical, but the therapists are professionally trained in children's massage therapy. The salon offers haircut, hair spa, make-up, foot spa, and other harmless primping services that purportedly boost self-confidence among kids. The wellness clinic monitors immunization, weight and growth, nutrition, and developmental milestones. Little Lambs emphasizes its role as "in addition to, NOT instead of" medical practice, combining preventive and therapeutic efforts to maintain and promote children's wellness.

PRICES: Infant massage, P250 (30 mins); Shiatsu and Swedish massage for ages 2 to 19, P280–300 (1 hour); well-baby check-up, P300.

PAYMENT: Cash. WEBSITE: littlelambspa.com ADDRESS: G/L MJB Bldg., 220 Tomas Morato Ave. cor. Lascano St., Quezon City T: 413-4478 OPEN: Mon–Sat, 11 a.m.–9 p.m.; Sat/Sun, 11 a.m.–8 p.m.

Malabon Zoo and Aquarium

U B V W

SPECIALTY: Coastal town zoo and homegrown animal sanctuary

Malabon Zoo started out in the late '60s as the backyard of animal lover Manny Tangco and was home to a private menagerie of the exotic and

Philippine endemic. He eventually expanded and opened the place to the public. Though a relatively small zoo, Malabon Zoo and Aquarium boasts a good collection of tigers, lions, dogs, monkeys, snakes, fish, and birds. The entire place is tranquil and lush with greenery. A mini library holds has books that you can read mid-tour of the zoo.

PRICES: Admission, P120.

PAYMENT: Cash. ADDRESS: 1 Gov. W. Pascual Barrio Potrero, Malabon T: 941-8393, 948-9866 M: 0917-899-5126 OPEN: Mon–Fri, 8 a.m. – 5:30 p.m.

Manila Ocean Park's Oceanarium

U B V W

SPECIALTY: The first major oceanarium in the country.

Manila Ocean Park has seven sections featuring all sorts of marine life in simulations of their natural habitat. The first part of the oceanarium is a vast exhibit of aquariums featuring an amazing array of tropical saltwater and fresh water fish one only gets to see in dive sites. Other sections feature multiple species of seahorses, sea anemones, star fish, corals, jelly fish, sea snakes, giant shells and shellfish, etc., fishing grounds with popular Pinoy fish, and a janitor fish foot spa. The most impressive spectacle, however, is a 25-meter long, 220° underground glass tunnel from where you can watch more than a hundred species of magnificent marine predators like sharks, stingrays, and barracudas zoom or leisurely glide past or overhead, just a glass partition away.

PRICES: Admission, P400 (adults), P350 (children under 4.5').

PAYMENT: Cash. WEBSITE: manilaoceanpark.com EMAIL: reservations@manilaoceanpark.com ADDRESS: Behind the Quirino Grandstand, 1 Rizal Park, Luneta, Manila T: 567-7777 OPEN: Daily, 10 a.m. – 9 p.m.

Legend: U=*Unique,* B=*Budget* V=*Variety* W=*With workshops/training/classes*

Manila Orchidarium & Butterfly Pavilion

U B V W

SPECIALTY: Orchid and butterfly conservatory in a tranquil botanical garden in the heart of busy Manila.

Located inside Luneta Park, Manila Orchidarium & Butterfly Pavilion is a one-hectare botanical garden that feels more like a rainforest. It is a refuge for growing and sustaining natural and cultivated orchids as well as a diversity of exotic and endangered flora from the Philippines and the rest of Asia. Its landscape is designed for leisurely promenades, with walkways under flower and vine trellises and bridges built over man-made ponds and waterfalls. The park has recreational facilities for children, such as wall climbing, fishing, butterfly watching at the pavilion (where kids can observe butterfly eggs turn caterpillars, then from pupae to butterflies), and weekly orientations that teach school-aged children about nature and water conservation. Parents can enjoy a soothing barefoot "acupressure" walk at the Reflexology path that's lined with healing stones, or have pastries and coffee at the in-house Spanish-Filipino café, Barbara's.

PRICES: Admission, P100 (adults), P60 (students and senior citizens with respective I.D.); wall climbing, P50; fishing, P25.

PAYMENT: Cash. ADDRESS: F. Teodoro Valencia Circle, Rizal Park, Manila T: 527-6376 or 78 OPEN: Tue–Sun, 9 a.m.–5 p.m.

Manila Soccer Academy

U B V W

SPECIALTY: Kiddie soccer camp for both beginners and advanced players.

Held at a vast playing field of one of Manila's swankiest neighborhoods, Manila Soccer Academy is one of the few major soccer programs that offer out-of-school soccer training. Doting, well-heeled parents watch from the sides as their little ones train to become future Beckhams. Heading the program is Ricardo Venus, a coach with over 20 years and licensed by the Asian Football Confederation, and former player for the Philippine National Football team. Kids get to play in soccer matches against other schools in and outside Metro Manila. A training program usually lasts up to mine weeks and is culminated with a soccer festival. Boys and girls attend the same classes and are segregated only by age group. Summer programs from March to May get filled easily, but there are programs scheduled year round. Call MSA for updates.

PRICES: Soccer class for Manila Polo Club members, P3,400 (9 sessions), P5,850 (18 sessions), P6,240 (24 sessions); for non-members, P3,675 (9 sessions), P6,210 (18 sessions), P6,790 (24 sessions). Required uniforms, P800 (a set of jersey and shorts).

PAYMENT: Cash. EMAIL: manilasocceracademy@gmail.com ADDRESS: East Polo Field, Manila Polo Club, 17 McKinley Rd., Forbes Park, Makati T: 828-8674 M: 0917-841-5530, 0921-249-2353

Maya Kitchen Family

U B V W

SPECIALTY: Summer cooking and baking classes for the whole family with recipes made easy.

Kiddie culinary courses are grouped into three classes: Junior Culinary Workshop (ages 7 to 11), Young People's Cook-in (ages 12 and up), and the most unique of the lot, Parent & Child Cooking. Junior Culinary Workshop covers kitchen sanitation and safety, kitchen measurements and conversion, table setting, and one cooking demo. Young People's Cook-in, on the other hand, covers basic cooking and baking techniques, with hands-on sessions that let students prepare quick and simple dishes like soup and dessert. Both workshops take a total of four sessions, with four hours a session. Parent & Child Cooking involves at least one parent in the class and isn't really about cooking per se more than it is about how parents and kids can bond over real duties and active roles in the kitchen. Classes cover meal preparation, simple cooking and garnishing, and simple baking with icing decorating. Parent & Child Cooking usually takes about two Saturday sessions, with five hours a session. All workshops are typically offered in the summer, but special schedules can be booked.

PRICES: Junior Culinary Workshop and Young People's Cook-in, P4,800 (4 sessions); Parent & Child Cooking, P3,000 (2 sessions). Tuition fees will be a bit higher for specially scheduled classes.

PAYMENT: Cash, check. WEBSITE: themayakitchen.com ADDRESS: Maya Kitchen Culinary Arts Center, 8/L, Liberty Bldg., 835 A. Arnaiz Ave. (Pasay Rd.), Legaspi Village, Makati T: 892-5011 loc. 108, 892-1185

Museo Pambata

U B V W

SPECIALTY: Interactive children's museum on Filipino culture and heritage as well as a science and technology. There are breathtaking showcases of miniatures, life-like and life-sized dioramas, and unique gadgets and experiments that kids can freely tinker with.

PRICES: Admission, P100; free for children under age 2, museum workers, and teachers with valid I.D.

PAYMENT: Cash. WEBSITE: museopambata.org EMAIL: info@museopambata.org ADDRESS: Roxas Blvd. cor. South Drive, Manila T: 523-1797 to 98, 536-0595 OPEN: Tue–Sat, 8 a.m.–5 p.m. (Aug-Mar), 9 a.m.–5 p.m. (Apr-Jul); Sun, 1 p.m.–5 p.m. Closed for lunch during summer.

My Little Art Place

U B V W

SPECIALTY: Basic to advanced fine arts workshops for kids and teens.

Though they do offer the standard painting, drawing, and creative crafts class, they also have art workshops not normally available to kids, such as Pen and Ink drawing, photography, oil pastel, watercolor technique, oil and acrylic, sculpture, and Anime and Comic Strip art. Call or check website for updates on workshop schedules.

PRICES: Workshops, average of P6,000 (8 sessions totaling 24 hrs).

PAYMENT: Cash, bank deposit. WEBSITE: mylittleartplace.multiply.com EMAIL: mylittleartplace@gmail.com ADDRESS: 222 Wilson St., Greenhills, San Juan T: 409-4122 M: 0922-806-4007

My Masterpiece

U B V W

SPECIALTY: Holistic creativity workshops for kids and teens

More devoted to harnessing creativity, imagination, and free play in children than training them on a particular skill, the workshops here integrate various art disciplines such as Visual Arts, Imaginative Writing & Storytelling, Music & Movement, and Creative Drama. Specialty classes formatted as kiddie social events include Ballet Tea Parties and Dance Culture Classes; while others, like the Speech classes, are more straightforward (classroom format). My Masterpiece also has party packages for both big bashes and intimate playdates. Call or check website for class updates and schedules.

PRICES: About P9,000–11,000 for a program (13 weekly sessions totaling 19.5 hrs, inclusive of materials, portfolio, and the student's developmental profile); P500–600 a session for one-off themed workshops (e.g., Halloween crafts, Christmas décor-making) and specialty classes.

PAYMENT: Cash. WEBSITE: mymasterpiece.info EMAIL: mymasterpiece@me.com T: 395-5028 M: 0915-432-7439, 0917-528-7301
Three workshop venues: VALLE VERDE I (call for exact address)
CREATIVE PLAY Cor. SCHOOL ADDRESS: Forbes Town Center, Burgos Circle, The Fort, Bonifacio Global City, Taguig KEYS GRADE SCHOOL ADDRESS: 951 Luna Mencias cor. Araullo Sts., San Juan

---

Ninoy Aquino Parks

U B V W

SPECIALTY: Tranquil botanical sanctuary with mini zoo, man-made lagoon, and other nature-themed facilities amidst busy Quezon City.

Just two blocks from mall giants TriNoma and SM North EDSA is this 80-hectare park and conservation site housing a botanical garden with 38 plant species and over 2,000 forest trees, a mini zoo and wildlife rescue center, a man-made lagoon, picnic gazebos, a kiddie playground, a rock garden, and a crafts village. The park façade and entrance are nondescript, which maybe explains why the vast property is mostly ignored despite a high-traffic location. The few who do frequent the place, however, like it for precisely this reason. Hidden in plain sight and uncrowded, Ninoy Aquino Parks is an accessible escape from noise, traffic, and pollution—truly a secret garden within the city.

PRICES: Admission, P8 (adult), P5 (kids). Parking, P15 flat rate.

PAYMENT: Cash. ADDRESS: North Ave., Diliman, Quezon City T: 924-6031 to 35 OPEN: Daily, 7 a.m.–6 p.m.

Peak Performance

U B V W

SPECIALTY: Kids dance classes using a combination of jazz, bellydance, and hip-hop for kids ages 5 to 12; cultural dances such as Hula, Tahitian, and traditional Chinese for kids. Cardio dance, cardio boxing, cardio hip-hop, and stretch-and-tone workouts for adults.

PRICES: Walk-in rate, P380 for any class; P1,300 a month for 4 sessions.

PAYMENT: Cash, check for complete sessions. WEBSITE: peakperformance.asiapad.com EMAIL: peakperformance@asiapad.com ADDRESS: Peak Performance, 2/L McGwen Bldg., 16 Don A. Roces Ave., Quezon City T: 413-3466 M: 0917-624-7534 OPEN: Call for updated class schedules.

Philippine Air Force Aerospace Museum

U B V W

SPECIALTY: The only aerospace museum in the country.

The first floor houses interactive displays of modern aerospace science, including aircraft parts, while the second level is an exhibit of Philippine Air Force history and cultural contribution to the country, complete with a life-like diorama. The third floor has a deck with a first-rate view of the entire air base. Don't leave without climbing onto the F Sabre Jet simulator (with a 135-degree view) or the bomber aircraft, all set for a "pretend flying" experience. A 50-seater theater that shows war movies is open to film aficionados. Also make a quick stopover at the adjacent PAF's Aircraft Park, where 18 kinds of military aircraft had been permanently parked for public viewing.

PRICES: Entrance fee: P20; use of jet simulator, P100–150.

PAYMENT: Cash. ADDRESS: Villamor Air Base, Pasay
T: 853-5023 OPEN: Mon–Fri, 9 a.m.–5 p.m.

Philippine Science Centrum

U B V W

SPECIALTY: First "hands-on" science museum in the country.

There are 15 galleries housing over 200 hands-on demonstrations on Earth Science, Bodyworks, Lights, Vision and Perception, Mechanics, Liquids, Mathematics, Electricity and Magnetism, and a themed Children's Gallery (for kids ages 2 to 9) featuring a Rock Wall, Pillow Geometry, and the Bernoulli Challenge among others. More interactive and futuristic demo areas have been added, such as the 3D animation IBM Try Science Kiosk, the Wonder House which challenges you to keep your balance as in the Hollywood film The Matrix, the literally hair-raising Van De Graaff Generator, and the Meralco Corner which demonstrates the entire process of electricity generation and distribution.

PRICES: Admission, P100 for a 1.5-hr visit. Free admission for teachers and kids under age 2.

PAYMENT: Cash. WEBSITE: science-centrum.ph ADDRESS: E-Com Bldg., Riverbanks Center, 84 A. Bonifacio Ave., Barangka, Marikina T: 942-5136, 942-5091; OPEN: Mon–Sat, 8 a.m.–5 p.m.

San Miguel Great Food Club's Kid's Kitchen Camp

U B V W

SPECIALTY: Usually held during summer, San Miguel's Kid's Kitchen Camp holds three-day hands-on cooking and baking workshops where kids ages 6 to 11 get to prepare simple full-course meals.

PRICES: A 3-day session, around P6,000.

PAYMENT: Cash. WEBSITE: mygreatfood.com ADDRESS: Legaspi cor. Eagle Sts., Bagong Ugong, Pasig T: 640-5453, 672-8558 OPEN: Check out website or call for schedule updates.

SM Science Discovery Center

SPECIALTY: The first interactive science center in the country, with high-tech facilities that are both educational and entertaining especially for kids

Enjoy nine stations in all: the Imageport gives you a glimpse of the art of digital imaging and photography; Virtual Reef lets you explore the underwater world; check scale city models at City Science; Media City is for computer whiz kids and gamers; Transport Nation features flight simulators and automobile; Grossology! teaches human anatomy in a fun way; Earth Experience will give you a peek at life around the world through web cams and videos; Planetarium gives a 40-minute videography of life in other planets; and Robots, Inc. introduces you to R2D2 and C3PO and helps you understand robot technology.

PRICES: P350; no entrance fee for children below 2 ft.

PAYMENT: Cash. WEBSITE: smsciencediscovery.com EMAIL: info@smsciencediscoverycenter.com ADDRESS: Levels 1 and 2, Southside Entertainment Mall, SM Mall of Asia, Pasay T: 556-2153, 556-0331 OPEN: Daily, 10 a.m. – 10 p.m.

SOFA (School of Fashion and the Arts) Kids Fashion & Art Camp

U B V W

SPECIALTY: Fashion and art camp for kids aged 6 to 12 with activities such as bag making, application of embellishments on clothes, etc.

PRICES: P1,500 (1 session) to P8,000 (8 sessions).

PAYMENT: Cash. WEBSITE: sofamanila.com EMAIL: info@sofamanila.com, sofamanila@gmail.com ADDRESS: 55 Paseo de Roxas Ave., Makati T: 892-8807 M: 0917-5018136 OPEN: Call or check out website for schedule updates.

Tech 4 Kids

U B V W

SPECIALTY: Multimedia workshops on digital photography and editing, website developing and design, video game development and design, computer animation, and advanced robotics for kids and teens. No previous training required.

The Tech4Kids teaching staff consists of industry experts, consultants, and professionals who work for companies here and abroad. All classes are activity-based and culminate with an original creation by the students.

PAYMENT: Cash. WEBSITE: tech4kids.com.ph ADDRESS: 3/L Victory Christian School, 339 Robinsons Circle, Captain Henry Javier Drive, Pasig M: 0917-5010845 OPEN: Call or check online for schedule updates.

Airsoft

U B V W

SPECIALTY: Sport in which the players simulate combat, warfare, or other military scenarios using authentic military tactics and replica weapons.

Airsoft guns use 6mm BBs made of ABS plastic as ammunition, which generally weigh from .12g to .43g on average. It has gained a cult following ironically among people in non-combative industries like advertising, medicine, and the corporate world. There are now organized teams and games, with vacant lots, abandoned buildings, and warehouses often serving as game site. Organized games usually enforce an FPS limit of 320 to 420. FPS (feet per second) refers to the speed at which a bullet travels, and the limit is considered a safe enough velocity to guard against serious injury, given the proper protective gear (helmet, fiberglass face mask or goggles, vest). Without protective gear, an Airsoft bullet traveling at 320 FPS can bruise or break skin. Live bullets form real guns, which embed themselves in or rip right through flesh, typically travel at a minimum of 900 FPS. Some organized Airsoft games have FPS limits higher than 420 because the game venue is wide and open. During organized games, a medic and/or marshal are usually present. If you're interested to try Airsoft out, you can contact existing Airsoft teams and organizations through their websites.

PRICES: Joining fees, gear rental, and use of the game sites are usually paid upfront in cash. Game fees, typically P100; gun rental, typically P500.

WEBSITE: filairsoft.com (most active airsoft website and online community), acmairsoft.org, airsoft-community.net, mag.popularairsoft .com (online magazine), airsoftxtreme.net (online magazine).

The following are Airsoft game sites and details; there are usually guns and gear for rent in these sites. If you just want to observe first, you can visit game sites on weekends from 10 a.m. onward.

Army Adventure Zone

Headquarters of team War Pigs, this open field has rich shrubbery and wrecked large-scale vehicles for obstacles and hiding places. Also has a jungle area. FPS LIMIT: 450 ADDRESS: C5 (southbound), Taguig (past Kalayaan Ave., right after Heritage Park) M: 0922-249-4653

Borden Gamesite

Claims to be one of the biggest Airsoft sites in Metro Manila, with mixed urban and jungle setting. FPS LIMIT: 450 ADDRESS: Alabang-Zapote Road, Las Piñas (across the demolished Philips plant near Petron) M: 0917-852-9438 (host Team Laspag)

Cainta Airsoft Community Game Site

Boasts indoor practical/combat shooting ranges apart from the outdoor game site. It also has indoor playing areas for room-clearing game components (entering a room with hostiles inside).

FPS LIMIT: 450 WEBSITE: caintaairsoftcom.multiply.com ADDRESS: Batangas St. (near J. Abad Santos Ave. and Ipil St., 200 m from SM San Lazaro and Rizal Ave.), Cainta, Rizal M: 09 19-647-3554, 0916-715-0809, 0927-335-2679, 0922-835-2679

Camp Echo Trail

Site with mixed close quarters battle and mini jungle mode. Food and drinks available on site. FPS LIMIT: 450 ADDRESS: Tandang Sora Ext., Quezon City M: 0927-701-3389

Camp Masada

Four-hectare hilly jungle hosted by Team Apocalypse. FPS LIMIT: 500 ADDRESS: Litex Road, Fairview, Quezon City (near La Mesa Dam, beside Violago Homes) M: 0917-531-1307

Camp Mckoy

A 3,360 sqm concrete lot ideal for urban setting games. FPS LIMIT: 320 ADDRESS: 964 Marcos Highway (right after Barrio Fiesta), Quezon City M: 0917-936-1152

Camp Urban Zone

Vast open-air venue. FPS LIMIT: 550 ADDRESS: North Ave. (beside TriNoma), Quezon City

---

D'Backyard

Vast but secure field with trees, thick shrubbery, sand bags, obstacle courses, sniper towers, and snacks and drinks for sale. FPS LIMIT: 450 WEBSITE: saga.atwebpages.com ADDRESS: 9 De Pebrero St. (inside the Correctional Institute For Women compound), Mandaluyong M: 0916-717-9410, 0916-384-4583

D' Warehouse

Home to Team Renegades, this bi-level warehouse hosts several rooms and obstacles, perfect for close quarters battles. Ample parking available. FPS LIMIT: 450 ADDRESS: Quirino Highway, Talipapa, Quezon City (beside Rubberworld M: 0919-680-6016

Dog Pound

Mixed jungle and urban site, home to the K9 Troopers team. FPS LIMIT: 450 WEBSITE: teamk9.proboards.com ADDRESS: 67 T. Santiago St, Veinte Reales, Valenzuela M: 0928-722-1665

Forest Camp

Home to Team Talahib, the site is a vast outdoor venue lush with tropical shrubbery and greenery, and installed with some urban obstacles. FPS LIMIT: 430 ADRESS: National Ecology, Mini Forest Park, East Ave., Quezon City M: 0919-405-7021

Mastac Gamesite

Ideal for jungle, close quarters battles, and fortress assault modes. FPS LIMIT: 450 ADDRESS: Putatan, Muntinlupa M: 0917-857-3214, 0915-480-9371

Poly Makati (old Makati Polytechnic)

Bi-level indoor site perfect for close quarters battles. Snacks and drinks available. FPS LIMIT: 400 WEBSITE: tech05.multiply.com ADDRESS: Malugay cor. Mayapis Sts., Makati

---

Pugad Lawin 3

Run by Team OB, snacks, drinks, and gun rentals available. FPS LIMIT: 450 ADDRESS: MWCI Compound, Balara, Quezon City M:0927-683-7559, 0917-851-2339

Sitting Ducks Airsoft Game Site

Has clean toilets, drinks and snacks for sale, and tents for staging areas (i.e., demilitarized zones with chairs and tables where non-ingame players can rest). FPS LIMIT: 400 ADDRESS: E. Rodriguez Jr. Ave., Quezon City M: 0915-867-7595, 0921-768-4977, 0927-299-3749

Sureshock Airsoft Game Site

More than 3,000 sqm of a shaded jungle environment with bunkers, tree-house sniper towers, and all sorts of covers. Vast guarded parking and food and drinks for sale are available. FPS LIMIT: 450 EMAIL: sureshockairsoft@yahoo.com ADDRESS: Rizal High School, Dr. Sixto Antonio Ave., Caniogan, Pasig M: 0917-964-4716, 0922-806-4824, 0922-778-8123

Team Bayani Indoor Airsoft Speedball Gamesite

Monthly mini tournaments are played here, and there's a maintenance crew that sweeps out bullets and rearranges kill houses, sniper towers, and other simulation structures after each game. FPS LIMIT: 450 WEBSITE: bayanicup.page.tl ADDRESS: J.P. Rizal St., Brgy. Kalumpang, Marikina T: 646-1629 M: 0919-661-9557

The Kingdom

Home to the Camanava Seals, it has 13 hectares devoted to five jungle game areas with urban ruins, a guarded parking lot, gear rental, food stands, and a marshal present at every game. FPS: 450 ADDRESS:328 Quirino Highway, Quezon City M: 0927-655-4077

Tigerland

Managed by Airsoft team Down South Recon, Tigerland is a four-hectare undeveloped subdivision with urban and jungle settings, an extensive range of obstacles, sniper towers, bunkers, and fox holes. It has spacious parking and a shop selling and renting out gear as well as drinks and snacks. FPS LIMIT: 450 WEBSITE: downsouthrecon.proboards.com ADDRESS: Villa Viena 1 Neopolitan, Regaldo Ave., Fairview, Quezon City (near SM Fairview) M: 0918-939-3565

Vanagard

Covered site for close quarters battles. FPS LIMIT: 400 ADDRESS: 8th Ave. cor. 7th St., Caloocan M: 0928-504-3029

Zone Juan

Managed by Spearhead Team, the site has mixed urban and jungle set-ups, ample parking, comfortable rest areas, and a small shop carrying snacks, drinks, and packed meals. FPS LIMIT: 450 WEBSITE: spearheadteam.wetpaint.com ADDRESS: Ugong, Valenzuela-Q.C. boundary

---

Airsoft Gear

Airsoft guns can go for as low as P5,000 to as high as P25,000 and up, depending on the make. It's the protective gear you don't want to scrimp on. Choose high-quality masks made from fiberglass; airsoft bullets can break inferior masks made from plastic. Below are some shops in the city that offer gear, upgrade parts, and repair.

AIRAMCOR
Grace Park, Caloocan
T: 692-6433
M: 0917-899-3515

AIRSOFT ARMORY
Salem Complex,
Domestic Road, Pasay
T: 851-6260
M: 0917-622-1552

AIRSOFT ONE
KY Bldg, Cubao, Q.C.
T: 726-2568

AIRSOFT PHILIPPINES
Anapolis St., Greenhills,
San Juan T: 722-5595
M: 0917-893-9790

BROJAMES FARMERS
Farmers Plaza,
Cubao, Q.C.
T: 912-1557
M: 0928-376-8521

G PROJECT
T: 646-8879
M: 0916-617-7882

GEAR UPS
gearups.multiply.com
M: 0906-488-5708,
0927-286-2407

TACTICAL GEAR DEPOT
Lazcano St., Q.C.
T: 928-4183 loc. 116
M:0922-899-0082

LYNX FIREARMS
Araneta Center,
Cubao, Q.C.
T: 912-5364

MY AIRSOFT SHOP
South Triangle, Q.C.
T: 489-5817
M: 0917-834-6768

TLP BUNKER
Nuevo, Makati
M: 0917-856-6366

TUK'S SHOP
Malate, Manila
T: 525-6380
M: 0928-500-1904

XTREME TOYS
tacticalhobbies07@
yahoo.com
Araneta Ave., Q.C.
(across Nacional
Funeral Homes)
T: 474-5208

YOUNG GUNS
Mother Ignacia St.,
Timog, Q.C.
T: 416-7688
M:0906-511-4475,
0922-228-9443

Aqualogic Swim Company

U B V W

SPECIALTY: Instruction of efficient swimming method for all ages (even infants), aqua aerobics classes

Unlike conventional swimming classes where strokes are learned visually and by rote, Aqualogic's approach more easily compares itself to learning a dance and claims to help seasoned swimmers unlearn bad habits while providing new swimmers with the right foundation in swimming technique. Aqualogic Swim Company incorporates a method of swim training called Total Immersion, said to increase the learning curve by concentrating on decreasing water drag and increasing efficiency and grace in the water. Success rates vary a person, but there are those who claim to have learned to swim from scratch after just 10 day s with the program. Aqualogic got its training in Total Immersion from Florida's Lifestyle Swim School, a leading school on swim instruction for children and on creating unique programs that cater to the needs of every age. At Aqualogic, infants and toddlers ages 6 to 35 months, as well as kids ages 3 to 12 years, are made comfortable in the water through innovative use of colorful toys and interactive games. Those looking for an alternative fitness program can try AquaFitness, a fun and effective form of exercise that makes creative use of the natural resistance and buoyancy of water. It aims to improve all the components of fitness: muscular endurance and strength, body composition, aerobic capacity, flexibility or joint mobility, and neuromuscular coordination. But not only is it an effective way to tone up and burn calories, compared to other fitness routines, it is safe enough and presents the least amount of stress and risks to the elderly, pregnant women, or those recuperating from major physical injuries and cardiovascular diseases. Schedules of children's and adult's classes can vary a month depending on the number of attendees, available slots, and weather conditions, so it's best to call first before enrolling.

PRICES: Annual registration fee is P500. Classes for one month, two 1-hour sessions a week: P6,850 for Aqua Tech Adult (per session P950),

P5,250 for Aqua Kids, P5,850 for Aqua Babes. Please call to inquire for special rates, promos, and discounts.

PAYMENT: Cash, check, credit card accepted. WEBSITE: aqualogicswimco.com EMAIL: aqualogicswimco@gmail.com, admin .aqualogic@gmail.com ADDRESS: 902 Amethyst St., Posadas Village, Sucat; T: 703-6386 M: 0917-8582782; Makati Shangri-La Hotel, Ayala cor Makati Aves., Makati; T: 814-2539, 813-8888 loc. 7087 or 7088; Galeria de Magallanes, Magallanes Village, Makati; T: 852-4670; Richmonde Hotel, 21 San Miguel Ave., Ortigas Center, Pasig; T: 638-7777

Bikram Yoga Manila

U B V W

SPECIALTY: Bikram yoga.

Bikram Yoga is a series of 26 postures (including two breathing exercises), each of which stretches, strengthens, and prepares specific muscles, ligaments and joints for the next posture. It is suitable for all ages and levels of ability, and some especially take to—while others find it difficult to overcome—practicing Bikram in an especially heated room (38°C, humidity level at 60%). Practicing in such palpable heat is a characteristic to Bikram and is used to facilitate stretching and sweat-induced detoxification.

PRICES: Introductory yoga-all-you-can one-week package, P1,000; yoga-all-you-can for a month, P5,000. Per class, roughly P250–300 for regular attendees (4–5 times a week).

PAYMENT: Cash. WEBSITE: bikramyogamanila.com EMAIL: info@ bikramyogamanila.com ADDRESS: 15/L, 88 Corporate Center, 141 Valero St. cor. Sedeño Streets, Salcedo Village, Makati T: 889-0126 OPEN: Mon–Fri, classes start as early as 6:30 a.m. and as late as 8 p.m.; Sat/ Sun, classes at 9:30 a.m. and 3 p.m. ADDRESS 2: 5/L CKB Centre, 203 Tomas Morato Ave., Quezon City T: 376-4632, 415 – 8910 OPEN: Mon–Fri, classes start as early as 6:30 a.m. and as late as 8 p.m.; Sat/Sun, classes at 9:30 a.m. and 3 p.m.

Legend: U=Unique, B=Budget V=Variety W=With workshops/training/classes

Bliss Yoga

U B V W

SPECIALTY: Classes on traditional yoga, yoga modified for different levels and needs, Pilates, and specialty yoga classes like Trance Dance yoga.

Held at a posh penthouse studio in Makati, Bliss Yoga's classes include ANUSARA (Sanskrit for "flowing with grace" and "following your heart," a derivative of hatha yoga), Bhakti Urban Flow (nonreligious chanting integrated into vinyasa yoga), Gentle Flow (a "relaxing" type of yoga where the body is supported with props and the poses are held for extended periods without the need to use substantial muscular strength; ideal for those with injuries, the elderly, and beginners), Heate Flow (a challenging 75-minute vinyasa flow class done in a heated room), Pilates, Power Yoga (Ashtanga yoga centering on posture, breath, and the development of both strength and flexibility), Radiant Flow (breath work and poses that promote flexibility), basic and advanced Vinyasa Flow (focuses on posture, breath, and proper body alignment for each pose), Yoga Fundamentals.

Bliss occasionally has guest yoga instructors that teach unique specialties—a class on Trance Dance Yoga and a workshop on Breath and Meditation are just some of the specialty classes that have been held here.

The studio has a juice bar and café that can cater even to strict vegans, a corner selling yoga apparel and accessories, and spa-like locker and bathroom facilities. You can reserve a slot for any of their classes online and their website is always updated with class schedules; you can even click on each class to learn more about the type of yoga it focuses on and on the teacher to view their profile and credentials.

Bliss will provide you with any required gear for each class—yoga mat, props, towels; though it is ideal for you to buy your own mat. Paid parking is available in the building, check out the website for designate slots.

PRICES: Drop-in, P500/day; one-week package, P1,000 (good for 7 consecutive days); 10 Series package, P4,500 (good for 45 consecutive days, lets you pick up to 10 of Bliss's scheduled group classes); one-on-one private session, P2,000; private group package, P1,500 (minimum 6 people).

PAYMENT: Cash only, check for annual fee. WEBSITE: blissyogamanila .com EMAIL: inquiry@blissyogamanila.com ADDRESS: 28/L Trident Tower Penthouse, 312 Sen. Gil Puyat Ave., Makati T: 753-1954 M: 0926-711-7462 OPEN: Daily. Classes start as early as 6:30 a.m. and as late as 8:30 p.m.

Club Intramuros Golf Course

U B V W

SPECIALTY: Night golf.

When the Spanish conquistadors built Intramuros four centuries ago on top of the ruins of Raja Sulayman's kingdom, little did they know that something as random as a golf course would someday sprout at the perimeter of its walls. It's simply not something you expect to see next to plazas, baluartes, and churches. But the Americans, when they took over, thought the protective moat around the walled city was a sorry waste of space; so in 1907, they turned it into a fairway. Club Intramuros is the oddest golf experience in Metro Manila, with centuries-old walls on one side and the bustle of city traffic on the other. At some point, a busy road actually needs to be crossed to finish all 18 holes. It's a small but challenging course, and the best part is, they let people play at night.

PRICES: Green fees for locals on weekdays are P1,100 for day golf, P1,500 for night golf. On weekends, this goes up to P1,350 for day golf, P1,700 for night golf. Green fees for foreigners on both weekends and weekdays are P1,800 for day golf, P2,650 for night golf.

PAYMENT: Cash, credit card for greens fees. Cash for caddies' fees. ADDRESS: Bonifacio Dr. cor. Aduana St., Intramuros, Manila T: 527-6613 OPEN: Mon, 10 a.m.–7 p.m.; Tue–Sat, 6 a.m.–7 p.m.; Sun, 6 a.m.–2 p.m.

Coach Now

U B V W

SPECIALTY: Two-day coaching boot camp for aspiring or beginner basketball coaches by top local coaches like Joe Lipa, Jojo Villa, Lito Vergara, Rico Perez, Ed Cordero, Norman Black, Ronnie Dizer, Patrick Aquino, Jude Roque.

PRICES: P3,500 for 2 whole-day seminars, inclusive of lunch.

PAYMENT: Cash, check. WEBSITE: icancoachnow.com EMAIL: mike@redmediacrm.com ADDRESS: Redmedia Solutions, Inc., 317A Computer Kingdom, Mile Long Bldg., Amorsolo St., Legaspi Village, Makati M: 0922-8262621 OPEN: The boot camp is usually held on two consecutive days, 8 a.m. – 5 p.m.

Cockfighting

U B V W

SPECIALTY: Derby.

Animal rights activists have succeeded in having cockfighting banned in the United States and Europe, but not in the Philippines where the biggest enthusiasts run big business and government. Danding Cojuangco, Jorge Araneta, and Manny Pacquiao are just a few of the big names associated with the sport. In some provinces, cockfighting is much bigger than basketball. Breeders say the thrill comes from "playing God," in the test of skill to see who can breed, raise, and train the bird who will slaughter all others in the cockpit. For the ordinary farmer or laborer, the sport represents the promise of instant wealth. Prize money can run up to millions for the owner of the victorious bird. Spectators, meanwhile, get their high from winning and losing bets. Whether you agree with it or not, cockfighting is a fascinating sport that reveals many things about Philippine culture and society. Two of the best places to experience it are the Roligon Mega Cockpit in Parañaque and the Araneta Coliseum.

PRICES: Tickets to Sunday hackfights at Roligon go from P200 to P300 for derbies. For inquiries about international cockfighting events at the Araneta Coliseum, log on to www.ticketnet.com.ph

PAYMENT: Cash only (Roligon); Ticketnet accepts credit card. ADDRESS: Araneta Coliseum, Cubao, Quezon City T: 911-5555 ADDRESS: Roligon Mega Cockpit–505 Quirino Ave., Tambo, Parañaque T: 851-2275, 833-1638 OPEN: Call for latest derby schedules.

DMF Drift

SPECIALTY: Drift car parts and services, drift lessons.

DMF Drift is an all in one high performance shop, garage and school that caters to all your drift needs and wants, from getting a car to setting it up and customizing it to your own specs, all the way to learning and practicing on its own custom-made drift track (the only one in the city). Many of the country's top drifters are DMF Drift "alumni."

PRICES: Drift car and set ups range from P250,000 onward. One-day drift basics class, P13,500 (includes use of the school's competition-ready drift machine).

PAYMENT: Cash, check. WEBSITE: dmfdrift.com EMAIL: info@dmfdrift.com, dmfdrift@yahoo.com ADDRESS: 170 Katipunan Ave., Cor. Boni Serrano Ave., Blue Ridge, Quezon City T: 383-0808 M: 0917-8490734, 0928-502-4352 OPEN: Mon–Sat, 2 p.m.–7 p.m.

Ezkrima

SPECIALTY: Sabre fencing lessons

Ezkrima offers basic sabre fencing lessons for both adults and kids as young as age 7. (Sabres are considered to be "cutting" weapons, as opposed to the épée and the foil which are "thrusting" weapons.) Founders of the club are former members and gold medalists of the national team; they also trained Ezkrima's current instructors. Ezkrima has two class venues in Metro Manila and offers free 1 day trials for you to determine whether or not you'd like to pursue lessons. Gear and required outfits can also be purchased from them.

PRICES: 1-time Ezkrima membership, P3,500; once to twice weekly trainings, P1,700-2,700 a month, respectively. Fencing gear: P950 (glove), P1,300 (saber), P2,900 (mask), P2,800 (jacket), P2,000 (pants, which you'll need if competing). Students can start out with just a saber and a glove. Other equipment can be purchased later.

PAYMENT: Cash. WEBSITE: ezkrima.com ADDRESS: Campanilla St., Dasmariñas Village, Makati. Schedule Tue and Thu, 6 p.m.–7 p.m. (age 7–11), 6 p.m.–7:30 p.m. (age 12 and up) ADDRESS: Club 650 Libis, Quezon City. Schedule Mon and Wed, 6 p.m.–7 p.m. (age 7–11), 6 p.m.–7:30 p.m. (age 12 and up)

Good QI Circle

U B V W

SPECIALTY: Noontime tai chi or meditation on weekdays when you need a quick sanity fix in the middle of a rough day.

Makati office drones will be pleased to know that a wellspring of calm exists in a building squarely in their midst. The Good Qi Circle is a yoga studio, tai chi studio, and meditation center rolled into one convenient venue. The atmosphere is so laid-back, some people walk in straight from the street, kick off their shoes, and have a round of tai chi without changing out of their day clothes. In traditional Chinese culture, qi ("chi") is believed to be the life force that governs the flow of the universe. When a person's qi is depleted or imbalanced, he experiences weakness. People must regularly gather qi, store it, and keep it balanced to live in harmony with the world and with themselves.

PRICES: Tai chi, yoga, and meditation classes cost about P350 per session. Monthly and three-month packages are also available.

PAYMENT: Cash, check. WEBSITE: goodqicircle.com EMAIL: inquiry@goodqicircle.com ADDRESS: Unit 506 Greenbelt Mansions, 106 Perea St., Legaspi Village T: 818-1111 loc. 239 or 250 OPEN: Mon–Fri, 7:30 a.m.–10 p.m.; Sat/Sun, 9 a.m.–12:30 p.m.

Karting

U B V W

SPECIALTY: Karting lessons and circuits for both grown-ups and kids

Go-kart racing enthusiasts have argued that karting can be a good training sport for those who want to become great Formula One drivers. But even without the aspiration to be the next Michael Schumacher, Mika Hakkinen, or Kimi Raikkonen, karting is still a fun, adrenaline-pumping activity that's safe for even kids to enjoy. Unlike other motor sports competitions, karting provides a controlled and closely monitored environment. Kids as young as age 6 can try start out on cadet karts or join a join a cadet class, where they learn all the necessary safety protocols of karting.

PRICES: P200–500 a 5–10-minute round (includes helmet, race suit and shoes, and gloves); additional fees for rental of extra gear like balaclava (head sock worn under the helmet), neck support, and rib cage protector.

PAYMENT: Cash.
WHERE TO ENROLL: PHILIPPINE INTERNATIONAL KARTING ASSOCIATION (PIKA) T: 813-1618, 812-6335; TUASON RACING SCHOOL 640 Boni Ave., Mandaluyong; T: 531-2962; tuasonracing.com; trpteam@yahoo.com
KARTING TRACKS: Boomland Kart Track Boom na Boom, CCP Complex, Roxas Blvd, Manila M: 0919-8581511; Power Kart Track Rockwell Center, Makati; T: 808-3290 M: 0917-535-4080; Manila Speedzone Bonifacio Global City, Taguig; T: 881-9682 M: 0920-926-6236

Krav Maga

U B V W

SPECIALTY: Extensive and intensive Krav Maga classes for civilians (age 16 and up) and professionals like law enforcers, military, bodyguards.

Unlike traditional martial arts that integrate some level of pageantry into their own range of offense and defense tactics, Krav Maga ("contact combat" or "close combat"), which was developed by Hebrew boxer and wrestler Imi Sde-Or in defense of the Jewish quarter in Batislava during an anti-Semitic period in the 1930s, is a modern, reality-based method of street fighting featuring simple movements that can be learned in a relatively short period and are designed to be easily remembered during high-stress situations. In the civilian classes, one is taught how to neutralize threat in a variety of street-tested real-life scenarios such as close-quarter confinement, multiple attackers, weapon-less defense against an armed attacker, etc. Classes for men and women do not significantly differ in what is being taught, but women are taught specialized techniques catering to their physique, especially for sexual assault scenarios. And if female students are comfortable enough, they are made to do drills in mixed classes. Krav Maga Philippines is the only Krav Maga training center in the country certified by the International Krav Maga Federation to train civilians, professionals, and other instructors. The training center also offers Krav Maga fitness programs which are designed to develop and strengthen core muscles (especially abdominal and back) against injuries and train them to endure stress and pain. The fitness program prominently uses the kettleball—a cast-iron cannon-ball looking weight with a handle. Kettlebell workouts are intended to increase strength, endurance, agility, and balance, channeling both muscular and cardiovascular systems. Krav Maga classes are held Monday to Friday, 7:30 p.m. to 9 p.m., and every Saturday from 10:30 a.m. to 12 nn. There are 10-day crash courses that require a minimum of 10 students and custom-tailored and -scheduled courses that require a minimum of 16 students (ideal for call center workers). Programs that require fewer days but more training hours a day are also available.

PRICES: P15,000 (6 days a week for 6 months), 9,000 (6 days a week for 3 months), P3,500 (twice a week for a month), P2,000 (once a week for a month). There are no per-session rates.

PAYMENT: Cash. WEBSITE: kravmaga.ph EMAIL: contact@kravmaga.ph ADDRESS: Asuncion Badminton Center, 20 E. Maclang cor. P. Guevarra Sts., San Juan T: 726-5021, 723-6053 OPEN: Mon–Fri, 7:30 p.m.–9 p.m.; Sat, 10:30 a.m.–12 nn.

LazerXtreme

U B V W

SPECIALTY: Inspired by the phaser guns of Star Trek, Laser Tag, is a combat-simulating game where opposing teams try to tag each other with infrared "guns" (much less painful than Paintball or Airsoft since there is no solid impact).

Scores are kept track of and the hits or tags are recorded through an infrared sensor worn by each player. Usually having a modern industrial feel, laser tag gaming arenas are filled with metal ramps, walls, and rails. They are also usually lit by black light during the game, so the sight of multiple infrared beams shooting out makes for a very space-age visual feast.

RATES/PRICES: About P200 per person per game, inclusive of infrared gun and use of the site.

PAYMENT: Cash. ADDRESS: 4/L Activity Center Wing, Market! Market!, Bonifacio Global City, Taguig T: 856-6467 M: 0917-852-9379 OPEN: Daily, 10 a.m.–9 p.m.

Makati Golf Club

U B V W

SPECIALTY: Golf lessons

A lot of business deals are sealed on the golf course, so why not put a golf course where the business deals are? Makati Golf Club is just a driving range, but its location on the periphery of the central business district means busy executives who get a sudden urge to hit some balls can easily hop over during lunch break, or right after clocking out at 5:00 p.m. There are restaurants and a snack bar to keep food and drink flowing, giving the place a pub-like atmosphere that has putting in place of pool.

PRICES: Lessons for beginners are offered at P1,200 a hour, plus P300 a hour for use of the driving range.

PAYMENT: Cash. ADDRESS: 7232 Malugay St., Brgy. Bel Air, Makati T: 830-2222 OPEN: Mon–Sat, 6 a.m.–11 p.m., Sun, 6 a.m.–10 p.m.

Manila Yacht Club

U B V W

SPECIALTY: Sailing lessons.

Maritime history on Manila Bay has seen balanghays arriving from Borneo, Spanish galleons sailing for Acapulco, and dogfights between the Japanese and Americans in World War II. Manila Bay is one of the best natural harbors in the world, and to fully appreciate it, you need to go beyond humdrum ferry rides. You must be the captain of your own ship, so to speak. The Manila Yacht Club lets you do this through private sailing lessons that can be organized at your convenience.

PRICES: 15 hrs, P4,000. This includes the use of a little dinghy. Lessons on a platu (a small sailboat that can fit up to 6 people) cost P5,000 a session, or P15,000 for a 5-day lesson that can be split between 3–4 people.

PAYMENT: Cash. WEBSITE: manilayachtclub.com.ph ADDRESS: 2351 Roxas Blvd., Manila T: 526-7868 OPEN: Can adjust to your schedule.

Movement

Y U V W

SPECIALTY: Classes in dance, fitness, and martial arts—including specialties like Vegas Strip, baby ballet, and Zumba (workout program that integrates Latin dance and music).

PRICES: Unlimited dance classes, P2,888 a month, P400 a day.

PAYMENT: Cash only. WEBSITE: movementdancestudio.com EMAIL: movement_inc@yahoo.com ADDRESS: 29/L Union Bank Plaza, Meralco Ave. cor Onyx St., Pasig (basement parking available) T: 944-8075, 474-4283 M: 0908-234-4114 OPEN: Mon–Sat, 10 a.m.– 10 p.m. (classes usually last 1.5 hrs). Call or check out website for class schedule updates.

Parkour Philippines

U B V W

SPECIALTY: Drills and meet-ups by enthusiasts of Parkour, a noncompetitive but rigorous discipline of "free running" across realistic urbanscapes.

In parkour, you not only run along a straight path or a circuit, you also negotiate all sorts of obstacles like stairs, ledges, buildings, rails, gates—which means that you also climb, swing, pull up, leap, jump, roll, etc. Strength, balance, agility, and enough spatial awareness to anticipate your next maneuver are key qualities of traceurs (practitioners of parkour, French slang for "to go fast"). During first chase scene of the 2006 James Bond film Casino Royale, parkour stunts were exhibited by the character being pursued by James Bond.

Even without official local presence by way of a training center, parkour already has quite a following, with Parkour Philippines serving as a venue for beginners and enthusiasts to meet up, do drills, and pool information (videos, documentaries, tutorials, etc.)

WEBSITE: pkph.multiply.com EMAIL: teng_al@yahoo.com, info@pkph.net

---

Peak Performance

U B V W

SPECIALTY: Modern dance (jazz, hip-hop), cultural dance (Chinese, Hawaiian, Bellydance), and integrative cardio (cardio striptease, cardio kickboxing, cardio dancing), yogilates, pilates. Unlike fitness gyms that happen to have dance classes, Peak Performance is first and foremost a dance studio that happens to have fitness and cardio elements to their dance programs. Call to inquire about updated class schedules.

PRICES: No joining fees or annual membership fees. Or you can avail of a Peak Pass to get 4 to 20 sessions on any class at lower in rates. Walk-in rates, P380 a session. Package rates, P1,350 (4 sessions), P2,700 (8 sessions).

PAYMENT: Cash, check for complete sessions. WEBSITE: peakperformance.asiapad.com EMAIL: peakperformance@asiapad.com ADDRESS: Peak Performance, 2/L McGwen Bldg., 16 Don A. Roces Ave., Quezon City T: 413-3466 M: 0917-624-7534

Power Kite Manila

U B V W

SPECIALTY: Lessons in power kiting (which is like paragliding, only you launch from a skateboard instead of a speedboat and you're hoisted up in the air by a big kite acting as a parachute); other kite-related activities like kite landboarding, kite buggy, kiteboarding, and static power kiting.

PRICES: P500 a session.

PAYMENT: Cash. WEBSITE: powerkitemanila.multiply.com EMAIL: bobbyjones1205@yahoo.com ADDRESS: SM Central Business Park I, Mall of Asia, Pasay M: 0917-979-5204 OPEN: Sat/Sun, 4 p.m.–6 p.m.

Pulse Yoga

SPECIALTY: Wide variety of yoga classes, from Ashtanga, Hot, Hatha, Vinyasa, Yin, and Power yoga to Pre-Natal and Kids' yoga; both mat and equipment-aided Pilates; and specialty yoga classes (pre-natal, kids, yoga instructor training). Check out website for updates and promos.

PRICES: Walk-in, P500; one-week package, P1,200 (for as many classes in a span of a week); monthly package, P4,000. Call Pulse yoga for one-on-one sessions or corporate packages.

PAYMENT: Cash only, post dated checks for annual fees. WEBSITE: pulse-yoga.com EMAIL: info@pulse-yoga.com ADDRESS: 23 Florida St., Greenhills, Mandaluyong T: 721-7900 M: 0917-847-8573 OPEN: Mon–Sat. Classes start as early as 6:30 a.m. and as late as 8 p.m. See directory for other branches.

Run Rio

SPECIALTY: Website dedicated to all things running by high-speed road-runner and running coach Rio De La Cruzhas. Has updates on marathons and races (course maps, registration details, and race results), online shops, running clinics, runners' blogs, and a host of resources on running.

WEBSITE: runrio.com EMAIL: feedback@runrio.com

Tuason Racing School

SPECIALTY: Professional racing school offering courses in go-kart racing, circuit car racing, rallying, and formula car racing. Instructors have extensive professional racing backgrounds coupled with training in prestigious racing schools abroad (e.g., Skip Barber, Richard Petty, Michael Andretti). Apart from on-site training, students also get simulated race experiences with occasional sessions held in professional-spec tracks.

PRICES: Introductory courses (karting, touring car racing, etc.), P12,000 and up (includes manuals/registration materials, safety gear like helmet and suit, instructor's fee, use of vehicle, drinks and lunch, gift packs, race track fee, and certificate). Keep tabs on their website for special promos!

PAYMENT: Cash only, post dated checks for annual fees. WEBSITE: tuasonracing.com, also on Facebook. EMAIL: info@tuasonracing.com ADDRESS: Warehouse 13, La Fuerza Compound, 2241 Chino Roces Ave. (Pasong Tamo), Makati T: 817-7795 OPEN: Mon–Sat. Classes start as early as 6:30 a.m. and as late as 8 p.m. See directory for other branches.

Urban Golf

U B V W

SPECIALTY: The first and only indoor golf lounge in the Philippines that boasts over 40 of the world's top professional-grade and "fantasy" (think Pebble Bach) golf courses with the use of single-screen, triple-screen, and 3D simulators. Also offered are golf swing diagnostics, consultation with professional golf instructors, and drinks and light snacks served to you on the virtual green by in-house bar caddies.

RATES/PRICES: P900 and hour.

PAYMENT: Cash. WEBSITE: Facebook ADDRESS: 12 Jupiter St., Makati T: 896-4965 M: 0908-378-5831 OPEN: Daily, 11 a.m.– 11 p.m.

DIRECTORY OF BRANCHES, RESELLERS, RETAILERS

Shops & Services

ALOHA BOARD SPORTS

- G/L Alabang Town Center, Muntinlupa T: 566-0195
- 2/L SM Mall Of Asia, Pasay T: 804-0627
- 2/L TriNoma, EDSA cor. North Ave., Q.C. T: 901-6052
- 4/L SM Megamall, Mandaluyong T: 470-3175
- Five-O Skate Shop, Forbes Town Center, Taguig T: 856-9616

AMBASSADOR

- G/L Park Square 1, Makati T: 815-9170
- 421 Dasmariñas St., Manila T: 241-3875, 241-3876
- V-Mall, Greenhills, San Juan T: 721-4935
- Market! Market!, Taguig T: 893-0667

ANG PAMBANSANG TSHIRT

- SM Kultura, SM Makati Annex, Ayala Ave., Makati
- Kultura Megamall, G/L SM Megamall Bldg. A, EDSA, Mandaluyong
- SM Kultura, 2/L SM Mall of Asia, Pasay
- Team Manila, 2/L Powerplant, Rockwell, Makati

AVANT

- 2/L Alabang Town Center, Muntinlupa T: 809-5544
- M2/LTriNoma, EDSA - North Ave., Q.C. T: 901-3550, 901-3553

AZTA URBAN SALON

- 2/L Metrowalk, Meralco Ave., Pasig T: 631-7915
- Robinsons Metro East, Marcos Highway, Pasig T: 682-2107
- Eastwood, Libis, Q.C. T: 678-6527
- Alabang Town Center, Muntinlupa T: 659-2249

BOOKSALE

Valenzuela

- SM Valenzuela, McArthur Highway

Las Piñas

- SM Southmall, Alabang-Zapote Rd. T: 800-36-31
- G/L M-Star Mall, Phil-Am Life Village, Pamplona

Makati

- UG/L Makati Cinema Square, Don Chino Roces Ave. T: 844-4081 loc.133

Mandaluyong

- G/L Star Mall, EDSA cor. Shaw Blvd.
- G/L EDSA Central Cinema, Shaw Blvd. T: 632-94-07
- Cherry Foodarama, Shaw Blvd.
- LG/L Bldg. A, SM Megamall, EDSA cor. Julia Vargas Ave. T: 633-1752

Manila

- Robinsons Place, Ermita T: 536-78-59
- LG/L SM Manila, Concepcion cor. San Marcelino and Arroceros Sts., Ermita T: 404-0777
- SM Lazaro, Felix Huertas cor. A. H. Lacson Sts., Sta. Cruz
- Pedro Gil cor. Leon Guinto St., Paco
- B/L Isetann Food Court, Isetann Ext., Cinerama Complex, Quiapo
- 4/L Isetann Recto, Isetann Ext., Cinerama

Complex, Quiapo
• G/L Rustan's Supermarket, Harrison Plaza, Malate
• Stall G2-CG/L Times Plaza Arcade, U. N. Ave. cor. Gen. Luna and T.M. Kalaw Sts., Ermita

Muntinlupa

• 2/L Alabang Town Center, Muntinlupa
• B/L Metropolis Star, SLEX cor. Alabang-Zapote Rd., Muntinlupa
• G/L Festival Supermall (near foodcourt), Filinvest, Alabang T: 807-5630

Parañaque

• President cor. Aguirre Aves., BF Homes Phase I

Pasig

• G/L Robinsons Metro East, Marcos Highway, Pasig T: 682-9379

Quezon City

• 2/L Ali Mall, Cubao
• Shopwise, Cubao T: 911-1731
• LG/L New Farmer's Plaza, Cubao
• G/L Big R Lobby, Robinsons Place, Novaliches T: 930-6795
• SM Centerpoint, Araneta cor. Ramon Magsaysay Aves.
• 2/L SM City Annex, SM North EDSA, North Ave. cor. EDSA T: 456-8695
• L/G SM Fairview, Quirino Highway cor. Regalado Ave., Lagro T: 418-9814

San Juan

• G/L Shoppesville, Greenhills T: 724-9049

BOSE

• 269 Connecticut St., Greenhills, San Juan T: 724-9566, 724-7527
• LG/L SM City, North Ave. cor. EDSA, Q.C. T: 453-0636, 442-0353
• 3/L Robinsons Place, Pedro Gil cor. Adriatico Sts., Manila
• 3/L Bldg. A, SM Megamall, Mandaluyong T: 634-8484
• 3/L Festival Supermall, Filinvest, Muntinlupa T: 850-3638
• 2/L North Wing, SM Mall of Asia, Pasay T: 556-0825
• 2/L Glorietta 3, Makati T: 816-7590

BOUQUET DE BONBONS

Milkyway Deli

• 2/L Milkyway Bldg., 900 Pasay Rd., Makati T: 843-4124, 843-7124
• Powerplant, Rockwell, Makati T: 756-5026
• G/L V-Mall, Greenhills, San Juan T: 726-5541

Terry Selection

• Unit 2. Bldg. B Karrivin Plaza, 2316 Don Chino Roces Ext. (Pasong Tamo Ext.), Makati T: 844-1816
• LG/L The Podium, ADB Ave., Mandaluyong T: 638-5725 to 26

CANON PHILIPPINES

• Marvin Plaza Bldg., 2153 Don Chino Roces Ave., Makati T: 884-9000

CONLINS COFFEE WORLD

CW Lifestyle Café

• 2/L SM Mall of Asia, Pasay T: 556-0230
• G/L South Quadrant, SM One Ecom Center, Mall of Asia, Pasay T: 801-8611
• UG/L SM Southmall, Alabang-Zapote Rd., Las Piñas T: 801-8611

Alessi

• Bldg. 5 unit 1E10-1E11, Bonifacio High Street, Taguig T: 856-4452

Conlins Elements

• LG/L Greenbelt 5, Makati T: 729-9698

Rustan's

• G/L Alabang Town Center, Muntinlupa T: 850-5532 loc. 127
• 4/L Home Appliances Section, Makati T: 813-3739 loc. 264
• 4/L Home Appliances Section, Shangri-La Mall, EDSA cor. Shaw Blvd., Mandaluyong T: 633-4636

DESIGNS LIGNA

• 3/L Greenbelt 5, Makati T: 729-1025
• 4/l Bldg. B, SM Megamall, Mandaluyong T: 634-0704

DIFFERENT BOOKSTORE, A

• G/L Serendra, Bonifacio High Street, Taguig T: 856-0330, 909-5079
• 2/L Eastwood Mall, Libis, Q.C. T: 709-1995
• 2/L V-Mall, Greenhills, San Juan T: 727-3917

DORY'S LAMBANOG

Kultura Filipino

• UG/L Bldg. A, SM Megamall, Mandaluyong T: 667-3914, 667-3975
• 2/L SM Makati, EDSA cor. Ayala Ave., Makati T: 892-1024, 892-1027
• 2/L SM City, North Ave. cor. EDSA, Q.C. T: 442-0166, 442-0017
• 2/L North Wing, SM Mall of Asia, Bay Blvd., Pasay T: 556-0416 to 17

Tesoro's

• 1325 A. Mabini St., Manila T: 524-3936 to 40, 522-1580
• UG/L Alabang Town Center, Muntinlupa

FILED

Luna (folders)

• 2/L Serendra, Bonifacio High Street, Taguig

Fully Booked (folders)

• Unit R5, Promenade, Greenhills, San Juan T: 724-4057
• R3/L Powerplant, Rockwell, Makati T: 756-5001 to 04
• Bldg. 6902 Bonifacio High Street, Taguig T: 858-7000
• 3/L The Block, SM City, Q.C. T: 442-0107

Nothing But Water (beach bags)

• 3/L Robinsons Galleria, EDSA cor. Ortigas, Q.C.
• 2/L Alabang Town Center, Muntinlupa T: 635-3588
• M2/L TriNoma, EDSA cor. North Ave., Q.C.
• 2/L Glorietta 3, Makati T: 894-0278

FIRMA

• G/L Greenbelt 3, Makati T: 757-4009 to 10
• 3/L M3 TriNoma, EDSA cor. North Ave., Q.C. T: 916-7257
• 4/L Rustan's Dept. Store, Ayala Ave., Makati T: 813-3739 loc. 259

FULLY BOOKED

• 2/L Gateway, Araneta Center, Cubao, Q.C. T: 913-4543
• G/L South Wing, SM Mall of Asia, Bay Boulevard, Pasay T: 556-0264
• G/L West Facade, EDSA Shangri-la Hotel, 1 Garden Way, Ortigas Center, Pasig T: 632-0837,631-9840
• Lobby, TriNoma, EDSA cor. North Ave., Q.C.
• Space B1-12, Greenbelt 5, Makati
• 4/L Eastwood Mall, Libis, Q.C.

GREAT TOYS

• Unit LC-29 & 30, 3/L Shoppesville,

Greenhills T: 571-8268M: 0906-348-7085, 0922-857-6268
• 3/L Waltermart Mall, Pasay Rd. (beside Don Bosco), Makati T: 345-8697M: 0906-348-5407
• Star Sports, 2/L Festival Mall, Filinvest, Muntinlupa T: 659-2843 M: 0932-613-0046
• Club650 Sports Center Parking Lot, 150 Libis, Q.C. T: 972-1570 M: 0922-564-7478

HOBBES & LANDES

• 3/L Greenbelt 5, Makati T: 757-4241, 728-2401
• G/L The Promenade, Greenhills, San Juan T: 722-6469
• R2/L Archaeology Wing, Powerplant, Rockwell, Makati T: 756-5119, 757-0263
• G/L Alabang Town Center, Muntinlupa T: 807-6519
• Main Mall, SM Mall of Asia, Bay Boulevard, Pasay T: 556-0578
• 3/L The Podium, ADB Ave., Mandaluyong T: 631-6189
• 4/L Shangri-la Plaza Mall, EDSA cor. Shaw Blvd., Mandaluyong T: 637-2069 Unit 3046
• Level M3, TriNoma, EDSA cor. North Ave., Q.C. T: 901-3650

ILLUSION LENS

• All Fully Booked, Hobbes & Landes, and National Book Store branches (see all in directory).

CVC Supermarket

• 289 Paso de Blas, Maysan Rd., Valenzuela

Compex Retail

• 4/L Bldg. B SM Megamall EDSA, Mandaluyong T: 633-1861
• 3/L Virramall, Greenhills, San Juan T: 584-18-75
• 3/L Robinsons Place Manila T: 567-26-63
• Unit 2085-2086 2nd Floor SM Southmall Las Piñas City T: 801-78-73
• Stall 14 Park Square I Ayala Center Makati T: 892-83-82 to 83
• 538 Annex I Bldg., SM City, Brgy. Sto. Cristo, Q.C.
• 3042 Level 3 Festival Supermall Muntinlupa T: 659-13-75

E-Media

• 2/L Unit 124 Cyber One Mall, Eastwood, Q.C.
• 2/L Theatre Mall, Greenhills, San Juan

Powerbooks

• G/L Corte de las Palmas, Alabang Town Center, Muntinlupa
• 4/L Robinsons Place Manila
• Festival Supermall, Filinvest, Muntinlupa
• 2/L Glorietta 3, Makati
• 2/L Greenbelt 4, Makati
• SM Central Business Park, Bay City, Pasay
• G/L Bldg. A, SM Megamall, Mandaluyong
• 6/L Shangri-la Plaza Mall, EDSA cor. Shaw Blvd., Mandaluyong
• M3/L TriNoma, EDSA cor. North Ave., Q.C.

INFOMAXX

• P-2B Park Square 1, Makati T: 815-0571, 815-8749
• 2/L Greenhills Theater Mall, Greenhills, San Juan T: 722-1566

JAY CEE KAY STATIONERS AND ENGRAVERS

• LG/L Service Town, Alabang Town Center, Muntinlupa
• 2/L Shoppesville,

Ortigas Ave., Greenhills, San Juan

JEWELMER

- 2/L Entertainment Mall, SM Mall of Asia, Pasay T: 556-6344
- Mezzanine, Manila Peninsula Hotel, Ayala cor. Makati Aves., Makati T: 844-0347, 843-4778
- G/L Alabang Town Center, Muntinlupa T: 772-3529
- EDSA Shangri-La Hotel, Mandaluyong T: 634-3596
- G/L Glorietta 4, Makati T: 729-6735
- 6762 Ayala Ave., Makati T: 810-0266 to 69
- Makati Shangri-la Hotel, Makati T: 813-5027
- 2/L Bldg. B, SM Megamall, Mandaluyong T: 633-8166

LAY BARE WAXING SALON

Quezon City

- G/L Jovita Bldg., Tirad Pass cor. Banawe, Sta. Mesa Heights T: 740-4031
- 3/L Don Antonio Sports Center, Commonwealth T: 428-9477
- 2/L NBC Square, 88 Congressional cor. Mindanao Aves. T: 920-5794
- Village Center, Libis T: 709-1915
- B/L SM City Fairview Annex 2, Regalado cor. Quirino Ave., Fairview T: 418-3606
- M/L AC Bldg., #38 Scout Ybardolaza T: 416-0998

South

- 195 Aguirre St. cor. dela Rama, BF Homes, Parañaque T: 466-7865
- 126 Doña Soledad Ave., Better Living Subdivision, Parañaque T: 776-5945
- Unit 9 Main Bldg., Susana Arcade, Alabang-Zapote Rd., Almanza, Las Piñas T: 994-7191

Central Manila

- 2/L Citiplace, 8001 Abad Santos St., San Juan T: 726-6479
- Upper Ground, Star Centrum Bldg., Buendia cor. Malugay St., Makati T: 840-2571
- 5081 Filmore cor. Fahrenheit Sts., Palanan, Makati T: 833-7915
- 2/L Pearl Plaza, 8101 Pearl Drive, Bgy. San Antonio, Ortigas Center, Pasig T: 470-2762
- 3/L Market! Market! (near elevator), Taguig T: 556-0743
- M/L Burgundy Transpacific Place, Taft Ave., Manila T: 353-5304

LOMOGRAPHIC EMBASSY MANILA

- Fully Booked branches: Bonifacio High Street, Greenhills, Gateway, SM The Block, and Shangri-La Mall (see Fully Booked in directory)
- Fortress Digital, 713 R. Hidalgo St., Quiapo, Manila
- Recreational Outdoor Exchange (ROX), Quadrant 1, Bonifacio High Street, 5th Ave., Taguig
- Brat Pack, Robinsons Place Manila
- Brat Pack, Greenbelt 5, Makati
- Republik, Cybergate Mall, Libis, Q.C.

MESSY BESSY

- G/L Main Aisle, TriNoma, EDSA cor. North Ave., Q.C.

Rustan's Flower Shop

- G/L Powerplant, Rockwell, Makati T: 897-8053

• G/L Rustan's Department Store, Ayala Ave., Makati T: 812-9706
• 4/L Shangri-la Mall, EDSA cor. Shaw Blvd., Mandaluyong T: 633-4658
• 2/L Rustan's, Alabang Town Center, Alabang-Zapote Rd., Muntinlupa T: 772-1015
• G/L St. Luke's Medical Center, Rodriguez Sr. Ave., Q.C. T: 726-4600
• G/L Asian Hospital and Medical Center, 2205 Civic Drive cor. Centennial Lane, Filinvest Corporate City, Alabang, Muntinlupa T: 771-0609

Make Room

• 4/L Powerplant, Rockwell, Makati
• G/L Bonifacio High Street, Taguig

Makeroom & More

• 2/L Bonifacio High Street, Taguig
• G/L Eastwood Mall, Eastwood, Libis, Q.C.

Beauty Bar

• 2/L Greenbelt 5, Makati
• G/L Lifestyle Wing, Powerplant, Rockwell, Makati T: 898-2042 to 43
• 3/L Shangri-la Mall, EDSA cor. Shaw Blvd., Mandaluyong T:632-7903
• G/L The Podium, ADB Ave., Mandaluyong T:633-7808
• 3/L TriNoma, EDSA cor. North Ave., Q.C.
• G/L Corte delas Palmas, Alabang Town Center, Muntinlupa T: 842-8350

NATIONAL BOOK STORE

Caloocan

• 2/L Ever Gotesco Grand Central, Rizal Ave. Ext. T: 363-5455
• G/L G 10 Old Victory, Rizal Ave., Monumento T: 332-1206, 332-1207
• Puregold Price Club Bldg. cor. Zabarte Rd. T: 355-2527, 355-2564

Las Piñas

• UG/L SM Southmall, Alabang-Zapote National Rd. T: 806-8093, 806-3403

Makati

• G/L Greenbelt I, T: 812-3950 to 51
• R2/L Lifestyles, Rockwell Center, Amapola cor. Estrella Sts. T: 897-4346
• Petron Square Bel Air, Sen. Gil Puyat cor. Makati Aves. T: 897-6744 to 45

Taguig

• G/L Market! Market!, Bonifacio Global City

Malabon

• G/L Malabon Citisquare Annex, C4 cor. Dagat-Dagatan Ave. T: 287-2864

Mandaluyong

• G/L Robinsons Place Pioneer T: 687-4421
• G/L, Shangri-La Mall, EDSA cor. Shaw Blvd. T: 633-4434
• G/L EDSA Central Square, Shaw Blvd. T: 631-5414
• G/L Bldg. A SM Megamall T: 636-7025, 636-7028

Manila

• G/L Harrison Plaza, M. Adriatico St. T: 525-8205, 526-1857
• 1921 C.M. Recto Ave. cor. Morayta T: 735-5631
• 701 Rizal Ave., Sta. Cruz T: 733-8256, 733-8257
• G/L Robinsons Place T: 536-7893, 536-7896
• UG/L SM City Ermita T: 524-1615, 524-1509
• G/L SM City Lazaro, Sta. Cruz T: 786-2519, 786-2522
• G/L Tutuban Centermall I,

Divisoria T: 253-1912
• G/L Madison Bldg., 2574 Taft Ave. T: 536-2913
• G/L, Robinsons Place Otis, Pandacan T: 559-0598 to 99

Marikina

• G/L SM City Marikina, Marcos Highway T: 477-1863

Muntinlupa

• G/L Casa Filipina Arcade, Alabang Town Center T: 842-6188
• G/L, Festival Supermall, Filinvest T: 850-3578
• G/L Metropolis Star Alabang, SLEX T: 809-9437
• G/L SM Supercenter Muntinlupa, National Rd., Tunasan T: 659-1536

Parañaque

• UG/L SM City Bicutan T: 776-0194
• G/L SM City Sucat T: 829-7712
• Jaka Plaza, Dr. A. Santos Ave., Sucat T: 829-4901
• G/L Shopwise Bldg., Dr. A. Santos Ave., Sucat T: 826-1300, 826-5614
• G/L Puregold Bldg., Dr. A. Santos Ave., Sucat T: 829-4901

Pasay

• G/L Metropoint Mall, EDSA cor. Taft Ave. T: 833-9145
• G/L J.W. Diokno Boulevard, Mall of Asia Complex T: 556-0529, 556-0531

Pasig

• G/L Danny Floro Bldg., C. Raymundo Ave., Caniogan T: 640-1698
• G/L Ever Gotesco, Ortigas Ave. Ext. T: 656-6716
• UG/L Robinsons Metro East, Marcos Highway, Santolan T: 682-4989

Quezon City

• UG/L Ali Mall, Araneta Center, Cubao T: 911-1585
• Unit 604,Eastwood Cybermall, Libis T: 687-6158
• 297 Katipunan Ave., Loyola Heights T: 920-1066 to 68
• UG/L New Farmers Plaza, Araneta Center, Cubao T: 421-1229
• 12 Congressional Ave., Project 8 T: 426-7247
• Sct. Borromeo cor. Quezon Aves. T: 373-3454, 373-0852
• G/L Robinsons Place Novaliches, Quirino Highway, Novaliches T: 935-4649
• G/L–2/L Robinsons Galleria, Ortigas Ave. cor. EDSA T: 632-0554, 632-0555
• UG/L SM City Fairview, Quirino Highway cor. Regalado Ave. T: 418-4953, 417-5463
• UG/L SM City, North Ave. cor. EDSA, Pag-asa T: 920-9388 to 90
• 2/L SM Centerpoint, Aurora Boulevard cor. Araneta Ave., Doña Imelda T: 716-1122, 715-0581
• General Roxas St., Araneta Center, Cubao T: 912-7135, 911-2261 to 68
• M1/L, TriNoma EDSA cor. North Ave., Barangay Bagong Pag-asa T: 901-5750 to 52
• 136 2/L New Annex Bldg., 252-254 SM City, North Ave., cor. EDSA
• G/L The Capital Towers, E. Rodriguez Ave. T: 722-0026

San Juan

• 2/L 53 A. Velason's Bldg., Annapolis St., Greenhills T: 725-1166
• 12 Missouri St., North East Greenhills T: 726-4746

Taguig

• G/L Market! Market!, Bonifacio Global City

T: 886-6611, 886-6613
Valenzuela
• G/L SM Supercenter Valenzuela, MacArthur Highway, Barangay Karuhatan T: 291-2901, 291-1786, 291-0947

COLUMBIA DIGITAL

(authorized Philippine distributor and service center of Nikon SLRs)
• 129 G. Roxas St. San Francisco Del Monte, Q.C. T: 363-5315, 363-0892

ORIENTIQUE

• 304 Home Precinct, Filinvest Ave., Westgate, Alabang, Muntinlupa T: 771-1062, 771-0660
• 52 Katipunan Ave., White Plains, Q.C.

PC CORNER

• G/L Fabricare Bldg. Alabang-Zapote Rd., Las Piñas T: 772-3416
• 3/L V-Mall, Greenhills, San Juan T: 727-4087

PC EXPRESS

• 431 Shaw Blvd., cor. Ideal St., Mandaluyong T: 718-2828, 718-3838, 718-3939
• 2/L Goodyear Hi-Performance Center, Alabang-Zapote Rd., Las Piñas T: 772-2282 to 85
• 2/L Golan Plaza, 333 Katipunan Ave., Loyola Heights, Q.C. T: 433-6800, 433-6802
• 2250 Don Chino Roces Ave., Makati T: 893-9537, 893-7652
• 2/L PARCO Bldg.,4 EDSA cor. Connecticut St., Greenhills, San Juan T: 726-0410, 726-5918
• Buwayang Bato cor. Sheridan Sts., Mandaluyong
• 369 Executive Bldg., Sen. Gil Puyat Ave. (Buendia) cor. Makati Aves., Makati T: 750-2616 to 17
• 2/L Alabang Town Center, Muntinlupa T: 807-6492, 807-8037
• 4/L Market! Market! 26th St. cor. C5, Taguig T: 856-6118

PC GILMORE

• LG/L SM Cubao, Q.C. T: 986-1314
• Unit B Sunbest Bldg. Lot 5 & 7, Blk 1 Brgy. Greater Lagro, Quirino Highway, Q.C. T: 418-7536
• 144 West Ave., near cor. EDSA, Q.C. T: 924-5914 M: 0922-599-8053
• 19 1st St. cor Gilmore Ave., Brgy. Valencia, New Manila, Q.C. T: 411-0786, 470-2154
• 4/L Annex 1 Bldg., SM City, North EDSA, Q.C. T: 441-1368
• Unit V338 3/L V-Mall, Greenhills, San Juan T: 727-8988, 727-9088 M: 0922-811-3616
• Unit 113 Aurelio Bldg., 1 Rizal Ave. Ext., Grace Park, Caloocan T: 361-1902, 367-0672 M: 0922-746-5474

POWER BOOKS

• G/L Alabang Town Center, Muntinlupa T: 850-5662/63
• 4/L Robinsons Place, Ermita, Manila T: 567-1931/33
• Festival Supermall, Filinvest, Muntinlupa T: 850-8221
• 2/L Greenbelt 4, Makati T: 757-6428/29
• Mall of Asia, Pasay T: 556-0244/45
• G/L Bldg. A SM Megamall, Mandaluyong T: 635-2898 to 99
• 6/L Shangri-la Mall, EDSA - Shaw Blvd., Mandaluyong T: 638-0025
• M3/L TriNoma, EDSA - North Ave.,

Q.C. T: 943-1581/82

PROUD MAMA STORE

Hobbes & Landes
- Bonifacio High Street, Taguig
- 3/L Greenbelt 5, Makati
- G/L The Promenade, Greenhills, San Juan
- R2/L Archaeology Wing, Power Plant Mall, Makati

Rustan's Department Store
- Alabang Town Center, Muntinlupa T: 850-5532 loc. 113
- Gateway, Araneta Center, Cubao, Q.C. T: 911-2401 loc. 138
- Ayala Center, Makati T: 813-3739 loc. 231
- Shangri La Plaza Mall, EDSA cor. Shaw Blvd., Mandaluyong T: 633-4636

Babyland
- Eastwood Mall, Libis, Q.C.
- Facilities 548 Center, Shaw Blvd., Mandaluyong T: 531-1217, 531-1367
- 3/L Festival Supermall, Filinvest, Muntinlupa T: 772-1543
- Shoppesville, Greenhills, San Juan T: 727-5276
- 2/L Alabang Town Center, Muntinlupa T: 807-2264

Big & Small Co.
- 2/L Glorietta 2, Makati T: 867-2024
- 3/L Greenbelt 5, Makati
- 3/L Alabang Town Center, Muntinlupa
- 3/L Market! Market!, Bonifacio High Street, Taguig
- M1/L West Wing, TriNoma, EDSA cor. North Ave., Q.C.
- Gateway, Araneta Center, Cubao, Q.C.
- V-Mall, Greenhills, San Juan T: 725-1244

Plume Shop
- 83 Katipunan Ave., White Plains, Q.C.

Procreation
- Shangri-la Mall, EDSA cor. Shaw Blvd., Mandaluyong

Sueño
- 1344 Filmore St., Palanan, Makati M: 0916-877-8662

PUNCH DRUNK PANDA

Power Mac Center
- 2/L Greenbelt 3, Makati
- 3/L Powerplant, Rockwell, Makati
- 2/L SM Mall of Asia, Bay Blvd., Pasay
- 4/L SM Megamall, Mandaluyong
- 3/L TriNoma, EDSA cor. North Ave., Q.C.

Lapdance Bags
- 3/L Gateway, Araneta Center, Cubao, Q.C.
- G/L TriNoma, EDSA cor. North Ave., Q.C.

The A Shop
- G/L Eastwood Mall, Libis, Q.C.
- 2/L The Podium, ADB Ave., Mandaluyong
- Ayala Ave., Makati T: 812-8682

Analog Soul
- Powerplant, Rockwell, Makati
- 2/L TriNoma, EDSA cor. North Ave., Q.C.

SIMPLE SHOES

Recreational Outdoor Exchange (ROX)
- Quadrant 1, Bonifacio High Street, 5th Ave., Taguig T: 856-4639

Res|Toe|Run
- G/L Glorietta 4, Makati T: 817-8850
- G/L Robinsons Galleria, EDSA cor. Ortigas, Q.C. T: 635-0289
- 2/L, Robinsons Place, Pedro Gil cor. Adriatico Sts., Manila
- 2/L TriNoma, EDSA cor. North Ave.,

Q.C. T: 901-3654

Rustan's

• Alabang Town Center, Muntinlupa T: 850-5532 loc. 113
• Gateway, Araneta Center, Cubao, Q.C. T: 911-2401 loc. 138
• Ayala Ave., Makati T: 813-3739 loc. 231
• Shangri La Plaza Mall, EDSA cor. Shaw Blvd., Mandaluyong T: 633-4636

SM KULTURA

• UG/L Bldg. A, SM Megamall, Mandaluyong T: 667-3914
• 2/L SM Makati, EDSA cor. Ayala Ave., Makati T: 892-1024, 892-1027
• 2/L SM City, North Ave. cor. EDSA, Q.C. T: 442-0166

STOKED INC.

• 4/L The Podium, ADB Ave., Mandaluyong T: 683-07-36
• G/L Promenade Area, Alabang Town Center, Muntinlupa T: 772-17-63
• 2/L Bridgeway, Greenhills, San Juan T: 723-92-86
• G/L Gateway, Araneta Center, Cubao, Q.C. T: 911-85-25
• G/L SM Mall of Asia, Pasay T: 556-01-46
• 2/L M2 TriNoma, EDSA cor. North Ave., Q.C. T: 916-97-08
• G/L Bldg. 1 Bonifacio High Street, Taguig T: 856-40-13

SUGARFREE & BLUE

• 3/L SM Sta. Mesa, Aurora Blvd., Q.C. T: 713-2877
• 2/L, Festival Supermall, Corporate Ave. cor. Civic Drive, Filinvest, Muntinlupa
• Shoe Center, Ali Mall, Araneta Center, Cubao, Q.C.
• Shoe Center, Greenhills, San Juan

SWITCHRINGS Chocolate Clothing

• 3/L SM Megamall, Mandaluyong T: 637-5172
• 2/L Power Plant, Rockwell, Makati T: 897-0825
• 3/L Robinsons Galleria, EDSA cor. Ortigas, Q.C. T: 637-9638
• 2/L Eastwood Walk 2, Libis, Q.C. T: 687-6779
• 2/L Main Mall, SM Mall of Asia, Pasay T: 556-0312
• 5/L Shangri-la Plaza Mall, EDSA cor. Shaw Blvd., Mandaluyong T: 633-5447
• 3/L The Podium, ADB Ave., Mandaluyong T: 633-5390
• 5/L The Block, SM City, North Ave. cor. EDSA, Q.C. T: 442-0118
• 2/L Rustan's, Gateway, Araneta Center, Cubao, Q.C. T: 911-2401
• 2/L Rustan's, Robinsons Place, Pedro Gil cor. Adriatico Sts., Manila T: 551-2788

Recreation & Activities

GALERIE JOAQUIN

(affiliate galleries)
• Galerie Joaquin, UG/L The Podium, ADB Ave., Mandaluyong T: 634-7954
• Galerie Raphael, 2/L Serendra, Taguig T: 856-3034
• Galerie Stephanie, Parc Plaza Bldg., Libis, Q.C. T: 386-8070, 709-1488
• Galleria Nicolas, 3/L Art Space, Glorietta 4, Makati T: 381-5800, 728-0124

PULSE YOGA

• 2289 UPRC III Bldg., Don Chino Roces Ext., Makati T: 468-4165 M: 0917-837-8573
• 45-A Broadway cor. 11th St., Q.C. M: 0917-847-8573

INDEX

SHOPS & SERVICES

APPAREL, ACCESSORIES

MOMS, KIDS

PERSONAL CARE

INDEX

LIFESTYLE, SPECIALTY SUPPLIES

COLLECTIBLES, GIFT IDEAS

F&B, FOOD PREP, INGREDIENTS

LUNCH-OUTS & LIGHT BITES

EAST

EAST MEETS WEST

RECREATION & ACTIVITIES

ART, CULTURE

ENTERTAINMENT, PERFORMANCE ARTS

SPECIALTY WORKSHOPS/ ACTIVITIES

FAMILIES, KIDS, PARKS

FITNESS, SPORTS, WELLNESS